Chasing Empire across the Sea
Communications and the State in the French Atlantic, 1713–1763

Drawing on a vast array of official correspondence, merchant's letters, ship's logs, and graphic material from archives and research libraries in Canada, France, and the United States, Kenneth Banks details how France, as the most powerful nation on the Continent and possessing a tradition of maritime interest in the Americas and West Africa dating back to the earliest years of the sixteenth century, seemed destined to take a leading role in exploiting and settling the Americas and establishing posts in West Africa. That it largely failed to do so can be explained in large part by problems emanating from information exchange in an early modern authoritarian state. Banks provides a historical context for the role of communications in the development of the imperial nation-state and offers an Atlantic World perspective on the growing body of literature revising the historical role of absolutism.

Banks defines and applies the concept of communications in a far broader context than previous historical studies of communication, encompassing a range of human activity from sailing routes, to mapping, to presses, to building roads and bridges. He employs a comparative analysis of early modern French imperialism, integrating three types of overseas possessions usually considered separately – the settlement colony (Canada), the tropical monoculture colony (the French Windward Islands), and the early Enlightenment planned colony (Louisiana) – offering a work of synthesis that unites the historiographies and insights from three formerly separate historical literatures. Banks challenges the very notion that a concrete "empire" emerged by the first half of the eighteenth century; in fact, French colonies remained largely isolated arenas of action and development. Only with the contraction and concentration of overseas possessions after 1763 on the Plantation Complex did a more cohesive, if fleeting, French empire first emerge.

KENNETH J. BANKS is assistant professor in the Department of History, Mars Hill College, North Carolina.

Chasing Empire across the Sea

Communications and the State in the French Atlantic, 1713–1763

KENNETH J. BANKS

McGill-Queen's University Press
Montreal & Kingston • London • Ithaca

© McGill-Queen's University Press 2003
ISBN-13: 978-0-7735-2444-6 ISBN-10: 0-7735-2444-4 (cloth)
ISBN-13: 978-0-7735-3160-4 ISBN-10: 0-7735-3160-2 (paper)

Legal deposit fourth quarter 2002
Bibliothèque nationale du Québec

Printed in Canada on acid-free paper.
First paperback edition 2006.

This book was first published with the help of a grant from the Humanities and Social Sciences Federation of Canada, using funds provided by the Social Sciences and Humanities Research Council of Canada, and with funds provided by the Faculty Enrichment and Renewal Committee of Mars Hill College.

McGill-Queen's University Press acknowledges the support of the Canada Council for the Arts for our publishing program. We also acknowledge the financial support of the Government of Canada through the Book Publishing Industry Development Program (BPIDP) for our publishing activities.

National Library of Canada Cataloguing in Publication

Banks, Kenneth J., 1958–
Chasing empire across the sea : communications and the state in the French Atlantic, 1713–1763 / Kenneth J. Banks.

Includes bibliographical references and index.
ISBN-13: 978-0-7735-2444-6 ISBN-10: 0-7735-2444-4 (bnd)
ISBN-13: 978-0-7735-3160-4 ISBN-10: 0-7735-3160-2 (pbk)
1. France – Colonies – Administration – History – 18th century. 2. France – Colonies – America – History – 18th century. 3. Communication policy – France – History – 18th century. 4. Government correspondence – France – History – 18th century. 5. Commercial correspondence – America – History – 18th century. 6. Travelers' writings, French – History and criticism. 7. France – Foreign relations – 1715–1774. I. Title.

JV1816 B35 2002 325'.32'094409033 C2002-903479-5

This book was typeset by True to Type in 10/12 Sabon

To the memory of my father

Contents

Tables and Maps

TABLES

MAPS

Preface

When I first started working on this project as a graduate student in 1992, I met a senior scholar in front of the order desk of the French Archives Nationales, which then held the majority of the colonial records prior to 1789. She politely inquired about the area of research I hoped to tackle, and I proudly declared, "Why, the first overseas French empire, madame." She became animated and began giving me many helpful hints as to where I might find more information on Napoleon and Haiti, his plans for Egypt, the sale of Louisiana, and so on. Surprised, I exclaimed, "Oh, madame, I mean the first one: Canada, Acadia, Louisbourg, the Îles du Vent ..." She looked at me quizzically and then thoughtfully smiled. She wished me good luck in my efforts and pulled away to fetch her dossier.

For many scholars, and still within the French popular mind, no French empire existed until 1802. Before then were the *vieilles colonies*, it is true, but this collection of territories, which stretched from the rich entrepôts of India to the vast claims in the North American interior and today comprises about a quarter of Canada and half the continental United States, hardly counted as an empire. This book examines the role of transatlantic communications in creating and maintaining French imperialism during the height of France's first overseas empire in the eighteenth century. As the most powerful nation on the Continent, and with a long interest in colonial exploration and adventurism dating from the early sixteenth century, France seemed destined to take a leading role in exploiting and settling the New World. That it had largely failed to do so by the end of the eighteenth century and had ceded much of its dynamic to Great Britain is well known. But disagreement over why France achieved mediocre results remains.

The study is comparative in a field that has been virtually devoid of such analysis. The early modern phase of French expansion has generated few surveys and virtually no in-depth studies. Those in the *vieilles colonies* have long remained isolated as three distinct historiographies: New France for Canadians, Louisiana for Americans, and the prerevolutionary and revolutionary Caribbean, focused on Saint Domingue, for French scholars. While scholars in each field have made valuable contributions to the others, a true synthesis of experience is lacking. This situation is highly unfortunate, for the French colonizing experience differed as much geographically and economically as the English and Dutch, yet shared some fascinating similarities in social structure with the Spanish and Portuguese.

This work has been in itself a transatlantic journey, pursued in primarily three countries, and leaving a trail of intellectual adventure and frustration, lost friendships, and new loves and colleagues, with joy and pain at every turn. My list of debts is long, but it must begin with Professor James Pritchard. I am only now beginning to appreciate the full extent of the meticulous training he imparted to me, his grasp of the larger context of French maritime history, his patience with my first crude papers. His uncanny ability to slice through my fuzzy concepts and cut to the heart of larger intellectual tasks has made this a far better and more stimulating work than it would otherwise have been. He has remained an encouraging supporter throughout, while providing tough but fair criticism. To him I owe more than thanks can say. Professor David Eltis opened the dimension of slavery and the Caribbean to me and offered timely criticism, advice, and endless encouragement. The members of my doctoral dissertation board, especially J.F. Bosher and Anne Godlewska, suggested some invigorating paths for me to follow. Klaus Hansen may not see the connection, but his stimulating seminar on antebellum America prompted my initial interest in the relation of communications to social order. Sir J.H. Elliott's probing questions on the depth and breadth of exchanges between the Americas and Europe at the America in European Consciousness Conference at Providence, Rhode Island, in 1991 sparked my initial enthusiasm for this study. And to repay two old but cherished debts, I would like to thank Robert Tittler and Joan Sherwood of Concordia University in Montreal for igniting my interest in history and setting me on a new life path.

Many colleagues during my graduate days at Queen's University helped to clarify my methodology and conceptualization. In particular, I would like to thank Michael Boudreau, Andrew Nurse, William Cormack, and Danny Samson. In France I would like to single out the gracious help of M. Henri Gradis, who unhesitatingly placed his family's archival resources at my full disposal. Professors Bernard Bailyn and David Hancock at the Harvard Atlantic Seminar of 1997 offered many penetrating insights, which have greatly enhanced my understanding of the Atlantic world. I also benefited enormously from conversations with David Armitage, Nikolaus Böttcher, Laurent Dubois, Thomas Fröschl, Nancy L. Hagedorn, Andrew O'Shaughnessy, and James Robertson. I am grateful to Leslie Choquette for providing several helpful suggestions for earlier versions of what became chapters 3 and 6. Cornelius Jaenen, Lloyd Kramer, Rosemary Brana-Shute, Wim Klooster, and Colin Coates shared insights, and this book has benefited enormously from their help. I would like especially to thank Bertrand van Ruymbeke for his unfailing goodwill and keen interest in this project and for doing yeoman service in his critique of chapter 1. Finally, I am indebted to the three anonymous readers for McGill-Queen's University Press, who provided generous, extensive, and thoughtful criticism. Any flaws or errors are mine.

Every scholar builds up an enormous number of debts to those often unsung heroes of academia, the archival, library, and support staffs. The staffs of the Archives Départementales de Gironde in Bordeaux and the Archives de Commerce et Industrie de La Rochelle are to be commended for running friendly and highly efficient archives. In North America I also extend my thanks to Ralph Stenstrom at the Beinecke Collection at Hamilton College; to Kate O'Rourke at the National Archives of Canada; and to Ross Hough and Eric Leinberger for their work on the maps. My sincere thanks go also to the staff of Special Collections at Douglas/Stauffer Library at Queen's University, to the University of North Carolina at Asheville's Ramsey Library, and especially to Bobbie Williams of Renfro Library at Mars Hill College's interlibrary loan department for her thorough-going efforts in obtaining a treasure trove of obscure works at a moment's notice.

The School of Graduate Research at Queen's University generously supported the initial research for the dissertation, including a Senator Frank Carrel Fellowship and a travel grant to France in 1992. A Social Sciences and Humanities Research Council of Canada doctoral fellowship helped fund a long period of research in Canada and a second trip to France, while an Ontario Graduate Scholarship supported the final year of doctoral work. Most of all, at Mars Hill College I would like to thank Dr Lyn White, Dean of Arts and Sciences, and Dr Tom Plaut, Dr Don Russell, and the members of the Faculty Enrichment and Renewal Committee. Dean White and the committee have been instrumental in shaping an appreciative and vibrant environment for scholarship at Mars Hill College, particularly in new and innovative areas. They provided generous funding and wonderful moral support at a critical stage of final research, revising, and publication of the book.

At a personal level, I would like to thank my late father, Raymond E. Banks, and my brother Joel for puzzling over some early drafts. My mother, Judith Jeppesen, has helped at some critical moments. My late Uncle Richard and Aunt Edie made Paris less lonely, and my cousin Bar made it more interesting. Ross Imrie and Catherine O'Grady provided bed, board, and brandy during several long, invaluable research trips to Ottawa. My greatest debt is to Tracey Rizzo, my colleague, best friend, and partner, who provided constructive criticism, made innumerable helpful suggestions, and gave soulful encouragement and inspiration at many critical moments of despair and shared in all the joys. Her intelligence, love, enthusiasm, and *zèle* dance on every page.

A Note on Terms and Translations

I have translated all passages from the original eighteenth-century French. Some terms, such as *huissier* or *commis*, seemed best left in French, however, since the English equivalent (town crier, clerk) failed to translate directly or capture the nuanced meaning in French. Other terms have been anglicized, but translated so as to avoid arousing associations with English or American positions. I have reluctantly used "secretary of state," with its American connotations, since it is more accurate than the ubiquitous "minister," but less cumbersome than *secrétaire d'état*. However, the reader will find "Bureau of Colonies" and "Marine," instead of "Colonial Office" and "Navy," both terms that conjure up imperial British institutions.

Some terms need special attention. "Marine," when used without qualification, refers to the bureaucratic institution comprising the secretary of state, officers, and clerks in France directly charged with maritime and naval operations. Of course, the Marine was composed of many people with their own ideas and agendas; but since the initiatives for the vast majority of actions and observations are not clearly articulated in the official correspondence, I believe it best to ascribe many of these actions to a collective bureaucratic "consciousness." I do not mean to imply by so doing that the Marine existed as a group of anonymous people working in perfect harmony and concert; like any government agency, it had its share of factional strife and intra-agency competition. I have ascribed actions or words to specific individuals, usually the secretary of state himself, only when I believed that a given piece of correspondence directly reflected his views. I have tried to reserve the term "New France" as a catch-all administrative reference to all the colonies in North America (Canada, the vaguely defined interior posts of the Great Lakes drainage basin and beyond, or *pays d'en haut*, Île Royale, Louisbourg, Louisiana, and the French fishing shore on Newfoundland) and to employ specific colony names where these seemed more accurate and appropriate. "Îles du Vent" refers to all the islands making up the French administrative area in the great arc of the Lesser Antilles, from (originally) Sainte Croix in the north to Grenada in the south, and including the two main colonies of Guadeloupe and Martinique.

The term "Creole" has a complicated history, and traditions on its use differed from island to island and in each mainland colony. I use the term in the far more restricted sense employed in the eighteenth century to refer to those born in the American tropics, and who lived most of their lives there. In this more limited sense, the word "Creole" implied specifically one not from the "metropolis," that is, France itself. However, I have chosen to employ the more current term "free black" instead of the eighteenth-century "free coloured."

Working on both sides of the Atlantic, as it were, reveals slight but interesting differences in names. For example, the spelling of the name "Beauharn*o*is" for the governor general of New France and "Beauhar-n*a*is" for the intendant at Rochefort may confuse some readers, who may naturally think these represent two distinct families. They are in fact brothers. The variation in spelling can be accounted for by differences between Canadian and French historians. Technically, the latter (the French spelling) is correct, but the former is so common among North American historians that I have not tried to impose any standardization.

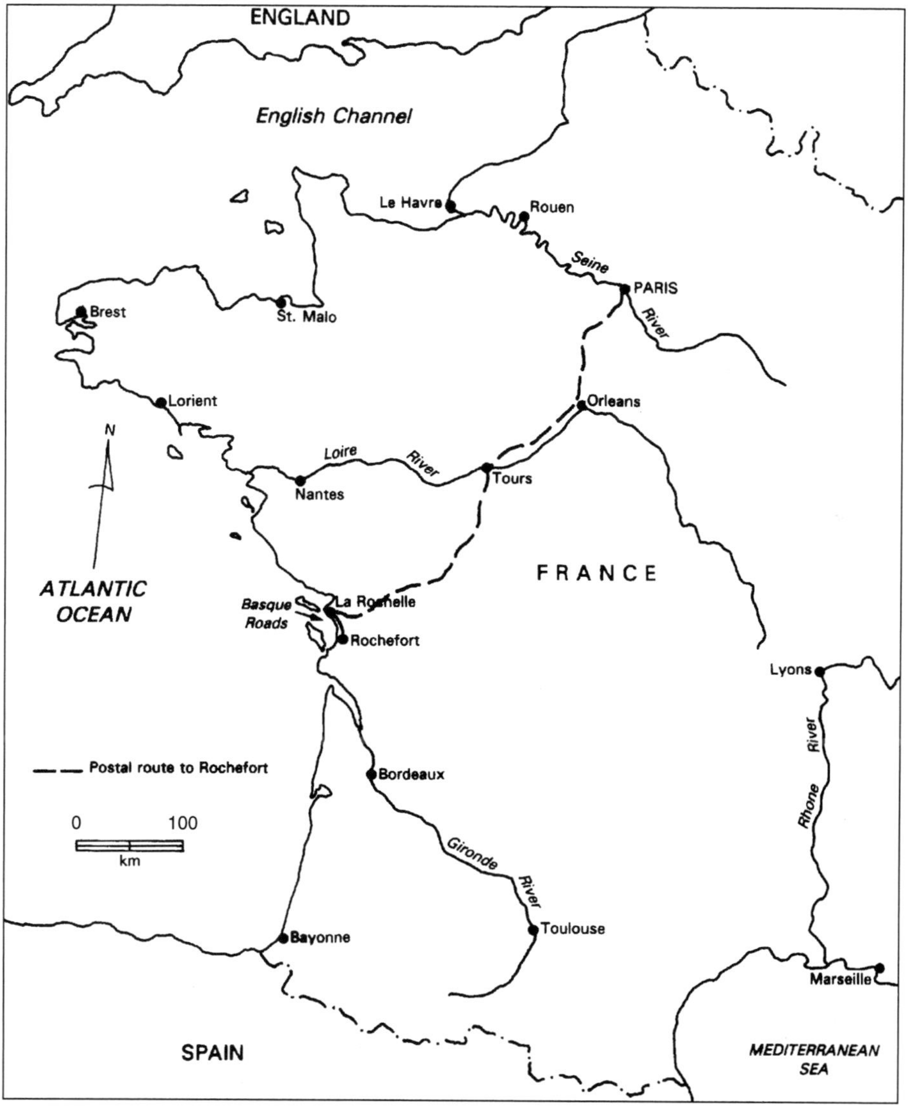

Map 1 Major towns and ports of eighteenth-century France

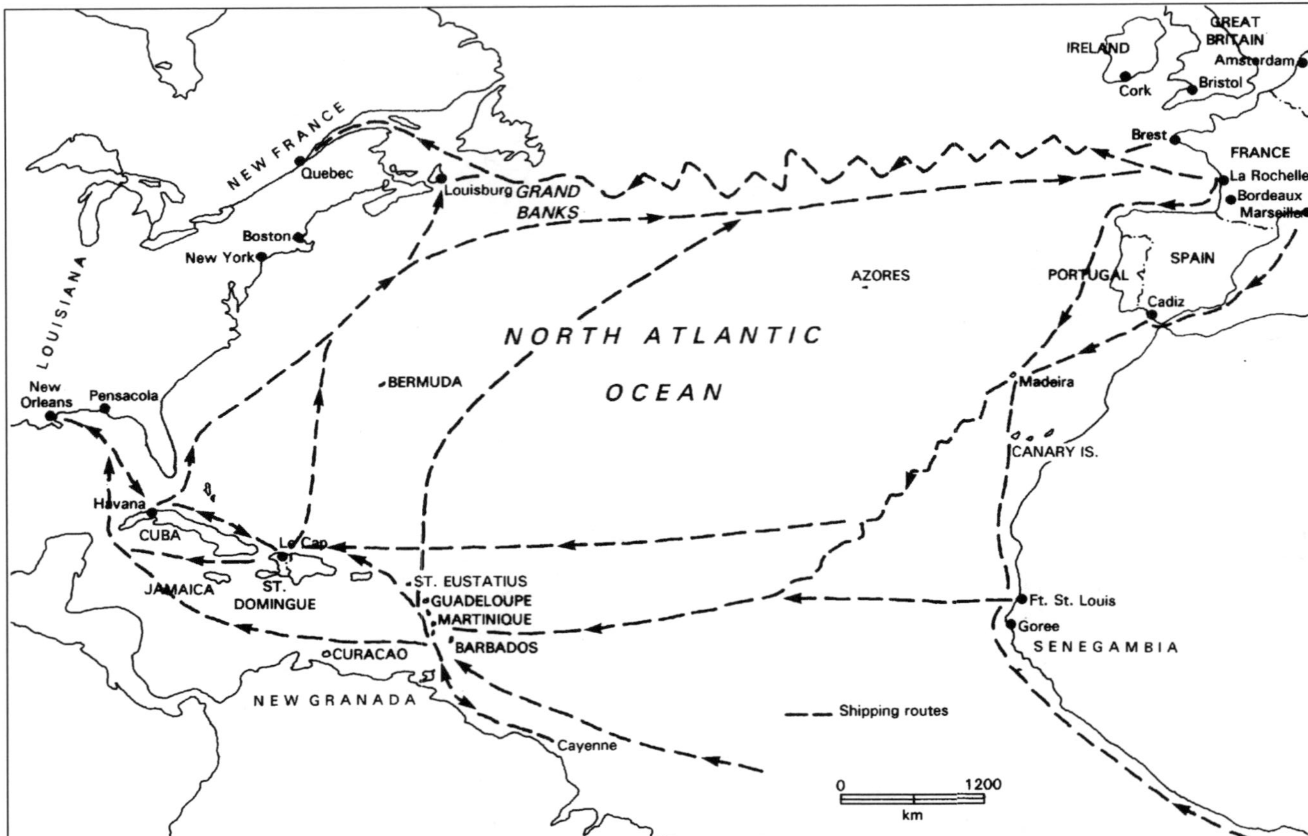

Map 2 Sailing routes and ports of the French Atlantic, c. 1745.

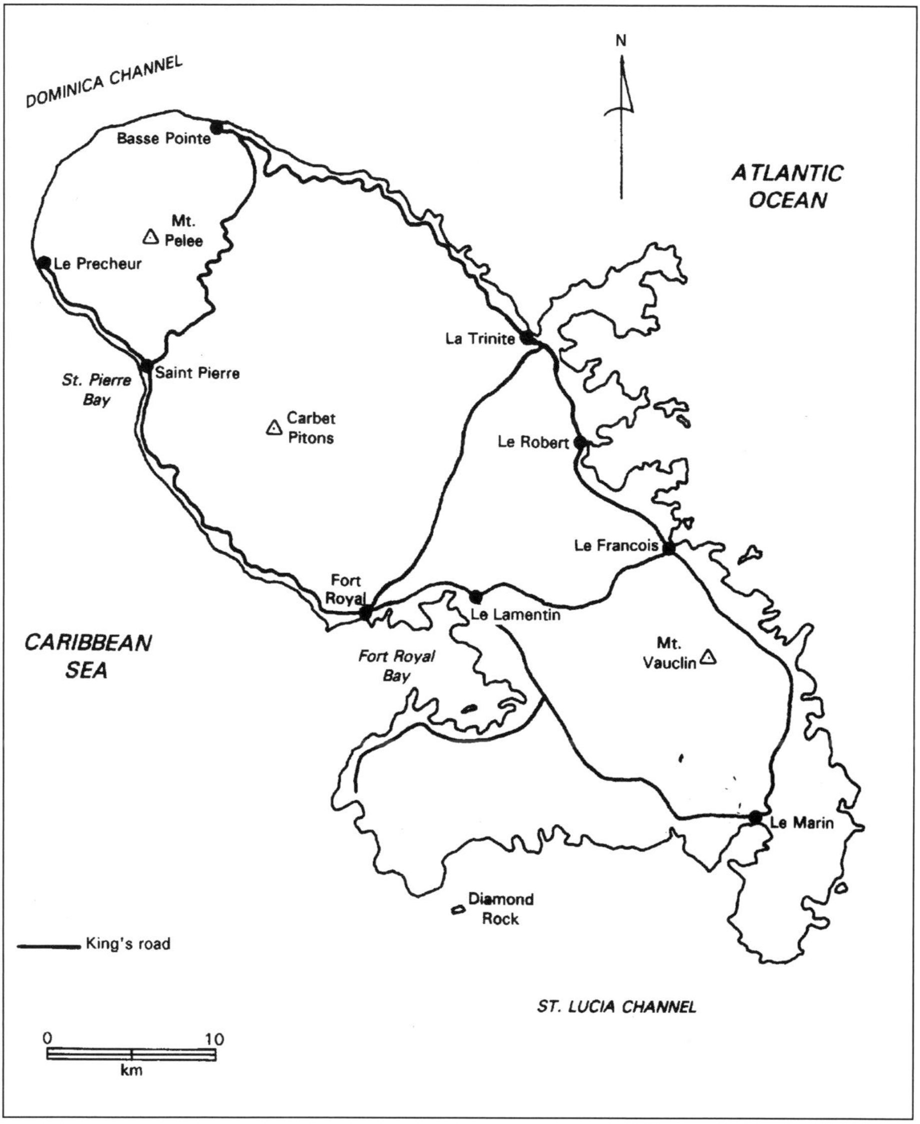

Map 3 Martinique in the eighteenth century.

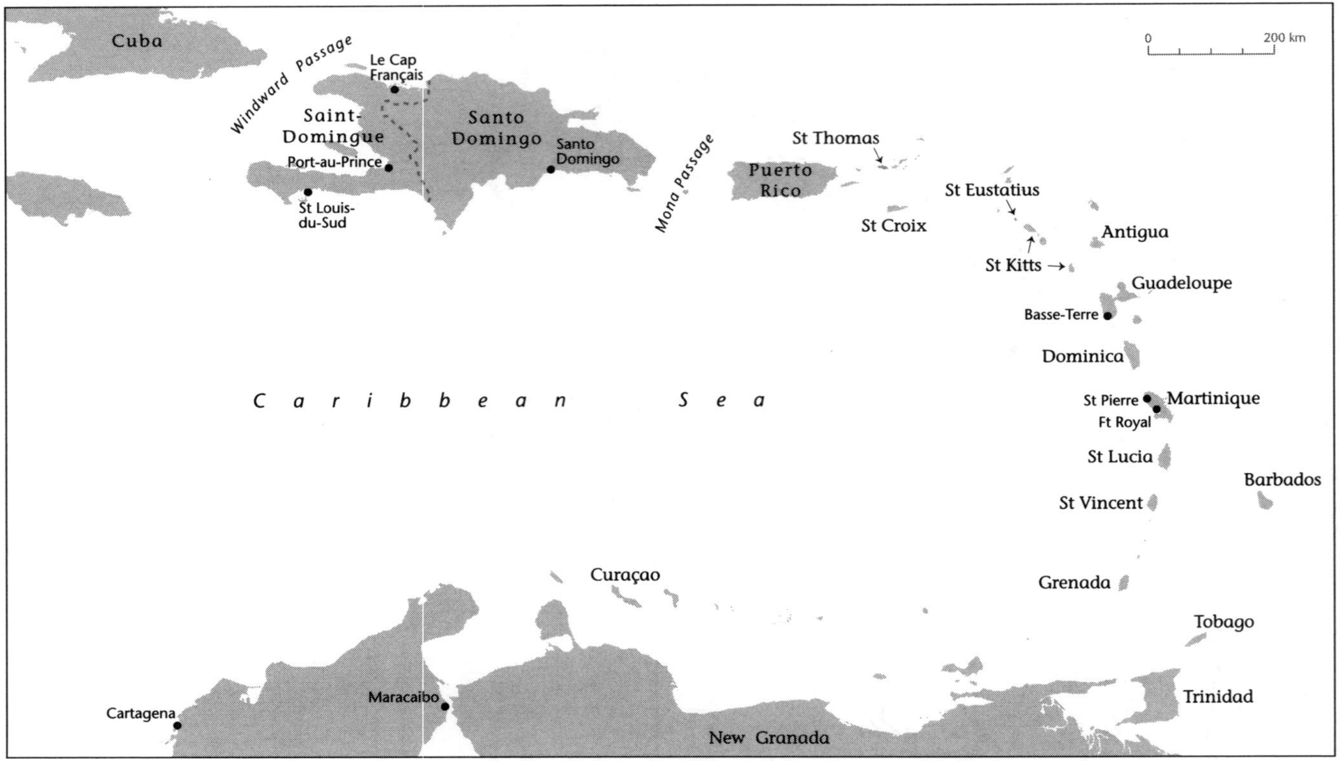

Map 4 The Îles du Vent and Saint Domingue in the eighteenth century.

Map 5 Canada, the Illinois Country, and Louisiana in the mid-eighteenth century.

Chasing Empire across the Sea

Introduction

In the heart of the long Canadian winter, Mathieu Benoist Collet and a clerk, Nicholas Gaspard Boucault, left the warm hearths of Quebec to visit the surrounding parishes. Governor General Philippe de Rigaud de Vaudreuil, Marquis de Vaudreuil, under orders from the Marine Council (a royal advisory body that combined the Navy and colonial affairs), had directed Collet to undertake an inspection in order to ensure that "all parish districts of the Colony are regulated by the same conventions as those observed in France."[1] He and his clerk were sent to find out the extent of each parish as actually experienced by the habitants, the number of families, and whether the people had any difficulty reaching divine services or priests. Above all, they were to listen: what did the common folk complain of?

At their first stop, in neighbouring Sainte-Foy, Collet and Boucault arrived early, but waited for over five hours for representatives of the seigneurs of the parish, the Jesuit order, to arrive; none did. Meanwhile, they warmed themselves in the tiny foyer of the local curé's cabin, speaking to some of the leading farmers in the area. The farmers, or habitants, listed the boundaries of the parish according to the *côtes*, or survey lines, although they disagreed over whether the Côte Saint-Michel marked a boundary or not. Some forty families inhabited the area, they said, and given the siting of the village in the middle of the parish, the curé was not far from anyone requiring solace or the last rites. Everyone present agreed that the situation was convenient for all. Then three men, two of them brothers, spoke up. Yes, they announced, they had in fact encountered some trouble. Part of the land they rented lay in the neighbouring parish of Lorette, and the Jesuits there insisted they go to the church located in that village, even though it was nearly twice as far as the chapel in Sainte-Foy. During the spring thaw, engorged streams completely cut them off from services; and it did not seem right, they added, that they paid the tithe to the Jesuits, since they never saw them, and the Jesuits were too far away to come to their aid in an emergency anyway. They knew at least seven other families who had the same problem. The men all agreed that this ridiculous state of affairs should not continue, and the more they talked, the more they wanted something done. Boucault wrote furiously. By five in the afternoon, another frosty night had tightened its grip on the land. Collet hastily read the proceedings back and asked if they had recorded the information correctly. Everyone attested to its accuracy, and most signed with an X by the light of a small oil lamp. Collet and Boucault then trudged out into the night and mounted their horses. They still had nearly an hour's ride in the stone-cold blackness to their next stop.

By June 1721, the two had collected hundreds of pages of similar testimonies for the Quebec military district alone, which Collet then summarized in about two hundred tightly packed folio pages. He delivered the results to Intendant Michel Bégon, who ordered a copy made to be forwarded to France. It arrived later that fall, and clerks in the new offices of the Bureau of Colonies, on the Rue Coquillière in Paris, neatly copied and annotated the document, and sent another condensed report to the Marine Council and the original to the archives nearby in the former Augustine monastery of Notre-Dame-des-Victoires, which had housed the Marine's papers for over twenty years.[2] Authorities used Collet's lengthy memorandum to either confirm or, more accurately, demarcate eighty-two parish boundaries in Canada and to try to address the serious problem that spiritual comfort reached only a fifth to a quarter of the population.[3]

This mundane episode in the life of an eighteenth-century French colony calls attention to a little studied but essential aspect of what might be called the "French Atlantic": the role of transportation and information exchange in the creation of a transoceanic administration. Outlined in this introductory anecdote are several of the basic components of this world: the desire by the metropolis to reconfigure the colony (in this case, the colonial landscape) according to its own patterns; a reliance on a clear hierarchy of command to communicate orders and receive reports, which in turn relied on the regular crossing of ships back and forth across the Atlantic to carry orders and receive reports; the use of written records and legal documents according to prescribed formulas; the intensive work of recopying written documents, which required literate clerks housed in permanent offices; the interdependence of church and state in creating reports in simple ways that we might overlook today (for example, the curé providing a warm "office" for the local depositions); the ability to carry out information-gathering missions in harsh climatic conditions over sustained periods of time and the assumption that basic transportation (horses, in this case) would be available; the storage and retrieval of records from more than one centralized depot; and perhaps most surprising for those unfamiliar with French colonial administration, the necessity to contact, listen to, and accept the judgments of local people in gathering the information upon which the state made many of its decisions. This last point is crucial, for it alerts us to a significant level of trust and cooperation between "the state" (through its colonial representatives) and free colonial inhabitants. Finally, Collet and Boucault's project accomplished its goal by providing information used by the state to make informed decisions. Individually, each of these aspects of the survey is unremarkable; collectively, they demonstrate the crucial importance of communications in binding metropolis to colony. It is from such ordinary projects of information gathering, analysis, and dissemination that a French Atlantic came into existence in the late seventeenth century and expanded until partially dismembered by the Treaty of Paris in 1763, which ended the Seven Years War.

Communications – gathering, analyzing, displaying, storing, and disseminating information and representations of authority – lay at the heart of the state's task in building an overseas empire. The early modern French state fostered the use of information and royal ceremony and symbolism within France itself in a highly rigid, hierarchial form, employing the paternalistically centred family as a model, and adapted to the needs of an authoritarian state with a new and burgeoning bureaucracy. And within France, the state largely succeeded. But it could not marshall and direct colonization and rule colonial possessions as easily because of a variety of constraints on obtaining and digesting information. The issue was not, as many historians have blithely assumed, that the colonies were too far away and were ignored by the king, leaving local officials perpetually awaiting orders or free to create their own mini-tyrannies. Such situations did occur in some extreme cases, but in most colonies the state played an active and highly interventionist role. Constraints on state control, and the royal authority that undergird that control, arose from quite a different source: the challenge of trying to absorb, comprehend, evaluate, and coordinate a very complex number of tasks in a wide variety of climates across a vast ocean which most state officials leaders never saw or experienced first-hand.

The difficulty of mastering communications emerged in a variety of different modes and circumstances. The outfitting of ships by a single, small administrative staff required a tremendous amount of attention and energy, and the efforts at coordinating the movements of vessels for different locations left little scope for imagination, poor reports, and ad hoc solutions to unforseen problems. Learning about new and often dangerous geographies and hydrographies required time and cooperation from the sailors and colonists who actually travelled the routes and understood the advantages and challenges. Lavish state ceremonies orchestrated in France to awe the king's subjects could not be easily duplicated in the colonies. Instead, colonial authorities used public celebrations and ritualized announcements as a way of addressing colonial issues and augmenting their own prestige, often in subtle ways. The state required continual reports explaining the behaviour and morals of new subject populations, the majority of whom in Louisiana and the Antilles were coerced labourers. At the same time, it enforced strict policies on separating them in order to prevent communication and potential collusion between the free, but at times "unruly," lower orders of colonial society and marginalized members such as soldiers, convicts, and especially slaves. These last three groups formed what might be termed a "marginalized estate," collectively comprising a level of society that did not have a direct equivalent in France. The state also faced a challenge from two other colonial populations. Since colonial and metropolitan merchants and agents controlled their own extensive networks of transatlantic and regional shipping, as well as commercial information, they were in a position to influence state policies and avoid state regulations. Finally, colonial elites rarely provided a unified front of royal authority, even though they were drafted into the administrative hierarchy. Reports by underlings, public disagreements between elites, dissension over promotions, even the sheer volume of information the state collected on its colonies either led to public disagreements between officials, which always raised the spectre of social disorder, or created inertia in decision-making when metropolitan officials were presented with conflicting evidence. As I hope to suggest in the following chapters, collectively these conditions and problems limited the extension of the French state's power overseas.

The existence of an early modern "French overseas empire" and what relation it has to an early modern "French Atlantic" remains unclear. The problem is more than semantic. As Anthony Pagden has shown, "empire" evoked the legacy of both Rome's *imperium* and the centuries-long search for a Christian *monarchia universalis*; beginning with the Iberian explorations of the Atlantic in the fifteenth century, monarchies interpreted "empire" according to specific cultural and political needs.[4] In the Anglo-American Atlantic world, John Brewer, David Hancock, and Marcus Rediker, among others, have described the wide and pervading base of administrators, merchants, and sailors who grasped the idea of an expanding Anglo-American empire in the eighteenth century, even if some, such as pirates, explicitly rejected membership. More importantly, both Brewer and Eliga H. Gould have underscored the prime importance of a public in both creating and supporting concepts of imperial destiny in the first British empire. Some British historians, led by David Armitage and Ned Landsman, have also argued for an Atlantic dimension to be consciously integrated into the study of 'Greater Britain.'[5] Other historians have convincingly traced other Atlantics, such as the black or "plantation Atlantic" described by Philip Curtin, David Eltis, John Thornton, and Paul Gilroy, among others.[6] In the hands of such scholars, there is a distinct discourse over the meaning and even timing between "empire" and "Atlantics" as a "system" of interaction.

"Empire" is an elusive term to describe France's overseas possessions before 1830. French authors and officials in the seventeenth and eighteenth centuries did not refer to a "French overseas empire," nor did they demonstrate any awareness of, or interest in, an imperial system or destiny. A version of "empire" seems to have coalesced in France only after 1763, and it is defined universally and overwhelmingly in negative terms, gaining momentum with the appearance of Abbé Guillaume-Thomas-François Raynal's *Histoire philosophique et politiques des deux Indes* (first published in 1770). Only toward the mid-eighteenth century did a minority of military thinkers, such as the Marquis de La Galissonière, envision an integrated imperial whole, when he argued in favour of fortifying and preserving Canada as a means of supplying French soldiers to the Caribbean and forcing Great Britain to divide its military attention between the Continent and North America.[7] However, nowhere in his extensive memorandums did La Galissonière discuss, explicitly or implicitly, a French "empire." Along both sides of the Atlantic littoral, French administrators treated overseas colonies, posts, and trading companies as an unsorted collection of peoples and possibilities, and they received "assembled bits of attention" from the state, to borrow Jacob Price's characterization of the French tobacco monopoly under Colbert.[8] The ambiguity of empire is reflected in the historiography of France's pre-1830 overseas possessions.[9] For example, in a recent article, Dale Miquelon employed the term to capture the essence of an imperial vision sketched by French negotiators in the Treaty of Utrecht which ended the War of the Spanish Succession (1702–13). However, "[t]he empire," he noted, "was one of colonial possessions considered individually valuable for their sugar, fur, or fish, but which were not integrated into a well-articulated imperial system."[10] A central concern of this study is to understand why, to paraphrase David Parker, the French empire was always in the making but never made.

A study of transatlantic communications is one way of shifting the emphasis away from a more narrow study of political institutions and bureaucrats to the interaction of metropolitan officials, free and unfree colonists, and French and foreign traders, within a broader geographic and economic domain: the French Atlantic. The idea of a French Atlantic is gaining some currency among scholars. For example, Silvia Marzagalli tentatively accepts that, "if something like a *French Atlantic* existed," it comprised a "common, interrelated historical area along the shores of France and the New World ... and [had] some relevance for both partners," and that it dated from between the early seventeenth century and some point between the end of the Seven Years War in 1763 and the independence of Haiti in 1804.[11] To recognize the existence of a "French Atlantic" is, first of all, to understand the possibilities and limitations of seaborne communication; after all, without seaborne contact, and the institutional infrastructure and social values that support it, overseas dominion would not exist. Since Fernand Braudel's work on the Mediterranean in the sixteenth century and Jacques Godechot's perception of a unified Atlantic civilization in the late 1940s, oceans and great seas are now viewed less as obstacles to contact than as highways merging different economies, creating new cultures, or even pollinating revolutionary movements.[12] As Anne Pérotin-Dumon has reminded us, this idea is hardly new; it can be traced back at least to Adam Smith and Wilhelm von Humboldt. What is new is the idea of humans interacting, albeit under unequal conditions, within a vastly larger network of contact made possible by sea: "People and ocean together made up the network, and throughout the network, it was people who carried ideas."[13]

The emphasis on geography and travel as tools of empire is essential to my own understanding of the "French Atlantic." Within the French Atlantic, the range in climate and topography must have been daunting to any eighteenth-century administrator, ranging from ice floes to equatorial rain forests, from rocky islets to humid swamps and tundra, across two major oceanic wind and current systems and another half-dozen major regional subsystems. Geographically, the French Atlantic encompassed a wide swath of territory under direct or indirect French influence. This area included the ports and their hinterlands of France's Atlantic littoral (called the Ponant), Marseille in the Mediterranean, and the centre of administration at Paris/Versailles; the French slaving posts of West Africa, from the Senegambia to the Bight of Benin but centred at Fort Saint Louis and later Gorée; North America, with three affiliated settlement colonies of New France (Canada, Louisiana, and Île Royale), plus "British-occupied" Acadia and the crucial fisheries of Terre-Neuve (Newfoundland); the Caribbean, centred on Saint

Domingue (Haiti after 1804) in the west and Martinique, Guadeloupe, and their dependent islands in the eastern arc of the Lesser Antilles; and the anemic colony of Cayenne on the South American mainland. As we shall see, learning how to pilot through these regions proved itself to be a formidable obstacle to creating a coherent administration.

As a cultural, political, and economic entity, the French Atlantic shared at least six other dimensions that gave it coherency and unique colonies. First, a single state agency, the Marine, based in Paris but attached to whatever palace the court happened to occupy at the moment, managed all colonies, provided defence, and tried to enforce the state's economic policies. In this respect, it functioned in a way very similar to the Spanish Council of the Indies.[14] However, the Marine also encompassed two branches of the Navy (a "blue water" fleet and a fleet of Mediterranean galleys), a network of maritime arsenals and ordnance suppliers, a coastal defence network, maritime courts, and a bureau to register and supervise the training of all deep-sea sailors. Technically, the interests of colonists were handled by a secretary of state for the Marine, a position reserved for the high nobility, which usually allowed access to the king through several councils (described in chapter 2). The primary role of the Marine therefore ensured that a distinct military ethos permeated many of the connections across the French Atlantic. A second characteristic was that the French Atlantic was a "national" French Atlantic, at least by the early eighteenth century. Parisian French became the standard language, colonial administrators were drawn from across France and trained in different regions in order to enhance priorities based on the national vision set by the court, and French settlers from distinct regions merged their inherited traditions within an increasingly "creole" or "habitant" one. Third, legal economic activity, woven together by a largely mercantilist set of policies, not only tied the French and colonial areas mentioned above together but embraced a select number of foreign ports such as Cork in Ireland, Cadiz in Spain, Amsterdam, and Hamburg. A fourth aspect was that the Gallican church and the vociferous ecclesiastic debates that raged within its ranks, particularly over Jansenism, influenced spiritual and family life, ultimately over both free and unfree colonists.[15] Fifth, a distinct set of legal codes – two Code Noirs (1685 and 1724) policing the conduct of slaves, a network of admiralty courts, and the Coutume de Paris – created a single and largely unified legal tradition. Finally, and alone among the colonizing powers in the New World, the French state consciously pursued policies of close diplomatic ties with independent Native nations in North America to enhance trade and security. In considering the French Atlantic as a distinct entity, it is also useful to see it as part of a larger transatlantic, transnational, and cross-cultural Atlantic zone in the 1500–1800 era, one layer of many other "Atlantics," which, if laid like transparencies one top of another, formed the "Atlantic world."

The Marine, as a dynamic and developing state organ in the early modern era, relied on the collection, processing, analyzing, and selective redistribution of massive amounts of information in order to direct the French colonial world. Of course, the rise of information-fed bureaucracies of nation-states is arguably one of the foremost defining aspects of the early modern French state itself and a mark of more recent studies of what historians call, now with qualifications, "absolutist France."[16] Orest Ranum, for example, has argued that the form of state control achieved under Louis XIV constituted an entirely new form of monarchical government by developing an intense preoccupation with data collection from across the kingdom, a will to enforce strict and uniform standards of morality, and the subservience of art and ideas to the needs of state glorification.[17] Added to his work have been studies exploring the complex relations of patronage and clientage as the basis of power relations in the seventeenth century. Sharon Kettering, William Beik, and J. Russell Major, to name only three of the more prominent scholars, have shifted attention from analyses of administrative structures to "networks" or "webs of influence" that operated through reciprocal bonds of personal loyalty, although they reach different conclusions about the political uses of such networks.[18] It is with this important emphasis on the primary role of information and controlling communication by centralized, permanent bureaucracies staffed increasingly by highly trained, literate personnel that I use the term "state." Clearly, the French monarchy established a fully functioning information-gathering and taxing bureaucracy unlike any other then existing in Europe. How, then, did the French state apply this new type of information bureaucracy to its overseas possessions? And how did the state's attempt at monopolizing communications condition the development of colonies?

Studies of the relationship of communications to imperialism have not been well received by historians until recently. For example, the later work of Harold Adams Innis on the relationship between communications media and imperial systems has long been recognized by communications researchers as an innovative set of studies, but few historians have appeared interested in his work.[19] However, studies emphasizing communications have slowly trickled into historians' consciousness. Jürgen Habermas has probably provided the greatest impact by uniting three aspects of communication that historians had previously treated separately: the sites of discourse (newspapers, salons), a particular mode of discourse (validation by reasoned critique), and communications actors (a specific class, the bourgeoisie). In defining his concept of the "public sphere," Habermas argued that the rise of long-distance trade, national markets, and internationally exchanged printed sources of news were inseparable.[20] In another direction, Roger Chartier has argued in favour of developing a methodology for determining representation in and appropriation of historical texts. The value of his approach lies in conceptualizing the intended audience of any piece of information or ritual as an important component in the formulation of the specific act of communication itself.[21] More recently, Daniel R. Headrick has has persuasively argued that "information was the lifeblood of European imperialism" in the nineteenth century, since new or improved communications by rail, steamship, and undersea cables allowed knowledge of technology applied in one region or continent to be cheaply and easily adapted and deployed in another.[22] Taken together, these studies have opened new doors in the historical research of communications. For the first time, historians have begun to perceive communications as an evolving human environment, continually re-forming and re-formed by the interplay of social interaction.

No longer does the older concept of communications as simply writing, printing, and transportation – the means of imparting messages from sender to receiver – hold sway among communications researchers.[23] James Carey has been among the most influential theorists in refining the concept of communications. He has distinguished between communications' two roles, a "transmission" component (dissemination of information) and a "ritual" component (sharing and legitimizing belief systems). For example, a newspaper has two communications roles: a transmission role in efficiently disseminating content, which can be quantitatively measured in a variety of ways, and a ritual role, where "news is not information but drama" and through which a reader finds in its narratives confirmation (or rejection) of his or her own perception of reality and place in society.[24] Carey's interpretation encompasses both the exchange of messages and the formation, maintenance, and re-formation of community as a result of changing patterns of such exchanges. His ideas place communications much closer to an ethnohistorical emphasis on intercultural exchange, where speech and non-verbal actions are examined to understand the dynamics of social and political change. The concept of communications used in this study emphasizes the dynamic and even volatile nature of mixing ideas, customs, and emotions among people and groups in specific places and times. Like a door opening between two adjoining rooms, communications is that third sphere created by the interaction brought into being from the first two.

My main interest in this study is to understand how the French Atlantic worked at its territorial, economic, and demographic height, between 1713 and 1763. I have relied mainly on internal official correspondence, which is remarkably partisan and riven by a pervading sense of the metropolitan as normative "Self" trying to ameliorate the colonial, Creole "Other." I have supplemented this information with officials' private correspondence, travel accounts, merchants' letters, ships' logs, local court records, analysis of graphic materials such as maps, and royal ordinances and laws. I decided to concentrate on three types of colonies as models: the French "mainland" colony of Canada, the tropical sugar islands of the Îles du Vent (French Windward Islands, which included Guadeloupe, Martinique, and the latter's dependencies in the Lesser Antilles chain), and the curious mixture of the two that became Louisiana. The documentation on all three is extensive – the official documents contained in Creole writer Médéric Louis Elie Moreau de Saint-Méry's collection on Martinique alone runs to more than 10,400 folio pages – and is relatively easy to access. I decided not to include what became France's greatest single New World producer, and one of the most inhuman prisons and cemeteries for hundreds of thousands of African and Creole slaves, the colony of Saint Domingue. Its huge size – it effectively incorporated three different colonies – its vast (and uncatalogued) written material, and its unique and complex history, would, I felt, muddy any clarity that might be achieved in a comparative study. Therefore this book is in no sense a "definitive study," but rather an extended essay serving as an introduction to what I hope will become a larger domain of inquiry. For this reason, I have tried to indicate throughout the book potentially valuable paths for others to follow.

The study begins with a brief overview of the formation and development of the French Atlantic from 1604 to 1763, for those unfamiliar with the French colonizing experience, and its relation to early modern French state-building. Chapter 2 examines the transmission of a single item of news, the proclamation of the Peace of Utrecht in 1713, ending the War of the Spanish Succession, and how the Marine organized the details for sending royal ships to the colonies. The third chapter provides an outline of basic transportation routes by land and sea, emphasizing patterns of contact and the environmental challenges associated with building and maintaining infrastructure, such as ports and roads. In chapter 4 I consider the state's use of processions and public ceremonies in the colonies, showing how these were modified by colonial officials for their own purposes. The following chapter suggests ways in which the state used its control over communications to impose social order on unruly imported and marginalized populations, including convicts, soldiers, and especially slaves. Chapter 6 stresses the accommodation that the Marine made with merchants, who enjoyed access to their own extensive transatlantic network of contacts. Finally, chapter 7 explores what I term the "information-patronage" relationship between local governing elites and the Marine, based on a basic exchange of information in return for appointments and promotions.

The challenges posed by transatlantic communications impinged on, modified, and increasingly undermined the French state's control over its colonies during the first half of the eighteenth century. Rethinking the use of technical and symbolic means of communication in that century will, I hope, provide a historical context for current debates over the aftershocks of colonization and the meaning of freedom within an "information age."[25] Collet and Boucault's survey of 1721, humble as it might seem, shows in a benign way how the eighteenth-century French state tried to control movement and information exchange in order to fully master its overseas peoples.

CHAPTER ONE

The Rise of the French Atlantic to 1763

Even as King François I challenged the Iberian monopoly on transatlantic voyaging and conquest by demanding to see the clause in Adam's will that reserved half the world to the king of Spain,[1] French sailors were cruising the Grand Banks for fish, trading for spices and perhaps slaves in West Africa, and collecting dyewoods from the coast of Brazil.[2] Yet sixteenth-century French kings, nobles, merchants, and fishermen were sporadic exploiters of the newly opened shipping routes and reluctant to seek the broader coalitions of talent, experience, and capital that colonial enterprise demanded. Religious strife, succession disputes, and armed Spanish opposition from the mid-sixteenth century further limited trading and settlement ventures, leaving what appears to be, from an imperial vantage point, a series of failed experiments. This chapter provides an overview of the evolution of the French Atlantic from the early seventeenth century to 1763, the end point of this study. My goal is to supply both a basic narrative of major political, economic, and military developments and to suggest the close connection between changes in France itself and colonial development. The growth of a French Atlantic mirrored the dynamic environment of French political culture, that often-elusive combination of ideology, leadership, administrative innovation, and authoritarian repression that marked the later *ancien régime*. In a sense, the French Atlantic provided a refracted image of the growing French nation-state during the 1600–1763 period, its leading personalities, its priorities, and its creeping paralysis.

PHASE ONE: PARTNERSHIPS, 1600–1642

Henri IV's (1598–1610) abjuration of Protestantism played a major part in cementing the authority of the monarch in all aspects of French life. In the late 1590s and into the first decade of the seventeenth century, Catholics and French Protestants (or Huguenots) joined talents, capital resources, and crews to venture overseas. In addition, arguments by Jean Bodin that a sovereign should and must wield unlimited power to ensure domestic tranquillity[3] helped calm the fears of merchant investors, who risked depredations by other nations or, worse, other French towns. The settlement expeditions in the region between the Orinoco and Amazon Rivers in South America[4] and the appearance of permanent colonies in the Bay of Fundy and along the St Lawrence River in North America has prompted some historians to declare this era the genesis of French overseas imperialism, and even of a coherent imperial policy.[5]

In 1603 the admiral of France, the Duc de Montmorency, granted to Pierre de Gua, Sieur de Monts, his vice-admiral for Acadia, a monopoly over trade, mining, and fishing in the northern lands, together with the obligation to settle at least sixty colonists. Forming an association called the Compagnie de la Nouvelle France, which drew on La Rochelle merchants experienced in American coastal fur trading, de Monts sailed, along with his young but experienced lieutenant, Samuel de Champlain, to construct a post at Port Royal (Nova Scotia) in 1604.[6] Henri IV revoked the monopoly upon the protests of Saint Malo, whose merchants had been excluded, in effect opening all transatlantic trade to many French ports. This ruling marked an important watershed, a switch from a monarch's support of regional interests to the state's desire to harness and balance competing interests. In the next two critical years, Champlain resurrected a dream dating back to Jacques Cartier's expeditions (1534–42) of harvesting furs in the St Lawrence River valley. He leapfrogged over fur-trading Basque competitors at Tadoussac to found a small settlement (*habitation*) on the promontory of Stadacona in 1608, which he called Quebec.[7] With the assistance of Algonquian-speaking peoples, the post hung on and even grew large and productive enough to attract the notice of Scottish privateers in 1629. Champlain understood the need to create a network of information for the colony to succeed: he regularly corresponded with the Rochellais merchants who extended credit, sought out Huron and Montagnais leaders to enhance gift-exchange and cement alliances, made regular personal representations at court (seven journeys in twenty years), published his own lively accounts and maps of the region, and encouraged the circular letters of others, such as Marc Lescarbot's *Histoire de la Nouvelle France*, to tap into the powerful and wealthy network of the French Counter-Reformation in order to bring Catholic missionaries to the colony.[8] Despite his devotion and energy, by Champlain's death in 1635 the colony numbered hardly more than 170 people.

The assassination of Henri IV in 1610 ushered in a short period of political instability, which ended with the majority of the young Louis XIII and the appointment of a new, aggressive, and visionary first minister, Jean-Armand du Plessis, Cardinal de Richelieu, chief minister of France from 1624 to his death in 1642. Richelieu brought to his post an unusually strong maritime heritage.[9] As the leading advocate for reducing Spanish and Austrian Habsburg power by any means at hand, he led an elite group of councillors and courtiers known as the "Bons français," often in opposition to the Dévot party, a powerful faction of great nobles and some financiers led by the queen mother, Marie de Médicis, who urged the spiritual renewal of France and closer ties with the pope.[10] Richelieu's plans to break Spanish power led him to grasp the importance of developing French maritime power, in part to choke off the Spanish flow of silver from its American colonies.

While Richelieu is known more for what he proposed than what he accomplished, his influence on colonial and maritime affairs cannot be underestimated. He awarded himself the grandiose title of "Grand Master and Superintendent General of the Navigation and Commerce of France" and set about to institutionalize and rationalize royal control over an invigorated French Navy and its main ports, more than tripling the Navy's budget in the process.[11] Along with Michel de Marillac, the keeper of the king's seals, a powerful official close to the king in 1626, he formulated the massive administrative document known as the Code Michaud, which aimed at improving French naval and seaborne commercial power. Among its 461 provisions, it laid the theoretical foundation for merchant-state cooperation by outlining forums for consultation with merchants, allowing nobles to enter into seaborne commerce without derogation, called for crown-funded schools for navigators and shipboard artillery cannoneers, and the creation of a census and registration of all French mariners (presumably to tap those with transatlantic experience), and even ordered pilots returning from overseas voyages to write, or have written, a precise report on their navigational observations.[12]

In colonial affairs, Richelieu created new state-supported monopoly companies to buttress the small posts recently founded in New France and Acadia and to penetrate further into the Spanish West Indies.[13] Most importantly, he destroyed the power of Huguenot La Rochelle, capturing it in 1629 and bringing it – and by extension, its Protestant connections with the new French colonies in America – under direct royal supervision.[14] After La Rochelle's conquest, there was no doubt that settlement and trade in the Americas would be Catholic and approved only by the crown. Of less immediate impact but with major consequences later, Richelieu engineered a partial restruction of the increasingly complex French taxation system, and he introduced the use of intendants in the provinces from 1634 to supervise tax collection.[15] The former provided the state with a stronger system to fund its colonies; the latter gave the crown a loyal reporter, tax supervisor, and social leader in the French provinces. The use of intendants later became a cornerstone of the colonial administrative system under Louis XIV.

Guiding Richelieu's administrative innovations were a number of fiscal and economic policies, which have been collectively labelled "mercantilism" by later economic theorists and historians. While a complex and far from static doctrine, it can be summed up as a system that "conceives of the state as a merchant, seeking always to achieve a surplus of exports (sales) over imports (purchases)."[16] The more the state helped to increase its wealth, by either increasing internal commercial activity and the exports of items such as wool or wine or decreasing the imports of resources such as bullion, metals, and timber, the more its subjects profited and the more the state gained in tax revenue. For the state, monopoly companies were simply easier to tax than individual merchants, and the vogue for creating large monopoly companies to develop overseas settlements gained prominence from the 1620s on. One early advocate of mercantilism, Antoine de Montchrétien, an obscure member of the lower nobility in seafaring Normandy, proclaimed that France possessed a natural calling to be a seafaring nation, with its "two doors giving issue to the two ends of the earth ... by which [our] noble peoples can carry the lily-decked oriflamme to every corner of the world."[17] In short, mercantilist ideas made colonies appear to be far more attractive to the interests of the state.

The founding of colonies in the West Indies reflected the new weight of the state's interest. After escaping from a Spanish galleon in 1624, Pierre Belain d'Esnambuc, an impoverished Norman noble, landed on the small island of Saint Christophe (St Kitts) in the Lesser Antilles chain.[18] An English group had already landed there four years earlier, and, in imitation of early Virginia, introduced slave- and indentured servant–cultivated tobacco. Sniffing the possibilities, d'Esnambuc left some men to stake a claim and learn tobacco production, returned immediately to France, sought and finally received an audience with Richelieu, and convinced the cardinal not only to grant him a monopoly for a tobacco colony but to invest 10,000 livres in it. The grant for the Compagnie de Saint-Christophe in 1626 included clauses typical for a seventeenth-century overseas monopoly company, including title from the crown to develop any lands occupied, a monopoly over import trade, quotas for sending new settlers (532 were taken in the first year), and a pledge to convert Native peoples (usually denoted as "savages") to Christianity. By 1634 it had become common knowledge that the colonists sold nearly all their tobacco to Dutch ship captains. Richelieu revoked the charter and established another, the Compagnie des Isles de l'Amérique, with many of his own clients as directors. From this company sprang initiatives for two new French possessions, Guadeloupe and Martinique, both settled in 1635.[19] Within seven years, smaller parties from these two islands carved out small farms on neighbouring Dominica, Saint Barthélemy, Sainte Croix, Saint Martin, Grenada, and Tobago, all at the expense of their Carib inhabitants. A few even ventured as far as La Tortuga, an island off the northwestern tip of Spanish Hispaniola.

Many of the French emigrants to the West Indies came as indentured servants, French labourers who exchanged the price of their passage for a commitment to work in the new colonies, often for a three-year stretch. Indentured servants came from different regions, but as with settlers for New France, many were from Paris or the Norman, Breton, and increasingly Poitou ports, although they might be the offspring of parents with roots in rural villages.[20] However, the commercial success and the provision of enslaved labour for these early colonies depended far less on either the French state or its ports than on Dutch ship captains and commercial connections. The Dutch not only purchased cargoes of tobacco for competitive amounts, but according to one early chronicler of the French West Indian colonies, Father Du Tertre, a Dutch refugee planter from Brazil named Tetzel first introduced sugar plantation agriculture to Martinique.[21] Within thirty years, sugar had emerged as the most profitable colonial product from the French islands, and the slave trade had begun as a crucial underpinning of the sugar plantation economy.[22] By the time of Richelieu's death in 1642, an estimated 3,000 French men and some women lived in the West Indies, along with approximately 1,200 imported African or black Brazilian slaves, while all of New France still counted barely 360 French men and women.[23]

While Richelieu's policies and those of the Dévot party clashed in France, in New France they found enough room for accommodation. In 1627 Richelieu streamlined the colony's charters by creating the Compagnie des Cents-Associés (Company of One Hundred Associates) the better to exploit the fur trade.[24] But with the loss of the Quebec post and Acadia to Scottish Protestant pirates between 1629–1632 – a direct result of the crown's attack on Huguenot La Rochelle – the company lost everything it had invested and was forced to lease out trade and settlement rights. In doing so, it inaugurated one of the more unusual aspects of New France: the granting of sub-fiefs to French seigneurs, who were then obligated to bring out a set number of settlers with them. Although medieval institutional forms such as the payment of *foi et homage* to the company by the seigneur or of customary dues by the settler were recorded, it is now generally conceded that settlers actually paid little, if anything, and moved relatively freely from seigneur to seigneur.[25] Despite its long-term impact on land settlement patterns, the seigneurial system was a temporary expedient, not a full-scale effort to export European feudalism to the New World.

The Dévots proved temporarily to be even more effective at launching overseas enterprises. Beginning in 1610, they sponsored Jesuit and Récollet priests to proselytize, first in Acadia, next in the St Lawrence valley posts, and from 1625, in the many Native villages throughout the vast territory woodlands of the *pays d'en haut*.[26] French Jesuits applied the same methods of close, appreciative study of new peoples and their languages, on the one hand, and relentless attacks on their traditional belief systems, on the other, that had proven to be so successful in the East Asian missions. By the 1640s they had established a number of settled villages among France's greatest Native ally at the time, the Huron nation, in what is now the Lake Simcoe region of Ontario.[27] To help support the missions, the Jesuit missionaries themselves penned a series of letters in the field, collectively known today as the *Jesuit Relations*, which their superiors edited in Quebec and sent back to France to be published. Vividly and richly written narratives, they described in exacting detail the lives, rituals, political organization, and torture of the peoples the Jesuits encountered, as well as the proselytizing efforts of the missionaries themselves. These works inspired a great number of prominent lay men and women (including many wealthy widows) to support evangelization efforts in New France; mission villages, colleges, a seminary, and hospitals were all built at least in part to aid the thrust of Christianity in the New World. In the spring of 1642, another Dévot-sponsored group, the Société Notre-Dame de Montréal, planted a "New Jerusalem" closer to the Iroquois and Huron of the *pays d'en haut* (and further from brandy-bearing fur traders) at a strategic site upriver christened Ville Marie. The fur-trading potential of the post was quickly recognized, however, and it grew into the opposite of a spiritual mission – the brandy-soaked town of Montreal.[28] Nevertheless, the institutional success of the Dévots, in comparison to the anemic support offered by either the French state or major port towns, reflected the wealth and high calibre of organizational skill possessed by the movement within France upon the death of Richelieu.

INTERREGNUM, 1642–1664

France underwent tremendous internal strife during the period from the late 1630s throughout the minority of Louis XIV until the mid-1650s, culminating with the outbursts of provincial civil war known as the Fronde (1648–53).[29] No such uprisings occurred in the colonies, largely because the collapse of royal authority and the diminishing of Dévot support allowed company governors to purchase what they exercised in fact: mastery over their respective domains. The scattered posts of the Americas were thrown onto their own resources, a situation that did not decisively change until the advent of direct crown rule in 1664. During this short period, mercantile links with either Dutch or, more rarely, French ship captains provided the only consistent contact with Europe. French colonists survived by turning inward, forging security alliances, moving, and pursuing trade contacts, often outside state desires.

In New France, chaotic conditions across the Atlantic forced the French company holding the fur monopoly to lease it back in 1645 to a New France group, the Community of the Habitants in 1645; in effect transferring trade rights back to the major fur merchants in the colony, their Jesuit supporters, and their primarily Rochellais creditors. Factional disputes erupted between fur-trading families and between the Jesuits and a new religious order, the Sulpicians, who haggled over a proposed bishopric for the colony. At the same time, tensions escalated between the Huron, Erie, Neutral, and Ojibwa and their French allies, on one side, and the Iroquois Confederacy, on the other. The Iroquois and the Huron engaged in a series of vicious, semi-genocidal wars, which resulted in the destruction of most Huron villages and the dispersion of the survivors in 1650s.[30] The Iroquois then turned their attention on the French settlements in the St Lawrence and came very close to eliminating the French settlers. As William Eccles has noted, dwindling military support from France prompted the trial-and-error creation of a tough Canadian-born militia to defend French posts and attack Iroquois villages.[31] But the militia were too few to prolong their tenuous hold for long. By the time of Louis XIV's assumption of the personal command of France in 1661, colonial leaders had appealed vigorously to the crown to stabilize trade, settle internal disputes, and above all, send military reinforcements. New France looked to the king as a saviour, a situation quite different from that in the French Antilles.

In the Antilles between in 1648 and 1651, Richelieu's successor disbanded the nearly bankrupt Compagnie des Isles de l'Amérique and sold the trade and colonization rights to the individual governors of the main islands. Saint Christophe, the most populated and largest exporter, went to its governor, de Poincy, who then resold it to the Knights of Malta, while the governors of Guadeloupe (de Houel) and Martinique (du Parquet) purchased the rights to their islands.[32] Although ships from Dieppe, Le Havre, Saint Malo, and increasingly Nantes and La Rochelle called at the French islands, the clear commercial winners in these transactions were the Dutch merchants from Amsterdam and Middleburg. By the early 1660s, one French estimate, although undoubtedly inflated, placed the value of Dutch trade in sugar, tobacco, indigo, and some cotton at over 3,000,000 livres per annum, with sugar alone accounting for two-thirds of the total. French settlers paid for the rise in sugar production with blood. The French ruthlessly cleared the islands of their Carib inhabitants, first on the Caribbean side of each island (Basseterre) and then on the Atlantic (Cabesterre). Whole villages were torched, and French colonists slaughtered men, women, and children indiscriminately. By 1658, the last pockets of Carib resistance had been subdued or forced to flee to Dominica and St Vincent. As sugar monoculture gobbled up land from Martinique down to Grenada, the number of slaves brought by Dutch ships also increased sharply.

Two other movements in the Greater Caribbean reflect the wide spectrum of responses to the evaporation of state support in the nascent French Atlantic. On the one hand, colonists themselves began to organize themselves into distinct, rudimentary governing units. This activity is best demonstrated by events on Spanish Hispaniola. From the 1640s, small groups of men, the majority from the French islands, began to settle in the wilder region of the island, vacated by the Spanish since the 1620s and largely untouched by other European authorities or monopoly companies.[33] They lived by growing tobacco, smuggling goods to Spanish colonial towns, and roasting the meat of wild cattle and drying hides over smouldering open-pit fires called *boucans*.[34] These "buccaneers" gradually coalesced into a potent and aggressive force numbering at least two thousand well-armed men by 1655. In that year, English Puritan forces evicted the Spanish from Jamaica, and most of the English- and Dutch-speaking buccaneers removed to that island; the French stayed behind at the stronghold of La Tortuga.[35] The nucleus of a new but clearly unruly French settlement – the Saint Domingue coast – had emerged by 1660, independent of, and highly antagonistic to, the crown's authority or state-granted monopolies.

At the other end of the spectrum, metropolitan colonizing efforts were redoubled in the northeastern corner of mainland of South America. This region, known to the French as Cayenne, continued its early tradition as the pre-eminent graveyard of preplanned French settlements. Three different consortia of Normandy merchants backed by powerful courtiers and Parisian financiers launched colonizing expeditions in 1643, 1651–54, and 1656. Each one fell prey to a combination of factional strife, epidemics, despotic rule, and stout resistance from neighbouring Gailibis peoples.[36] In the last instance, hopeful colonists encountered the remnants of the second expedition at Martinique and, learning of the rosy future awaiting them, mysteriously slipped away. The failure of these three initiatives marked the last time when private interests would inaugurate French colonizing efforts. Henceforth, colonization would be the state's domain.

PHASE TWO: ABSOLUTISM, 1664–1683

The ascension of Louis XIV in 1661, along with the rise of his chief administrative officer, Jean-Baptiste Colbert, initiated the first attempt to integrate all of France's overseas dominions into a single, integrated political entity under direct royal authority. There is no doubt that royal authority and priorities replaced local leadership in all colonies, or that the full array of a centralized royal administration was exported virtually intact to the colonies. More than any period during the *ancien régime* either before or since, the first half of the Sun King's reign saw the implementation of a genuinely absolutist power structure in the French Americas. During this short era, it appeared that the colonies would be the realization of Louis's desire to organize France around the royal person and permanently enshrine belief in the divine right of the monarch, even if this proved more difficult to enforce within France itself. Yet we must keep in mind that this moment proved to be relatively brief, ending effectively with Colbert's death in 1683.

Louis introduced four broad but far-reaching administrative and political initiatives that directly recast the French Atlantic. First, the king became his own first minister, and re-organized his top echelon of administrators in 1661 so that four secretaries of state reported directly to him. Each secretary now handled a specific domain and was expected to offer counsel from a national perspective. Colonial matters, eventually subordinated to the portfolio of the secretary of state for the Marine, therefore could be brought directly to Louis's attention as pertaining to state interests. Secondly, he centralized command over information flows from the lower echelons upward. Information about the colonies and issues pertaining to them now flowed to the secretaries of state from their clients, relatives, and associates, and they in turn assessed and passed on information from their own network of clients, relatives, and friends. In effect, Louis tapped into, and could influence, the vast client networks of each secretary of state. Thirdly, he firmly brought the French clergy under his control, ceaselessly championing the divinity of his royal person, bullying the French clergy into supporting the Four Gallican Articles (1682), which diminished the pope's control over the French regular clergy and lay orders, and campaigning against the Jansenists, a movement of theologians and priests who opposed state control over religion. Never again would the church be able to organize or maintain its own overseas projects, and all missionary activity, down to the recording of parish baptisms, would henceforward serve state interests. Finally, Louis insisted that all colonies be brought under direct royal jurisdiction and not remain the provenance of companies. He personally appointed, or approved the appointment of, colonial governors and, for the first time, intendants and lesser officials; supported the adoption of uniform taxing structures, codes, and regulations to govern the colonies (such as the Coutume de Paris);[37] and eventually allowed only orthodox Catholics to wield any semblance of power or privilege in his name overseas. For the first time, metropolitan-trained personnel, for the most part, were to harmonize rule in the colonies with rule and conduct in France. However, all these major initiatives must be placed in the context of Louis's slight interest in maritime or colonial affairs. As Denis Dessert has noted, the king spent more time concocting names for his ornate flagships than learning or thinking about naval strategy, coastal defence, or colonial development.[38]

If Louis conceived of the grand scheme on the canvas, to Colbert fell the task of painting the details. Historians through most of the twentieth century viewed Colbert as a kind of self-made bourgeois who worked hard to curtail the feudal nobility and advance the interests of his own order, the middle class.[39] Recent work has completely debunked this myth.[40] As a young man, Colbert had ample resources at his disposal, having been raised in the tightly knit world of Parisian finance; as one historian has observed, "It was [the] family which made Colbert, not the reverse."[41] By the time Colbert officially took command of the Marine in 1669, he had aggressively recruited his extended kin to occupy key positions in all the main Atlantic naval bases of Rochefort and Brest and the Ponant and Levant offices of the Navy, and had forged alliances through marriages of close relatives to six major military commanders and several major court financiers.[42] Among his highest priorities was rebuilding the Navy itself.[43] During the reign of Louis XIV, the Marine constructed, purchased, or captured nearly 380 naval vessels; some 98 ships of the line (those carrying 40–100 cannon) were brought into service between 1661 and 1677 alone.[44] Colbert expanded the naval port at Toulon, built new arsenals at Rochefort in Poitou and at Brest in Brittany, and employed several thousand shipwrights, artisans, labourers, and clerks. For the first time, royal ships possessed the infrastructural capability to sail regularly on the Atlantic Ocean. To nationalize and routinize the culture of the Navy, he instituted a new code, which appeared near the end of his life in 1681.[45] However critical these improvements were, they were still inferior in terms of overall state policies. As Jean Meyer has ruefully noted, Louis XIV lavished as much money on his palaces as on the Marine; and in a typical year, the Army devoured 47 per cent, or 54 million livres, of the state's budget, while the Marine had to be content with only 9.5 per cent (10.9 million livres).[46]

Colbert linked his understanding of naval affairs directly to his concept of state power: the more commercially successful a country, the stronger its tax and customs base and therefore its ability to be materially self-sufficient during periods of war. To paraphrase, commerce was war by other means.[47] With this world view, colonies might assume a far more preponderant role in supporting the state. Colbert broke decisively with Richelieu's obsession with Spain, a declining power by the 1660s, and focused instead on the wealthy and powerful merchants of the Netherlands. To compete with the Dutch, he organized several companies, including a West India Company (Compagnie des Indes occidentales, 1664), which also managed, under close state supervision, all American colonies. He also created two major companies for the sole purpose of supplying African slaves to French Caribbean plantations, the Senegal Company (1673) and the Guinea Company (1685), officially chartered just after his death.[48] To enforce their monopoly, French naval commanders seized the Dutch post of Gorée in Senegambia in 1677, turning it into one of the primary French slaving stations; it became the nucleus of French imperialism in nineteenth-century West Africa. At least 2,824 slaves were transported by 1700 before war ended slaving operations, drawing roughly equally from the Senegambia and Bight of Benin regions of West Africa.[49]

Even before Colbert launched his ship-acquisition program, he sent out a major expedition in 1664 under Alexandre de Prouville, Sieur de Tracy, with six ships, 1,200 soldiers, and orders to enforce the king's new presence overseas. This epic voyage to the Americas took three years to complete.[50] De Tracy first sailed to Guiana, where he repossessed the old French post from a small Dutch garrison without firing a shot. He then sailed north to Martinique and Guadeloupe, where he installed the new governors and appointed local commanders who took an oath to the king, settled several outstanding and divisive lawsuits, and imposed an embargo on Dutch goods on behalf of the newly christened Compagnie des Indes. He then landed in New France in the fall of 1665. Early the next year and aided by veteran reinforcements sent from France (the Carignan-Salières regiment), de Tracy led an expedition deep into Iroquois lands to burn their villages and execute as many warriors as possible. The raid was more symbolic than devastating, but it did have the effect of building loyalty among the habitants to the new king and led to an alteration in Iroquois diplomacy, which grudgingly accepted permanent French settlement in the St Lawrence valley.

De Tracy's expedition established a temporary political and military stability in the new crown colonies. In New France, peace negotiations with the Iroquois paved the way for a period of rapid expansion in the fur trade and extended voyages of exploration for traders under the grasping direction of Governor Louis de Baude, Comte de Frontenac. Bent on monopolizing the fur trade beyond Montreal, Frontenac established his own private post at the eastern end of Lake Ontario (Fort Cataraqui, now Kingston, Ontario) and a short-lived one near Niagara Falls.[51] In 1673 trader Louis Jolliet and the Jesuit father Jacques Marquette accompanied several Native traders and warriors down the Mississippi to what is now the Arkansas River. Within four years, Robert Cavelier de La Salle, an officer, fur trader, and client of Governor Frontenac's, descended the Mississippi to within a few days of the Gulf of Mexico and claimed the northern Gulf coasts for France. By 1685, a network of French fur-trading posts dotted the eastern Great Lakes region and the main tributary rivers. Colbert, who had ordered that French settlements and traders venture no farther than Montreal, accepted the failure of confining the fur trade to the St Lawrence valley and instead tried to limit it by licensing only twenty-five canoes each year.[52] Immediately a huge illicit trade arose, conducted by unlicensed traders called coureurs de bois; many of them gradually settled among Native peoples around the Great Lakes or further south at the juncture of the Mississippi and Illinois Rivers (the Illinois country). Some French traders ventured down to the new settlements in coastal Louisiana after 1700. The only foreign incursion into this fur-producing area took place far to the north, where in 1670 the English Hudson's Bay Company built three small posts to tap a vast area of prime fur trapping.

Ironically, the Caribbean did not benefit as much from the enhanced power of the Navy and proved to be more exposed to attack. During the Second Anglo-Dutch War (1665–67), French settlers, using their shaky alliance with the Dutch as an excuse, chased the English from Saint Christophe and then, aided by regular forces from France, raided the islands of Antigua and Montserrat as well, only to return all possessions at the Treaty of Breda (1667). At the same time, resentment over the high prices and heavy-handed purchasing policies of the Compagnie des Indes led to major revolts by poorer whites on Martinique in 1665–68 and in the French settlements on Saint Domingue in 1670.[53] French colonists on Martinique beat back an invasion by the famous Dutch admiral de Ruyter in 1674 during the last Dutch War, a defeat that marked the advent of a long tradition of Creole pride in the ability of colonial militia to defend the islands unaided. As we shall see in chapter 7, this myth became a contentious issue between metropolitan and colonial leaders during the Seven Years War. Further Dutch attacks in 1676 gained tiny Tobago (only to lose it again two years later), but failed to dislodge the French buccaneers from their base at La Tortuga. The French were no more successful, failing on two separate occasions to capture Dutch Curaçao (1673 and 1678). Even more devastating than these attacks was Colbert's decision to introduce a tobacco monopoly in 1674, which led to an economic depression on Saint Domingue and a rise in raids upon Spanish Caribbean settlements by the buccaneers.[54]

A new order of imperial expansion called for a new type of royal agent, and under Colbert a new group of professional transatlantic bureaucrats arose to serve as a bridge between colony and court. A brief outline of the career of *robe noblesse* Michel Bégon serves as a good example.[55] Cousins of Madame Colbert, the Bégon family can be traced back to the mid-sixteenth century as treasury officials in Blois. After legal studies in Paris, Michel Bégon (the fifth so named) returned to Blois in 1662, rising to become the president of the Blois court. In 1677, when Bégon had reached the relatively advanced age of thirty-nine, Colbert assigned him to be the *commis du trésorier*, or treasury officer, at the Mediterranean naval base at Toulon. After he had served brief stints at the new naval base in Brest and at the strategic English Channel port of Le Havre, Colbert offered him the post of intendant of the American Islands, which at the time included all French possessions in the Caribbean from Grenada to the buccaneer stronghold of Saint Domingue. From his base at Saint Pierre on Martinique, Bégon commanded similar duties as any intendant in France. In addition to acting as the principal judge in his jurisdiction, they included *la police*, which covered all tasks associated with regulating social interaction and keeping social order: setting market days and rules, ensuring fire prevention, regulating building codes, instituting new public infrastructure such as bridges, water canals, and town squares, overseeing the marriages of the *filles du roy*, prosecuting smugglers, settling land disputes, and directing the introduction of new crops – in short, all operations not directly connected to defence.[56]

But Bégon also supplied information on specifically colonial problems, sending reports on sugar-cane production with an eye to lowering costs and searching for saleable by-products, writing extensively on the introduction of new crops and industries such as tanning, presenting planters' complaints about the high cost of French goods and low prices for colonial products, supplying suggestions on how to augment French indentured servants and African slaves, and reporting regularly on the morality of all colonists – free whites, indentured labourers, and slaves. In the course of his tour of duty, he began building a library that would grow to over seven thousand volumes (requiring the services of a professional librarian to catalogue it), and he continually plied his subordinates and contacts to send him "curiosities," such as an intact birchbark canoe and a sealskin coat. Upon returning to take up a post in Marseille, Bégon continued an interest in New World flora, collecting hundreds of American plants transported in pots on the king's ships.[57] One of his botanist friends, Father Plumier, even named a "plump and fleshy" plant with colourful flowers plucked in Saint Domingue the "begonia" in the intendant's honour.[58] Once back in France, Bégon ended his career as the intendant of the main naval arsenal at Rochefort, from which sailed the majority of the king's ships for the Americas, a post he held from 1688 until his death in 1710. In the 1690s, merchants of La Rochelle enlisted Bégon's support to gain entrepôt status in the transatlantic trade, knowing that he would be sympathetic because of his Caribbean posting and that he held the ear of the new secretary of the Marine, the elder Pontchartrain.[59] In short, informing well and being well informed on transatlantic issues comprised the sinews of power for overseas administrators such as Bégon.

PHASE THREE: EMPIRE DEFINED, 1683–1713

While Colbert institutionalized the absolutist state in France's overseas colonies and laid the foundations for an overseas empire, those institutions had to be maintained and the empire augmented to truly glorious proportions. It was left to his successors, his son, the Marquis de Seigneleay, and the father and son team of Louis and Jérôme Phélypeaux, Comtes de Pontchartrain, to inaugurate significant imperial expansion. This era, which remains poorly studied, witnessed the formal incorporation of Saint Domingue, the dramatic explosion of sugar monoculture and the subsequent rise in slave exports, the first tenuous post in Louisiana, the foundation of the Great Lakes post of Detroit, a treaty with the Five Nations Iroquois that freed New France to successfully confront Anglo-American colonists in the northeast, and the creation of the huge stone harbour-fortress of Louisbourg on the new colony of Île Royale. The younger Pontchartrain also instituted the most important French transatlantic administrative innovation by creating a Bureau of Colonies, organized for the first time according to rationalized division by geography and function and staffed by career specialists who helped ensure a remarkable continuity in policy throughout the eighteenth century. However, this seeming coherency of an imperial vision suffered greatly from the perceptible decline in the influence of the French Navy after defeats experienced in the early 1690s. Added to this was the impact of the departure of several noted Huguenot commanders after the Revocation of Nantes (1685) and the restriction of the officer corps to the nobility, which greatly reduced the advancement of experienced seamen from bourgeois or commoner families.[60] From this point forward, France ceded to Great Britain a naval supremacy that it never fully recaptured. It is this awkward combination of expansion and retrenchment that stamps the war years from 1689 to 1713 as a turning point from Louis XIV's pursuit of glory on the seas to the cutthroat race for Atlantic trade.

The wars of the second half of Louis's reign scarred and bled France, and provided the background upon which our understanding of colonial developments must be based. The Nine Years War (also called the War of the League of Augsburg, 1688–97) began as an attempt by Louis to consolidate his hold in the German Rhineland in September 1688, as well as to counter the growing influence of Austrian emperor Leopold I in central Europe. The short-lived dynastic unity of England and Holland cemented in 1688 by the Dutch stadtholder William of Orange to guarantee the succession of his Protestant English wife, Mary, to the throne greatly enlarged the power of France's enemies.[61] The French Navy won a resounding initial victory at Béveziers (Beachy Head) in July 1690, but followed this with the "unfortunate day" at La Hogue (May 1692), which forced Louis to shelve plans to invade England. Poor harvests, famines, and riots from 1694 limited the state's ability to conduct war on land, let alone at sea.

The War of the Spanish Succession (1702–13) strained French resources and its people even further. As the Nine Years' War ground to a halt by 1696, it had become clear that the aging Spanish Habsburg king, Charles II, would die without an heir. As a member of the Austrian branch of the Habsburgs, Leopold I was a distant heir to the Spanish throne; but Louis XIV's grandson had the stronger claim, since he had married the Spanish Infanta. For the first time, European rivals not only considered political ramifications within the Continent but, more importantly, eyed the richest and most populous "Europeanized" settlements, those of Spain in the Americas. London's merchants in particular coveted the right to trade goods and slaves to the Spanish colonies, a licence known as the Asiento. Either a Franco-Spanish superpower would emerge, or the merchants of England and Holland would finally be seated at the feast of Spanish colonial piastres. When Charles died in early 1702, the same coalition from the previous war, minus Spain, reformed to oppose Louis. From the beginning, French generals lost battle after battle – Blenheim (1704), Ramilies (1706), Oudenarde (1708), and Malplaquet (1709) – but Spanish forces decisively defeated the British in 1710, forcing the war into a stalemate. Throughout France, meanwhile, economic devastation, riots, and famine reappeared and ravaged several regions; Louis became widely despised.

These two long wars of attrition eventually became colonial wars of attrition. Settlers in New France faced a series of attacks by the Five Nations Iroquois up the St Lawrence River, including the massacre of four hundred people at Lachine (near Montreal) in 1689, and a concerted invasion effort by militia from New England sailing down the river the next year. The colony's militia defeated both attacks, and from 1693 they mounted their own destructive raids into the Iroquois heartland and all along the New York and Massachusetts frontiers. By 1701 the governor general of New France, Louis-Hector de Caillière, succeeded in reaching an agreement with four of the Five Nations (the Mohawk, allied to the Anglo-Dutch in New York, abstained) to maintain neutrality in future European wars, thus buttressing New France's beleaguered position. During the next war, with most of the Iroquois Confederacy safely pursuing a policy of neutrality, French *troupes de la Marine* and the Canadian-born militia carried war deep into the Anglo-American frontier regions, burning farms and trade posts in upper New York and western New England, including the infamous assault on Deerfield, Massachusetts, in March 1704, killing forty-seven and taking more than a hundred captive. In retaliation, Anglo-American forces took Port Royal, in Acadia, and again prepared to descend on Quebec. An expedition to dislodge the French under Admiral Hovenden Walker finally left Boston in the late summer of 1711, only to be scattered by a storm and wrecked in the treacherous waters of the St Lawrence in September. To the north, Pierre Le Moyne, Sieur d'Iberville, launched raids against the Hudson's Bay Company and eventually pried all its prized fur forts from its grasp by 1696.

In the Caribbean, English, Dutch, Spanish, and French forces pillaged one another in a frenzy of thinly disguised buccaneering raids, culminating in the spectacular capture of Spanish Cartagena in 1697 by a combined naval-buccaneer army led by Baron de Pointis. The raid netted more than ten million livres for the victors. French privateers continued their raids in the subsequent war, where d'Iberville, shifting attention to the tropics, captured and ransomed the English island of Nevis, and took off an additional 1,400 slaves to be sold in Martinique. In the South Atlantic a small French squadron under the famed commander René Duguay-Trouin emulated Ducasse's sack of Cartagena by capturing and ransoming Rio de Janeiro in Portuguese Brazil in 1711. At peace negotiations in the Dutch city of Utrecht, France permanently lost Acadia and its nearly two thousand inhabitants, as well as the strategic fishing bases on Terre-Neuve (Newfoundland). Only the craggy northern lobster claw–shaped Île Royale (Cape Breton) remained.[62] France also ceded its first Caribbean settlement, Saint Christophe, to Great Britain. Although Philip kept the throne, the British prohibited any union of crowns, and they won, among other privileges, the Spanish Asiento. When it was all over, even the Sun King admitted on his deathbed that he had been "too fond of war."

Perhaps because of the relentless problem of financing, Jérôme de Pontchartrain found New France difficult to support in any imperial policy. Cultural incomprehension also played a part. He considered Canadians to be aliens guided by "another spirit, other manners, other sentiments" than the people of France.[63] But he continued the same "compact colony" policy that Colbert had insisted upon, limiting colonists to the farmlands of the St Lawrence valley; low prices and a huge stockpile of pelts in La Rochelle and other ports during the war made this easier to accomplish. However, outside the Canadian heartland, Pontchartrain *fils* encouraged three new settlements that would greatly extend the French presence and influence in North America. In 1699 he ordered the founding of a new post by one of d'Iberville's younger brothers, Jean-Baptiste Le Moyne de Bienville, at Mobile, within reach of the Mississippi's marshy mouth. But the colony, numbering less than two hundred, barely survived the War of the Spanish Succession. The crown shed its losses by leasing it to financier Antoine Crozat in 1712. At the same time, Pontchartrain also authorized a scheming former fur-post commander, Antoine Laumet de Lamothe Cadillac, to build a fur post at the strategic narrows connecting Lakes Erie and Huron, close to the portages to the Wabash and Saint Joseph Rivers. From 1701 the post, called simply "The Strait," or Le Détroit, became a magnet of settlement for Huron, Wyandot, and Potawatami families and some French traders. Île Royale formed the third and final piece in France's burgeoning North Atlantic empire. Anticipating the loss of Acadia and the fishing posts of southern Terre-Neuve, Pontchartrain in 1712 ordered the transfer of French families from the main base of Plaisance to a new site that would become the nucleus of a massive stone harbour-fortress.[64] It would, he hoped, guard France's fishing trade in the North Atlantic, limit New England's expansion, and act as an entrepôt between Canada and the West Indies. Soon, hundreds of labourers and engineers swarmed over the site, raising the thick, grey walls of Louisbourg.

In the French Caribbean the Pontchartrains bowed to metropolitan pressures and extinguished sugar refining in the islands by 1695; henceforth they were to supply only raw sugar to refiners in Nantes, Bordeaux, and Orléans. The firm grip on the French Windward Islands of Martinique and Guadeloupe resembled the "compact colony" policy for New France, an attempt to keep colonies economically subordinate and territorial restricted in order to enhance metropolitan interests and control. However, the Pontchartrains, especially Jérôme, mitigated this policy by supporting the rapid development of Saint Domingue. With 27,000 square kilometres, about two and a half times the size of its chief competitor, British Jamaica, it possessed highly fertile soils and a climate ideal for growing sugar cane, and could be easily reached from France. Ducasse and several associates took much of their booty from the Cartagena raid and purchased land, slaves, boilers, tools, and draft animals to build sugar plantations in the colony's northern region around Cap Français (now Cap Haitien, Haiti). When Ducasse sent the first shipload of sugar in 1698 to La Rochelle, Pontchartrain (who knew him well) scolded him that "this can only be very prejudicial to the colonies of America," a reference to the sugar plantations of Martinique. Ducasse responded by providing the secretary of state with a detailed lesson in sugar economics, stressing the relentless need for new land to maintain high yields. Pontchartrain relented.[65]

By 1700, eighteen sugar plantations were counted in the colony. Despite the uncertainties and ravages of war, this number had jumped to 138 by 1713. Their slaves produced 7,000 tonnes of raw sugar by 1714, less than 10 per cent of the total sugar exports from all the Americas, Brazil (the largest exporter) included. The number of smaller plantations, such as those producing indigo, also increased dramatically during the war. The number of slaves consequently grew as well, rising nearly eightfold from 3,400 in 1687 to 24,000 by 1713, and then doubling again to 47,000 in just seven years.[66] Most of the slaves were shipped on French vessels, but a significant number arrived on Dutch ships. This sudden sugar revolution on Saint Domingue, and the Pontchartrains' role in that growth, remains to be systematically explored by historians, as does their part in expanding France's imperial domain more generally. Despite the circumscribed role played by the Navy and the neglect of older colonies, by 1713 the French state could now claim to have an imperial domain of American colonies administered by a central agency, strategically interconnected, and with the promise of economic integration, ranging from the icy waters of Louisbourg in the north to tropical Cayenne on the South American mainland in the south.

PHASE FOUR: PAX ATLANTICUM, 1713–1744

In September 1715 Louis XIV died, and an entirely new era emerged overnight in France. The late king had survived all his male children; only one great-grandson was still alive, a bare five years old when his guardian, Philippe d'Orléans, Duc de Bourbon, took control of the state. Philippe itched to relax the sober and tense religious atmosphere of the Sun King's later reign. But with his grip on power very insecure, he moved cautiously. He first placated the kingdom's provincial *parlements* by reinstating the right of remonstrance, and then sought to avoid any confrontation with England, now united (with Scotland and Wales) as Great Britain, going so far as to sign a treaty of cooperation in 1717. The British, in any event, had their own worrisome succession problems over the claim to the throne by the Stuart prince, Charles. When Philippe d'Orléans died in December 1723, the young Louis XV assumed the throne and called upon his tutor, seventy-three-year-old Cardinal Fleury, to manage affairs of state. From 1726 to his death in 1743 (aged ninety), Fleury resolutely kept France out of any major confrontations. Only two minor European wars claimed the attention of either crown until 1739, when powerful London merchants shoved Britain into war with Spain over greater access to markets in Spanish America. This era of political stability, christened the "Long Peace" by historians, gave birth to a dramatic rise in Atlantic commerce, a burgeoning slave trade, and the beginnings of mass consumerism based on colonial products. To the surprise of many contemporary observers, France emerged economically strong and politically stable from war, and began to surpass Great Britain in terms of colonial exports by the 1730s. From 1713, European dynastic issues would no longer overshadow colonial commercial ones; too much money was at stake.

During the Long Peace, the northern third of France and most coastal regions began a tremendous social and economic transformation. From Paris to the Flanders border, urban artisans and rural families gradually switched from crafting goods and cloth in small shops or at home, for use in family households, to piecework manufacturing, especially to produce cloth for national markets or for export. Urban centres connected with the Atlantic colonial trades grew at rates never before experienced: Bordeaux, for example, shot from 20,000 in 1700 to over 45,000 by 1750, drawing on much of the countryside of southwest France.[67] In the process, two Frances were emerging: a dynamic urban network, fronting on the Atlantic and based on transatlantic trade, and a more stagnant, agricultural interior of local markets and subsistence farming.[68] All the tropical products of the French Americas quickly passed from coveted luxuries to daily necessities between 1700 and 1730. And of all the products, sugar became the foundation upon which the edifice of France's, and Europe's, Atlantic prosperity rested. Artisans and labourers, even in the most remote regions, began to buy colonial sugar, either to consume directly or as a sweetener for two other American-produced products, coffee and chocolate, as well as for the great Asian export, Indian tea. By 1700, London alone boasted nearly five hundred coffee houses, and sweetened coffee powered sharpened discussions in all French salons.[69]

Sugar production rose steadily in each of France's colonies and was either absorbed within France or sold to central and southern Europe. Although the Îles du Vent furnished the bulk of colonial produce as late as 1730, as early as 1714 Nantes's merchants had already identified Saint Domingue as their greatest market for slaves and return cargoes.[70] Colonial planters experimented with a variety of other crops: cocoa became a major export for Martinique until a blight destroyed trees in the mid-1720s, but coffee brought from the king's gardens at Versailles and transplanted in 1721 replaced cocoa after 1727. By 1750, Martinique exported more coffee by value than sugar.[71] Tobacco consumption also steadily increased, so that on the eve of the Revolution, French men and women consumed at least 15 million pounds annually, mainly as snuff. Other products included indigo for making colourfast blue dyes, cotton (the second largest export from Saint Domingue in the 1780s), and spices, such as nutmeg, a specialty of Grenada. Although Louisiana failed to become the major producer of sugar and silk it had been expected to, it did export more mundane products such as hides, corn, and lumber to Saint Domingue and lower grades of tobacco and indigo to France.[72]

The inauguration of commercial prosperity brought greater efforts by the state to profit from that prosperity in the form of greater policing of trade. Increased restrictions led directly to colonial protests, particularly under the Regency, when a series of ad hoc regulations were first introduced. These revolts differed significantly from the more common protests by urban dwellers or soldiers over high food prices and food scarcity that had erupted during the long war years.[73] The immediate causes, length, and seriousness of revolts differed greatly in each colony, but the common factor was the efforts made by the Marine Council, or the companies to which it had granted colonial trade monopolies, to wring greater amounts of revenue or state-sponsored work from colonists during peace than they had been used to. The responses ranged from a mild protest by peasants near Montreal over the corvée (1717),[74] to complaints over alcohol price increases in Louisbourg (1720), to more general protests over low salaries and high bread prices by soldiers and sailors in Louisiana (1723), to the most serious revolt on Saint Domingue, which started in November 1722 and lasted for a year. The main issues animating agitation centred on the Regency's attempts to lower purchasing power by colonists and the arrival of new administrators under a reorganized monopoly company, the Compagnie des Indes, which threatened low, fixed prices for tropical products, higher selling prices for slaves, and exemption from export duties for company agents only.

Behind the popular agitation, Charles Frostin has asserted, Saint Domingue's major sugar planters engaged in a "game" of exciting continued popular agitation in order to reform the colony's political structure into a French province with its own powerful and semi-autonomous parliament (*pays d'état*).[75] But the most famous revolt occurred in the Îles du Vent in opposition to a new entry tax (*octroi*), which had sparked several protests by the colony's Superior Council in 1715, and a popular protest on neighbouring Guadeloupe in the same year. But two years later a much wider revolt began over food shortages and the setting of high prices, both of which were widely attributed to officers of the Marine Council. In May 1717 colonists pounced on Governor General La Varenne, Intendant Ricouart, and their staffs as they toured the southern side of Martinique, marched them back north to Saint Pierre, and placed them on the first ship sailing back to France. Although it was initiated by artisans and small planters, major planters quickly usurped the movement, dubbed the Gaoulé (rabble-rousing), for they feared (according to their written depositions) that violence might escalate. A free assembly (but orchestrated by the major planters) elected a prominent planter, Jean Dubuc Létang, to lead the rebels. He skilfully deflected popular rage away from attacking the king's fortress at Fort Royal, identifying the new colonial officials as the culprits instead, and negotiated a quick disbanding of the rebels after the two had sailed. The revolt had the temporary effect of throwing all ports in Martinique and Guadeloupe open to British ships. The court decided not to hunt down or imprison any of the agitators, and Dubuc received an immediate pardon.[76]

In response to this insurrection, and in order to create more uniform guidelines to augment metropolitan-colonial exchange, the young Comte de Maurepas, secretary of state for the Marine, composed a set of a set of colonial trade regulations known as the *Exclusif*, which were finally promulgated in October 1727.[77] To keep the sugar mills turning required construction lumber, wood for fires, mules, and cheap food, especially protein sources, to feed slaves. Although French authorities and financiers hoped for an intercolonial trade between New France (grain, lumber, and ships), Louisbourg (fish), and its sugar islands, New England merchants were better positioned to provide these essentials, giving rise to a vast and still poorly understood clandestine trade. According to Paul Butel, the enormous and fast-growing British protected market in colonial produce remained the greatest strength of the British Atlantic economy.[78] However, smuggling drew the French West Indies into this market and away from France's trade in continental Europe. Maurepas insisted on a doctrinaire mercantilist view of trade as far as the British were concerned, although as he matured, he supported free trade when it came to the Spanish colonies or valued allies such as Ireland.[79] Smuggling firmly emerged as a crucial underpinning of the French Caribbean economy. In dozens of isolated coves and in all harbours on the French islands, a dependence verging upon sympathy developed for Anglo-American merchants, who were seen as distinct from and superior to British or British-Caribbean ones.

But French planters also received considerable aid from the state in another form: legal impediments slowing debt repayments.[80] Although profits on an efficiently run sugar plantation could amount to 15 per cent per year, planters spent far more on lace, wine, fine furniture, and other luxury goods, in addition to slaves and capital improvements such as tools, mills, and building supplies. Payments to metropolitan merchants could be legally forestalled for at least eighteen months, and a delay of three years or longer was not uncommon. It became increasingly difficult for French merchants to collect debts, even before the onset of war after 1744, since colonial officials, who also benefited from lax repayment, blunted colonial laws. Slaves and land, the two most valuable pillars of the plantation economy, could not be seized to settle debt payments in most jurisdictions.[81] The debt issue became bitterly contested between metropolitan merchants and colonial planters and brokers. The Marine, caught in the middle, never successfully resolved the problem.

It is one of history's greater ironies that the first French domain of commercial enterprise to be unfettered by the state was the French share of the African slave trade. In 1716, new regulations advocated by the Regency opened slaving to all French merchants so long as they fitted their ships out in the ports of Rouen, Nantes, Bordeaux, and La Rochelle. Within ten years the latter three ports, along with newcomer Saint Malo, emerged as the major suppliers of African slaves to French America. Nantes became by far the largest, transporting 48 per cent of the 363,781 slaves known to have been sent to French America between 1701 and 1763.[82] Although French traders roamed the entire length of the Atlantic littoral of Africa, most slaving operations tended to concentrate on two major stations: the older slave-trading fort at Gorée in Senegal and a newer one at Ouidah (Dutch, Juda; English, Whydah). In consequence, the number of plantations in the French Antilles increased dramatically on all major islands. French slaves were forced to work in gruelling, factory-like environments to produce a variety of tropical products in settings foreshadowing the Industrial Revolution. One observer on Saint Domingue wrote of the "chaos and noise of the sugar mills alongside the carts trundling along with their crops ... one can occasionally and indistinctly hear blows being dealt to animals and Negroes. From ovens and boiler rooms, plumes of smoke can be seen extending high into the distance and falling to the earth, or rising in the form of dark clouds."[83]

At the start of the boom in 1713, Martinique possessed between 250 and 300 sugar plantations; this number increased to 437 by 1730, although it declined to 324 by 1754, on the eve of the Seven Years War, as coffee replaced sugar as the island's most valuable export. Guadeloupe experienced more rapid growth, rising from 130 plantations in 1713 to 252 in 1730 and to 333 by 1754. In the same years, Saint Domingue grew yet faster: from 138 plantations in 1713, it had 339 by 1730, and this number nearly doubled again to 600 by 1754.[84]

Unlike the Caribbean, New France more closely reflected the changing composition and economic dynamics of old France. Under Intendant Gilles Hocquart (1729–48), the state funded select industries with imperial needs in mind, such as an iron forge near Trois-Rivières and shipbuilding at Quebec, and it encouraged a trade in exported wheat from the Montreal district to Louisbourg and even the French Windward Islands. Consistently harsh winters and high costs greatly hampered the possibilities of the wheat trade, and colonists fell back upon furs.[85] Competition with Anglo-American traders in Lake Ontario brought commercial friction and the building of two new posts in the mid-1720s, Anglo-American Oswego and French Fort Niagara, both on the New York side. The search for new sources of high-value furs and the desire to bring more Native peoples into the French alliance led to the planting of additional posts beyond Detroit. These created friction with anti-French nations. New France's *troupes de la Marine* fought at least three wars with the Fox nation (1716, 1727, 1731), and under Governor Bienville, Louisiana's forces pushed the Natchez into war (1729-31) and fought the Chickasaw in two costly and fruitless campaigns (1736 and 1739–40). French motives had other sources: the Regent supported exploration beyond the Great Lakes, convinced of the existence of a Western Sea, equivalent in size to Hudson Bay, which opened on the Pacific. Maurepas, an honorary member of the French Académie des Sciences and a noted supporter of mapping projects, funded further explorations, culminating in the expeditions by Pierre Gaultier de La Vérendrye and his sons to voyage through the area north to Lake Winnipeg and west along the Missouri River, sixty years before Lewis and Clark.[86]

French North America's two newest colonies provided mirror images of growth. While the decision to plant Île Royale sprang from strategic considerations, the fortress port of Louisbourg quickly emerged as an important fishing port and as a key entrepôt for French ships on the transatlantic run.[87] Louisiana, which appeared to have a much brighter future, staggered from one unrealistic plan by the state to another. The nadir was reached early under the Regency, when John Law, a Scottish adventurer and friend of the Regent, introduced reforms that paved the way to creating paper currency and a national bank for France. However, promise turned to fiasco, as Law tried a variety of expedients to pay off France's huge war debt by selling certificates in a single state monopoly based on developing Louisiana. He added more and more colonial monopolies to the original, taking on all their debts and selling more stock, which speculators drove to absurd heights. The financial edifice collapsed in mid-1720, leaving 2.5 billion livres in unpaid debts, and many tens of thousands of investors, both noble and bourgeois, lost heavily.[88] In the meantime, Louisiana had become a dumping ground for France's undesirables, whether salt smugglers, prostitutes, or black sheep from noble families. Even the slave trade failed to provide it with the labour crucial to development and ceased to attract any ships after 1722. Plagued by revolts and desertions by its soldiers, unprofitable, and under siege from the Natchez nation in 1729, the colony's owner, the Compagnie des Indes hastily gave it back to the crown in early 1731. It became synonymous with broken dreams in Abbé Prévost's popular novel, *Manon Lescaut* (1731).

PHASE SIX: EMPIRE DECLINED, 1744–1763

The Long Peace did not see growth in one conspicuous area: the French Navy itself. Louis XV limited the Marine to a paltry 9 million livres per year after 1726; in comparison, it received 22 million in 1700 in anticipation of war. Of the total, only 2.5 million, less than a third, went to colonial administration and infrastructure.[89] When war finally did break out between Great Britain and Spain in 1739, France found itself in a vulnerable maritime position. It is a measure of the importance of Atlantic commerce that, unlike in 1702, conflict erupted initially between Great Britain and Spain over the Asiento and colonial trade in 1740, and only later became conjoined with European dynastic politics. Bourbon France finally joined with its Bourbon Spanish ally in the early spring of 1744, and for the next twenty years, the main belligerents either fought or tiptoed through a very precarious peace. This era also saw a major transformation of political culture within France, and these changes are inseparable from changing knowledge about French America and a rethinking of imperialism more broadly. During the War of the Austrian Succession (1744–48), Louis XV maintained a generally positive perception of the monarchy, enhanced by his personal appearance on the battlefield of Fontenoy (1745) but weakened by his well-known disregard for religious functions and his flagrant womanizing.[90] At war's end he engaged in a series of confrontations with the Parliament of Paris, leading to the resignation of its members in late 1756, during the start of a new round of war. In January 1757 a failed assassination attempt on the king resulted in the sudden throttling of the slight efforts at political discourse that had begun to emerge. Meanwhile, many officials at all levels became increasingly aware of and anxious about the troubled financial situation of the state. Nearly solvent by 1744, in part because of the spectacular growth in colonial commerce, the state again faced huge debt loads after 1748. Financial reform became the watchword, and along with this, the desire to effect structural reform within each ministry by officials, some nobles, and many members of the provincial parliaments.[91] In the Marine itself, the stability achieved under Maurepas ended with his sudden dismissal in mid-1749 over an unwise (leaked?) poem poking fun at Louis XV's powerful mistress, Madame de Pompadour. From 1749 to 1761 the Marine had no less than six ministers, each one attempting to overhaul the structure of the central bureaucracy and establish his own internal and overseas patronage networks. While the French Navy rearmed from 1744 with remarkable success, thanks in part to the continuity provided by the lower echelons of officials and clerks, the Marine and the colonies under its control consistently lacked funding, accountability and close supervision, and a coordinated set of directives and policies until the Duc de Choiseul assumed control in 1761, adding the Marine to his other portfolios of War and Foreign Affairs.[92]

A sea change in perceptions of the value of overseas domains also occurred in the 1744–63 period. At exactly the same time as Great Britain experienced an outpouring of popular support for parliamentary culture and imperial expansion,[93] capped by the victories achieved in 1745–48 and again by 1762, France underwent the reverse. Lacking any popular medium for discussing the value of empire and with overseas dominion the political preserve of the Marine, the majority of the literate French public appeared to consider colonies as distant, mysterious, and increasingly superfluous domains. From the 1720s on, veiled critiques of French political culture and society became progressively bolder, moving from Montesquieu's criticism of French monarchy through the eyes of a foreigner (*Persian Letters*, 1721), to Voltaire's appreciative account of England (*Letters on the English*, 1733, which led to his exile), to Françoise de Graffigny's ingenious denunciation of both French patriarchal institutions and imperialism in *Letters from a Peruvian Woman* (1747), and back to Montesquieu in his *Spirit of the Laws* (1748), which stopped just short of demanding a constitutional monarchy in France and contained lengthy critiques of several underpinnings of French colonialism, including monopoly companies and slavery.[94] Although none of these works were written expressly about colonial ventures, they all posed a similar question about empire: if metropolitan society could not be accepted as morally good and politically valid, how could the imposition of that society overseas be justified? Voltaire neatly encapsulated the disenchantment with imperial pretensions in 1761 by dismissing the war in North America, and imperialist ventures generally, as conflicts over a "few acres of snow."[95] In short, these writers increasingly identified empire as harsh, barren, costly, and as something that would surely melt away. Undoubtedly the price to keep them was far too high. It is with this turbulent mixture of disillusionment with the monarchy, calls for financial reforms, growing domestic repression, and anti-imperialism that France entered what became a great international battle with Great Britain in 1744.

In that year the colonial theatres of war immediately reverted to raids among outlying settlements in New York and Massachusetts and privateering in the Caribbean and from Louisbourg. Anglo-American forces, determined to end the depredations of Île Royale's corsairs, captured Louisbourg after a seven-week siege, the only major operation in North America. A French convoy sent in 1746 to retake the fort ended in horrific disaster, with the majority of men dying of typhus aboard ship as they waited to launch the assault.[96] By mid-1747 the British Royal Navy effectively blocked both French merchant vessels and France's Navy, leaving the French Americas temporarily without French contact and supplies. French merchants in the Caribbean alleviated the problem by trading with the Dutch entrepôts of Saint Eustatius and Curaçao, much to the exasperation of the Marine and French metropolitan port merchants. Peace came early the next year with the treaty of Aix-la-Chapelle (1748), where negotiators swapped Madras in India for Louisbourg in North America. But colonial trade quickly surpassed even the high levels of the pre-war years. The war did produce a notable change in French imperial thinking under the influence of Roland-Michel Barrin, Marquis de La Galissonière. During his brief tour as interim governor of New France (1747–49), La Galissonière devised the first interconnected imperial plan insisting on the colony's strategic value. New France, he argued, not only produced excellent, hardy soldiers who could be useful in all French colonies, but it forced Britain to keep soldiers and spend money in the Americas that would otherwise be deployed in Europe.[97] His views became the basis of the Marine's new policies and were in the process of implementation when the next war erupted.

The Treaty of Aix-la-Chapelle had left many territorial questions unresolved in both Europe and North America.[98] The most dangerous concerned the broad expanse of the Ohio valley. Anglo-American provinces coveted the area for land sales and future immigration from the increasingly crowded seaboard, while French authorities desired the area for bases to thwart British fur traders, as a bountiful homeland for its Native allies, and as a strategic marchland to limit Anglo-American settlement. After a brief skirmish in the summer of 1754 between the Virginia militia (led by a young George Washington) and French *troupes de la Marine* under Villiers de Jumonville, both combatants rushed regular land armies to North America: 8,000 British and 4,000 French regular soldiers the following year. In the meantime, Anglo-American militias also struck in American-controlled Acadia, where British general Charles Lawrence ordered the forcible deportation of up to 18,000 Acadians and the laying waste of their farms.[99] By the late winter of 1756, events on the Silesian border between Prussia and Austria had again overtaken the clash in the upper Ohio. France, engineering a "diplomatic revolution" by uniting for the first time with its traditional enemy Austria and with its old ally Russia, faced Great Britain, Prussia, and an assortment of smaller German states. The Dutch remained doggedly neutral.

North America became the main theatre of war for the first four years. In 1756 and again in 1757, the combined forces of French regular troops, the Canadian-stationed *troupes de la Marine*, Canadian militia, and Native allies, drawn mainly from Native Catholic settlements in the Montreal area, defeated British armies far superior in size. They chased the British Army and American militia from the Ohio valley, routed Anglo-American soldiers, and even built a small navy to master Lake Ontario. Louisbourg remained impregnable; only on the Lake Champlain frontier did French forces suffer an early setback. An inconclusive battle at Lake George resulted in the capture of the French general, Baron Jean-Armand de Dieskau, who sat out the rest of the war as a British prisoner. The French Army hastily assigned Louis-Joseph, Marquis de Montcalm, then in France, to replace him in late 1756. The next year, Montcalm captured the strategic British fort of William Henry, just south of Lake Champlain, placing Anglo-American forces in New York and New England on the defensive. However, the ascent of William Pitt the elder to the position of prime minister in late 1757 completely changed the British position. Pitt clearly made North America the primary target, and he threw far more money, British regular soldiers, and, most importantly, the full weight of the Royal Navy into the task of defeating the French forces overseas as soon as possible.[100] The results were immediate and decisive. A combined British-American colonial force took Louisbourg in July 1758 and Fort Frontenac on Lake Ontario in August, and forced a retreat from Fort Duquesne (Pittsburgh, Pennsylvania) in the upper Ohio valley.

The situation worsened for the French in 1759. The British and American forces completed the sweep of Lake Ontario by capturing Fort Niagara in July, then a British force of 8,000 regulars under General James Wolfe laid siege to Quebec, capturing the city after a famous (or notorious) fifteen-minute battle on the Plains of Abraham immediately outside Quebec's walls on September 8, 1759. Ironically, both Montcalm and Wolfe were wounded in the battle and died shortly thereafter. The remnant of New France's forces retreated to Montreal to await a relief convoy in the spring. But the British Navy, after inflicting severe defeats on the French Navy off Lagos, Portugal (August 1759), and at Quiberon Bay (north of Nantes, in November), shattered any hopes of a French maritime relief effort. It arrived in Canada first, and after a tense summer of manoeuvring, British forces swamped the surviving French army and Canadian militia at Montreal in September 1760. New France now faced an uncertain future as Great Britain's newest colony.

The French position in the Caribbean proved to be very different. Privateers from both sides roamed about at will; one historian estimated that French privateers, mostly from Martinique, captured over 1,400 British merchant ships.[101] However, by 1757 most French merchant ships, as well as the French Navy, were again bottled up in their ports, and the islands were hard-pressed to import food and basic supplies, let alone export sugar and coffee. Only after the fall of Louisbourg did Pitt shift attention to the French West Indies. On January 15, 1759, British naval forces numbering nineteen ships and frigates and at least 7,500 sailors and soldiers made an amphibious assault near Fort Royal and bombarded Saint Pierre, before moving on to Guadeloupe.[102] A vicious, punishing war endured on the island for three months, as British troops systematically burned outlying plantations, seized any slaves captured and sold them off the island, and carried out arbitrary executions.[103] Once the island was secure, however, the British commander, General John Barrington, not only granted highly favourable capitulation terms, but allowed London merchants to offer Guadeloupe's planters healthy prices, extended credit, and full access to British sugar markets. The conquered planters were only too happy to oblige. Within three years, a veritable revolution in sugar production took place on Guadeloupe. British slave ships landed over 27,500 slaves, and the number of plantations, which had dwindled to 185 on the eve of the capture, soared to 446, surpassing in number and production for the first time those on Martinique.[104] News of events filtered back to Martinique via small coastal carriers and through French contacts in London; the island's planters, starved for markets and at times near starvation, took careful note. When a second, larger British force attacked Martinique in January 1762, the island fell in just three weeks. Militia units deserted in most districts, and the southern (and most productive) half of the island sued for peace on terms similar to Guadeloupe's, in defiance of Governor General Levassor de La Touche's insistence on prolonging war. For the next sixteen months, Martinique's major planters also benefited from British markets and elevated slave exports, which, according to one French estimate, reached six thousand.[105] Only Saint Domingue escaped the Royal Navy, although its privateers ravaged coastal areas. Alarmed by the entry of cheap French sugar, planters on Jamaica and the other British sugar islands mounted a successful campaign to rid the empire of the new possessions.[106] At the Peace of Paris in 1763, Great Britain agreed to return Martinique and Guadeloupe, but kept New France, Île Royale, the Caribbean islands of Grenada, Saint Vincent, and Dominica, Senegal, the major French territories in India, and a small collection of other posts. Louisiana, by a secret agreement reached in 1761, reverted to Spain in compensation for the loss of Spanish Florida to the British. The recently installed minister of the Marine, the Duc de Choiseul, welcomed France's loss, predicting correctly that the removal of the French threat from North America would considerably weaken Anglo-American bonds with Britain.[107]

Throughout the seventeenth century and until 1713, the colonies had clearly been subordinated to metropolitan France, forming an early "Greater France," to borrow Robert Aldrich's term.[108] After 1713 it became increasingly clear that each colony, while remaining a political satellite of the state's Marine and relying on France for funding, protection, and cultural cues, pursued under colonial leadership its own economic and political agenda. These agendas did not embrace cooperation or coordination among the colonies, let alone with France. Let us return to the watershed year of 1713, when the French Atlantic first became a territorial reality. How did the state articulate its vision of rule in the colonies, and how did it try to institute control over them? What obstacles did it encounter? We begin with the complex problem of how news travelled across the Atlantic in the eighteenth century.

CHAPTER TWO

Proclaiming Peace in 1713: A Case Study

On the morning of May 22, 1713, a Monday, thousands of Parisians thronged the Place de la Grève with tears in their eyes and joyous cries in their throats. After eleven long and brutal years, the War of the Spanish Succession had finally ended. A rumour had spread speculating that Louis XIV would announce the signing of a peace treaty at the Dutch city of Utrecht. The informed elite of Paris – royal officials, well-connected financiers, and bourgeois subscribers to one of the foreign *Gazettes* from Holland or Switzerland – already knew that the treaty had been signed more than a month before, on April 11th.[1] The celebrations were not for them, but for the illiterate mass of poorer Parisians, a reward for years of suffering and sacrifice.

According to an official report, the festivities began with the arrival at the Hôtel de Ville of seven royal heralds accompanied by a small musical battalion, composed of thirty-seven trumpeters, drummers, and pipers, and several companies of soldiers to keep exuberant merry-makers in check.[2] The royal officers were greeted at precisely 10 a.m. by city officials dressed in their traditional long, red robes. The municipal officials ushered the royal officers inside, where they gracefully received the proclamation from the king into their hands. Afterwards, the two sets of officials dined together on fresh fish and oysters, drank wine (white and red), and toasted the peace with shouts of "Long live the king!" The soldiers stayed outside, watching the celebrating crowds. At the end of the feast, civic officials and their heralds reassembled outside the Hôtel de Ville and marched in an order prescribed by tradition through the streets of Paris to announce the signing of the treaty to the people. The king's word passed ceremoniously from him through his intermediaries, to the city officials, and finally to his subjects. The procession stopped fourteen times, including at the Tuilleries, Grand Chastelet, Les Halles, the Pilory, Place Louis le

Grand, Pont Neuf, before the equestrian statue of Henri IV, and before the equestrian statue of Louis XIII at Place Royale, all places of social exchange or before landmarks of august royal authority.[3] At each stop, the officials made the same speech and read the proclamation to crowds of presumably cheering Parisians, although the account does not record any response from the people. As the cool of evening descended in shades of ever-darkening purple, the poor of Paris – apprentices, labourers, shopkeepers' wives, servants with some time off – wandered through the streets, drinking and singing, stopping to gather before noble *hôtels*, where they scooped up coins flung from the balconies above. The celebrations continued for three days, culminating in the singing of the traditional Te Deum at Notre-Dame Cathedral. Later that night, fireworks split the sky as noble revellers gathered at the home of the Duc de Tresmes, where an orchestra, the famed Vingt-Quatre Violons du Roi, played for the guests.[4] Although we have no accounts of the celebrations for the crowd, they may have helped themselves to free wine and bread provided in the city's main squares, as was the case during other similar state-sponsored celebrations.[5]

Three months to the day after the ceremonies in Paris, officials on the French island of Martinique sponsored celebrations in the two principal towns of the island, Saint Pierre and Fort Royal.[6] The governor general, Raymond-Balthazar de Phélypeaux du Verger, a cousin of Secretary of State for the Marine Jérôme Phélypeaux, Comte de Pontchartrain, had received the proclamation of peace from the king at least a month earlier, as well as letters from Pontchartrain instructing him to hold the "customary rejoicings."[7] Like the Parisian officials, Phélypeaux prepared the celebrations well in advance. In Fort Royal, the only town for which a detailed account still exists, the members of the colony's Superior Council, acting on behalf of the island's colonists, acknowledged receipt of the proclamation at the governor general's residence. Afterwards they marched with colonial officials in a solemn public procession to the parish church, stopping to read the proclamation aloud to those gathered in the town's square. Immediately after a performance of the Te Deum, the dignitaries and townsfolk, swelled to nearly two thousand with planters who had come from all over the island, gathered in the small town square to watch a fireworks display, managed by the king's soldiers, on the beach. The night ended with a round of parties thrown in the rented homes of planters, often a few rooms in boarding houses or above a tavern. Although aping Paris, the king's officials controlled the entire round of celebrations in the Îles du Vent.

The exact same proclamations and instructions for celebrations that were sent to Martinique were also drawn up at Versailles and sent to

Louisiana and Canada on the very same day. But the intended celebrations never took place in either colony.[8] Louisiana, the most recent and most promising of the Sun King's colonial projects, received the news only in early 1714. Although Governor Antoine Laumet de Lamothe Cadillac ordered the soldiers of the garrison of Fort Louis (near present-day Mobile, Alabama) to sing the Te Deum in the fort's small chapel, he lamented that "it is scarcely an occasion to celebrate because of the many hardships, for nearly everything is lacking."[9] In fact, he and the other colonists were facing starvation.

In Canada, no official celebrations were held at all. When the first merchant vessels anchored before Quebec in late June, Governor General Philippe de Rigaud, Marquis de Vaudreuil, learned along with the rest of the town that a peace treaty had been signed in April.[10] He waited for the king's ship to bring the official proclamation, but the ship never arrived.[11] The representation of royal power and the display of aristocratic grace and generosity of the Paris celebrants, so easily replicated three months later in Martinique, failed to be reproduced in Canada and Louisiana. Why did they not take place, and does their absence tell us something about the relative strength of royal authority in each colony? Did the lapse occur as a result of a unique combination of trying circumstances, or were such gaps in the expedition of royal orders endemic in the French system of colonial communications? Only the continual crossing of ships carrying the king's word guaranteed the presence of royal authority in the colonies. Should the flow be interrupted, colonial leaders found themselves isolated. Following the path of a single piece of news allows us to chart the problems of how the French state projected royal authority at the start of a spectacular period of French economic growth and colonial development. It can also help us appreciate the human labour and material cost of circulating information in the eighteenth century.

The infrastructure and coordination required to send the king's word overseas could be extraordinarily complicated. The treaties signed in 1713–14 and collectively known as the Peace of Utrecht (the companion Treaty of Rastadt was signed in 1714) are ideal for a case study of news dissemination for several reasons. The French proclamation was a single document, which called for a response. Tracking its progress through the French bureaucracy and over the ocean to each colony is relatively easy. Both the state and colonial officials understood the importance of the news for a variety of reasons: privateers had to be called back, merchant ships reloaded, militias disbanded. The news also provided an opportunity to display the king's concern for his overseas subjects (by giving them peace), and it supplied an occasion for colonial elites to publicly display their closeness to the sovereign. Also, the treaties and the accompanying king's instructions travelled on both land and sea, allowing a comparison of the relative efficiency of communications between the land-based royal postal system and the use of king's ships on transatlantic routes. By identifying the opportunities as well as the limitations of a single piece of information, we can better judge the efficiency of transatlantic information within an emerging imperial, and authoritarian, system.

A NEW ORDER

Peace negotiations to end the War of the Spanish Succession lasted nearly as long as the war itself.[12] By 1704, France had already lost effective use of its Navy and was halted on land at the battle of Blenheim. Secret peace overtures began in 1705, but England and Holland did not respond with any serious counter-proposals until the fall of the Duke of Marlborough in 1711. The articles for a possible ceasefire between France and Great Britain were agreed to in April 1711, and preliminary negotiations opened in July of that year. General peace negotiations began in Utrecht the following March. These discussions led to a ceasefire in Flanders in June 1712 and a four-month general ceasefire in August. The principal combatants prolonged this ceasefire for another four months in November. The Treaty of Utrecht, therefore, was not signed with a sudden gasp of exhaustion by each side. Instead, nearly two years of proposal and counter-proposal preceded the signing of the treaty early on the morning of 12 April 1713.

Throughout the later stages of the war, Pontchartrain informed French colonial leaders of the progress of negotiations. In August 1712 he sent word to all American colonies that a peace treaty would be signed shortly and ordered an immediate halt to all raids and privateer operations.[13] He sent the same letter to the governor and *commissaire-ordonnateur* in Saint Domingue via Martinique, since this colony remained under Martinique's jurisdiction until 1714. The orders reached Martinique by a merchant vessel that arrived in early December 1712. Accompanying this letter of peace was another containing instructions to celebrate France's latest victories in Flanders.[14] At least two months prior to the letter from France, however, Phélypeaux had already received word from his counterpart in Barbados that a treaty would probably be signed within months. Between them, they agreed to extend the ceasefire then in effect in the Caribbean for six weeks longer than the date set in Europe, an example of how colonial leaders set their own agendas "beyond the line." In Canada, Pontchartrain's letter reached wily Governor General Vaudreuil overland via Boston, probably carried through the winter forests by Abenaki warriors or hunters.[15] Vaudreuil withdrew his forces slowly in order to wreak as much damage as possible on New England's outlying settlements, violating the spirit, if not the directives, of Pontchartrain's letter.

As for the newly commissioned governor of Louisiana, Cadillac spent the fall and winter of 1712–13 overseeing the loading of cargoes in several French Ponant ports. While in port, he wrote Pontchartrain several times, outlining his future plans for the colony.[16] Although his ship, *Le Baron de la Fauche*, was only the fourth to sail for the colony in nine years, a new commercial monopoly seemed to promise invigorated efforts at developing Louisiana through regular trade and contact.[17] Cadillac clearly understood that the court would reach a peace with Great Britain. By the end of March 1713, all three colonial leaders were therefore well aware of the definitive move toward a treaty. When the announcement of the treaty's signing arrived in their colonies later in the year, it did not have any value as news; the letters, if they received them, merely confirmed what most colonists already knew. Within the broad framework of an impending peace, colonial officers made their decisions by sifting through a variety of news sources and acted according to intuition and local circumstances. Pontchartrain's letters contained legitimating, rather than urgent, information. All news has a variety of uses, and official pronouncements may not be the most critical.

Immediately upon the signing of the treaty at Utrecht, clerks for the negotiators set to work to copy the document and brief reports; messengers awaited to take them. The news reached the king at Versailles on the evening of the 14th, brought by the Marquis de Torcy's own messenger.[18] De Torcy, the chief French negotiator, found the event so anticlimactic that he did not preside over the final signing of the treaty and passed over any description of the occasion in his memoirs.[19] Within days of receiving word, Pontchartrain's own secretaries began to copy out the proclamation and letters that notified colonial leaders of the substantial rearrangement of France's American colonies.

CLERKS AND CORRESPONDENCE

As in all other aspects of *ancien régime* political life, the form of the peace proclamation reflected the king's role as sole lawgiver and final judge of his subjects, for all announcements were essentially pronouncements of law. A bewildering hierarchy of letters existed for official documents during the *ancien régime*, and the nuances of each still elude current scholarship. However, some basic characteristics are understood.[20] The vast majority of orders and judgments were issued in two ways: through general and specific sealed letters (*grandes* and *petites lettres patentes)*[21] issued by the King's Chancellery, which included ordinances and edicts applicable to the entire kingdom, or more commonly, through direct royal orders, called *lettres closes*.[22] The colonial proclamations of peace issued to the governors and intendants on May 22, 1713, follow the format of the *lettre close*.[23] Only a few of these were actually written and sealed in the king's presence. The vast majority were countersigned by one of the king's secretaries of state, and were used mainly for urgent notices, passports, ordering of payments, or circular letters concerning routine administrative practices. Secretaries specially skilled in copying the king's signature signed them, and secretaries of state such as Pontchartrain kept several hundred blank letters in their offices for use within their departments. In all probability, royal clerks drafted the proclamation according to a traditional format and presented it to Louis XIV for his approval. A second set of royal letters, destined for the governors and intendants of Canada, Louisiana, and Martinique, accompanied the proclamations. These were written nine days later, on May 31, 1713, and again the king likely did not see them, though they were issued in his name. Since these were addressed to specific persons and struck a more personal tone, they resembled the form of a *lettre de cachet*.[24] In each, Louis XIV notified the recipient that, after he had asked "our Lord for the grace to halt a war so long, so terrible, and so bloody," God had allowed the other princes to re-establish a "a perfect understanding" with him. So that no mistake might be made, the document listed the nations signing the treaty and ended with orders for the official addressed to publicly attend the singing of the Te Deum of thanksgiving in the principal church of each colony, along with the "customary rejoicings."[25] Letters to the governors contained additional instructions to proclaim the peace to all French subjects and to halt all hostile actions.

Pontchartrain prefaced each of these letters with yet a third letter. He emphasized the importance of proclaiming peace promptly and asked the governors to ensure that the proclamation be made the day before the celebrations. He also wanted to know "in which manner the common people of your jurisdiction have received this agreeable announcement." Letters to the intendants included orders to make powder (for fireworks) and "other supplies" available for the necessary celebrations.[26] The most striking aspect of these letters is the concern with public presentation. A proclamation of peace did not merely inform the colonists of a cessation of war; it was a staged event, similar in function and even style to contemporary press conferences or photo opportunities. It is not clear if Pontchartrain stipulated the timing of celebrations because traditional practices in France were not followed in the colonies, or because he was concerned that governors, such as

Vaudreuil in Canada, might drag out hostilities for their own purposes. But it is clear that the state had a keen interest in orchestrating the reaction of its overseas populations.

The task of actually composing and writing each of the proclamations and accompanying instructions fell to the clerks of the newly created Bureau of Colonies, established by Jérôme de Pontchartrain on January 1, 1710.[27] For reasons that remain unclear, but probably were a response to war, the younger Pontchartrain drastically remodelled the Marine bureaucracy inherited from his father. Gone was the old and cumbersome division between Ponant and Levant; instead, he created individual bureaus organized by function and appointed knowledgeable staffs of clerks to run them. Like many early modern institutions, it had one foot in the past and one in the future. For example, while all the colonies came under one agency, certain aspects, especially import tariffs and direction of state-supported companies, still remained in the hands of the controller general of France, and the French Council of Commerce (one of the king's councils) acted as a kind of pressure group for French ports involved in overseas commerce.[28]

Pontchartrain placed the bureau in the hands of a career administrator with the understated title of chief clerk (*premier commis*). During the eighteenth century, these *premier commis* and the common clerks who worked under them emerged as powerful men with extensive connections at court, specialized knowledge of maritime issues, and financial interests in the colonies, although the extent of these last remains poorly known.[29] The court valued their expertise because they could act as advisers and because of the administrative continuity they provided during periods when the secretaries of state were increasingly enmeshed in court intrigues. Although the first *premier commis* for the Colonies, Moïse-Augustin Fontanieu, had occupied his post only since November of 1710, he had long been a client of Pontchartrain's, having served as treasurer for the Marine since 1701.[30] He retained at least these two posts until his death in 1725.[31] Fontanieu's extensive knowledge of naval affairs, the more important merchants, and Parisian financiers allowed Pontchartrain to delegate lesser chores to him, such as the appointment of minor officials and the arrangement of the details for financing at least some of the voyages of the king's ships.[32] How many ordinary *commis* staffed the bureau at this early stage of its development is unknown. However, it was undoubtedly lower than the approximately five main clerks in each of the Marine's offices (including the Bureau of the Colonies) by the mid-eighteenth century.[33] Members of this small group occupied an extremely crucial position in colonial affairs, since they dictated what information and projects the secretary of state and the king would see and how these would be presented, and relayed back to colonial officials how the ideas were received.

The year 1713 appears to have been only slightly busier than others in Louis XIV's later reign for the Bureau of Colonies. In this year its clerks wrote out a total of 760 letters on 606 legal-size folios (1,212 pages) to the colonies and to French ports, principally the king's naval arsenal at Rochefort. However, this number represents only those letters actually copied into the bureau's register. The original letters were written twice and sent as duplicates to ensure that at least one arrived at its destination. Urgent news was sent as many as four times, all by different routes.[34] If it is conservatively estimated that each letter to Rochefort was written out twice (one to be kept, one to be sent) and those for the colonies three times, then the Bureau of Colonies produced a minimum of about 3,170 handwritten pages of recorded correspondence in 1713 (see table 2.1). The number is probably much higher for two reasons. First, a quick comparison of the bureau's letter register with the one kept at Rochefort reveals that Intendant François Beauharnais in fact received 568 letters from Pontchartrain over the course of the year, not the 280 recorded in the bureau's register. While many of these dealt with issues such as ordinances on coastal fishing and the impressment of sailors which were not under the jurisdiction of the Bureau of Colonies, these letters often included one or two paragraphs discussing the outfitting of colonial-bound ships.[35] Second, the recorded letters also refer to private letters not bound in the register, and many of these were copied and sent by Pontchartrain's clerks as well. The total volume of correspondence from this one bureau could conceivably mount to between six and seven thousand pages. The writing style of the recorded letters indicates that at least two clerks scribbled on colonial matters, one with a very refined hand, the other with a rougher script, perhaps a junior clerk. Even if a third clerk existed, these numbers indicate that each clerk copied out just over one thousand pages, and possibly double that amount, over the course of the year.

The volume for each destination indicates the priorities placed on maintaining overseas contact. The letters to Rochefort and other French points concerned with outfitting the king's ships collectively accounted for the largest share of the correspondence, comprising 225 (37.1 per cent) of the 606 folio pages and 440 (57.9 per cent) of the 760 letters. Of the French-bound letters, two-thirds were destined for Intendant Beauharnais at Rochefort. These letters were short and contained specific instructions for outfitting and cargo purchases or, less often, were concerned with buildings and personnel problems in Rochefort. Most of the other letters were sent to various nobles, clerics, and financiers in

Table 2.1
Volume of correspondence of the Bureau of Colonies, 1713

Destination	*No. of Folios*	*Per cent*	*No. of Letters*	*Per cent*
Îles français de l'Amérique[1]	225	37.1	440	57.9
New France (Canada)	118	19.5	126	16.6
Louisiana	10	1.7	15	2.0
St. Domingue	114	18.8	73	9.6
Martinique and the Îles du Vent	122	20.1	81	10.7
Cayenne	10	1.7	21	2.8
Indes Orientales	7	1.2	4	.5
Total	606	100.0	760	100.0

SOURCE: AC, B, vol. 35, [1713]. In addition, a single letter was written to the "Indes d'Espagne" (presumably the Spanish Main), but not included in the microfilmed set analyzed at the National Archives of Canada in Ottawa.

[1]Correspondence pertaining to the Marine's shipping to colonial ports.

and around Paris. The efforts to coordinate money, people, and cargoes proved to be a very complicated undertaking and required constant attention to resolve an interminable number of problems: freight rates, objections by merchants, passage for clerics, poor cordage or tar, clarifications about fund allocations. The size of this correspondence points to two contradictory trends: the relative ease of contact with Rochefort allowed Pontchartrain, in contemporary parlance, to micromanage certain operations; but at the same time, the marshalling of money and goods to repair, man, and supply the king's ships on a schedule, even during peace, proved in many respects more complicated than attempts to direct colonial life.

Letters to French colonial officials were longer and mixed specific requests or orders with more general guidelines or observations. Of the 321 letters written, Canada led with 126 (16.6 per cent), compared to 81 for Martinique (10.7 per cent), 73 for Saint Domingue (9.6 per cent), 21 for Cayenne, and only 15 for Louisiana. The number of folio pages, however, demonstrates a more even distribution: 122 folios (20.1 per cent) were sent to Martinique compared to 118 folio pages (19.5 per cent) to Canada. While the discrepancy between the numbers of letters and folios may simply reflect a difference of form rather than substance, it also appears that Pontchartrain addressed a larger number of different correspondents in Canada. This volume of correspondence far outstrips England's contact with its colonies. As Ian K. Steele has shown, an estimated 3,720 letters were written by both American colonial governors and the Lords of Trade between 1675 and 1737, an average of just 52 per year.[36] The Bureau of Colonies clearly kept a more wary eye on colonial affairs than did its English counterpart.

The rhythm of correspondence indicates how closely metropolitan communication followed colonial needs. The imminent departure of a ship threw the Bureau of Colonies into a frenzy of letter-writing. Of the 126 destined for Canada, nearly two-thirds of the total (78) were written in the two weeks prior to the anticipated departure of its ship in late June. Since communications with the French Antilles could be maintained year-round, clerks could space copying out accordingly: 40 per cent (34 letters) were written in the two weeks prior to an April departure, and just 14 per cent (11 letters) before a September departure. These optimum departure times were in turn dictated by colonial seasons, a reminder that royal bureaucracies adjusted to nature, and not the reverse.

This brief outline of the correspondence of the Bureau of Colonies in 1713 underscores the efficiency with which a small office managed colonial affairs for France. Only a few people were required to handle a broad range of concerns; whenever problems arose, they could be dispatched surprisingly quickly. More importantly, the coordination of shipping, not the management of the colonies, consumed the largest single amount of time, energy, capital, and paper. This is the first indication of a dilemma for the strict managment of an overseas imperial domain: the volume of correspondence within France was high because outfitting royal ships was a collective endeavour that drew upon a diverse range of people and resources: merchants from La Rochelle, Bordeaux, Saint Malo, and other ports; Rochefort's own intendant and port officials; a wide number of naval officers; Parisian financiers; and religious authorities from dioceses across France. The bureau's correspondence system, which coordinated and arbitrated between different groups within the kingdom to ensure orderly contact with the colonies, thus served as a microcosm for the coordination and arbitration functions of the king for the kingdom.

MESSENGERS AND MAIL

Once written in the bureau's rooms at Marly, where Louis XIV spent the spring of 1713, the letters were either entrusted to confidants and special messengers or carried by regular post[37] (see map 1). Historians often envision land travel as a slow and arduous process at the mercy of the seasons, serving only as a supplement to river transport until the "great restructuring of roads" inaugurated in the mid-eighteenth century.[38] It is true that in the spring of 1713, heavy rains had turned all roads leading from Paris and Versailles into ribbons of mud. However, the condition of roads did not appear to hinder messengers or France's well-organized (and highly profitable) postal system. Correspondence between the Bureau of Colonies and Rochefort suggests that, as frightful as roads undoubtedly were by current standards in the West, the king's correspondence galloped with impressive regularity across *ancien régime* France. Exactly how the proclamations travelled from Marly to Rochefort remains a mystery. We do know that the bureau had three potential methods of sending mail. The first relied on personal contacts between Pontchartrain and colonial officials to carry dispatches. For example, when the king's lieutenant on Guadeloupe, Louis-Gaston de Cacqueray de Valminière, was about to leave Paris in January of 1713, he informed Pontchartrain of his imminent return to the colony and asked several favours. Pontchartrain thanked him for his courtesy, promised to make solicitations on Valminière's behalf, and forwarded several dispatches to him to carry on to Rochefort, where he was to take ship for Martinique.[39] Information exchange could thus be closely bound with clientage.

The other two options for carrying correspondence relied on less personal connections: the French postal system and the extensive network of king's roads. Under Louis XIV's secretary of state for War, François Le Tellier, Marquis de Louvois, the postal system had been expanded to help coordinate the movements and supplies of increasingly larger and larger French armies. Louvois reorganized the old postal system in 1691, and by 1713 it had emerged as a highly profitable venture. According to Eugène Vaillé, the postal service operated as a semi-autonomous department within the royal bureaucracy, employing its own inspectors and messengers and settling disputes in its own court system, an arrangement not unusual for ancien regime monopolies and institutions. Rates for mail carriage based on travel to and from Paris were published annually from 1708. Some twenty-two great roads, or *grands chemins*, radiated from Paris to connect the whole country, and along both these and the secondary roads, postmasters spaced about five kilometres apart provided the necessary change of horses for carriers and messengers.[40] This system, with slight modifications, remained intact until the Revolution.

In 1713 the *Almanach royal* listed daily connections for mail to each of the royal palaces and two departures per week from Paris to La Rochelle and Rochefort. Messengers also arrived in Paris twice a week from Bordeaux and most parts of Guyenne. We know, as well, that the distance between Paris and La Rochelle was ten days by carriage in 1765, when improvement of the great roads had begun. Messengers travelled an average of about forty-seven kilometres per day, an impressive distance for eighteenth-century land travel.[41] Two types of letter carriers used these roads: the *chevaucheurs de l'écurie du roi* (literally, "riders from the king's stables") and the routine couriers employed by the postal service. The king's messengers (a non-venal post reserved for nobles) formed an elite corps of just eleven men, and each minister of state claimed at least one. In 1713 Sauveur Jussau served as Pontchartrain's messenger.[42] However, Pontchartrain dispatched a special courier only twice (in February and again in July), both times at critical periods prior to ship departures. The first was too early for the proclamation to be sent, and the second too late.[43] It appears that these important proclamations were sent via ordinary post.

Knowing that the letters were carried by the postal service does not tell us how frequently or easily correspondence flowed between Versailles/Marly and Rochefort. We know from René Mémain's work that, in the year 1680, couriers lugged mail three times per week between Paris and Rochefort in each direction, taking four to six days to complete the journey each way; express messengers accomplished the trip in two to three days.[44] However, knowing the frequency and length of time of postal trips does not tell us how quickly mail was actually answered; it only indicates how fast a letter could theoretically reach its intended recipient, if written and posted on the same day, if read on the day it arrived, and if acted upon on the same day.

The Marine's correspondence between Pontchartrain's clerks and Beauharnais's clerks at Rochefort indicates that this theoretical rate of exchange rarely occurred. Letters might be held up in a postal bureau, stopped at an inn until roads became passable, or simply sit upon arrival for days – or in a few cases, weeks – before the recipient returned from a voyage or simply found time to read them. The problem is important, for by assuming that eighteenth-century correspondents could and always did act immediately within the potential speed of news distorts the actual pace of human interactions. A more accurate method is to track what is termed here the "response time" of a given piece of correspondence. In official correspondence, and in most private correspondence, often the first item mentioned is the date when the preceding communication was penned to the recipient. "Response time," refers to the time between the writing of the initial letter and the action of responding to it by the recipient. While the empirical base is small in this case, this method has the advantage of being precise, is applicable to any exchange in which dates of correspondence are known, and most important of all, demonstrates the wide variability possible for acting on discrete pieces of information. Tracking the flow

Table 2.2
Response time between the court and Rochefort, 1713

	Court to Rochefort			*Rochefort to court*		
Month	No.	*Var. (days)*	*Ave. time*	No.	*Var. (days)*	*Ave. time*
Jan.	3	11–20	15	5	10–27	15
Feb.	4	8–14	11½	5	7–38	15
March	4	8–24	12½	4	8–12	10
April	8	5–14	10	6	5–17	10½
May	4	10–13	12	4	8–15	11
June	4	8–24	11½	5	4–25	12½
July	3	8–23	13½	4	3–13	6
Aug.	4	4–35	18	5	10–15	13½
Sept.	1	8	8	3	10–16	15½
Oct.	1	31	31	4	8–27	14½
Nov.	4	9–62	26	–	–	–
Dec.	1	12	12	3	9-15	12

SOURCES: Rochefort IE, vols. 81–3, Dispatches from the court to the intendants; ibid., vols. 342–3, Letters from the intendants to the court; and AC, B, vol. 35, [1713].

KEY: No. = number of dated letters; var. = variation between slowest and fastest response time in days; ave. time = average response time, rounded to nearest half-day.

of letters over the course of a year also indicates periods of seasonal disruptions or intense shipping activity.

The results suggest a smoothly run communications system, despite the bankruptcy of the treasury and the poverty of France at the end of a long war (see table 2.2). Beauharnais's clerks in Rochefort consistently acted on orders within two weeks after the Bureau of Colonies sent them. On the two known occasions that Pontchartrain sent his own courier, the response time was cut to a mere four days. In the opposite direction, the bureau could rely on receiving reports from Rochefort within two weeks. More importantly, while great variations in individual response times exist, ranging from between three and sixty-two days, the average response times for each month, and in both directions, are strikingly consistent. These conclusions suggest that some issues received priority, while others could be placed aside for periods of slower activity. Less obviously, the figures provide a measuring stick by contemporaries for acceptable communications: the Bureau of Colonies and the intendant at Rochefort could be assured that most issues would handled between one to two weeks; any time beyond that suggested a problem, or that the recipient had become sloppy or preoccupied, and called for a prompt. The very consistency of contact is noteworthy. Road conditions apparently had little, if any, influence on the flow of official correspondence, although the wet months of early fall and winter tended to increase time. This impression is reinforced by the fact that, although Pontchartrain often stated his impatience for news, none of the letters examined ever mentioned poor road conditions or confusion in the posts as problems. The Bureau of Colonies–Rochefort contact is consistent with other examples. For example, William Beik showed that the response time between Jean-Baptiste Colbert and the intendant of Languedoc in 1675 took between two and three weeks.[45] From the Bureau of Colonies to the Ponant, the state demonstrated an assured grip on internal communications, despite the bleak year of 1713.

ROCHEFORT AND THE FRENCH ATLANTIC

The real complications in information exchange began after the dispatches reached the king's naval arsenal at Rochefort. Fifty years before, this slumbering town had occupied a patch of muddy terrain between the Charente River and a wide expanse of wild and dreary marshland. In 1666 Colbert selected the site for a new base.[46] It lay only twenty-five kilometres from the spacious and sheltered stretch of the coast known as the Basque Roads, where warships by the dozens might drop anchor safe from attack and secure from storms. The bustling commercial port of La Rochelle lay only thirty kilometres away to the northwest; upriver to the east was the city of Angoulême, famous for its iron and cannon foundries. Construction of Rochefort's dry docks, rope works, king's storehouses, and officials' homes began in 1669. The town had grown to the respectable size of 15,000 by 1713, yet Marine officials in Versailles fretted that Rochefort would never fulfill its vital role. Groundwater rotted walls, river mud clogged dry docks, and fevers from the swamps surrounding the town earned it the title of the "graveyard of the Navy" among officers and sailors alike.[47] Rochefort's buildings always appeared to be dilapidated, and the periodic cramming of tons upon tons of ships' supplies into the already crowded warehouses gave rise to storage congestion and easy theft. In the mid-eighteenth century, one intendant characterized Rochefort as "little more than a chaotic farmyard."[48]

There is no reason to believe this description was any less applicable in 1713. Maintenance of royal buildings and docks had ceased since 1704 because of a lack of money, and fire destroyed part of the town in 1706. The Marine's credit had sunk so low that merchants began refusing its bills, and port labourers balked at loading ships when their pay was slow in coming. In addition, a series of poor harvests had struck the region during the war and diminished food supplies.[49] It was against these harsh conditions that the officials and labourers of the port struggled to outfit royal ships for the colonies in 1713.

The end of war brought increased demands to resupply the colonies. Canada, Louisiana, Cayenne, Saint Domingue, and Martinique (along with its dependent islands) were all to be sent new troop detachments, uniforms, muskets, shot, and thousands of barrels of flour in case the ceasefire broke down. A new crop of colonial officials sprang up to replace those worn down by the war, and they began arriving in Rochefort to await the ships that would carry them to their new assignments. Contracts had to be negotiated with merchants in La Rochelle, Bordeaux, and other ports for return cargoes of colonial sugar, cocoa, and furs to help defray the cost of voyages. When it became clear by February that a treaty would be signed, other pressing matters arose. The bureau knew that the British would probably receive title to Saint Christophe in the Caribbean and to Acadia and Terre-Neuve in North America. The governor general of the Îles-du-Vent, Phélypeaux, would need time to arrange the transfer of the French settlers from Saint Christophe to a new home, as well as call back Martinique's highly successful privateers.[50] Terre-Neuve's situation caused great anxiety in the bureau because the French post of Plaisance (Placentia), which provided some protection to the invaluable cod fisheries of the Grand Banks, would have to be abandoned. The small community and its tiny garrison would have to be evacuated to a new port somewhere on Cape Breton Island (now renamed Île Royale), all at the king's expense. As 1713 progressed, the search for a new and strategically situated port, and the ship to carry the refugees, supplies, and soldiers to build it, increasingly taxed Pontchartrain's time and patience.

Readying the ships for the colonies followed a routine arrived at by trial and error over the previous forty years. Colonial seasons dictated the ideal departure dates, and these in turn determined the pace of careening, refitting, victualling, manning, and loading. Ships left for Martinique and Saint Domingue twice yearly, once in mid- or late March and again in early to mid-September. The March departures allowed them time to cross the Atlantic, unload supplies and load a new crop of colonial sugar, and then depart the Antilles before the *mauvais temps* (hurricane season) began in mid-July. The September departures allowed ships to arrive in the Antilles shortly after the hurricane season ended by mid-October.[51] Sailing to Louisiana imposed a similar regimen, since the same violent storms that struck Martinique also lashed the northern Gulf coast.[52] Canadian-bound ships followed a very different schedule. By 1713, officials strove to ready ships for departure by late May in order to allow plenty of time to cross the

Atlantic, unload supplies and load furs, and depart before ice formed on the St Lawrence River and the sharp northeast gales slashed sailors and sails by late October.[53] However, the Marine usually found it impossible to ready a ship for the Canada run so early. These departure dates served more as theoretical statements of ideal goals than as rigid guidelines. Imperial designs and colonial shipping demands seldom complemented each other in reality.

OUTFITTING THE NEWS

By December 1712 the colonial intendants had sent Pontchartrain reports listing the supplies needed for each colony, along with cost estimates. In addition, Intendant Beauharnais at Rochefort provided appraisals of the seaworthiness and cost of repairing each ship, along with his recommendations for that year's itinerary. On January 20, 1713, Pontchartrain wrote to Beauharnais with his assignments. He switched *L'Héros*, which had supplied Quebec the year previously, to the Martinique run and designated *L'Afriquain* to sail for both Quebec and Plaisance. But the secretary of state allowed only the paltry sum of 35,000 livres for careening, repairing, and outfitting both ships, with *L'Héros* to receive the major part of the money and priority in outfitting. Beauharnais also received orders to draw up contracts with Rochellais merchants to provide ships' supplies. Finally, Pontchartrain notified Beauharnais that the Louisiana-bound *Le Baron de la Fauche* had left its home port of Saint Malo and was slowly fighting through winter storms off Brittany's Cape Finisterre to reach La Rochelle. There it would load its main cargo of uniforms, muskets, and Native trade goods.[54]

Problems over cargoes, repairs, and ship assignments arose immediately. A messy lawsuit had developed over *L'Héros*'s previous shipment, and the creditors had sent a complaint to the king, effectively placing the ship's destination temporarily in doubt.[55] Worse, poor weather had slowed the ship's careening. Pontchartrain nevertheless pressed Beauharnais to finish the work quickly, for he wished to send Governor-General Phélypeaux of Martinique the news of the extension of a ceasefire with Portugal.[56] News that port officials at La Rochelle had detained the ship for Louisiana to unload several tons of the new *commissaire-ordonnateur* Jean-Baptiste Duclos's private freight allotment, apparently including several kinds of trade items, forced Beauharnais to visit the town and investigate.[57] The imminent signing of the peace treaty sent Pontchartrain scrambling to find a new port to replace Plaisance sooner than expected. Instead of the original single ship for Canada, he decided to send two, one to supply Canada and another, *Le Samslack*, to evacuate Plaisance and transport its inhabitants and a contingent of workers to a yet to be determined harbour on Île Royale. In conjunction with this project, he also ordered Beauharnais to contact key Rochellais merchants for their ideas on the best site for a new port.[58] On the basis of these discussions, Beauharnais wrote back and recommended Baie des Espagnols, but noted that several other harbours, including Baie des Anglais (more commonly referred to as "Havre des Anglais") the future site of Louisbourg, would be suitable alternatives. By late February, Pontchartrain began urging Beauharnais to speed up repairs to *Le Samslack*, using what soon became a familiar refrain: "Time is extremely pressing!"[59]

A bleak winter turned into a more promising spring. Although Beauharnais had not told Pontchartrain of *L'Héros*'s progress, by early April the latter guessed that it was ready to hoist sail. On April 9 Pontchartrain sent all the Antilles dispatches to Rochefort by his own courier. Beauharnais's confirmation that workers had completed *L'Héros*'s outfit crossed in the mail. Rough seas and stiff contrary winds kept the ship in port another week, but it finally sailed from the Basque Roads on April 17, a month later than the anticipated departure date.[60] However, Pontchartrain only wrote of the treaty's signing to Beauharnais on April 22, and the proclamations destined for the colonies were not penned until May 22.[61] Even though Pontchartrain's guess for the departure of *L'Héros* had been accurate, his latest dispatches were dated April 6th.[62] The peace proclamations and Pontchartrain's orders regarding Saint Christophe would have to travel on a merchant ship, since the next royal vessel would sail only in September.

How then did the announcements arrive in the Îles du Vent? There is some evidence that they were rerouted back through France to be place on board another merchant vessel. Pontchartrain sent a letter of introduction to Governor-General Phélypeaux for one Sieur de La Mothe (not related to Lamothe Cadillac). Phélypeaux responded on August 12, announcing that La Mothe had indeed arrived, as had several letters, including the peace treaty.[63] At about the same date, Intendant Vaucresson reported that several of Pontchartrain's winter dispatches had reached Martinique on July 14 by a merchant vessel from Le Havre. It is quite possible that La Mothe carried the dispatches. Another set of dispatches, including instructions on the transfer of Saint Christophe and new regulations on Anglo-French trade, were carried by the captain of a Marseille merchant vessel that dropped anchor at Saint Pierre in early September.[64] Clearly, the Marine depended on merchant vessels leaving from ports throughout France to carry official mail, especially to a colony as readily accessible as Martinique. While it is not clear whether the Marine paid for the service or whether merchants, as dutiful subjects, were expected to provide it at no charge, this example underscores the interpenetration of royal and mercantile interests in maintaining colonial contact. However, though the state needed merchant ships in times of peace, merchants did not need those of the state.

Throughout February and early March, the Louisiana-bound *Le Baron de la Fauche* remained tied up in La Rochelle, where presumably Duclos fumed over the removal of his goods. The ship finally made a last call back north at Brest; it then began its Atlantic crossing on March 18, bound first for Le Cap Français on Saint Domingue. Like *L'Héros*, this ship left too early to take the proclamations. However, Crozat already had another ship, *La Louisiane*, scheduled to leave Port Louis in June. The records on this second ship have thus far proved elusive, but it was the only vessel scheduled to call at Louisiana that left late enough to carry the proclamations. Either it or another merchant vessel may have halted at Le Cap and transferred the dispatches to a smaller vessel.[65] Despite the new Cadillac-Crozat company, regular and consistent contact with Louisiana was already beginning to prove just as difficult as under royal auspices.

Meanwhile, the preparations for the Canadian-bound ships continued. Difficulties in rounding up reluctant sailors and contrary winds hampered the ship destined for Île Royale, *Le Samslack*. It finally sailed for Plaisance in mid-June, two and a half months behind schedule.[66] Pontchartrain would not know of its fate, nor of Île Royale's, until late October, when a fishing boat brought news of the successful removal of the settlement.[67] As for Quebec's ship, *L'Afriquain*, financial problems dogged its preparations from the start. The refit of *L'Héros* had been somewhat cheaper than expected (perhaps because it was not completed), and Pontchartrain directed Beauharnais to use the remaining 10,000 *livres* for *L'Afriquain*'s outfitting. But the intendant reported that the money could only cover the ship's repairs and not the cost of supplies. Pontchartrain briefly considered changing *Le Samslack*'s itinerary so that it would anchor at Quebec first in order to embark a detachment of *troupes de la Marine* for the new post. But he changed his mind two days later and ordered Beauharnais to round up private cargoes to underwrite *L'Afriquain*'s cost. They exchanged a flurry of letters on contract options, but the ship's designated captain complained of the "exorbitant" demands of La Rochelle's merchants. Pontchartrain again ordered Beauharnais to use the leftover *L'Héros* funds. In late April, Beauharnais repeated that the funds were insufficient. For the next two weeks Pontchartrain sought in vain to interest other parties in *L'Afriquain*, including return cargoes for the monopoly Compagnie du Castor. Meanwhile, he still pressed the intendant to ready the ship for departure by mid-June.[68] During this period,

Pontchartrain wrote letters to Canadian officials, to be sent on private ships, informing them of events at Utrecht and indicating that the year's supplies and dispatches would arrive on *L'Afriquain*.[69] However, on the last day of May, Beauharnais received word from Pontchartrain that the king had cancelled plans to send a ship to Canada for that year. Although he did not provide the king's reasons, clearly the Marine's credit had run too low to finance a separate voyage; Pontchartrain, we may assume, actually cancelled the voyage. Instead, he ordered Beauharnais to contract with two solid Rochelais merchants long familiar with the Canada trade, Fleury and Pagés, to take most of the supplies and the dispatches.[70]

Unknown to the secretary of state, Beauharnais had taken the initiative and had already negotiated a contract on June 2nd with a Rochelais merchant named Faures de la Grivolière, owner of *Le Prince*. The terms of the deal were better than the usual ones offered by Fleury and Pagés, Beauharnais explained, and the ship awaited only the royal cargo to sail. Pontchartrain quickly approved this *fait accompli*.[71] In late June and early July, he forwarded the dispatches for Canada to Rochefort. Included were copies of the peace treaty itself, so that the colony's officials could study the clauses on the cession of Acadia to Great Britain. *Le Prince* finally departed La Rochelle in mid-July, a full six weeks behind its original sailing date.[72] By mid-July all the three sets of proclamations were on ships headed across the Atlantic for the Caribbean and North America.

MIXED RESULTS

The first batch, as we have seen, reached Martinique sometime between mid-July and the first days of August, in the middle of the hurricane season. Governor General Phélypeaux immediately set to work to ensure that the celebrations were as carefully orchestrated as those held in Paris.[73] He appointed the date for festivities to coincide with the feast of Saint Louis on August 25th, one of the most important feast days in France. Copies of the proclamation were sent ahead of time to Guadeloupe and Grenada, so that all three governors would announce the celebrations at the same time for the same day. The one-day gap between the announcement and the commencement of festivities remains puzzling; it is the only order to do so in colonial dispatches until at least 1763. Officials in both France and the colonies had ample time to prepare festivities. One might speculate that by announcing the treaty and the orchestrated celebrations at the same time, Pontchartrain hoped to dissuade rowdy colonists from launching their own impromptu gatherings.

On the morning of August 25th, the main festivities began at the capital of Fort Royal and in the main port of Saint Pierre. The members of the Superior Council assembled at their usual meeting place at four o'clock in the afternoon and then marched to the governor's residence, located inside the fort itself. There Governor General Phélypeaux first formally read them the proclamation, after which the king's prosecutor agreed to abide by the terms on behalf of the council members and the colonists. The councillors reassembled outside the fort and then marched in procession to the Capuchin church of Saint Louis to the sound of seven cannon salvos. There the governor general and Intendant Vaucresson joined them, and together with nobles drawn from across the islands, they sang the Te Deum of thanksgiving as ordered. After services, a final procession marched the short distance to the central *place d'armes*. At eight o'clock in the evening, the governor general, intendant, and Capuchin superior together ignited the traditional bonfire, while the fort's garrison and the local militia unit fired several musket volleys into the air. As the smoke lingered on the darkened beach, guns from some forty merchant vessels anchored in Fort Royal Bay answered with their own salutes. Because the celebrations were held during hurricane season, Fort Royal's harbour was unusually crowded, although no king's vessel lay at anchor: *L'Héros* had already departed for Saint Domingue. A fireworks display followed, fired from a "structure" (a triumphal arch?) adorned on four sides with symbols and inscriptions in Latin attesting to the new amity between the kings of France and Great Britain and the return of wealth and prosperity to the king's loyal subjects. A figure representing Public Order stamping out Discord decorated the top of the structure. Although no lavish official dinners were reported, Phélypeaux and Vaucresson both related that celebrations had ended by two o'clock in the morning. Similar celebrations took place on the same day in Saint Pierre. Phélypeaux reported back to Pontchartrain that he was pleased with the display of fidelity and honour shown the king, although he noted with his usual candour that "people here have displayed their great joy for the increase in the selling price of their sugar, cocoa, and indigo, and the decrease in the price of food; they have no other concerns save these."[74]

In a later letter, Phélypeaux reported his displeasure over only one thing. He had not received a copy of the treaty itself, as had his counterpart on Antigua, Lieutenant-Governor Matthew Douglas. Not only had Douglas obtained the treaty in early July, but he received copies in both English and Latin. Most important of all, he had also received a copy of the commercial treaty, which appeared to proclaim freer trade between the French and British islands.[75] This was not at all Louis XIV's intention, and the prior restrictions were quickly reimposed for the colonies within two years. The new ordinances became the tinder that eventually ignited the planter revolt on Martinique known as the Gaoulé of 1717.[76]

In stark contrast to Martinique's lively events, the proclamation of peace produced barely a ripple of relief in Louisiana and Canada. As we have seen, settlers in Louisiana greeted the news with little joy in the rough-hewn post of Fort Saint Louis, which Cadillac and Duclos had proclaimed the seat of government. Governor and *commissaire-ordonnateur* had begun bickering on the Atlantic crossing, and their relations worsened upon arrival, forcing colonists to publicly choose loyalties.[77] The display of elite unity that the celebrations were supposed to help reinforce were impossible under such conditions.

No celebration took place in Canada at all, for *Le Prince* never reached North American waters. On August 26th, Intendant Beauharnais reported to Pontchartrain that the ship had put into Brest a few days previously, partially flooded. Its captain, one Sieur Raudouin, reported that after the ship had fought stormy seas for two months, a series of great waves had smashed the mainmast, and the crew had barely managed to bring the stricken vessel back to port.[78] Beauharnais urged that another royal ship then at Brest, *Le Milfort*, be quickly loaded so as to arrive at Quebec before winter. But at that moment, shipwrights and labourers were preparing it for a second voyage to Martinique and Saint Domingue, and its itinerary could not be changed.[79]

In Quebec, Canadian officials still expected the arrival of *Le Prince* in the fall. Since *Le Samslack* reached Plaisance in late July, it is probable that Governor Philippe Pasteur de Costebelle at Plaisance (who did receive an official proclamation) sent a copy via a small coasting vessel to the capital.[80] But Quebec's officials received no further word. Governor General Vaudreuil and Intendant Bégon wrote Pontchartrain on November 15 by the last ship to leave the harbour that they had given up hope of seeing *Le Prince*. What had happened? they asked. Without the official proclamations, no royal celebrations took place, although officials clearly knew that peace had been signed. It was not until the following year, on March 22, 1714, that Pontchartrain explained the fate of *Le Prince* to Bégon, promised him that copies of all the 1713 dispatches would accompany those of 1714, and pledged that the ship for Canada (*L'Afriquain* again) would depart France much earlier. He tried to correct the situation by sending orders to sing another Te Deum, this time to celebrate the peace of Rastadt with Austria, the final peace treaty signed at the end of the War of the Spanish Succession. These dispatches did reach Quebec, but in September 1714, seventeen months after the Utrecht treaty had been signed.[81]

While we may be reasonably sure that Canadians held their own private celebrations upon the first receipt of the news, the official correspondence is strangely quiet on the issue.

It is highly significant that Quebec's officials did not bemoan the fact that royal ships could make only one voyage per year. Storms, shipwreck, and hazardous coastlines were simply part of the challenges and sorrows of life. What did upset them was the too often tardy arrival of the king's ship late in the navigation season, a situation that they knew could be remedied by more careful attention to outfitting and coordination on the part of the secretary of state and the intendant at Rochefort. Much the same could be said for Louisiana, even at this early date. But Saint Pierre's situation was entirely different. Even in the event that the king's ship missed important freight or news, the Bureau of Colonies could forward these on another vessel within six months. Moreover, a wide variety of merchant vessels sailed throughout the year to the Îles du Vent. The ability to send information and supervise the colonies depended on the regularity and consistency of contact, not upon the distance or length of sailing time between France and its colonies.

The snapshot of communications efficiency provided in this case study indicates important differences in information flows between the home country and its colonies. Exchanges between French and British colonies showed that royal news openly competed with foreign sources, a situation absent in most of France itself. There the court, whether at Versailles, Marly, or elsewhere, supervised and coordinated symbolic displays in most parts of the nation, thanks to a productive and increasingly centralized bureaucracy and by relying on relatively efficient courier and postal systems. This organizational finesse stopped at France's shores. Beyond, bourgeois merchants provided the only consistently reliable method for transporting and distributing news. The crown could only establish an effective presence when its own ships and officials could travel to the colonies and back fast enough to keep the court's attention focused on specific issues for long periods of time. A six-to-eight-month gap between the issuing of orders and receipt of feedback seems to have been the limit for effective counteraction. Only with the Îles du Vent and Saint Domingue would such close contact operate, and it should not surprise us that instructions were followed the most closely in the Îles du Vent. Louisiana and Canada, progressively further away and more difficult to reach, were the only two French colonies in the Americas that could not receive, react to, and have confirmation of orders within a six-to-eight-month period. The state could be only as strong as its most recent dispatches.

CHAPTER THREE

Sea and Land Connections

A light wind from the northeast stirred the rigging of the king's ship *Le Chameau* on the morning of July 2, 1720. Father Pierre-François-Xavier de Charlevoix, respected Jesuit historian and geographer, watched as sailors slowly turned the capstan bars around and around, lifting the ship's heavy black anchors from the green-grey waters off Île d'Aix. Charlevoix had sailed twice before to New France, and he looked forward to this voyage. The first three days were pleasant sailing, but on the fourth day the skies filled with rain and the seas began to rise. Charlevoix lay in his bunk, desperately seasick. For nearly six weeks the ship rode out the waves, tacking against the heavy winds and high seas, until at long last it emerged into a cold, grey world draped in fog. The pilot proclaimed himself certain they were near or on the Grand Banks off Newfoundland – but where exactly? For a week *Le Chameau* wandered, never glimpsing the sun, while a knotted rope was dropped over the side to take soundings. On August 16 the rope reached 400 feet deep and came up grey with sand, confirming that the ship had drifted onto the richest fishing banks in the world. The sailors raised several rounds of hearty cheers. But that night a thunderstorm "louder than a hundred cannons" pounded the ship, and Charlevoix feared they might be driven ashore and ground into "bait for the cod." *Le Chameau*, again wrapped in misty layers, sailed blindly on. Charlevoix tried to relax by scanning the waves for the fantastic battles between giant swordfish and whales that he had so often heard about. Three days later the dawn watch suddenly cried, "Land! Land!" The crew and passengers rushed on deck. To their great surprise, they found themselves in a quiet inlet ringed by jagged rocks. Incredibly, the ship had entered this natural harbour without the captain or pilot realizing it. Not two cannon shots away, a small English ship rode at anchor, just as surprised to spot them. The pilot learned from the

English that the ship had drifted into a small harbour somewhere between Cape Race and Cape Broyle, on Newfoundland's east coast.

With a better idea of their position and with a sharp reprimand from the captain still stinging his ears, the ship's pilot redrew their course to the south and then southwestward, steering into the Gulf of St Lawrence. Soon after they entered, an iceberg "taller than the towers of Notre-Dame" suddenly loomed out of the fog and nearly collided with the ship. The pilot, ever more cautious, guided *Le Chameau* gingerly between the low islands scarring the gulf's waters and the rocky shoreline to the north. Finally, after another full day and night of sailing, the ship entered the great St Lawrence estuary. For the next three weeks, it sailed slowly upriver, its pilot watching for familiar landmarks but wary of shoals and treacherous currents. On September 22 *Le Chameau* finally skirted Île d'Orléans, an island the habitants still thought to be haunted by sorcerers, and dropped anchor in Quebec's harbour the next morning. Charlevoix praised God and blithely noted the end of a "long and trying voyage" of eighty-three days.[1]

Charlevoix's account fits neatly into current perceptions of eighteenth-century sea travel, since it is filled with dangers, close calls, and fantastic sights. As with many other aspects of transportation in the period, historians have assumed much and imagined more. Yet we know surprisingly little about actual routes, navigational conditions, or anchorage problems faced by the thousands of mariners and their passengers who crossed the Atlantic. This ignorance stems in part from a heavy reliance on diaries and memoirs by occasional travellers, for whom the sea often held terrifying associations, and from rarely consulting the records of mariners, for whom crossing the Atlantic represented, as Dale Miquelon has put it, "business as usual."[2] The same problem of sources might be said to apply to other primary means of transportation – lake and river transport, and roads. How did the nature of these routes construct the reality within which metropolitan and colonial officials could efficiently use information, perceive problems and opportunities, and act upon them? This question cannot be reduced to a tidy formula which supposes that longer and longer distances created less and less state control. Eighteenth-century officials did not share current notions of acceptable speed; instead, each route created its own assumptions about speed, ease of use, and risk, and, in so doing, conditioned expectations of what might be reasonable rhythms of information exchange. We need to examine not simply length of routes, or even difficulty, but also frequency, perceptions of safety (which is related to, but independent of, difficulty), and commercial or strategic considerations. What is more, new geographies called, at least initially, for an accumulation of knowledge that could only be gained through ongoing experience by people actively using new forms of transportation technology and the routes themselves. How did mariners, canoe paddlers, or couriers adapt to these routes, stamping them with their own traditions? How did the state accommodate to or use this local knowledge?

To explore these questions, this chapter first examines the transatlantic system of oceanic routes used by French ships. These absorbed the most attention and protection from the state. Secondly, it outlines the development of water and land transportation routes within each colony. For a variety of reasons, lake and riverine traffic remained the method of choice within all French colonies until 1763, although a nascent road system had been firmly established in all colonies on the eve of the Seven Years War. Those colonies with an easily accessible riverine/land network, and which required cooperation from colonists to construct and utilize, such as Canada and Louisiana, appear to have forged greater independence from the state. In contrast, seaborne contact lent itself to greater state intervention, as in the Îles du Vent.

FRANCE'S ATLANTIC RIM

Until the work of Fernand Braudel on the Mediterranean Sea attracted attention in the 1960s, historians envisioned oceans more as barriers than as bridges, a hindrance to trade and settlement.[3] This view still persists. One noted maritime historian has even remarked, "It cannot be denied that the Atlantic Ocean curbed the development of New France."[4] Historians of *ancien régime* France rarely mention transatlantic contacts and navigation at all; if they do, they emphasize the crowded conditions and hazards of French ports.[5] The belief that oceans have played a divisive or, at best, hindering historical role has been challenged only recently by historians interested in transatlantic ties of kinship, patronage, and spiritual community.[6] The most meticulous work on the actual movement of peoples and information across the ocean in the colonial era remains Ian K. Steele's *The English Atlantic*.[7] Steele dismantled the assumption of the perilous, isolating ocean by showing that contact in the Anglo-American Atlantic became easier, routine, and more frequent between 1670 and 1740. Two of his perceptions are applicable to this study. First, by debunking the myth that early transatlantic communications "were slow, infrequent, and dangerous," he showed that eighteenth-century observers had their own concepts of fast and acceptable levels of contact.[8] Secondly, he divided the Atlantic into four well-defined routes used by all English ships: a "Sugar route" to the English West Indies, a "Tobacco route" to the Chesapeake, a "Western route" to the northern mainland colonies, and a "Northern route" to the Newfoundland fisheries and Hudson Bay. In turn, a knowledge of the physical limitations of these routes allowed Steele to plot the movement of politically sensitive information for a specific event, the Glorious Revolution of 1688.[9]

A similar set of sea routes reached across the North Atlantic from France to its American colonies. First, a Canadian route, consisting of two segments, between France and the colonies of Île Royale and Canada; second, an Antillean route to the French West Indies from Grenada in the south to Saint Domingue in the northwest, and which ships used to reach Cayenne on the South American mainland; and third, a Gulf route to Louisiana, which, although an extension of the Antillean route, required different navigational knowledge and posed far greater challenges. Scholars have examined only the first, the Canadian route, in any detail, with an eye to understanding early colonial trade, and some details of the Louisiana run have been imperfectly sketched out.[10] The most economically important and greatest route in terms of shipping, the Antillean, has received very little attention. All three routes imposed their own geographic logic not only on modes of travel but also on the very mechanisms of royal authority. There existed a direct relationship between the ease and frequency of oceanic contact and the desire to ensure royal command. As we shall see, however, easy and frequent access for the crown could also apply to those opposed to the crown's interests.

The navigational challenges to extending royal authority began on the coasts of France itself. Despite mile after mile of sheltered bays and artificially protected harbours, French mariners and Marine bureaucrats faced one overwhelming fact: the kingdom had poor access to the Atlantic Ocean (see maps 1 and 2). The prevailing westerlies and the Gulf Stream combined to slow and even batter ships as soon as they sailed beyond sight of land. Brittany's ports of Brest and Lorient (the chief port of the Compagnie des Indes) were especially notorious for delays.[11] Off La Rochelle and Rochefort, ships might wait at least a month for the western winds to change, as a very frustrated Lieutenant Rossel of the king's ship *L'Orox* did in the late summer of 1737, when he waited more than four weeks for a breath of wind to power his ship out of La Rochelle.[12] Even entry into the open Atlantic seldom guaranteed smooth sailing, as we saw in chapter 2, when the ship carrying the official proclamation of the Peace of Utrecht to Quebec left La Rochelle in late July of 1713, only to limp back into Brest nearly two months later, de-masted by storms.[13]

Access to the Atlantic from French ports on the Mediterranean coast (the Levantine ports) proved as difficult. Ships sailing from Marseille and Toulon not only faced extremely light and unpredictable winds, but often had to run the gamut of unfriendly Spain, the Barbary States, and after 1704, the English choke point at the Straits of Gibraltar. Reaching the Atlantic Ocean from these two Mediterranean ports could be wildly unpredictable: Carrière showed that the time needed for the voyage could range between five and nine weeks, although one king's ship accomplished it in four.[14] None of the French ports could boast a decided advantage over any other in the kingdom for launching transatlantic voyages. Even more surprising, French ports had no distinct advantage over the ports of the British Isles or Holland in reaching the open Atlantic through the English Channel. Both England and Holland could utilize the winds of the North Sea to sweep around the British Isles, and ships from western England and Scotland used an even quicker shortcut through the Irish Sea.[15] Ships could reach the Americas, from Canada to Cayenne, as easily from London or Amsterdam as from Brest or Bordeaux. Wind and current combined to level the playing field or rather, the sea room – for navies and merchant fleets for each of the transatlantic routes.

THE CANADIAN ROUTE

The route to Canada required two stages.[16] As we saw in Charlevoix's account, vessels leaving France's Ponant ports steered directly westward into the Atlantic Ocean, making long tacks against the headwinds and fighting heavy seas and storms as they went. If the daily positions on such a trajectory were plotted on a map of the North Atlantic Ocean, a ship's progress would show a line of weaving zigzags and drunken loops. After four to six weeks, and about 3,400 kilometres later, ships finally entered the cold and fog-enshrouded world of the Grand Banks. Once arrived on these teeming fishing grounds, veteran sailors treated first-time passengers to a "sea baptism" by the master of the Grand Banks, Bonnehomme Terreneuve. Few descriptions of such rituals remain, but Peter Moogk has translated one anonymous diarist's impressions from the 1750s. According to the author, the ceremony began by

> disguising an old sailor with a large, fur-lined, hooded coat, a pair of high boots, a white wig on the head ... with a helmet and stocking cap, and a large, white false beard. The sailor thus attired descends from the main topmast, where he dressed himself, and, with the aid of ropes and pulleys, he slides down to the foot of the foremast ... near the mainmast the initiate is held in a sitting position on the edge of a tub filled with [fresh sea] water. There Bonhomme Terreneuve makes the candidate swear an oath to keep the secret [of

this ritual] from those who have not yet passed this latitude, with a [further] promise to never touch any sailor's wife ... if the initiate has not taken the precaution of giving a coin for a drink, he is at once tipped over into the tub by the two men holding him.[17]

The ritual not only reminds us that navigation was as much a social as a technical feat, but also that contemporary mariners themselves divided the Atlantic into two segments, a familiar "European" sphere and a more supernatural "American" one. Such customs, which turned the world upside down, where sailors might dunk aristocrats, also presaged the powerful role of transportation labourers in the New World. The journey back to France from the Grand Banks followed the same route, but the eastward-flowing Gulf Stream and prevailing westerlies aided the return voyage, chopping off about ten days on average (see table 3.1). While rough and posing considerable discomfort to both passengers and sailors alike, this first part of the transatlantic crossing posed very few navigational hazards and did not require sailing near enemy territory.

The second stage of the voyage, into the heart of Canada, proved to be far more dangerous and required considerable knowledge of the Gulf of St Lawrence's hydrography. As Charlevoix's account graphically showed, crossing the gulf of St Lawrence and navigating up its wide estuary was the equivalent of walking blindfolded and barefoot in a room of jagged glass. While the distance travelled measured only about 1,450 kilometres, or about one-third of the North Atlantic portion, it consumed at least the same amount of sailing time. The journey from the Grand Banks to Quebec took a minimum of three weeks and might last up to six. The return journey consumed less time, so long as it did not commence much later than the onset of icy northeasterly winds by mid-to-late October.

Upon entering the Gulf of St Lawrence, ships encountered a dismaying range of navigational obstacles. These included contrary winds, which might send a ship scurrying for the shelter of a wooded inlet, halting progress for days or even weeks; sudden, violent squalls with blinding rain; sharp, often uncharted rocks; a maze of shifting sandbars; and maddening deflections of the compass near the iron-enriched land of the Canadian Shield. But fog proved to be by far a navigator's greatest foe. Up to the 1760s, pilots determined their position either by taking bearings from the sun, usually at midday, or, more commonly when near land, by steering from one recognized landmark to another. Fog obscured both methods. Captains could either drop anchor and wait until visibility returned or proceed slowly, taking soundings every few minutes and presumably praying just as often. Once past the

Table 3.1
Sailing times between selected Atlantic ports

Departure Port	*Arrival Port*	*Kms*	*No.*	*Outward* (*in weeks*)	*Return*
La Rochelle/Rochefort	Quebec	4,850	10	6–12	4–6
La Rochelle/Rochefort	New Orleans	9,100	14	14–21	9–12
La Rochelle/Rochefort	Saint Pierre	6,600	18	5–9	6–10
La Rochelle/Rochefort	Louisbourg	4,100	-	4–8	2½–4
Louisbourg	Quebec	900	-	2–5	1½–2½
Louisbourg	Saint Pierre	3,350	-	4–7	4–7
Bristol	Barbados	6,500	-	8–9	6–7
Bristol	Kingston (Jamaica)	7,600	-	9–11	12–14
London	Boston	4,550	-	8–9	4–5

SOURCES: Sailing distances based as closely as possible on actual routes; distance calculations from *Distance between Ports*, 1965, H.O. Publication no. 151 (Washington: U.S. Naval Oceanographic Office, 1965). Sailing times drawn from AC, C8A, vol. 46; C11A, vols. 67, 79; and C13A, vols. 15, 16, 20, 28; AM, 4JJ, liasses 15 (logs nos. 18, 19); 18 (logs nos. 53, 57, 66, 81); 29 (logs nos. 39, 42, 44, 47, 50, 55); 34 (logs nos. 4, 4bis, 5, 5bis, 6, 7, 8); and NAC, MG 18, J5, "Journal of *L'Héros*"; 1712'; Charlevoix, *Histoire et description générale de la Nouvelle France*, 3: 47–69, 446–99 passim; Hachard, *Relation du voyage des dames religieuses*, 26, 44–74 passim; PAC *Report*, 1905, "Journal of the 'Formidable,' 1757"; ibid., "Journal of the 'Inflexible,' 1757." Also used in calculations were Butel, *Négociants bordelais*, 224–6; Cavignac, *Jean Pellet*, 52–5; Clark, *New Orleans, 1718–1812*, 50; Mathieu, *Commerce entre la Nouvelle-France et les Antilles*, 116–20; Maupassant, "Armateurs bordelais," 170–5; Miquelon, *Dugard of Rouen*, 172–89; Pritchard, "Ships, Men, and Commerce," 29; Proulx, *Between France and New France*, 54–7; Surrey, *Commerce of Louisiana*, 76–81. Sailing times for English ports from Steele, *English Atlantic*, 23–7, 31–2, 51, 58–60, and 334n4.

massive island of Anticosti in the northern reach of the gulf, ships followed the rocky northern shore of the St Lawrence estuary, gradually arching southwest, pulled by strong tides and struck by sudden cross-currents, especially at the entrance to the powerful Saguenay River. In the late seventeenth and early eighteenth centuries, Canadian pilots familiar with this tricky stretch were stationed at the nearby post of Tadoussac during the summer to await French vessels. However, the Marine discontinued the practice in the 1730s in conjunction with improved knowledge and practical experience among French pilots.[18] Further upriver, just north of Quebec, another great challenge lay in wait. Here Île d'Orléans forced the river to make two swift-flowing branches. At the island's northern tip, ships needed to cross from the northern shore of the river (where treacherous tidal flats began) to the deeper and more sheltered waters off the southern shore. In between lay the "Traverse," a notorious sandbar-choked channel that snared even local ships when weather conditions turned ugly. Once ships completed this last, delicate manoeuvre, the spacious and secure anchorage of Quebec welcomed them. Until the advent of steamships in the 1830s, ocean-going vessels could sail easily only a short distance past the town. The direct firepower, and prestige, of the king's ships effectively stopped at Quebec.

Obtaining the necessary navigational knowledge to sail the gulf and river of the St Lawrence required consistent funding, years of experience, and the coordination of nautical skills between colonial and metropolitan mariners. Even then, pilots made grave errors. At least thirty-three major vessels are known to have sunk in the river between 1650 and 1760. The actual number is probably higher, and an unidentified number ran aground temporarily.[19] Shortly after uniting the colony to the crown in 1664, the state took a direct interest in systematically training pilots for ocean voyages and for charting Canada's waters. In 1671 it supplied money to the colony to hire a professor of mathematics and navigation to teach at Quebec's college. In 1685–86 Jean Deshayes undertook an extensive triangulation survey of the St Lawrence and the Gaspé Peninsula, supplying the basic knowledge for the most accurate map of the river, still in use when Charlevoix sailed on *Le Chameau* over thirty years later. The Jesuits assumed responsibility for navigational instruction in 1701, and from 1708 they supplied their own highly trained French professors. However, the state failed to consistently furnish professors with proper texts and instruments, and the teaching of navigation remained hampered until at least 1748.[20]

Proposals to undertake the desperately needed hydrographic surveys of Canadian waters abounded under the Regency; at the same time it offered a prize of 100,000 livres to tackle the problem of accurately determining longitude. However, most of the state's attention in the 1715–23 period focused on charting the water around newly settled and strategic Île Royale. This attention did not prevent a ship's captain from complaining to the Marine that "the [Canadian] pilots know nothing there, and the charts are unreliable."[21] When *Le Chameau* tragically struck a reef in 1725, with the loss of 316 lives and the colony's annual supply of specie, the Marine, under the Comte de Maurepas, acted on several fronts. It doubled the salary of professors teaching navigation from 400 to 800 livres in 1727 in order to attract better qualified teachers, and it insisted that two pilots, one French and one Canadian, accompany all naval vessels.[22] More importantly, the disaster convinced both colonial and metropolitan officials to pursue a major mapping programme of the gulf and river of St Lawrence from

1731, directed by an energetic naval captain, Henri-François Des Herbiers, Marquis de L'Étenduère. Royal funds financed this scheme in part (how much is not known), and royal and Canadian sailors took soundings, a long and tedious labour.

The work paid significant results, with the compilation of a highly accurate set of manuscript charts, and supplied information eventually published in the *Hydrographie française* (1756), rushed into publication in time for the outbreak of war.[23] Pilots were still used during the war, since geography constantly altered and because of the dramatic increase in shipping; few merchant captains ferrying supplies had the opportunity to consult expensive sea atlases. The loss of Louisbourg required further modifications in setting courses to avoid contact with British warships. In the immediate aftermath of the defeat on the Plains of Abraham in 1759, Governor General Pierre de Vaudreuil-Cavagnial complained that French pilots were inferior to their British counterparts; we know that leading the corps of the latter was the young and gifted James Cook.[24] However, Vaudreuil-Cavagnial wrote this comment in the context of explaining how the British had caught the defenders off guard. A few months later, the value of these same pilots prompted the last commander of French forces in North America, Chevalier François-Gaston de Lévis, to withdraw them from above Quebec in May 1760 in case they were captured by the advancing British Navy.[25] The ignorant pilots of forty years before had become potential prizes in war, suggesting that the second segment of the transatlantic crossing had started to become completely reliable only at the very end of the French regime in North America. Constructing hydrographic knowledge proved to be costly and posed considerable challenges to coordinating a variety of talents, from initial training in mathematics to sea experience, and ending with publication. Progress could be measured in decades, and it cost lives to achieve.

It is no exaggeration to say that a safe anchorage was the most precious colonial possession by the state in each colony. Quebec's harbour lay between the town and Île d'Orléans, measuring five kilometres in any one direction. When the ice retreated by the end of April, ships anchored in cold, grey-green water up to a hundred metres deep, dropping and rising with tides of nearly five metres, threatened only by the biting northeasterly winds that started usually by mid-October.[26] During the summer shipping season, up to three dozen ships found enough space to manoeuvre easily. It was the very spaciousness of Quebec's harbour that made it so attractive as a military stronghold, as a strategic centre for organizing armies, and as the display case for the most important and majestic symbol of royal power in the colonies, the king's ships.[27] Ships were regarded as manifestations of the royal person, and since 1681, Marine rules had stipulated the protocol for etiquette and salutes by merchant vessels and colonial forts for entries, departures, and public ceremonies.

The spaciousness of Quebec's harbour could also lead to chaos if the ships were not spaced out properly. As traffic slowly grew, colonial officials created the position of port captain in 1711 to keep order among the anchored vessels.[28] The job was not easy. Port captains carefully recorded the entry and departure of all vessels, watched for and reported smuggling activity (minimal at Quebec), organized crews to clean the town's beach so that cargo might be landed quickly and safely, retrieved lost anchors (weighing at least 300 kilos each), and marked the more dangerous channels with buoys every spring. In addition, they might have to lead emergency salvage operations for distressed ships, a demanding and sometimes dangerous operation. For example, after the sinking of the king's ship *L'Éléphant* in September 1729, port captain Richard Testu de La Richardière made three salvage trips, including one of nineteen days, in miserably cold and very stormy conditions, to recover the ship's cannon, munitions, and iron fittings. According to the report, which singled him out for special recognition (and a bonus), the efforts made by him and his small crew saved the king at least 20,000 livres. Given La Richardière's salary of 500 livres per year at this time (1,000 livres in 1737), it appeared the Marine had a bargain.[29]

In the early 1730s, the Marine placed greater responsibility on the position; it evolved from being a harbourmaster to more of a master pilot and surveyor's post. The Marine assigned La Richardière two major projects. First came the long-term project to map the St Lawrence River in the 1730s, instigated by L'Étenduère. The second project, begun at the same time, called for the construction a dry dock near the intendant's residence to service the king's vessels.[30] But while the Marine supported the charting projects, it insisted that Quebec's citizens pay for the dry dock through a land tax, which residents accepted only grudgingly.[31] Most of the quays and shipyards were small, privately operated concerns, and individual merchants resented paying for a dockyard that would not benefit them directly. By the mid-1740s, the post of port captain appears to have evolved into something of a sinecure, although the last port captain in the French regime, French naval lieutenant Gabriel Pellegrin, peppered the Marine with intelligent memorandums on improving navigation during the Seven Years War. His advice did not garner the attention of the Marine in France, perhaps crowded out by the solicitations and projects of higher-ranking French naval officers.[32] The development of the port captain's role in Canada suggests a negotiated and mutually beneficial relationship between colony and state. As soon as the needs of both were met, and those who began the initiatives died or were transferred, communications improvement projects stagnated, a pattern repeated many times in the French American colonies.

Climate and seasonal variations also proscribed royal control over the timing of sailing. Unlike all other French colonial ports, Quebec was open to ships for only five months of the year, six at best. The harbour became a scene of frenzied activity that culminated with the arrival of the king's ship in September or even October, when it unloaded new recruits, military supplies, and the year's supply of silver and government bills of exchange.[33] Winds and freeze-up made contact by sea impossible thereafter. During the long winter months, news from Europe reached Canada overland from Île Royale, carried mainly by Abenaki warrior parties, or more often from the Anglo-American colonies, either north from New York via Montreal or from Boston, transmitted by either Iroquois or Abenaki trading or hunting parties.[34] In this way, Canada's officials remained for half the year dependent in part on past and potential enemies to piece together political events. The climatic constraints constantly frustrated both the colony's top officials, who needled the Marine to send the king's ship earlier in the shipping season. The advent of war after 1755 prompted one French officer to devise a scheme for two voyages a year to Canada. By departing France in late March, a ship could reach Canada in early May, soon after the breakup of ice; after discharging its cargo and leaving in early June, it could complete another loop between mid-July (when many of the king's ships actually sailed) and the end of October. The memorialist stressed that French fishing boats from the Ponant routinely timed their arrivals to coincide with breakup. Not only could the king's vessels copy their itineraries, but they should hire their captains as pilots.[35] Significantly, most of the memorandum stressed the need for the Marine to prepare ships and coordinate gathering and loading cargoes well in advance of the anticipated departure dates. As we saw in chapter 2, limited funding and the logistics of juggling repairs, supplies, and personnel on several major routes left little manoeuvring room to revise sailing schedules.

Given the difficulties of the St Lawrence passage, the value of ice-free and cod-rich Louisbourg as a port of call for French ships is readily apparent. The voyage from the Grand Banks to Louisbourg took a week at most; thus sailing time from France was roughly two-thirds that of the Canadian run, and navigating far easier. While figures on the number of vessels are scanty, it is estimated that between 130 and

150 trade vessels from France, the French Antilles, Canada, and (often surreptitiously) New England docked each year at Louisbourg during the 1730s. During the same decade, the port also sheltered up to 400 fishing boats.[36] All these ships were potential carriers and exchangers of news. Not only were valuable cargoes of cod and sometimes colonial produce available, but French masters and shipowners could dispense with the time, wages, and skills needed for the longer voyage to Quebec.[37] Benefiting from a lifetime of experience in Canadian waters as much as from disinterest by French merchants, Canadian masters dominated the Quebec-Louisbourg run from the mid-1720s. Jacques Mathieu has estimated that at least 200 small vessels plied between Quebec and Louisbourg in the first half of the eighteenth century. Some 52 were known to have operated during the busy season of war-related activity in 1755.[38] It was these smaller vessels that kept Canada well informed of events in Europe, the Anglo-American colonies, and the Caribbean on a weekly and even daily basis during the summer navigation season. But even during winter, Louisbourg served as a crucial news bureau for Canada. For example, in early 1758, during the height of the Seven Years War, its governor warned Governor General Vaudreuil-Cavagnial in Quebec of a probable attack on Louisbourg in the spring, sending the news with French merchants who first took a boat to Île Saint Jean (Prince Edward Island) and then struggled by sled up the frozen Saint Jean River to reach the hamlet of Kamouraska on the St Lawrence's southern shore. This tough voyage, in one of the coldest winters recorded in the eighteenth century, took nearly two months.[39] As New France's window on the Atlantic world, Louisbourg, through its merchants, filtered exchanges so that Canada often learned what Île Royale had already known at least three weeks beforehand. While Quebec never quite lost its prominent role as an Atlantic port, the state discovered that maintaining seaborne communications required large amounts of capital, supervision, and knowledge acquired after years of surveying, a tall order for a colony providing minimal economic dividends. In no other French American colony did the desire to control the hazards of the sea play as great a role in integrating colonial and metropolitan interests.

THE ANTILLES ROUTE

In complete contrast to Canada's circumstances were those of Martinique and the Îles du Vent. To begin with, the Antilles route was much simpler. As with the North Atlantic route, ships dodged storms across the Bay of Biscay and then headed south to Cape Saint Vincent, off southern Portugal. But the weather quickly improved thereafter, and by the time vessels passed Madeira or the Canary Islands, the winds were brisk, astern, and constant. Pilots simply steered a south-westerly course until reaching Martinique's line of latitude at about 14° 30' north, at which point they switched to due west until they sighted one of the Lesser Antilles islands.[40] Ships sailed the 6,600-kilometre route in five to seven weeks on the outbound journey. It felt much longer to seventeenth-century chroniclers, who estimated the distance closer to 9,000 kilometres[41] (see table 3.1). If bound for Saint Domingue, vessels followed the same Antillean route but simply turned due west upon reaching between 19 45' and 19 15' north latitude; this brought them directly to Le Cap. The Saint Domingue run averaged about one week to two weeks longer than that to Martinique.

Sailors initiated first-time passengers and sailors with a "baptism" when ships crossed the Tropic of Cancer at 23° 26' north latitude. Although similar to the one for Canada, it featured some differences. Veteran sailors would soot their faces with ash and adorn themselves with tridents, harpoons, sea pikes, and other marine tools, surround the initiate, and tie him (it is not clear if women were subjected to this ceremony) with sailing cord, blacken his face and upper body, and dunk him in a tub of cold, fresh sea water, long enough for him to start hyperventilating. Sailors then dragged the initiate out and held him kneeling before the chief pilot, who had also blackened his face and put on Neptune's crown, and who held charts, compasses, sextants, and other instruments of navigation in his hands. In this guise, the pilot demanded that the initiate swear on a chart to observe the rules of the sea and not divulge them to anyone else not having undergone the baptism. The demons of the sea released him only after he paid, or vowed to pay, a sum for brandy, after which he was let go, and resuscitated and cleaned up by the other passengers.[42] This homage to Neptune, with its symbolic rebirth from blackness into the light and warmth of the Tropics, also demarcated the boundaries between the Old World and the New. Unlike the Canadian ritual, with its Santa Claus–like figure, the emphasis on an ancient Greek god, played by the master of sea knowledge with his sceptre of sea charts, carnivalesque demons, and emergence from primordial blackness, suggests a desire to more completely "transform" the individual than its North Atlantic counterpart. It is tempting to speculate that for mariners, Canada appeared to be a colder version of France, while the Antilles were another level of existence altogether.

The return voyage back to France carried ships north, to arrive within twenty-four hours between the British islands of Montserrat and

Antigua (with its naval base), then past low-lying, virtually unpopulated, but dangerous Barbuda, and finally out into the safety of the Atlantic swells. Ships picked up the Gulf Stream several hundred kilometres to the southeast of Bermuda, and at between 26° to 30° north latitude they began to follow an arc-shaped course east-northeast back toward France.[43] This return journey averaged a week longer than the outbound one, about six to eight weeks in total. Favourable winds, which were not uncommon, could easily clip ten days from the voyage. To put the ease of the Antilles route into perspective, consider that ships sailing from France to Canada took the same amount of time to travel only half as far, or that if Antilles speed could be applied to the Brest-Bordeaux run (a mere 550 kilometres apart), the voyage would take only three days instead of ten to fourteen days. While the Caribbean islands of course afforded far richer cargoes, it may well be that French historians have underestimated the impact of easy oceanic access on economic and strategic issues.

The other major source of seaborne traffic for the Antilles comprised slave ships from West and Central Africa. These ships in effect navigated the mirror image of the European-Antilles route. If arriving from the Gold Coast, the Bight of Benin, or points further south, ships picked up the southeast trades along the southern rim of the West African coasts and sailed west and then northwestward, following the bulge of land and battling the Guinea current as they went, slowly arching to the north to clutch at the northeast tradewinds, and following them until they reached Martinique's latitude before turning due west. Depending on where the slave ship left the coast, the distance could range from approximately 7,100 kilometres off the Ivory Coast to over 10,500 kilometres from Luanda in Angola. These voyages ranged from seven to twelve weeks, but great variations were possible. Robert Stein found that one French slave vessel, departing from the Gold Coast, took an agonizing twenty-six and a half weeks (six months) to make the crossing. Ships loading slaves at the port of Gorée on the Senegambian coast simply sailed west directly, since it and Martinique lay virtually on the same line of latitude. This much shorter route stretched only 4,800 kilometres across the mid-Atlantic and enabled crossings of four to six weeks, although great variations were again possible.[44] For example, *Le Maréchal d'Estrée*, with 227 slaves on board, left Gorée on July 13, 1723, and arrived at Saint Pierre on Martinique only on October 23, after a passage of fourteen and a half weeks. The pilot recorded that the voyage took so long in part because the vessel kept moving between 14° 26' and 9° latitude, desperately searching for wind.[45] Aside from the problems of negotiating the often hazardous West African coastlines, straying into the dreaded Doldrums also posed major potential navigational problems to slave ships. This expansive sea region of little or no wind could becalm a ship for weeks on end in stifling equatorial heat. Unfamiliarity with the Atlantic's wind circulation in the seventeenth century entrapped many slave ships in the Doldrums, leading to the slow and ghastly death of many enslaved Africans and sometimes their European captors.

Whether sailing from Europe or from West Africa, once on the American side of the Atlantic and having sighted land, navigators had a choice. If they were headed for Saint Pierre, Martinique, or Guadeloupe, either the looming volcano of Mount Pelée or jagged Macouba Point (both on northern Martinique) served as a landmark. Pilots heading for Fort Royal searched for Mount Vauclin on Martinique's southern side (see map 3). Pilots simply followed the coastline, passing the thatched wooden houses and white parish churches that peeked out from the dark green shore. Saint Pierre Bay lay in a slight indentation on the island's northwestern side, adequately sheltered from the trade winds and powerful swells of the Atlantic Ocean, forming an open roadstead with no natural or artificial protective barriers.[46] However, the waters were gentle, and in contrast to the Ponant ports, winds blew continually from the east-northeast, allowing ships to sail in or out of port at any time of the day or night. The stronger shore breezes (*brises du large*) rose with the sun and died in late afternoon, only to be replaced by the lighter land breezes (*brises de terre*), which began in the evening and blew through most of the night.[47] The ease of entering and leaving the bay rendered it difficult to defend but ideal for smuggling, and few Caribbean anchorages were as accommodating for loading and unloading by lighters. The sandy bottom dropped away quickly, allowing the largest of merchant vessels to anchor within thirty-five metres of the surf, with tidal action so minimal as to be non-existent.[48]

Despite the inviting conditions, Saint Pierre's harbour remained virtually unsupervised. As the officially designated capital of the colony, Fort Royal boasted a port captain, but Saint Pierre did so only once. During the plague of 1720, the colony's intendant assigned a merchant captain from Le Havre named Filliol to inspect ships as they entered. He apparently succeeded at his task, as officials did not report any spread of the plague. During the Regency, several local sea captains had solicited to have the post created, but to no avail.[49] In 1728 Intendant Blondel wrote enthusiastically about Saint Pierre's excellent roadstead, but noted that it had become cluttered with discarded anchors. Fines had been instituted in 1681, but the regulations went unheeded, presumably because the no officials existed to enforce

Table 3.2
Ship arrivals at Saint Pierre compared with Fort Royal, 1733–1757

	Saint Pierre		*Fort Royal*		
Year	*No.*	*Per cent*	*No.*	*Per cent*	*Total*
1733	160	80.8	38	19.2	198
1735	166	83.4	31	15.6	199
1737	167	86.1	24	12.4	194
1745	82	56.9	56	38.9	144
1747[1]	70	100.0	0	0	70
1752[2]	126	76.4	39	23.6	165
1757[3]	139	97.2	4	2.8	143

SOURCES: 1733: AC, C8B 17, Record of ship arrivals, nos. 12–28, May 15, 1734; 1735: ibid., Record of ship arrivals, 1735, nos. 27–36, July 10, 1736. 1737; ibid., Record of ships for 1737, nos. 45–51, June 20, 1738. 1745: ibid., 21, Record of Commerce for 1745, nos. 17–34, August 12, 1746 [another 7 came from Holland, 1 from Ireland (Cork), and 1 from Bermuda, all to exchange prisoners]; 1747: ibid., Record of foreign ships anchoring in Martinique in 1747, no. 41, March 10, 1748. 1752: ibid., Record of commerce for 1752, nos. 61–72, October 25, 1753. 1757: ibid., 22, Record of foreign ships anchoring in Martinique in 1757, August 15, 1759, nos. 4–10.

[1] Foreign ships only.
[2] French ships only; port of arrival for non-French ships not indicated. Total number of recorded ship arrivals in both ports from all destinations in 1752 was 278.
[3] Foreign ships only.

them.[50] Saint Pierre thus stood in complete contrast to Quebec: it needed no infrastructure or any careful surveying to operate efficiently and safely. The ease of using Saint Pierre's harbour contributed greatly to its role as the commercial hub of the Îles du Vent, and explains why it drew a dramatically larger number of ships than did nearby Fort Royal (see table 3.2).

The king's harbour of Fort Royal, Saint Pierre's alter ego, lay only 43.5 kilometres away. Although *ancien régime* officials tended to see the two towns as opposites – the rowdy, dirty, money-grubbing port and the neatly designed governor's town with its great stone fort – Louis-Philippe May has pointed out that their ports, at least, were in fact highly complementary to each other and comprised a single economic and maritime unit. Fort Royal offered one distinct advantage over Saint Pierre's open roadstead. Surrounded by hilly land on all sides except for an opening to the west, Fort Royal Bay featured a hurricane-proof inlet. The fear of hurricanes dated from a particularly vicious storm in 1670, when all twenty-eight ships then in Saint Pierre's harbour were sunk or run aground and irreparably damaged. Upon receiving word of the disaster, Louis XIV's chief minister, Jean-Baptiste Colbert, decided to transfer the site of the capital to the safer anchorage at Fort Royal, already highly esteemed by mariners since the 1640s. Between 1713 and 1763, at least fiften hurricanes and major storms thrashed the Îles du Vent, sending ships scurrying each time from Saint Pierre to Fort Royal's sheltered waters; a hurricane on September 19, 1751, levelled about half of Saint Pierre, but visited only slight damage on Fort Royal.[51] However, the concept of how much damage hurricanes could do apparently took many years to become common knowledge at the Marine. In 1701, after more than sixty years of experience, a royal pilot still had to describe what they were and why they had to be avoided, in a memorandum to the Marine's clerks back in France.[52]

Fort Royal offered other advantages. Along with the security of a stout stone fort overlooking the bay and a patch of ground suitable for careening and repairing vessels, enclosed by an iron chain, the harbour also provided a near-ideal stage to showcase the arrivals and departures of the king's ships.[53] However, it proved to be no less polluted with debris than Saint Pierre Bay. In 1727 one of the king's vessels ran aground on a sandbar while taking Intendant Blondel on an inspection tour of the harbour. It required the better part of two weeks to refloat the vessel, an event, he noted with some chagrin, which caused great mirth among merchant captains watching the operation.[54] Missing from Blondel's report was any mention of a port captain. The Marine had paid for a port captain at Fort Royal since the 1690s, but such officials clearly played a minor role in the commercial and political life of French Caribbean ports. Scattered references indicate that they held the rank of lieutenant on the king's vessels and were in charge primarily of collecting entry and exit duties on ships in the harbour. In 1727 these duties brought in a paltry 3,000 livres.[55] Port captains also worked closely with the king's Domaine (customs) to deter smugglers, but most smuggling occurred everywhere on the island except (conveniently?) at Fort Royal.[56] Very few documents attest to their presence; they are not included on the yearly salary appointments, and none were used for any survey work. The last captain, one Sieur Bart (a great-nephew of the famous French corsair Jean Bart) was a former ship lieutenant who had settled on the island and obtained the post in 1758, with its annual salary of 1,000 livres.[57] His position seems to have been a mere sinecure. The striking difference between Canada's and Martinique's captains is indicative of the state's vastly different needs in each colony. The Îles du Vent posed no serious navigational challenges; colonists and metropolitan merchants did not require state help, whether it was in the form of pilots, port captains, or nautical instruction; further expense would have been superfluous.

Ports situated to the west of Martinique and Guadeloupe, from Saint Domingue to Vera Cruz and as far north as New Orleans, could be easily reached, but ships had to fight contrary winds and currents on the return to Îles du Vent. French naval and merchant vessels frequently used Martinique as a stopover before continuing on to the increasingly more dynamic markets of Saint Domingue. Pilots used a variety of routes to gain Saint Domingue; most commonly, they steered northwest via British Nevis, then turned west to skirt south of Sainte Croix and the southern coast of Puerto Rico, before either heading north through the Mona Passage if aiming for Le Cap, or continuing along Hispaniola's southern coast if making for Saint Louis-du-Sud, Léogane, or the smaller outports in the southern province (see map 3.3).[58] Ships completed the voyage to Le Cap in about ten days with good weather, and to Saint Louis-du-Sud, on Saint Domingue's southern coast, in eight to fourteen days.[59] Only smaller ships based mainly in Saint Pierre found a niche shuttling between the two colonies. The manoeuvres of the British Royal Navy during war could reverse the usual flow, so that Saint Domingue's ships often sailed east to avoid capture, putting into Martinique or Guadeloupe before heading across the Atlantic, and thereby informing the eastern islands of events near Jamaica.[60]

Unlike Quebec's port, all harbours in the Îles du Vent remained open all year. In Saint Pierre, casks of semi-refined sugar or sacks of coffee piled up in warehouses as early as January, often overflowing onto the beach by late March. Activity built until early July and the onset of the *mauvais temps*. Although authorities prohibited ships from anchoring during hurricane season from mid-July to mid-October, even official records show a reduction, not a complete halt[61] (see table 3.3). After October, French merchants and clandestine traders from New England again slowly invaded the islands. At all times of the year, ships could reach not only Saint Pierre and Fort Royal but the many smaller outports of the Îles du Vent as well, all quickly, safely, with a minimum of navigational expertise, and, best of all, with little or no supervision by colonial authorities. These other harbours tended to be either a Saint Pierre–like open roadstead or an enclosed harbour such as Fort Royal's. Roadsteads included Basse-terre and Saint François on Guadeloupe, while enclosed harbours included La Trinité (facing the open Atlantic) and Cul-de-Sac Marin on Martinique and the two "Carénages," one on Saint Lucia (today's Castries) and the other on Grenada (today's St George's). Despite containing small garrisons, all these ports were also active centres of this contraband trade.

Table 3.3
Monthly ship arrivals from France at Saint Pierre

Year	*J*	*F*	*M*	*A*	*M*	*J*	*J*	*A*	*S*	*O*	*N*	*D*	*Total*
1733	12	4	12	12	15	14	5	2	0	14	9	17	116
1745	0	2	3	5	3	1	0	0	0	0	5	2	21
1752	5	13	19	9	11	8	8	0	2	2	29	20	126

SOURCES: 1733: AC, C8B 17, Record of ships arrived, nos. 12–28, May 15 1734; 1745: ibid., 21, Rcords of commerce for 1745, nos. 17–34, August 12, 1746 [another 7 came from Holland, 1 from Ireland (Cork), and 1 from Bermuda, all to exchange prisoners]; 1752: ibid., Records of commerce for 1752, nos. 61–72, October 25, 1753.

Martinique and Guadeloupe possessed one further natural advantage in terms of navigation. In addition to its central position on a major east-west transatlantic route, the island lay astride a busy northwest-southeast intercolonial one. If we drew an imaginary line bisecting Martinique along this axis, we would see that the steady northeast trade winds blew perpendicular to this line. Because of the dynamics of sailing, ships could travel up or down this northwest-southeast axis with relative ease throughout the entire year.[62] All of Martinique's dependencies in the Îles du Vent lay on this line. These included the islands of Guadeloupe, Marie-Galante, Saint Martin, and Saint Barthélemy, together with the "neutral" (officially neither British nor French) island of Dominica to the north and "neutral" Saint Lucia and French Grenada to the south. Guadeloupe could be reached by an easy overnight voyage, while all the rest were within four days' sailing. The furthest, Grenada, took four to five days, although twice that long on the return trip.[63]

More importantly, all of Martinique's potential enemies and trading allies also lay along this northwest-southeast axis. To the north lay British Antigua, with its naval base at English Harbour, and the busy entrepôts of Dutch Saint Eustatius and Danish Saint Thomas. This sailing route extended even farther north to New York, Rhode Island, Boston, and of course Louisbourg.[64] South of Martinique, but still along this line, and to the east lay British Barbados, the first Caribbean port of call for many British warships; to the west of the line, but still within easy sailing range, was the other Dutch entrepôt of Curaçao and the larger cities of the Spanish Main, such as Puerto Cabello and Cumaná.[65] The line could be extended even farther south to French Cayenne, on the South American mainland.[66] Sailing along this axis proved so easy that, for example, an English captain bound from New

York to Louisbourg with a cargo of flour decided that it was safer and at least as profitable to escape a violent Christmas storm off Cape Sable and sail all the way south to Martinique to sell his cargo, an easy voyage of less than three weeks. Such rethinking in the teeth of storms was not unusual.[67] In this way, geography favoured Guadeloupe and Martinique as natural terminal points for New England's merchants. Like English Barbados, Martinique, with an advance position in the Lesser Antilles, served mainly as a transmission point of European news and products for ports to its lee, and it benefited from the intercolonial axis in trade, particularly with New England. However, the interaction worked two ways: the ease of the Antilles route invited greater metropolitan control, while the intercolonial route defeated the state's ability to enforce that control. This conflict lay at the very heart of the issue of illicit trade and, ultimately, of Creole autonomy in the islands, a point considered in chapter 7.

THE GULF ROUTE

Compared to both Canada and the Îles du Vent, New Orleans sat at the extreme end of the French American maritime world. In terms of navigation, the entire voyage from France was by far the most gruelling and unpredictable of the three routes, and it required four distinct stages (see table 3.1). The first two paralleled those for the Îles du Vent or Saint Domingue. Sometimes the king's vessels or French slavers found it just as expedient to enter the Caribbean Sea at the south between Grenada and Trinidad, follow the prevailing coastal currents and winds along the Spanish Main and Central America, and then turn due north at the Yucatan Peninsula to enter the Gulf of Mexico. From Grenada to Louisiana's ports took only three to four weeks at most.[68] On one occasion, a transatlantic crossing from Bordeaux to the mouth of the Mississippi via Grenada took only fifty-nine days with no stops, an astonishingly short trip.[69] More usually, ships ran down the wind upon reaching 19° 30' north latitude (the same latitude as Le Cap) and continued until they encountered the northern coast of Hispaniola. As we have seen, this portion of the voyage lasted seven to nine weeks outbound from France.

The third stage began after the ships left Saint Domingue's ports.[70] They pushed a thousand kilometres west, sometimes along Spanish Cuba's north coast but more commonly along its rocky southern shore and its dependable westward currents. Either route brought ships to within a few days' sail of Havana. Rounding Cape Saint Antoine at the island's westernmost point, pilots then steered northwestward and tacked a further one thousand kilometres miles against contrary winds and currents until they reached the sandy, flat, pine-covered shores lying between the Mississippi River and Pensacola Bay. This portion of the trip took between two and four weeks. Initially, ships anchored in a small harbour at one end of desolate Île Dauphin, at the entrance to Mobile Bay. From 1716 until 1722, most dropped anchor off Île aux Vaisseaux (Ship Island, Mississippi), when it appeared that Biloxi might become the colony's capital.[71] During this time, an assortment of officials, priests, and boatmen contributed their knowledge and memorandums toward understanding the region's geography in order to determine the safest and most accessible harbour.[72] Royal officials finally accepted Governor Bienville's unequivocal recommendation in 1722 that the site at the future New Orleans be made the colony's capital. Immediately, royal engineers and work gangs of slaves and some soldiers commenced building a small stone fort, La Balize (The Buoy), on two precarious dots of land at the only viable entrance to the Mississippi River, the Southeast Pass.[73]

Finally came the long and arduous 160-kilometre ascent up the Mississippi to New Orleans itself.[74] At La Balize colonial officials stationed a pilot (two after 1732) to guide ships up the river's continually reshaping course. The Mississippi's lower delta formed a vast, watery world, a region of thick air and tangled reeds, slimy ground, and shifting islets, which could disappear beneath two metres of water in the spring. But an even greater obstacle lay just upriver from the fort. A permanent sandbar (known simply as "Le Barre") limited passage via the Southeast Pass to ships drawing less than 3.5 metres. Since the keel of a heavily-laden warship or large merchant vessel often lay submerged 5 to 7 metres below the water-line captains were often forced to unload some or even all of their cargoes onto lighters or *bateaux*; the latter were flat-bottomed boats fitted with sails. This monotonous process added between one and two weeks to the voyage, and on one occasion about three.[75]

Once past the bar, ships struggled upriver, dodging half-submerged logs and thick clouds of mosquitoes along the way. It was not uncommon for adverse winds to strand ships for up to two weeks at a time at the 180-degree bend in the river known as the "Detour aux Anglais" (now English Turn), some forty kilometres below New Orleans. Here, in mid-1699, Bienville had bluffed an English captain and his men into believing that his small band of Frenchmen was the advance guard of a much larger army. The English turned back and, according to the story, lost Louisiana.[76] Only at this point did passengers and crews glimpse the first signs of the French settlement: two small and incomplete sets of earthworks on either side of the river and the first smattering of thatched slave huts and rough log cabins along the riverbanks. Important and weary passengers, as well as critical dispatches, could be put ashore at this point as well and proceed by horse or on foot to New Orleans. Although some historians have calculated that it was theoretically possible to sail to New Orleans from France in about twelve weeks, contemporary ships' logs show that the average crossing approached seventeen weeks, at least a month longer.[77]

Upon reaching New Orleans, ocean-going vessels dropped anchor just downriver of the *place d'armes*, or public square. Large dugout canoes with seating for four to six people (*pirogues*) or the *bateaux* from Illinois tied up farther upriver, opposite a muddy patch of ground that served as the town's market. According to an early observer, Antoine Le Page du Pratz, if the river was high enough, ships could be floated right up alongside the levee and unloaded by rolling barrels off long gangplanks.[78] The pilots stationed at La Balize supervised this anchorage from 1723.[79] The most important among them, Sieur Livaudais, served the Compagnie des Indes initially in the capacity of port captain but without the title and the royal pay of 1,200 livres, before becoming firmly attached as one of Governor Bienville's clients in 1731.[80] As with his counterpart at Quebec, his work included piloting ships upriver, taking regular soundings of the river to determine the safest channels, exploring stretches of the Gulf coast, and guiding ships downriver. The return voyage took ships back down the Mississippi with the aid of its powerful current, out into the Gulf, and with the winds to Havana. From there they picked up the Gulf Stream, entered the Bahamas Channel toward Bermuda, and then arched back to France across the North Atlantic. The return was far more predictable and required, on average, about four weeks less time.

Climate also complicated navigation to New Orleans. At least six major storms lashed the port between 1708 and 1750, dismasting ships and ramming them onto shoals or the shore each time.[81] The Mississippi's annual flooding regularly rearranged the coastline, rendering maps obsolete within five years, and made the use of pilots mandatory. Even the fort at La Balize moved. Within thirty years after its construction, it lay seven kilometres from its initial position relative to the Southeast Pass, permanently flooded by about a metre of water and slowly sinking into the delta. By 1760 an old hulk served as the "fort."[82] But the most difficult obstacle to navigation had nothing to do with navigating per se. Finding return cargoes to fill all of a ship's hold continually plagued the colony's officials and merchants for most years during the French regime. All ships, including royal warships, had empty holds to fill. Louisiana grew the same tropical items as other colonies and produced little that they needed.[83] As Saint Domingue began its rise to become the richest sugar-producing island in the Caribbean in the 1740s, merchants bound for Louisiana realized fatter profits at Le Cap or other ports in the colony. Contacts with Saint Domingue thus proved to be a mixed blessing. While New Orleans received valuable news from France or from other colonies and could sell construction supplies to Saint Domingue's planters, the latter colony devoured many of the goods and supplies destined for Louisiana.[84]

As a result, and because of the attraction of Spanish silver, French officials regarded Havana as a potentially valuable trading neighbour, although Spanish colonial officials remained cool to their overtures. While Havana served as a valuable source of news during wartime, its proximity to Jamaica exposed French ships to English privateers. A single capture could have serious consequences. For example, when Jamaican privateers captured the king's corvette *La Fée*, outbound from Saint Domingue in the early fall of 1740 (four years before any declaration of war), Louisiana's colonists were kept in the dark about British movements against the Spanish colonies, and possible French declarations of war, until the following March, when a merchant vessel from Saint Domingue finally anchored at New Orleans and brought updated news.[85] Le Cap thus acted as a kind of window for Louisiana to peer on activity in the greater Atlantic world in much the same way as Louisbourg did for Canada or Saint Pierre for the smaller ports in the Îles du Vent. Since reaching Louisiana required a long, tedious, and largely unprofitable voyage, both metropolitan officials in France and colonial leaders in Louisiana actively encouraged closer contacts with their Spanish allies in order to compensate.

LAKE, RIVER, AND ROAD IN NORTH AMERICA

From the Marine's point of view, seaborne routes were the most important and easily controlled links between France and each colonial port. Once it arrived, official information filtered down a hierarchy of agents under state command. But the ports also marked a critical transition point from metropolitan to colonial influence. Once royal orders and personnel reached the ports, colonial traditions, economics, technology, African slave labour, Native allies, and even the cooperation of colonists themselves increasingly dictated how, when and under what circumstances they circulated. Local or regional transport comprised two basic forms: water-borne transport by rivers and lakes, and roads. Water transport dominated, although roads played an increasingly larger role on the eve of the Seven Years War.

The construction of land transportation infrastructure in the colonies is best understood as an extension of a dynamic series of initiatives originating in France. Under Louis XV, an increasing number of administrators, and the king himself, demanded not merely to understand the extent of the kingdom but to grasp its potential and fully impose royal order in every corner. Although Colbert had initiated a number of large-scale communications infrastructure projects, notably the Canal des Deux-Mers,[86] it was in the eighteenth century that, as Daniel Nordman and Jacques Revel put it, "knowledge of territory became inseparable from the exercise of sovereignty."[87] Roads were an essential component of enhancing the state's knowledge. Despite the reliance on a feudal levy, the *corvée*, to provide labour for construction (from 1720), French roads and river routes improved dramatically. Under Philibert Orry, a former provincial intendant who became controller general in 1730, French engineers reorganized and built a new road system, creating a demand for more accurate mapping and surveys to accomplish the task. As a corollary to the extensive surveys undertaken for roadwork, the Cassini family, royal map-makers since the early reign of Louis XIV, published the first of their highly detailed and accurate maps of France by 1756. This infrastructure augmented more than mere transportation: as Daniel Roche has commented, roads and bridges "were like monuments [for t]hey etched the power of the monarchy into the landscape itself."[88] Not surprisingly, metropolitan intendants assigned to the colonies introduced transportation initiatives shortly after taking up their posts.

Constructing a similar network of roads in the wilderness of North America or the Antilles proved to be far more difficult, and less necessary, than in France (see map 4). In North America, the vast drainage area of the Great Lakes–St Lawrence and the Mississippi-Ohio river systems offered a dense network of reasonably safe, well-connected waterways easily accessed by birchbark canoes. One historian has estimated that the Mississippi-Missouri and Alabama river systems combined afforded 26,000 kilometres of navigable waterways.[89] From the earliest years of settlement in North America, French men and some women learned about and adopted a variety of Native technologies and developed skills to explore and trade in the *pays d'en haut*. In the French Antilles, local shippers, often freedmen, carried information and people from cove to cove. Recent research by Jeffrey Bolster has suggested that at least some African labourers brought maritime and boat-building skills and their own seafaring traditions from West African coastal regions, which they put to use, or were forced to use, in the Greater Caribbean.[90] In all three colonies, local knowledge by colonists, including slaves, and lower echelon officers was instrumental in propelling the king's word.

In Canada the riverine network centred on Montreal. To the south and west, river routes divided into three main branches: a northern route to Lake Huron, and on to the western end of Lake Superior, via the Ottawa River and Lake Nipissing; a second and more widely used Great Lakes route that led southwest via Lake Ontario and a portage at Niagara Falls to Lake Erie and then to Detroit; and a third route due south to Albany in the colony of New York, via the Richelieu River and Lake Champlain. In an effort to secure France's claim to the heart of North America, military officers carved out a fourth major route in 1749, which branched off from the Great Lakes route at Presque Isle (near Erie, Pennsylvania) to reach the upper reaches of the Ohio River. Along this route French soldiers and Native allies built a series of small posts to guard against British intrusion.[91]

From the earliest era of settlement, the birchbark canoe served as the workhorse of riverine transportation. According to Charlevoix, the largest held twelve people (two abreast) and 4,000 pounds of merchandise, yet drew only about twenty centimetres of water. Other sources record that many canoes averaged ten to fifteen metres in length, about the size of an ocean-going sloop. Strong paddlers averaged sixty kilometres a day if gliding with river currents or on calm lake waters, or about 100 kilometres with sails (all canoes carried them). Although the French quickly learned how to handle and then build canoes, Huron craftsmen, especially at the Catholic native settlements at Lorette outside Quebec and at Trois-Rivières, constructed the majority in the eighteenth century.[92] Builders used white cedar for the ribbing and covered it with a patchwork of birchbark pieces, sewn together with spruce roots and sealed with heated tree resin. So long as they were not continually punctured, canoes could last ten to twelve years. As Swedish botanist Peter Kalm pointed out, canoes were easy to fix anywhere, since all the necessary materials could be found not far from any riverbank.[93] Everyone travelled in them: officers, traders, missionaries, voyageurs, and emigrants of both sexes, although men predominated. The cost of using them as transportation is very difficult to determine; since expeditions were outfitted for trade or for ferrying missionaries, soldiers, and post supplies (or both), the costs of trade and military supplies, as well as food, are inextricable from transportation costs. To send information alone would be prohibitively expensive. For example, in 1757 French officer Louis-Antoine de Bougainville noted that the dispatch of a canoe with the specific purpose of carrying important military correspondence from Fort Frontenac (five days upriver from Montreal) to Detroit cost 2,260 livres one way for supplies and the salaries for the six to eight paddlers.[94] By 1700, mastery of native canoe technology and geographic knowledge helped establish Canadians as the preponderant European presence in the *pays d'en haut*.

In contrast to water transport, land transportation, using horses and wagons over roads and bridges, appeared only gradually in Canada and became a major factor only by the Seven Years War. Efforts to impede common habitants from usurping the privilege of noblemen by owning and riding horses were the basis of several local laws in the eighteenth century. But a system of regular land contact between Quebec and Montreal emerged only later. By 1757 Bougainville reported that posts to rent horses operated in the two towns, at a cost of 20 *sols* per league.[95] Constructing a road network required a high level of coordination to gather materials and labourers, placed tremendous strain on local resources, and required widespread cooperation from colonists to maintain. Colonial regulations closely followed French models in classifying roads into three basic types. King's roads (*chemins royales*) were the major highways of the era, constructed principally in France to speed troops, the baggage of court, and messengers across the kingdom, and were designed and paid for by the state; they served essentially the same purpose in the colonies. Connecting roads between towns or villages and the king's roads were called *chemins de communications* and were maintained by each parish, with labour supplied by the local militia company. Privately owned and used roads, or *chemins particuliers*, linked *chemins de communications*. In Canada, official correspondence also mentioned a fourth type, the *chemins de moulin*, which were really dirt pathways cleared and maintained by seigneurs to allow their farmers easy access to grain mills. More culturally distinct types of land transportation also developed in Canada, such as "ice bridges," cleared paths of snow marked with buoys for sleds and carriages.[96] Roads were expensive. Until the early eighteenth century most roads were restricted to the immediate region around Quebec, with a slight development on Montreal Island. In the early 1740s, soldiers and some requisitioned habitants were paid the low wage of 30 *sols* per day to clear a road from Chambly on the Richelieu River to Montreal, a project that took three months to complete and cost the crown, according to a recent estimate, 35,000 livres.[97] The responsibility for plotting the roads rested on the shoulders of the *grand voyer*, or royal surveyor, and roadwork progressed only when energetic or ambitious men held the post. The responsibility for supplying the labour to build and maintain them rested, however, on the collective shoulders of local parishes, which fulfilled a *corvée*, or tax of labour.[98] In return, these roads were open to all. The development of land routes was closely tied to the willingness of habitants to cooperate with the state and the negotiating abilities of the Royal Surveyor.

The construction of Canada's Quebec-Montreal road is a case in point.[99] Colonial officials had requested such a highway since the late seventeenth century, although it is not clear whether or not local parishes initiated the requests. Only with the appointment of a new royal surveyor, Jean-Eustache Lanoullier de Boisclerc, who worked under the direction of the new intendant, Gilles Hocquart, did work begin in earnest. The largest French colonial road-building project of its era, the road ran along the north shore of the St Lawrence River and required ten bridges from 14 to 20 metres long. Habitants completed work on it during the summer months of four successive years between 1732 and 1735.[100] Lanoullier and his assistant rode to the church or seigneur's house in the thirty-seven parishes involved to announce the project and requisition men for the task. While he marked out the section of the road within each parish, the men would either cut trees and pull out the stumps or cut cedar trees into timber for bridge boards. Farming, rain, and the summer's heat dictated the rhythm of work.[101] In August of 1735 Lanoullier tested the new road, making the 300-kilometre journey between the two towns in a horse-drawn carriage in only four and half days.[102] The road made little difference to travel, for canoes took the same amount of time (even upriver), and most people, goods, and messages still travelled by river. However, the habitants received other benefits in return, for the road opened up new areas for farming. As each section neared completion, settlers began taking up land concessions along or near it. In fact, Hocquart enthused over this aspect to such an extent that one suspects agricultural development was his prime motivation for supporting the project.[103]

In the 1740s Lanoullier continued to build or improve roads and bridges around the island of Montreal and in the Richelieu River valley, but road-building activity halted during the War of the Austrian Succession. The last major project, the "Justinian Way," running through the Beauce valley southeast of Quebec toward Abenaki lands, was completed at the height of the Seven Years War, during the summer of 1758. The active participation by local habitants, combined with massive state expenditures to build other roads, is in striking contrast with both France and the Antilles, where *corvées* generated vociferous opposition. Given that many farmers also belonged to a militia company, and thus understood the reality of attacks from the Anglo-American colonies and their Native allies, this cooperation is one of the best proofs of William Eccles's thesis that Canada was a colony with a peculiarly "military ethos" penetrating all levels of society.

In Louisiana, rivers also served as major highways. Early colonists, many of whom were Canadians, tapped into a long-standing tradition of river transport, from both neighbouring Native peoples and the coureurs de bois. They began bringing furs to d'Iberville's initial settlement at Fort Condé (near Mobile) as soon as workmen erected its palisade in 1701.[104] Convoys of up to twenty *pirogues* and flat-bottomed river boats supplied New Orleans with badly needed grain from the Illinois posts of Cahokia, Kaskaskia, and later, Sainte Geneviève (all near Saint Louis, Missouri, on either side of the Mississippi). These convoys usually left New Orleans between August and November, pushing slowly upriver at about six or seven kilometres per day, on a voyage that required three to four months to reach Fort de Chartres. The return trip could be considerably shortened; one missionary heard that the trip could be made in fifteen days by river pilots who knew the currents and safer channels. Starting in February or late March, boatmen could also use small sails, averaging thirty to thirty-five kilometres per day.[105] The important trading post and Native diplomacy centre of Mobile could also be reached by canoes from New Orleans, either by Lake Pontchartrain or by small sailing craft via the Mississippi and along the coast; either route took four or five days. Slave sailors manned ships for most regional traffic, along with a few soldiers and the occasional white sailor, and authorities also employed skilled workers to construct local craft.[106] According to Daniel H. Usner, the Compagnie des Indes favoured the use of slaves in order to reduce expenses.[107] However, officials regarded their dependability as suspect.

In comparison to water-borne transport, roads are barely mentioned in official correspondence relating to Louisiana. In 1735 shortly after the crown reclaimed the colony, the Marine issued regulations to ensure the surveying, building, and upkeep of roads, but these were ignored.[108] The Marine then approved the appointment of Olivier de Vezin as Royal Surveyor from 1747, four years after Governor Vaudreuil-Cavagnial and *commissaire-ordonnateur* Salmon had unofficially assigned him the task. However, eleven years later, in 1758, Vezin complained that he had not yet received any surveying tools, two desperately needed assistant surveyors (for land disputes), or his salary of 1,200 livres per year. He had spent the intervening period clearing a road parallel to the levee from about thirty kilometres below New Orleans to nearly seventy kilometres to the Côte d'Allemands (German Coast) above the town. But it remained virtually impassable because of regular flooding and the neglect by local planters in allocating their slaves to repair the road.[109] We also know that in 1741 a dispute arose between the king's lieutenant and a Pointe Coupée planter over repairs to a bridge on a public road,[110] but it is not clear from this account if the road was an extension from New Orleans. Another contemporary account suggested that elementary roads, or pathways, linked the villages clustered around Fort de Chartres in the Illinois country by the 1750s, the presence of which has been confirmed by recent archaeological work in the region.[111] These snippets of information reinforce the impression that, despite efforts by the state to institute secure land routes, riverine travel remained the transportation of choice for goods and people throughout lower Louisiana.

Most of our information on travelling in the North American interior is derived from explorers and missionaries in the seventeenth century. These accounts capture the dramatically new biological and cultural world for Europeans entering it for the first time. By the era of the Seven Years War, the regular movement of soldiers had helped regularize the route between Montreal and the entry to the *pays d'en haut* at Fort Frontenac (now Kingston, Ontario), a hard journey by canoe of eight to nine days[112] (see map 5). What did this world look like in the mid-eighteenth century, when travel routes and cultural interaction between Natives and Europeans had become more thoroughly integrated, even routine? How fully did the state control these routes? We have only two complete glimpses into interior travel in this period. Father Charlevoix, in his famous account of New France, describes his journey from Quebec to the Great Lakes and from there to New Orleans. He entered the area at the very beginning of the French post-building era beyond Detroit and south to the Ohio. His itinerary followed what gradually had become the major route linking Canada and Louisiana.[113] From Quebec to Montreal took an unusually long 10 days by horse and riverboat; Montreal to Fort Frontenac at the edge of Lake Ontario, 13 days by canoe; from there to Fort Detroit, across windy Lakes Ontario and Erie, 22 days; from Detroit to Kaskaskia, near the Mississippi, via the Illinois River and including several long layovers, 104 days; and finally from Kaskaskia to New Orleans, then still under construction, a long 38 days. If we keep in mind the necessity of resting, the desire to visit and record, and patient waiting out inclement weather or for comrades to catch up, Charlevoix completed the voyage from Montreal to New Orleans in just under ten months, of which six were spent actually travelling. His account, really the first to attempt an accurate assessment of fauna and flora and especially the Native tribes inhabiting this vast region, marks a transition between the earlier exploratory voyages by La Salle in the seventeenth century and post-revolutionary accounts by Americans, who took the basic transportation, cultural practices of Native nations, and geographic knowledge of the Great Lakes–Mississippi valley for granted. But how did travel occur at the height of French influence in the area?

A better glimpse is afforded by Jacques-François Forget Duverger, a French priest who journeyed from France to his new post among the Tamaroas people at Cahokia (near Fort de Chartres) in the Illinois country in 1753–54[114] (see map 4). His account is important because not only is it precise but it captures a metropolitan perception, albeit an idyllic one, of travel in the Great Lakes region in a time of transition. Leaving La Rochelle on June 25, 1753, Duverger arrived at Quebec on September 9 and wintered in the city. Here he enjoyed the small but lively cosmopolitan world of the pre-war capital, impressed with its churches and the high standard of conversation, and detailing exotic ailments such as frostbite. On April 22, he left Quebec for Montreal, taking the normal five days by a small sailing boat to reach the fur trade's capital. From here his interior travels began in earnest. Leaving Montreal proper, he took a carriage overland to the village of Lachine, a rendez-vous for many fur traders since the 1670s, where he encountered his first birchbark canoe. Lieutenant Péan, commanding a small company taking supplies to the French posts in the suddenly contested Ohio valley, brought news of Jumonville's ambush and invited Duverger to join his group for safety.

Leaving Lachine (eight kilometres southwest of Montreal) on May 10, Duverger with his compass and sighting tools in hand, the company paddled up the St Lawrence toward Fort Frontenac, reaching a camp near there May 16; they immediately turned south, passing near the English fort at Oswego (Chouegouen to the French) on May 20, before reaching French Fort Niagara on May 23. As a priest, Duverger at this time did little or no paddling; this left him time and energy to appreciate the "charming skies" and lake water "clearer than the fairest fountains," and to exclaim that "the agreeable nature of the country tempts one to voyage [by canoe] all one's life." At Niagara he witnessed his first Franco-Native conference, which he described as a "great feast." Leaving Fort Niagara on June 11, his party visited the Great Falls while making the obligatory portage around them, and then entered Lake Erie, where they heard more of Jumonville's death from a detachment of French soldiers returning from the Ohio posts. Duverger lingered here for a month, where the company were joined by a new brigade of twenty-three trading canoes and an estimated three hundred men (overloaded with thirteen men in each canoe) before finally reaching Presque Isle (Erie, Pennsylvania) on July 17, Sandusky on August 4, and, after a short cut through the small rivers of northern Ohio, Detroit on August 6. This portion of the journey took so long because harsh lake winds threatened to capsize the canoes nearly every day. Once arrived, Duverger found the post and region around Detroit enchanting, gushing that "truly Nature has refused nothing to make of this country the most charming in the world."

At Detroit he arranged to place his baggage on *pirogues* headed for Fort Ouiatanon; he set off with seven traders and officers on rented horses on September 3 and reached Fort Saint Joseph a week later. Along the way he slept under a bearskin blanket, marvelling that "one would think on this voyage we were lodging every night in the finest *auberges* as they have on the great roads in France." From nearby Fort Ouiatanon, Duverger exchanged his horse for a *pirogue* on October 3, although his account does not clarify whether this was the one that also carried his baggage. Storms of mosquitoes hounded the travellers whenever they camped on shore and pursued them until Fort Vincennes, which they reached on October 10. Here Duverger rested and enjoyed the enlightened company of the fort's commander and the local Jesuits for three weeks. On October 31 he joined a French officer and twenty-four soldiers in *pirogues* to make the final descent down to the Illinois country. For the first time on his travels, he noted their precautions to mount a guard against enemy Natives (whom he did not identify). On November 8 the detachment entered the Mississippi (Duverger found its water excellent to drink) and finally camped at Kaskaskia. From this hamlet, Duverger walked on foot to Fort de Chartres, where the post commander, a French officer with Irish roots, Mactigue de Macarty, received him in the evening and supplied him with a horse the next morning to take him to his new home at Cahokia.

Duverger's account provides valuable insights on several fronts. The trip took the better part of seven months, with major stops at key points to make further arrangements. Weather, as on the oceanic routes, played a crucial role in determining speed, safety, and comfort. The variety of transportation is significant. After leaving Montreal, Duverger travelled on carriages, canoes of different sizes, horses, Mississippi *pirogues*, and on foot. The fact that he could rent horses, as a modern traveller might rent cars, or send his baggage on riverboats, in the middle of the *pays d'en haut*, suggests a fairly sophisticated level of regularized transportation in the region by the 1750s.[115] Duverger demonstrates above all that the Great Lakes–Illinois country proved to be not only largely safe for travel but regularly criss-crossed by French troops, underscoring the impressive reach of the French state's authority into the heart of the North American interior. Native voyagers and villages, so paramount in earlier narratives of exploration, have receded into the background; Duverger encounters them in large groups only three times, all within or in sight of French forts. The very fact that his account is so sentimentalized and idyllic, ten years before Rousseau's *Émile*, attests to a subtle transformation from "traveller" to a pseudo-tourist.

Finally, Duverger's account stresses the opportunities for contact and even polite conversation in the *pays d'en haut*. Information, while subject to chance encounters, bounced in many directions and perhaps more quickly in this region than historians have tended to appreciate. His account also emphasizes the distinction between European and American modes of transportation and contact, hinged at Quebec or, alternatively, at New Orleans. Up to and within the capitals of Canada or Louisiana, European technology and transatlantic correspondence dominated; beyond the town, a non-European and culturally distinct type of contact, based on technology borrowed from North American Natives or on West African skills and labour, quickly rose to prominence, determined largely by the fur or hide trades and, from the 1740s, the logistics of military supply. At the same time, American interior transportation developed rapidly under French and Native alliances, but was increasingly reliant on European forms of exchange, well in advance of the Anglo-American emigration after the American Revolution.

COAST AND TRACK IN MARTINIQUE

In the Caribbean, French settlers had destroyed indigenous Carib transportation technology and skills by the mid-seventeenth century, leaving vestiges in the construction of boats and interior paths on many islands. Small and fast-flowing rivers hindered land transport, since they sliced islands into isolated coastal strips, particularly on mountainous Martinique, Basse-Terre island in Guadeloupe, Grenada, and the South Province of Saint Domingue. The sea provided the fastest and most economical means of transporting people, heavy loads of tobacco or sugar, and of course, correspondence; from the beginning of settlement, small coasting vessels dominated local and inter-island travel. Black freedmen and slaves provided most of the labour, skills, and even entrepreneurial management. They occasionally carried merchants and their letters,[116] and summaries of colonial expenses usually included some mention of "black proprietors of canoes" to carry officers and dispatches between the two main ports or, more rarely, to outlying ports on Martinique or to Basse-Terre on Guadeloupe. That freedmen actively participated in this carrying trade is borne out by official records, which often listed payments to "*patrons noirs*" for carrying officials, supplies, and dispatches in their boats, principally between Saint Pierre and Fort Royal.[117] In 1739, a typical year, the state spent 3,714 livres (1.5 per cent of the year's expenses).[118]

However, detailed accounts of operations are very rare. According to Father Jean-Baptiste Labat, a freedman man named Louis Galère operated the best service between Saint Pierre and Fort Royal in the 1690s and early 1700s. Galère charged white passengers 1 *ecu* for the thirty-kilometre, half-day voyage, a rate Labat considered quite reasonable. Within three years he had built up an operation of three or four boats, manned by a total of twenty of his own slaves (about five to each boat). His boats used a square sail and oars, and carried five passengers or the equivalent weight in goods. Each vessel left Saint Pierre no later than 4 a.m., arrived at Fort Royal by 8 a.m., and then departed there at 4 p.m., arriving back at Saint Pierre between 7 and 8 p.m.[119] By 1713, up to twenty-five such vessels plied between the two towns, although a hurricane that year demolished many of them.[120] In the 1750s Thibault de Chanvalon noted that only slaves served as sailors on the large number of small inter-island sailing craft. He carefully distinguished between passenger 'canoes' with two masts and six to eight oars and the lighter and more manoeuvrable *pirogues*, based on older Carib designs, with a keel and pointed at both ends.[121] As in Louisiana, slaves appear to have comprised the backbone of local seaborne transportation in the Îles du Vent, probably because their services were cheap, and the work attracted skilled slaves who benefited from relatively greater freedom. Colonial officials certainly considered them reliable, in contrast to official perceptions in Louisiana. While the use of slaves in such relatively free circumstances would appear to contradict the severity of the French labour regime, it may also well be that slave sailors formed an elite group within the slave community.[122]

As important as sea travel remained throughout the eighteenth century, roads assumed an increasingly important role much more than in North America. Most of our information is limited to Martinique. The island's roads began as a defensive system to ensure internal movements of the militia during the Nine Years' War (1689–97)[123] (see map 3). By 1695 an elementary network linked Saint Pierre and Fort Royal along the coast, Saint Pierre to Basse-Pointe on the Atlantic Ocean via the "Jesuit Trace," and the major towns of Le Français, La Trinité, and Le Marin, on the island's eastern side, to Fort Royal. In 1700 Trinité could be reached from Fort Royal in six hours by horse, a distance of about thirty kilometres over rugged terrain.[124] After 1700, however, the island's roads gradually fell into disrepair, even as officials shifted their emphasis from a defence network to a means of land development.[125] Wealthy plantation owners dispensed with roads, since they often had easy access to coves and inlets for shipping their precious cargoes of sugar. Poorer whites bought the much cheaper hillside properties to start banana, cacao, and, later, coffee plantations. They needed the roads, but could not underwrite their cost or supply enough slaves for the needs of the *corvée*.

As in Canada, the arrival of an ambitious new intendant energized the communications infrastructure. In 1724 Blondel created a set of regulations for road surveying and repair, projected ample labour from slave *corvées*, and used the talents of a new royal surveyor, Jean-Eustache du Joncheray, the son of the former surveyor who had created the original road system in the 1690s.[126] Although Joncheray quickly set out to revamp the road system on Martinique, his work never progressed much past the initial survey made between January 27 and April 3, 1727.[127] Outraged planters soon swamped the local courts with lawsuits over who should pay for the system. Blondel appointed a special commission in 1728, the *chambre d'arpentage*, to hear complaints over road payments (which were closely tied to land titles). The commissioners' work progressed very slowly; reports on the various cases appeared periodically in the official correspondence over the next thirty years.[128] Aside from its financing, the survey drew the ire of the planters because it impinged on their autonomy. Blondel blamed the inertia on the militia captains, reporting that traditionally they alone had the right to order road repairs. The result was that transgressors were not notified and fines remained uncollected. Of an estimated 5,976 livres of repair work to be done, Joncheray had been able to obtain a meagre 360 livres.[129] Within a decade, years of seasonal rains had washed out roads in southern Martinique, hindering the movements of the militias.[130] The use of slave *corvées* increasingly emerged as the most contentious issue over road repairs. On the eve of the Seven Years War, planters continued to balk at allowing slaves to be used, in part because of decreasing profits from sugar and coffee and in part from fear of allowing slaves from across the island to mingle and make contact with one another.[131]

The incomplete roads of Martinique were typical of the stillborn transportation infrastructure evident in all French colonies prior to 1763. It took time and the accumulation of knowledge to establish the best routes, and money and still more time to coordinate and build roads or clear harbours. Colonial authorities were still exploring and adjusting to new environments and social structures in the first half of the eighteenth century. In the meantime, colonists had developed their own routes by rivers or along coasts. While often more inconvenient, these had the distinct advantage of being unregulated by authorities. The royal road system had long served as an important arm of the

French state, helping royal and Ferme officials to exchange correspondence and easing the movement of royal armies and officials throughout the kingdom. Opposition by peasants to the *corvées* proved annoying, but could ultimately be controlled. In the colonies, roads were expensive and needed the cooperation of colonists to built and repaired.

All forms of transport, whether by road, lake, or ocean, evolved as an ongoing process of trial and error, discovery and refinement. Both Canada and Louisiana proved hard to get to by the ocean, but once port was reached, the strategic entry into two vast river-lake systems allowed an extensive, but in many ways superficial, influence by French missionaries, traders, settlers, and military officers. Only by the 1750s did interior traffic become fully linked and allow consistent communications between the Atlantic or Gulf ports and the interior posts and settlements. Distance did not curtail or mitigate state influence nearly as much as did adverse climate and commercial opportunities, both of which limited the regularity of contact. In this sense, the growth of Louisbourg shifted direct state attention away from Canada, as a result in great measure of its strategic position at the easily accessible tip of North America and the Grand Banks fishing grounds, and the subsequent ease of sailing to it. The Canadian heartland became, geographically speaking, Louisbourg's backyard until the 1750s. Is it mere coincidence that the Marine re-evaluated and re-emphasized Canada's strategic role at exactly the same moment as navigation both to and within Canada reached a level of routine safety, even though its economic production remained virtually unchanged? In contrast, the Îles du Vent, and Martinique in particular, offered far better opportunities for regular contact and for state influence than Canada and especially Louisiana. European captains and pilots, and through them French merchants and the state, seized upon and developed the easiest, safest, and most profitable navigational routes and anchorages first. Despite their obvious strategic advantage from the metropolitan perspective, the islands of the Îles du Vent offered many year-round opportunities for close and continual intercolonial contact, such as smuggling, and these in turn challenged state control.

In all three colonies, the state found that to control a colony efficiently, including sending troops, personnel, credit and money, and supplies, required that it expand its grasp of the colony's geography and enlist, or even co-opt, colonial leaders and elites, skills, and very often, colonial initiatives in order to do so. The state did not boldly determine colonial transportation infrastructure, but instead tended to pick and choose from a variety of options proffered by local officials and leaders. The projects with obvious advantage for colonists or colonial leaders were acted upon; those not meeting these requirements faded in the countless memorandums urging action. At the same time, knowledge of local geography opened doors to state service for talented men, such as La Richardière in Canada and Livaudais in Louisiana, or established and sustained free black entrepreneurs such as Galère in Martinique.

CHAPTER FOUR

State Ceremonies and Local Agendas

The spring sun had finally arrived to relieve Canadians of their long burden of winter.[1] In Lower Town, merchants gathered before the grey stone church of Notre-Dame-des-Victoires to arrange contracts for the season's shipments of furs and exchange the last morsels of stale winter gossip. Ice still clung to the edges of the river; no ships were yet in sight. Yet on this sun-dappled morning on the first day of April 1730, the town was already awake with excitement. News from New England, probably brought by a party of Abenaki warriors who had camped outside the town's walls the evening before, raced from door to door. What was afoot?

The answer came at noon. The cannon from the Château Saint-Louis's batteries fired salvo after salvo while the bells of Upper Town's churches chimed in discordant merriment to announce the news. Even by the time a crier and a drummer had been dispatched to make the official announcement in the streets, many of Quebec's people had most likely understood the meaning. The queen had given birth to a son. The future succession to the crown, and the very stability of France itself, had been assured. Governor General Beauharnois ordered a special service in the Cathedral to sing the traditional Te Deum, attended by himself, Intendant Gilles Hocquart, who had survived his first Quebec winter, the councillors and military officers wintering in the town, and any of the habitants who could squeeze in. Enthusiasm and an outpouring of love for the king characterized all levels of Quebec's society, at least according to the anonymous official who recorded events in fourteen folio pages.

The arrival of the news of the Dauphin's birth set in motion a round of celebrations that began in April, intensified in July, and eventually led to three weeks of official celebrations in September, coinciding with the arrival of the king's ship. The celebrations were similar to ones held in Paris and throughout France in the preceding autumn of 1729 and in the earlier part of 1730 in Martinique. What makes this document unique is its detail, which provides a rare and fascinating glimpse into the festive world of the French colonies. What prompted the recording of this particular event in such detail, when metropolitan authorities had not asked for it in the first place, and given that so few other colonial ceremonies barely rate a paragraph in the official correspondence. The celebration also raises two further important questions. First, did colonial public ceremonies merely copy French forms and traditions, or did they reflect their time and place? Second, how was royal power presented in the colonies?

CEREMONIES SERVING THE STATE

As in *ancien régime* France, most colonists learned of the world outside their direct experience through oral means, and not by the written or printed word. The situation of the sixteenth-century French peasantry described by Natalie Davis, where "oral culture [was] still so dominant that it transformed everything it touched," still characterized the eighteenth century.[2] The church had long recognized that ceremonies which combined voice and music, bursts of colour and shades of light, and the smell of incense created a powerful sensual impact, leaving lasting individual and collective memories. But ritual encompasses far more than religious rites. Anthropologist David Kertzer believes that making a distinction between religious and secular rituals obscures the similarities between them, for both serve to undergird traditional power. Rituals, he argues, are better explained as "symbolic behavior that is socially standardized and repetitive."[3] This broader conception of ritual invites us to explore "how the symbolic enters in to politics, how political actors consciously and unconsciously manipulate symbols, and how this symbolic dimension relates to the material bases of political power."[4] Force is messy and ultimately divisive; ritual is singularly alluring and costs less (in the long run), and by the very fact that it parades widely recognized symbols and is couched in a language of shared beliefs, it is very often a creative, unifying force.

Political rituals can be used in a variety of contexts and have a multitude of nuanced uses; they may even be contradictory. For example, Kertzer understands rituals associated with the death of French kings as a practical problem: late medieval processions featured both the dead king and an effigy of him treated as if it were alive; the one the mortal king, the other symbolizing the eternal being of the king. Ritual communicates authority achieved and sustained, claims to authority, to show power relationships within the power elite and to express relations between the powerful and the powerless, which, as Kertzer points out, is the essence of patron-client relations. Political ritual also transmits information: the participation or exclusion of a person or group in an event, such as the decision to attend or absent oneself from a funeral or to wear a clown's mask at a court hearing, can tell us much about their policies or commitment.[5] Processions and public ceremonies were the most effective means of communicating royal power in its most exalted form – majestic, beneficent, orderly.

As historians now appreciate, ceremonies mounted by the state were not mere circuses of entertainment, but complicated public interactions playing out social desires and tensions. They were often a means of enhancing royal prestige, articulating a community's hierarchy, and giving voice to common aspirations.[6] In describing a full town procession (*procession générale*) recorded by an anonymous bourgeois of eighteenth-century Montpelier, Robert Darnton recognized that such events constituted "a statement unfurled in the streets, through which the city represented itself to itself – and sometimes to God, for it also took place when Montpelier was threatened by drought or famine." In French towns, festivals remained a pillar of popular and often violent expression.[7] Royal and municipal authorities found order hard to instill, even during events celebrating royal prestige. Michèle Fogel has argued that public ceremonies existed as a "system of ritualized information." More than merely enhancing the stature of the monarch, they communicated the idea of legitimized state action.[8] Public ceremonies, she believes, reached their apogee as an instrument of state power under Louis XV during the War of the Austrian Succession.[9] Arlette Farge goes even farther in suggesting that despite the propensity to violence, elites and vulgar crowds constituted a "symbiotic relationship." They needed each other, elites reading for approval or basking in simple adulation, the crowd joining vicariously in the life of court society or simply to voice its disapproval. As one chronicler late in the *ancien régime* noted, "The court is most mindful of what is being said by the citizens of Paris ... 'What are the froggies [the common people] saying then?' was often the cry. And what a happy band they were [court society] when the froggies applauded their appearances or clapped their hands at the spectacle ... But occasionally their silence was punishing. In fact, they were able to tell what the people were thinking about them from their bearing; the happiness or indifference of the public had a distinct character."[10]

Farge's point is important, for it sensitizes us to read the official correspondence on public ceremonies very carefully. Crowd reactions or the actions of common people are rarely discussed in any length in the official correspondence from the colonies; yet the *menu peuple* (the little people) are constantly referred to in the dispatches as measures of policy. They appear as identifiable interest groups (particularly merchants and ship captains), as habitants or simply "the people" who commented on the efficacy of new regulations, or as a shadowy public, an ominous cloud on the political horizon: "The rumour in the town is ...," "It is said that ...," "There has been an outcry amongst the people ..." While we can rarely know the veracity of a given report on the public's response when we have so few, and all written by the authorities themselves, we can gain a very clear idea of what colonial officials hoped to achieve through ritual practices of power and whether they thought they succeeded.

The importance of ceremonies, and the state's use of them in France, does not necessarily mean they were used in the same way or with the same frequency in the French Atlantic. Colin M. Coates has artfully demonstrated how any event surrounding a public person, such as a funeral, could easily provoke a factional dispute between colonial leaders, which in turn led to rumours among the non-elites, who questioned – or worse, made fun of – the grasp of power about those involved. Rituals were crucial to these social displays of power. As Coates observed about the colonial (and, arguably, the French provincial) context, "the exercise of power required not only allies but also control of the metaphors of legitimate authority."[11] Elsewhere he makes the valuable point that struggles over rank and precedence were not simply amusing sideshows, but that "attention to ostentatious display could indeed be what politics was all about."[12] Habitants or *petits blancs* also read into public displays their own perceptions and hopes. As noted in chapter 2, white Martiniquais joyously celebrated the Peace of Utrecht in 1713 largely because they thought it would open up sugar markets while temporarily removing tariffs on French finished goods. Colonial capital towns in particular provided the only forums for presenting the majesty and power of the king in his American colonies, and by the same token, they were the only sites where that power might easily be contested.

This chapter presents colonial public ceremonies, not as direct imports from France imposed on passive *petits colons* and habitants, but as reconstituted celebrations that reflected particular colonial fears and concerns. The most important difference between France and its colonies lay in the relative emphases on cornucopia and martial themes. Celebrations in France portrayed the king as conscientious provider, while those in the colonies depicted him as gallant defender of his subjects. French ceremonies provided a legacy, a model that metropolitan officials tried to adapt to colonial realities for their own purposes, even as colonists reshaped them to fit theirs. There were also far fewer colonial ceremonies. In the few reports left us, officials stressed the loyalty and love of colonists for the king. The pattern of reporting suggests that the real value of public ceremonies in the colonies lay in enhancing the stature of newly appointed metropolitan officials, both in the colonists' eyes and in those of the Marine.

FROM CHURCH TO STATE RITUAL

Colonial authorities faced a daunting task in their attempts to recreate French public ceremonies as closely as possible. The church provided the essential ritual organization around which royal authority could be legitimately proclaimed both in France and in the colonies. King and church were so closely linked in the French mind that to celebrate one was to call upon the presence of the other. The church's calendar followed the seasons and set the rhythm of religious holy days, and these in turn regulated the calendar. Sunday mass always punctuated each week.[13] A.J.B. Johnston determined that the inhabitants of Louisbourg marked their year with twenty-seven fixed and ten movable feast days, each with a special mass in church; a few, such as the feast day of Saint Louis, were also celebrated with a special procession through the streets of the town afterward.[14] As well, the church provided the means and mental space in which colonists created their own ritual world beyond the state's hand. These celebrations or rituals are much harder to detect in the official correspondence, but they suggest a rich ritual life for both free and enslaved colonists. For example, when the people of Quebec learned of the wreck of the British expedition sent to attack them in 1711 (the ill-fated Walker expedition), even "the least devout were moved by the magnitude of this miracle." The town's merchants convened their own meeting and decided to make a "public endowment" of 6,000 livres to Notre-Dame-des-Victoires church in Lower Town, enough to pay for seven masses dedicated to the Virgin.[15] In addition, local colonial communities proclaimed and revelled in their own festivals based upon or coinciding with less prominent religious holidays. For example, in the two weeks leading up to Saint Louis's day on August 25, white planters throughout the Îles du Vent celebrated a string of festival days marked by visits and parties honouring the patron saints of various island towns (still known today on Martinique as *fêtes patronales*).[16] In Louisiana, white planters marked ownership of a new plantation by a series of symbolic rites of possession and a large banquet for friends and neighbours, usually after Sunday mass.[17] This degree of control over "celebratory time" by habitants and *grands* and *petits blancs* suggests that local officials intent on displaying royal authority faced limitations over when and where they could celebrate state events. The sheer number of religious celebrations and the large number of movable feast days gave officials the freedom to hold celebrations when it was most beneficial to make statements of the king's power. However, the state largely adapted to an traditional processional calendar; it did not set it.

In all colonial religious processions, the military played a far more prominent role than in France. In October 1702 Father Jean-Baptiste Labat recorded an account of a jubilee procession in Saint Pierre.[18] It began at the Dominicans' church in the Mouillage district and wound its way north along the Grand Rue to the Jesuits' church in the Fort district. White-robed children – Labat does not mention their sex or race – led the procession, followed by hooded monks of the three religious orders in the town and then by the governor general, the intendant, all four of the king's lieutenants, and several dozen royal and militia officers. The procession wound along the shore and then doubled back, thus passing Saint Pierre's fort twice and saluting it on both occasions. When it returned to the Dominicans' church for the final benediction, troops fired a thunderous salvo of exactly one hundred cannon shots from the shore batteries and three sets of volleys from a hundred muskets.[19] Labat emphasized the procession, not so much as marks of piety, but as a reflection of a more refined, orderly, and mature Martiniquais society which could compare favourably to France. Nevertheless, he did note that a large contingent of regular troops was stationed along the procession route to "hinder the crush of people."[20] For metropolitan observers such as Labat, clearly the home country set the standard of dignity. What he did not mention is that news of the declaration of war against England and Holland (the War of the Spanish Succession in 1702) had been received just before the pronouncements of the jubilee announcements from Rome, and fears of an English attack had rippled through the colony. While it is not certain, we can speculate that the procession served the dual purpose of celebrating not only the grace of God but also the might and protection of the king.

A religious procession fifty years later in Quebec featured a similar mix of religious and martial elements. According to visiting botanist Peter Kalm, the procession celebrating the Ascension of the Virgin Mary (August 15) in Quebec contained two distinct components. First marched children (boys and girls) in long white robes and priests carrying silver images of the Crucifixion, all followed by Quebec's bishop. Kalm continued: "After him marched the governor-general's private guard with guns on their shoulders, followed by the governor himself ... As the procession passed the castle the soldiers presented arms in salute, the drums were beaten, and the cannon roared from the forts, as was customary on such occasions."[21] In this case, church and state clearly worked hand in hand to reinforce each other's symbolic power. The conscious integration of spiritual and martial leadership is striking, an aspect lacking in similar reports from *ancien régime* France. On the frontiers of empire, the smells of incense and gunpowder mingled freely, reinforcing each other in public.

NUMBERS AND FUNCTIONS

The number of public ceremonies recorded for the colonies was far smaller than those for France (see table 4.1). While sources are scarce, they nevertheless suggest a major distinguishing characteristic between metropole and colony. In France, Jean Quéniart discovered that the municipal registers of Rouen recorded twenty-seven orders from the court to sing the Te Deum for military victories and peace treaties between 1702 and 1714.[22] In her more systematic analysis of the use of Te Deums, Fogel counted thirty-six ordered for Paris during the same period.[23] However, only three were recorded as being issued to Canada and the Îles du Vent before the Peace of Utrecht in 1713. During the War of the Austrian Succession, which Fogel studied even more closely, she found that Te Deums were ordered thirty times between the declaration of war in May of 1744 and the announcement of peace in January 1749.[24] During this time, the Marine issued orders for Te Deums in the colonies only four times, one for the victories of Ypres and Courtrai in Flanders in 1744, one for the king's recovery from illness in 1744, one for the victories of Fontenoy and Tournay in 1745, and one for the peace itself, signed in October 1748 but celebrated in the second half of 1749 in the colonies.[25] Taking into consideration that on two occasions one order encompassed two victories, the total number of events, thirty in France compared to just five in the Americas, underscores numerically the dramatic distance between observance of royal ritual in France and that in the colonies. When it came to the colonies, the court engaged in a limited use of wartime propaganda, for only the most important and positive events were celebrated.

Public celebrations in all their manifestations had two major functions. The first primarily helped to deliver information through official promulgations or statements, and the second to publicly display the hierarchy of elites. It is artificial to separate the two, for even when colonial authorities sat mute in church, they provided information that other colonists might speculate on, whether it be one's presence or one's seating position. For our purposes, however, it is useful to distinguish between one type of ritual, used primarily to inform colonists, and a second, more complex type, to reinforce colonial hierarchy.

Table 4.1
Colonial Te Deums

	Place and date celebrated			
Event	*Paris*	*Martinique*	*New France*	*Louisiana*
Utrecht, 1713	22/5/13	25/8/13	none	2/14
Fontarabia	?	after 24/6/19	?	after 24/6/19
Dauphin's birth, 1729	7/9/29	before 15/12/29	11/9/30	NR
Duc d'Anjou's birth, 1730	?	NR	after 30/8/30	NR
Ypres and Courtrai, 1744	20/7/44 17/9/44	10/1/45 no TD	NR	NR
Convalescence of king, 1744	25/9/44	28/2/45	NR	NR
Fontenoy and Tournay, 1745	19/5/45 26/6/45	26/2/46	NR	NR
Aix-la-Chapelle, 1748	12/2/49	12/5/49	27/7/49	26/8/49
Duc de Bourgogne's birth, 1751	19/9/51	2/52	before 2/8/52	13/2/52
Convalescence of king, 1752	?	14/12/52	NR	30/4/53
Minorca, 1756	before 21/7/56	after 31/7/56	before 12/9/57	NR
Cassel, 1761	?	after 17/4/61	NA	NR
Paris, 1763	17/6/63	16/7/63	NA	8/6/64

SOURCES: Paris: Fogel, *Cérémonies de l'information*, 450, 456–7; AN, K 1719, nos. 11, 15, 30, 34, 36; colonies: AC, B 35, ff. 526–6v., 270–70v., 354–54v.; 53, ff. 306v., 576–7v.; 54, f. 478; 111, f. 352; 116, ff. 35, 567v.; ibid., C8A 40, ff. 123–4, 202v.; 56, f. 245, f. 257; 57, f. 53. ibid., C11A 52, ff. 42–9; 85, ff. 206–6v.; 93, f. 76v; ibid., C13A 33, f. 55; 37, f. 52–3; O'Neill, *Church and State in French Colonial Louisiana*, 119.

KEY: dates arranged day/month/year; NR = no record found.

Again, both depended on the cooperation of the clergy. From the mid-1690s, Louis XIV prohibited French clergy from announcing judicial decisions or royal decrees. In the late-seventeenth century colonies, the parish priest disseminated the king's word by reading royal ordinances during high mass on Sundays, although in major towns the king's attorney read them aloud himself by the church door immediately after service. Regulations issued by the Marine Council under the Regency brought the colonies in line with France and marked a distinct inversion that placed the secular over the spiritual. In 1717 the council ordered that henceforth only bailiffs were to read out the decrees, using a clear, slow voice in public squares, in markets, and before public wells or church doors in the larger colonial towns.[26] A drummer usually accompanied them, and more rarely a trumpeter or fifer. These musicians were regular troops who received extra pay (20 *sols* per announcement in the French Antilles) for their services.[27] Copies of the ordinance were then nailed on the doors of royal buildings and churches, and this entire process constituted valid public announcement. The bailiffs also delivered court notices or summons to individuals, a task that marked them for popular insults, behaviour less acceptable when it came to parish priests. Peter Moogk has observed, "Invested as they were with the authority of the king's justice, these petty officials were inclined to be self-important and overbearing in the execution of their responsibilities ... Physical resistance against a bailiff was considered to be seditious." On Martinique an ordinance of 1719 threatened anyone insulting bailiffs on king's business with a stiff but undefined amount in fines and possible imprisonment.[28] Not only did information move irrevocably from within to outside the church doors, but the change made force, or threat of using force, associated with promulgating the king's word an issue in itself.

Official correspondence very rarely mentions how new regulations were made public, other than a perfunctory note that ordinances or announcements were to be "read, published, and affixed" in prominent public places. Apparently the system worked so well that authorities saw no reason to comment upon or improve it. Fortunately, we have a detailed description of one promulgation from Louisiana, recorded in full because of its sensitive nature. On February 28, 1751, King's Bailiff Marain Lenormand, accompanied by two drummers, read to the people of New Orleans "in a loud and intelligible voice" the preamble and all thirty-one articles of the new public-order regulations outside the doors of New Orleans's church after high mass. Lenormand and his men then strode to the "principal crossroads" of town, which meant specifically the intendant's residence and then the king's storehouse (the largest building in town and a principal site of trade), to repeat the same words. At each site they nailed the handwritten copies of the regulations on the main doors of the building. Lenormand followed up this first announcement by making the same circuit the next day. He may also have been checking to see if the contentious new rules had been ripped down during the night.[29] By combining visual and oral means and using either the church or the king's buildings as the setting, such public acts of communications conveyed a uniformity of the king's word to literate and illiterate members of colonial society, including slaves, free blacks and any Native traders or travellers in town, and at the same time they reinforced the moral, judicial, and even economic authority of the king in making the announcement.

Arguably the more important role for public ritual and celebrations lay in its use for determining colonial hierarchies, or the rank of officers and nobles. Rank ordained, in essence, the proximity one had to the king; metropolitan officials with court connections clearly enjoyed an advantage in this regard. But French practices collided with colonial traditions, and by the early eighteenth century, the growing presence of Creole officials necessitated clear guidelines for each colony. Governor General Raymond-Balthazar Phélypeaux du Verger requested the first such regulations in 1713, after his dignity had been slighted once too often by Martinique's Superior Council. The Marine issued similar regulations for Canada in 1716, and later to Louisiana in 1734 after its retrocession to the crown.[30] Again, the relationship of church and state figured prominently. For example, at mass the governor sat at his own prie-dieu closest to the epistle inside the choir, the intendant somewhat behind him, and the other officers progressively further away according to their status, with officers of the sword behind the governor general, starting with the governor of the district of king's lieutenant, and officers of the robe behind the Intendant. If the governor general was not present, then the governor of the district took his place, and everyone moved up a seat. In Louisiana, setting this hierarchy proved so difficult to sort out that a map of the main church was made to show who sat where.[31]

In the taking of communion, public assemblies, parades, and even ceremonial lightings of bonfires, regulations prescribed that the same hierarchy be followed. Public processions began with two columns, representing the nobility of the sword on the right and the nobility of the robe on the left, presumably determined by the direction of the march. In the nobility of the sword's column came first the governor's honour guards and then the governor himself, and on the left, and slightly behind the right column, marched the bailiffs (the chief bailiff, followed by the court clerk and then other bailiffs) and sergeants, followed by the intendant. These two columns were followed by others marching side by side: the king's lieutenant for the whole colony, the district governor, the king's lieutenant for the district, members of the Superior Council by seniority, the attorney general, the town major, and finally any local officials of the parish. The regulations are not clear as to who in this second large group of officers marched in which column. We do know that retired officers also marched, awarded a place matching their highest attained position in the processions.[32] As the king's personal representative, the governor embodied the sacredness of royalty in his person, and as with the king, his absence could not adequately be filled – his place might be taken by the intendant or simply left unfilled, his presence conspicuous by his absence. The 1713 regulations for the Îles du Vent featured an additional clause not found in either Canada or Louisiana: a fine of 500 livres levied on any person "of whatever station he might be" who occupied a pew or mixed with other ranks not befitting his social standing. The higher numbers of purchased nobility, the relative ease of claiming noble status because of the difficulty of providing documentation from France, and the ease of acquiring wealth apparently also invited usurpers to transcend their allotted station more easily in the French Caribbean.

Colonial clerks rarely provided details of colonial public ceremonies in the official correspondence. But there is one important exception. The arrival of a new governor in a colony were often reported in great detail. These reports, written by the governor's secretaries, constitute a uniquely imperial form of royal ceremony. As the king's representative, the governor used the occasion to enact a type of entry ritual that resembled the entries of French kings into conquered or recalcitrant towns. In these entries they symbolically reinforced the king's authority by making eloquent speeches, conducting highly public inspection tours, and renewing oaths of fidelity from the three estates. The reports contained the governor's first impression of his new command and allowed him to report on the mood of colonists. These ceremonies also allowed him to introduce himself to his new "subjects," stamp his own personality early on public life, and signal new directions in policy. But more than any other activity, a new governor took great pains to confirm the existing colonial social order at a delicate transitional moment in political life. In style these speeches and inspections resemble a cross between current press conferences and official fact-finding visits held by newly elected political leaders.

The arrival of Roland-Michel Barrin, Marquis de La Galissonière, as interim governor of New France in September of 1747 is a prime example.[33] Maurepas hastily pressed La Galissonière into service early in 1747 because the designated replacement for Beauharnois, the Marquis de La Jonquière, had been captured during a sea battle and would sit out the rest of the war as a British prisoner. Although the ships carrying La Galissonière arrived on September 18th, he did not disembark until the next day, allowing preparations for his entrance to be completed.[34] Upon his stepping ashore, a thirteen-gun salute thundered from the king's ship, answered by a twenty-one-gun salvo from the Château Saint-Louis. The court clerk (*prévôté*) of Quebec officially welcomed La Galissonière with a short speech, which was followed by another from the king's lieutenant for the city, symbolically uniting the robe and sword nobilities. From the harbour landing, La Galissonière and his retinue entered Lower Town, where the new governor reviewed the royal troops before a crush of the curious and excited citizens of Quebec, and met Intendant Gilles Hocquart and his staff. Together they walked up the steep street of the Côte de la Montagne to Upper Town, past double rows of the local militia presenting arms, on their way to Quebec's cathedral. Here La Galissonière kissed a silver cross laid on purple velvet, met the bishop and heads of the colony's regular orders, and heard mass. Afterwards, he marched over to the château to meet Governor General Beauharnois. Following a short display of the "customary ceremonies," for which unfortunately we have no detail, the old governor general took La Galissonière by the hand and brought him within the château's wrought-iron gates. Inside he received the respects of the members of the Superior Council and other colonists "of distinction" in the main audience chamber.

La Galissonière, we should note, met the important leaders of Canada in a specific order. He first met the king's judge, the *officiers de l'épée* and their troops, the *officiers de plume*, the clergy, and, in the company of the outgoing governor general, the other distinguished members of the colony. Finally, Beauharnois presented him to the members of the Superior Council, who represented the third estate in the colony. Thus he met the representatives of the king's military and administrative authority first, church representatives second, the colonial nobles third, and finally, the leaders of the third estate. The role of the habitants is especially interesting, for they were either recognized only in their capacity as military men or relegated to the status of props, a backdrop of enthusiastic onlookers for the actions of the elite in the foreground. This ceremonial hierarchy hints at a significant transatlantic change in the composition of the three estates. In Canada, the sword and the robe officers composed the first estate, and the clergy the second, while in the third estate, wealthy merchants assumed a highly visible presence. This ranking is in accord with Peter Moogk's research on how the people of Canada themselves viewed their social hierarchy, based on amounts of predetermined dowers in marriage contracts.[35] Moogk contends that high-born ecclesiastics (including nuns) and "transient French administrators" who did not marry in the colony would have belonged to the first group. The ceremonial itineraries of the new governor suggest that colonists may have observed overlapping social hierarchies; or, to be more precise, that certain public occasions called for composing the social hierarchy one way, and other occasions called for an adjustment, so long as the major divisions were not unduly stretched. As a final telling note, La Galissonière's introduction to the colony differed in only one way from equivalent ceremonies in other colonies. Most outgoing governors met their replacements immediately after the latter had landed on shore. La Galissonière himself did so with his successor, La Jonquière, and Vaudreuil-Cavagnial did so when Kerlérec arrived in Louisiana. The reasons for this change have not been recorded, but either Beauharnois was suffering from some mild illness (he was, after all, a month shy of seventy-six), or from the fact that La Galissonière was not, properly speaking, of Beauharnois's rank. The ancient governor general, well known for his exactness on matters of protocol, may have felt that La Galissonière should come to him.[36]

Aside from symbolically recreating the social order, a new governor could use the occasion to indicate shifts in policy. Governor Louis Billouart, Comte de Kerlérec de Kervasegan, studiously imprinted his mark as a conciliatory presence when he first arrived in New Orleans in 1753.[37] The acrimonious fighting between the departing governor, Vaudreuil-Cavagnial, and the recently deceased *commissionaire-ordonnateur*, Honoré Michel de La Rouvillière had poisoned relations in the colony, propagating the factionalism from the Bienville era. Upon meeting Governor Vaudreuil-Cavagnial, Kerlérec publicly assured him that the king was in no rush to change governments, thereby giving Vaudreuil-Cavagnial and his military and commercial policies the vote of the king's confidence. For the first several weeks, Kerlérec always made his initial inspections with Vaudreuil-Cavagnial and always kept him on his right. He also attempted to impress upon the white colonists an air of sincere concern and expansive good nature by engaging in a spirited exchange of compliments (*combat de politesse*) with the outgoing governor. He received the various "bodies" of the colony, including the Superior Council and representatives from the upriver plantations. Finally and most significantly, Kerlérec made a point of visiting plantations as far downriver as the English Turn, to meet with ordinary habitants and to "listen to their grievances, comfort them, and inspire them."[38]

Kerlérec cultivated the colonial elites as well. Within a week after his arrival, he gave two short speeches at his new governor's residence. First he addressed the clergy, acknowledging the conjunction of interest and responsibility of the nobility and the religious orders in properly guiding the colony, and complimenting the two notoriously understaffed, overworked, and divided orders, the Capuchins and the Jesuits, for their "proselytizing fervour and religious adherence to the faith," ending with a promise to support them in all temporal matters.[39] In the second speech the governor assured the Superior Council that "gentleness, sincerity, and steadfastness shall guide my steps in all situations."[40] He then pledged to learn all he could from Vaudreuil-Cavagnial about the colony's needs and to work closely with interim Creole *commissionaire* d'Auberville. He finished by stressing his desire to mark his career with service to the king and with earning the goodwill of the *commissionaire-ordonnateur* (whenever the new one arrived), the council, and the habitants of the colony.[41] Kerlérec's words to the colonists are especially noteworthy. This was the only occasion when speeches to them were recorded, however briefly. The governor emphasized his role as a moderating influence and mediating presence, a father who embodied reason and sought the good for his people. He laid out a type of contractual relationship between himself and the colonists: in return for fair and benevolent government, he expected to receive the respect and devotion of those under his command. At the same time, Kerlérec's report reassured Secretary of State Antoine-Louis Rouillé that he was conducting himself as a conciliator.

THE DAUPHIN'S BIRTH: THE CELEBRATIONS

Despite the prevalence of governors' arrivals in the records, the most exciting public ceremonies were reserved for royal affairs. Celebrations that connected the king's life to the colonist's and held it forth as a model for emulation provided one of the most powerful tools for aligning colonial society with that of the metropole. According to Orest Ranum, the state's desire to direct private morals came to be one of the quintessential characteristics of absolutist France.[42] By using public ceremonies to share joy in birth or marriage, grief in mourning, or exultation in victory, the royal family invited its subjects to participate vicariously in its own life, effectively joining interests. But the political dimension was never lost. Merchants great and small clearly understood the centrality of dynastic affairs to political and economic life. The birth of a male heir to the French throne brought joy because it guaranteed French political continuity, avoiding the wrenching power struggle between the houses of Bourbon and Orléans that might erupt into a vicious civil war over succession; at the very least, it augured well for keeping the myriad webs of patron-client networks more or less intact. One writer describing celebrations held for the Dauphin's birth may simply have observed an accepted truth when he stated, "A DAUPHIN alone can make us a perfect people: his birth calms our fears of the future, and displays for us now that which our grandsons shall have."[43]

That literate elites connected dynastic politics to their own well-being is amply demonstrated in the metropolitan and colonial ceremonies marking the birth of the Dauphin on September 4, 1729. In

France the official descriptions of the birth that circulated in Paris and Bordeaux reveal a careful manipulation of information in the state's interest. We have only detailed accounts printed with official approval; these cannot be regarded as providing some objective statement on the meaning of these events, but they can indicate how court society wished to present itself to the increasingly literate (and influential) members of the kingdom. The official account for Paris began by describing the period of the queen's pregnancy and her difficult labour early in the morning of the 4th (she gave birth at 3:45 a.m.), and it stressed the excited, doting role of the devoted husband and nervous new father, then nineteen years old.[44] As soon as one of the princes brought the news to the Hôtel de Ville in Paris later the same morning, the whole city, proclaims the official account, exploded in spontaneous celebrations. The streets were alive with people that night, as municipal leaders tossed coins to the poor from the steps of the Hôtel de Ville, distributed meat, bread, and wine from four major outdoor taverns (*fontaines de vin*), which had evidently been set up beforehand in anticipation of the great event, and sponsored a huge bonfire in the Place de la Grève. Some thirty-five minor "fountains" flowed in other parts of the city as well. Cannon thundered intermittently from several surrounding, unnamed citadels, and every church rang its bells for three successive days at every hour. At the end of the three days, Louis himself arrived in the city from Versailles to participate in the Te Deum of thanksgiving at Notre Dame Cathedral. After the service, the king dined with the municipal officials and then made a final appearance at Place Louis le Grand, throwing money and receiving the adulation of the assembled crowd, before returning to Versailles that night.

In Bordeaux, similar celebrations occurred several weeks later, but with a number of significant differences. A royal courier galloping to Spain stopped to relay the news to municipal authorities on the afternoon of September 7th. They made the information public by ordering the firing of cannon from the three royal forts that then still surrounded the town.[45] While preparations began for the official celebrations, various corporate bodies held a succession of church services and hosted dinners. Two hundred workers prepared the town hall for the main dinner, to be presided over by no less than full-length portraits of the king and queen mounted on a dais. Workers planted candles on every interior surface, and the hall's front facade and the clock tower were brightened with an additional five thousand lanterns. Hoisted above the entrance was a banner painted with the arms of France and a picture of the imagined baby surrounded by Latin and French inscriptions amidst a rain of fleurs-de-lys.[46] On September 22, the designated day for celebrations, at least twelve *fontaines de vin* delivered some

48 hogsheads of wine (depending on the measure, from 13,265 to 26,500 litres) in the major squares of the town. Throughout the night, artisan and bourgeois corporative bodies, as well as nobles, held their own dinners and balls, but the report made no mention of money tossed to the poor. Indeed, it boasted of the widespread active participation by all orders and corporations from the city, especially those of the third estate: "Even the humblest artisan desired to display his zeal for his Majesty, and for the August Prince ... all quarters of town resounded with cries of 'Long Live the King' ... being a public celebration, where all Orders took part, the town's officials supped with the Gentlemen, lawyers and distinguished bourgeois, who, the day before, were not present."[47]

The report singled out the final procession held by a youth group, the "Young Merchants," as especially exemplary. They had constructed a "triumphal cart" painted with an image of Minerva (representing France) in battle armour and drawn by eight sturdy horses. They marched in good order down Bordeaux's narrow streets, tossing "jellies" to young ladies as they passed.[48] In Bordeaux, as in Paris, the crowds sang, wine flowed, and people were described as well behaved and joyful. The striking difference between the Paris and Bordeaux reports is the active role of the shopkeepers and artisans' guilds in the latter. In Paris "the people" were largely passive receptacles of the king's bounty (or through him from the nobles). In Bordeaux the *menu peuple* actively created the celebrations and shared the bounty, manifesting the independent spirit still possessed by the city, but now turned, at least in the official report, to honour the king.

The proclamations for the overseas colonies were dated on the same day as those for all France, September 4, 1729. This is the only instance during the first half of the eighteenth century when clerks coordinated metropolitan and colonial news.[49] All letters were exact duplicates, with only the names of colonial officials changed. The orders included singing the Te Deum in the capital and other major towns, obligatory attendance by the governor general and intendant, cooperation with the Superior Council in planning bonfires and fireworks displays, and "rendering the other marks and displays of public rejoicing as is customary on such occasions."[50] The fact that instructions were vague but referred to previous celebrations is significant. Colonial authorities, it would seem, were not expected to duplicate metropolitan events, but to re-enact a more standardized set of symbolic references, perhaps allowing for local differences in the festivities planned for their colonies. There is no reference to celebrations in Louisiana's official correspondence, although this should not be surprising, since the news arrived during the crisis with the Natchez and Chickasaw in 1730.

The official announcements reached the French Antilles within ten weeks. In the Îles du Vent, the official dispatches ordering the Te Deums arrived at some point in mid- or late November, for the celebrations were held on December 5th.[51] The news arrived at a good time for white planters: the earthquakes, piracy, and uncertainty of the Gaoulé were far behind them, and the colony as a whole was launched upon its dramatic expansion of tropical exports at the expense of the British islands. As in France, officials proclaimed the news to the colonists by firing cannon from the royal batteries in Fort Royal, and the next day from those at Saint Pierre. Official reports do not mention other towns, but presumably forts from Basse-Terre to Grenada would have followed suit upon learning the news. At Fort Royal the governor general, the intendant, and the major planters (including the island's nobles) gathered to sing the Te Deum "with great attention" while soldiers set off fireworks in the town square.

Governor General Jacques-Charles Bochart de Champigny hosted a grand feast at the fortress attended by planters from every corner of the island. But it was the non-violent reaction of the humbler colonists that impressed him the most. He proudly noted that "not a single misfortune or disorder disrupted festivities, a rare thing in this country with such events."[52] The festivities were not confined to the capital, for, he wrote, "[t]here have been prepared at fort St. Pierre many great rejoicings for this happy occasion, [and] all people have exhibited the Utmost joy inspired in them by the love they have for the King and the benevolence of his government." This last comment is so similar to those found in the printed descriptions of Bordeaux's celebrations that one wonders whether Champigny or one of his clerks had a copy before him.[53] It is not surprising that he took credit for the lack of violence; the governor general had been promoted barely two years before, and he took every opportunity to demonstrate his firm hand over the colonists.

Official festivities were then, as now, political events that serve political ends within specific historical circumstances. To better understand the celebrations in Canada in 1730 and why they were seemingly of greater importance there than in the Îles du Vent, an appreciation of the colony's far more precarious military situation is necessary. Tensions with New York over control of the fur-trade routes across Lake Ontario and trading by British "interlopers" throughout the 1720s had led to the construction of two opposing forts (Niagara and Oswego) and an escalation of diplomatic tension in the region between the British and the French and their respective Native ally networks.[54] In addition, the expansion of French trade beyond the Great Lakes reopened conflict with a powerful Native adversary, the Fox nation. In the economic sphere, the colony had just begun to experience the first real expansion of commercial activity beyond subsistence farming and the fur trade. Under the encouragement of the new intendant, Gilles Hocquart, Quebec's shipyards had begun an ambitious shipbuilding program, royal monies supported the creation of a massive iron foundry in the Trois-Rivières district, and most important of all, a grain trade from the Montreal district to Île Royale and even Martinique had started.[55] In Quebec society the arrival of the amiable Hocquart put an end to three years of bitter disputes between Governor General Charles de Beauharnois and the former intendant, Claude-Thomas Dupuy.[56] Beauharnois himself was a breath of fresh air after the long, turbulent, and often decadent rule of Governor General Philippe de Rigaud de Vaudreuil (1703–25). At the same time, the sudden death of the elderly and acerbic bishop, Monseigneur Saint-Vallier, ended years of bitter fighting between Quebec's powerful and numerous religious orders.[57] A promising new metropolitan bishop, Pierre-Herman Dosquet, had just arrived, and he was eager to inject a more refined spiritual life into a land he clearly regarded as savage and degenerate.[58] In short, the colony was poised at the dawn of a new and exciting, but uncertain era.

According to the official account of the festivities marking the Dauphin's birth, officials trusted the news from New England enough to set in motion a round of initial celebrations and plans for more elaborate ones in the fall.[59] Confirmation from Louisbourg arrived shortly thereafter, and the official announcement came on July 31st, on the king's ship *L'Héros* (a replacement for the earlier vessel of the same name, which had sailed to Martinique in 1713).[60] Planning began in earnest in early August. Governor General Beauharnois proclaimed the news on the feast day of the Holy Virgin (September 8th) and announced that an even greater public holiday would take place in three days' time. The report does not indicate whether the chosen day held any particular symbolic significance. During the three days of celebration, all stores were to be closed and Quebec's bourgeois were ordered to light their homes at dusk with as many candles as they could find. The evening before the holiday, cannon from the governor general's château roared in repeated salvoes, and the regiment of regular troops (the *troupes de la Marine*) paraded through Quebec's streets to announce the commencement of festivities the next day.

As the sun rose the following morning, the sound of cannon fire again echoed in the streets of the town and across the harbour. All dignitaries, including the captain and officers of the king's ship, landed at

Quebec's small boat harbour (the one used by La Galissonière) at mid-morning to attend mass in the cathedral. In the afternoon a procession composed of the nobility, clergy, and representatives from "all Bodies" in the town walked in a procession between the major churches of Upper Town. Upon its entering and leaving the Recollet chapel, gunners and soldiers at the château fired muskets and cannon. The procession arrived back at the cathedral, where officials joined together to sing the Te Deum. After the service the procession marchers and the townsfolk attended a huge bonfire built in the square before the château. In front of its gate, workmen (presumably soldiers with the aid of some of the clergy) had constructed a triumphal arch consisting of three arches and four columns, decorated with classical and royal motifs such as cupids, fleurs-de-lys, and stars. The front panel featured a poem dedicated to the Dauphin. Latin phrases garnished all four sides, and candles lit up the entire structure for more than three days. As dusk came, both the Marine and militia troops began to shout "Long live the king!" The account noted that the assembled crowd answered these cheers with their own, which were "so general and in manner so natural, that it was easy to see that the Heart animated their acclaim." After firing more musket and cannon salvoes were fired, joined by *L'Héros* anchored in the harbour, candles appeared in every window. On Beauharnois's orders, soldiers ignited a fireworks display from the riverbank opposite the town. On this slope, lit torches formed the words "Vive le Roi" (Long live the king) clearly legible from at least 5.5 kilometres away. By 10 o'clock in the evening, the governor general's staff had prepared a sumptuous dinner for the nobility and clergy at the château. A formal ball began soon after, which lasted until dawn.

A week later Intendant Hocquart gave a similar feast, though not apparently as sumptuous, and on the same day the Recollets held a special mass to sing another Te Deum. As before, Beauharnois ordered that cannon fire should mark the eve of the celebrations and the dawn and dusk of the day, and that more fireworks should be set off, this time from the batteries near Intendant Hocquart's residence in the Palais district. On October 9 the commander of *L'Héros*, Henri-François Des Herbiers, Marquis de L'Étenduère, hosted a third dinner on board his vessel. As a mark of respect to the king's ship, all the merchant vessels then in port draped their rigging with flags and pennants. At 7 p.m. a discharge of muskets and cannon signalled all ships in the harbour to be illuminated, probably with small oil-burning lanterns (lampions) set on the decks and masts. The Jesuits held a third and final service to sing the Te Deum on October 15th, marking the end of festivities and the onset of another long winter.

THE DAUPHIN'S BIRTH: ANALYSIS

The exhausting rounds of celebrations can be divided into five component parts: the public processions, the Te Deums, the triumphal arch, the food, and the use of illumination and pyrotechnics (fireworks, bonfires, and the firing of muskets and cannon). The official account clearly expected the habitants to react in a traditional way to each feature. And while the same elements are to be found in Paris, Bordeaux, and Martinique, the Quebec celebrations uniquely emphasized security and prosperity. The report announced only one procession, beginning from the cathedral and passing to the Recollet's chapel, and from there to the Jesuits'. The route was short and remained confined to Upper Town, and so did not pass through the narrower streets of bourgeois Lower Town; instead, it began at the governor's château and passed it on the way back. Soldiers fired muskets and cannon each time. The Château Saint-Louis and the cathedral of Quebec – the twin pillars of Canada's society – figure prominently in the procession route as the two most important focal points of assembly. The procession began with the governor general's honour guard on the right side, followed somewhat behind by the bailiffs and sergeants of the intendant's administration on the left; then came Governor General Beauharnois and Intendant Hocquart, followed by all the other officers according to the regulations. Commander L'Étenduère of *L'Héros*, who also took part in the procession, probably marched just behind the governor general. It is not clear where the bishop of Quebec, who also ordinarily took part in the procession, marched. As the representative of the pope, he, along with a group of choirboys, may have led the entire procession. Behind this elite group came the members of the Superior Council and the other officers of the jurisdiction, of both the sword and the robe, all marching two by two, although the military were a step or two ahead of the administrative arm, in accordance with the 1716 regulations. Later celebrations with minor variations on Martinique repeated the same order.[61] Following the colonial officers were the colonial nobles and the representatives of Quebec's artisans. The report did not mention a bourgeois or merchant honour guard, although such a group existed nearly twenty years later to greet Governor La Galissonière on his arrival. As in France, this procession clearly paraded the elite in order of importance to Quebec's citizens. More importantly, it served to separate the first two estates and the literate bourgeois from the illiterate third estate into active players and a passive audience. This continuity in processional segregation remained unbroken in both France and its colonies.

Singing the Te Deum formed the traditional symbolic centre-piece of state celebrations. Music played a key role in French ceremonies known as "divertissements," and every dinner featured concerts and pieces from operas. No official gathering was considered complete without music, dancing, and carousing until dawn the next morning.[62] In France, musical directors of cathedrals were sometimes commissioned to write original scores for celebrations including the Te Deum.[63] According to Christian tradition, the Te Deum emerged as a dialogue between St Ambroise and St Augustine upon the latter's acceptance of Christ in AD 387. Charlemagne adopted and employed it for state occasions, beginning with his own coronation in AD 800. It later became the victory song of choice on medieval battlefields. Its use by the early modern French state dates from the time of Henri III in the late sixteenth century. Fogel has argued that, as a familiar and stirring musical form, the Te Deum offered the state an accessible avenue for identifying its less popular demands for money and military support during the Wars of Religion (1562–98) with the more popular pomp surrounding religious ceremonies.[64] By the death of Henri IV in 1610, the Te Deum had emerged as the main celebration for state occasions.[65] The report of the celebrations at Quebec specifically mentioned that music accompanied the singing of the Te Deum, suggesting that a new sophistication in colonial church music had been achieved.

Although the exact text of the Te Deum used at Quebec is unknown, thanks to Fogel's work, we can identify certain probable characteristics. The version most often used for state purposes was the Te Deum Laudamus, the form preferred by both Louis XIV and Louis XV.[66] The governor, the intendant, and many of the officers had undoubtedly heard a version of it when they attended court at Versailles. It begins with resounding praise of God the beloved:

> We praise you, O God! we bless you, O Lord.
> All earth adores you, O Father Eternal!
> All the Angels, the Heavens, and All the Powers.
> The Cherubs and Seraphins cry unceasingly before you:
> "Holy, Holy, Holy, is the Lord, the God of armies"
> Heaven and earth overflow with the majesty of your glory.[67]

The mixture of themes – adoration by the heavenly hosts, glory in the heavens and on earth, the association of God and armed might – makes it easy to meld the image of saintliness and righteousness with an all-powerful king, already identified as "His Most Christian Majesty." The song also reasserted the tacit paternalistic contract between king and subject:

> Save your people, Lord, and pour your blessings on your heritage.
> Conduct your children and raise them until they reach eternal bliss.[68]

One can appreciate how attractive this particular version could be for identifying Louis XV, "the Beloved," with the glory and conquests of his famous great-grandfather, while reinforcing a notion of his selfless love for his people.

The most arresting aspect of the report is the attention lovingly bestowed on the triumphal arch erected in front of the Château Saint-Louis. Officials often ordered the construction of symbolic sculptures for important occasions. While clerks rarely described them, reports for two have survived from eighteenth-century Martinique. The first was the Latin-inscribed scaffolding for the fireworks marking the Peace of Utrecht in 1713, mentioned in chapter 1, and the other an imaginative arch celebrating victories in the War of the Austrian Succession in 1745, described below. Nearly a third of the Quebec report is devoted to describing the arch, and the use and explanation of classical figures and motifs clearly indicates that it was meant to impress not merely the local literate elite but, probably more importantly, the chief clerks and secretary of state at the Marine, court nobles, and the king.

The arch formed a complicated piece of art with four columns supporting three arches. Each of the four columns featured a specific symbol or allegorical figure. As the eye moved from left to right, the arch showed a sceptre, Justice, Religion, and a crown. These were meant to be read literally. As the writer of the report explained, they signified that Justice and Religion would educate the new prince and serve to support and strengthen his future rule. A cupid floated above the middle arch, and from his mouth issued a banner with the following verse:

> The fable portrays Cupid [Love] in His youth
> In his world, this Child never changes
> Our Love [Cupid], dear Dauphin, has this One benefit
> It will be yours to command in later ages.[69]

The inscription includes a "jeux de mots" on the word *amour*, which means both love and devotion in the modern sense, but also the personification of Love (as Cupid) in the archaic sense. Latin inscriptions were another notable aspect of the art. Above the three archways floated a rainbow inscribed: "From all sides of France comes Hope and Love" in Latin along one edge.[70] Artists painted a scroll above the sea in the very centre of the rainbow, supported on either side by sailors blowing on conch shells. From the shells emerged a mist which formed the Latin "Vivat Delphinus" (Long live the Dauphin). Another sea, placed further back (its relation with the first is unclear from the description), showed the Dauphin and a rising sun (the prime emblem of both Louis XIV and Louis XV) and the motto "Master of all from sea to sea."[71] On the surfaces of the archways not given over to the rainbow were painted various arms of the royal family supporting ornamental globes, all entwined with golden fleurs-de-lys. Above these arms lay the figure of a *rénommé*, or winged female blowing on a trumpet, from which came the words "These are gifts from the gods." The use of the plural "gods" suggests a classically trained background.[72] The employment of Latin was not exceptional; as Kalm observed, all colonists, from voyageurs to noblemen, repeated Latin liturgical phrases, even if they did not know what they meant.[73]

On all four sides of the arch hung brightly lit chandeliers. Combined with the lanterns decorating the chateau's windows, the light "emitted a brightness and clarity so striking that one might mistake it to be midday in the middle of the darkest night."[74] Although it was meant to be lit only for the three days of official celebrations, the account noted that Governor General Beauharnois bowed to the "people's" demand and allowed the arch to remain lit for a longer period.

Aside from the impression the arch must have made on Quebec's people, its symbolism is noteworthy. Clearly, the designer came from a well-educated background in the classics, which suggests the influence of Bishop Dosquet. Its verses and symbols were designed to be appreciated not only by the colonial elite but by metropolitan officers, such as L'Étenduère, or visitors who might give an account when back in France. The strong marine motifs and the accent on world empire suggested by the Latin inscriptions ("from sea to sea"), as well as the globe motifs, appeared to spring from a more worldly imagination, perhaps that of Intendant Hocquart or his staff. That Beauharnois "bowed" to popular demand to keep the arch lit longer than planned underscored the burst of popular enthusiasm that runs as a sub-theme through the entire account. The writer of the report apparently wished to impress upon his metropolitan readers the fierce loyalty of the king's Canadian subjects.

Descriptions of food and dining were noticeably reduced in the Quebec report, in comparison with those for France. Only four dinners are mentioned: the governor's in April and again on September 11, one at the intendant's, and the one held by Commander L'Étenduère aboard *L'Héros*. The governor's meal is mentioned as a "souper" (traditionally a lighter evening meal) held at 10 in the evening, attended by so many guests that many were seated on the outdoor gallery of the château, with its cool breezes and the St Lawrence under moonlight. Officials did not provide food and wine to the crowds in either Canada or the Îles du Vent, although the governor of Île Royale at Louisbourg, a town in close contact with France, distributed wine from his own cellars on at least two public celebrations in 1752 and 1753.[75] After Beauharnois gave the first celebratory dinner, the report boasted,

"All the Bourgeois and artisans, justifiably penetrated with the same Joy, chose to do likewise, such that this part of the evening was enjoyed by all with diverse amusements and music."[76] Significantly, Quebec's bourgeois were expected to emulate the elite by holding their own smaller versions of feasts and parties.

The inclusion of pyrotechnics – bonfires, fireworks, and the firing of muskets and cannons – was not in itself unusual, as the French reports demonstrate. The account for Bordeaux mentioned that each musket was fired six hundred times, and each of the cannon in the three forts twenty times.[77] What is unique for the celebration of the Dauphin's birth in Canada is the use of thundering reports to mark every phase, as if they were a drumbeat setting the tempo of events. Soldiers fired salvoes on at least twelve different occasions during the course of the celebrations. Their noisy effect called attention to the initial announcements, marked both the commencement and end of festivities, and punctuated the chief moments of celebrations, such as the Te Deums. Aside from the drama provided by cannon fire, its symbolic use to celebrate dynastic continuity would be a natural part of the military ethos of New France. It is not hard to imagine that colonial leaders considered the use of cannon and musket fire a means to assuage colonists' anxiety over possible encroachments from their Anglo-American and Native enemies. People in Canada and Louisiana were quite aware of their precarious position in relation to the expanding mainland colonies, and Martiniquais feared the British Navy.

The orders to the intendant to make powder available for celebrations indicate not only how central pyrotechnics were but also how costly. The enthusiasm for using powder displayed by Bordeaux's municipal authorities was so great that Versailles ordered the intendant for Guyenne to curtail the number of festive days to celebrate the Dauphin's birth in 1729, in order to stop wasting expensive gunpowder.[78] The amount used in Quebec can only be guessed. While the report does not indicate how many salvoes in total were fired in Quebec, we do have a more comprehensive list from the last years of French Louisiana. Jean-Jacques Blaise d'Abbadie, the interim administrative leader of the colony who succeeded Kerlérec, recorded many of the numbers of cannon salutes given during the seventeen months of his administration. Beginning with his arrival in New Orleans, timed to coincide with the celebration of Saint Louis on August 25, 1763, at least 402 cannon salvoes were fired during the year ending on August 25, 1764. Half of these, 203 salvoes, were fired on the two feast days of Saint Louis celebrated during his tenure, while the second largest number, three sets of 21-gun salutes (63 in total), were reserved for the Corpus Christi (Fête-Dieu) on June 21, 1764.[79] Such numbers are in accord with the isolated reports provided by Johnston for colonial Louisbourg.[80]

Illumination has always played a dramatic aesthetic role in celebrations. In an era before widespread street lighting, the use of candles in windows transformed the darkened shapes of evening into a magical landscape of pinpointed light, in the same way that candles add a sense of warmth and intimacy in the vast and cold space of a gothic cathedral. Once again, the use of regulations and the threat of fines to ensure lighting is noteworthy. From these we may infer that the use of candles was not a traditional practice, or at least not freely engaged in by all the town's inhabitants. Candles were not cheap. The role of Quebec's people in this case is also suggestive of the use of their homes literally as a backdrop to the more important celebrations of its elite. The competition between townsfolk and garrison to shout louder and more energetic versions of "Long live the king" over the bonfire at dusk added an evocative and almost primal detail to the whole account. The combination of fire and voice at the transitional point between the solemn marches and songs of the day and the raucous feasting and dancing to come at night suggests a calculated effort to publicly evoke the king's presence before the elite retired to the château and the ball, leaving the streets to the habitants.

Unfortunately, the report does not describe the fireworks in detail. These could be quite complex and ingenious in execution, as a report from Martinique demonstrates. To mark the convalescence of the king during the War of the Austrian Succession, Governor General Champigny engaged an Italian architect to design the celebrations held at Fort Royal in February 1745, and he ordered the commissary of the artillery to provide gunpowder and other supplies. Labourers, presumably slaves and soldiers, erected an octagonal platform supported by six twenty-two-foot-high pillars on the savannah beyond the beach. On top of the platform rose a twelve-foot-high pyramid adorned with painted cupids around the base offering their hearts to an image of the sun at the top. About forty metres beyond this structure a large pond had been dug, and in the middle of it rose several rocks populated with figures of sirens, swans, ducks, frogs, and other "aquatic animals." At the start of the display, a "whirlpool" of fire in the shape of a dragon forced the figures to "plunge" into the water. Their flaming hearts then re-emerged, carried by the dragon to the image of the sun at the pyramid (perhaps connected by a rope and pulleys). The sun burst into a ball of fire, after which the dragon retreated to the brilliantly lit pond.[81] Encapsulated in this ingenious display is a fable describing how God's representative on earth, the Sun King, tamed an evil dragon (that is, England) which had persecuted God's innocent creatures.

Such a message would have had a powerful and satisfying resonance at the start of the first war in over thirty years.

More than any other aspect of the report about the celebrations in Quebec, it is the fact that it was written at all that arouses the greatest curiosity. The detail provided in the account is in itself interesting. Why were the celebrations recorded on this occasion and not on others? If such reports were indeed frequent, then why have so few survived in the official correspondence? Like modern-day media pseudo-events, the celebrations evidently were carefully planned, but it is less clear that they had an overt political agenda. Nevertheless, the celebrations in Quebec suggest some important divergences from practices in France. Unlike in France, the governor and not the municipal authorities (in this case, the Superior Council) clearly planned and directed celebrations and used soldiers as the principal labour to stage them. As in France, humble folk provided the background against which the supremacy of the nobility and the clergy was paraded, but with this difference: they were not beggars or the poor to be bought off, but an independent public whose incorporation into festivities authorities recognized and sought. The reporting of these events, like those recording the arrival of governors, served to reflect positively on the zeal of local officials in gaining and holding the loyalty of colonial subjects.

Festivities such as the celebration of the Dauphin's birth in 1729–1730 or those held upon the arrival of new governors demonstrate how little control metropolitan authorities in fact exercised over public colonial celebrations. As we have seen, the Marine's orders were not consistently carried out, in part because there appeared to be no major repercussions if local officials were amiss in their duties. More importantly, it would appear that colonial officials used public celebrations as a tool of statecraft, a means to whip up popular morale, and at the same time as an opportunity to demonstrate to the Marine their commitment and competence in handling colonists. Martial elements dominated royal celebrations and were important components of religious ones. In colonies such as Canada, where the division between rich and poor whites was not as sharply defined as in France, the governor did not seek to appease a riotous crowd, but instead to affirm a conjunction of interests. This appears to have been especially the case in Louisiana, where relative poverty acted as a kind of material leveller among white colonists. In the Îles du Vent, processions and state rituals tended to more faithfully transmit metropolitan models and concerns. Over time, a subtle shift in all colonies is evident, moving from strict metropolitan control over information presentation through rituals to the forging of coalitions of patriotic spirit by local leaders in the French Americas.

CHAPTER FIVE

Travel and Assembly, Disorder and Revolt

It was a pleasant evening for a walk along the levee that separated the wide Mississippi from the town of New Orleans. Étienne La Rue, the pilot of the ship *L'Unique* from Saint Domingue, strolled leisurely along the levee, walking stick in hand, humming a tune.[1] Even in the spring of 1747, the terrible war between France and Great Britain had not completely halted shipping between Louisiana and Saint Domingue. La Rue did not look exceptional, except that as a free man of colour, with the liberty to come and go as he chose, he offered a rare sight to the white population of New Orleans. In his pocket he carried two small hand pistols which he had purchased at an auction in town two days before and which he was now taking to a free-black smith he knew of for mending. As far as La Rue knew, there was nothing illegal about these; nearly everyone carried a weapon.

La Rue passed three soldiers walking in the opposite direction on the levee. They eyed each other; then La Rue bowed. The three hailed him. "Bonsoir, Seigneur Negritte!" said one, using the diminutive form of "Negro" as a racial slur. La Rue was about to pass on, but stopped and asked why they responded with such ill manners to him. The three soldiers slowly approached him and began to raise their voices. They accused La Rue of insulting behaviour. Suddenly one of the soldiers grabbed his walking stick and struck him with it. A fight ensued. The evening guard rushed in and, after more blows, pushed La Rue off toward prison. La Rue walked willingly beside him at first, but along the way he asked the guard to stop, remembering that one of the guns still had shot in it. La Rue discharged it off to the side of the road, but the guard, fearing an attack, drew his sword and beat La Rue to the ground. Other whites rushed to aid the guard, and La Rue was bound and this time dragged to the prison, beaten again, and thrown into a cell. At his trial before the Superior Council the following week, the soldiers and the guard persistently accused La Rue of a variety of assault charges, including attempted murder while drunk. Still, La Rue defiantly maintained his innocence and his version of the story. The crown dismissed all the serious charges, fined him only for carrying concealed weapons, and ordered the pistols confiscated and La Rue to pay court costs.

At first glance this verdict appears to reinforce the oppressive racial boundaries of a colonial society. Yet the punishment meted out to La Rue could hardly have satisfied the vengeful appetites of the soldiers, the guard, and the whites of New Orleans generally. Moreover, the length of the trial, the careful attention to verifying the facts, and the dismissal of the white soldiers' allegations – all capital offences – suggests that the council rendered a more subtle judgment. The decision clearly reinforced the subordination of free blacks, but it set free a skilled sailor from Saint Domingue, New Orleans's only link to France during wartime. What better way of keeping racial animosity alive while calming a potential backlash from either slaves and free blacks or white soldiers?

THE PROBLEM OF MOBILITY

Colonial authorities knew that they could play upon divisions among the lowest groups of society to suppress or at least help supervise the movements of other members. Even so, they feared that free social intercourse between them would lead to collusion. French soldiers and convicts, Creole free blacks and Creole and African slaves, and Native peoples, some enslaved, who lived under French jurisdiction together composed a large and largely illiterate underclass, varying in size and perceived threat by colonial officials in each colony. Together, they composed a type of "fourth estate" of the marginalized – necessary but barely tolerated colonial peoples who had no respectable place in traditional French society. Some had come voluntarily to live among the French; most had not.

These groups of marginalized colonials posed four fundamental problems to the maintenance of authority. First, the prosperity and security of the colonies clearly depended on them. While few recognized their bargaining power, authorities continually feared the potential of collusion. Second, the absence of the sorts of restraining social institutions found in France, particularly the network of strong village and town parish churches, removed a level of supervision and stable family formation for many. For colonial officials, most of these emigrants formed an identifiable but rootless and therefore dangerous group. Third, most of those brought to the colonies were young, unattached males (unattached by choice or force), the group most likely, as in France, to challenge authority. In Canada, André Lachance has found that nearly nine of every ten of those accused of crimes were single males, and nearly 40 per cent of that number under the age of twenty-five.[2] But even those not dragged before a law court could be disruptive: the travels of apprenctice glazier Jacques Ménetra demonstrates how a young male could use the fraternal contacts of his *compagnonage* to trace a circuit around France, engaging in spirited personal battles and provoking local authority as he went.[3] In Canada, Leslie Choquette has shown that artisan brotherhoods (*confréries*) were tolerated by colonial authorities in the seventeenth century, but that they survived into the eighteenth in a "substantially diluted form." Colonial authorities carefully regulated them precisely because their meetings quickly turned into forums for criticizing local officials and regulations.[4] Finally, many were cultural or phenotypically distinguishable from European French. Within the confines of the orderly society that the king and his advisers would have preferred to emerge overseas, there existed instead important elements that were identifiably alien, even though they had embraced the French language, laws, religion, and even respect for the king. Colonies with a growing class of free blacks and Catholic peoples settled into their own villages did not fit this pattern. They posed a wrenching social dilemma for white colonial officials: they should have possessed everything to become fully integrated into stable colonial society. While each group could be found throughout the colonies, ports and towns offered the greatest opportunities to oppose authority, allowing them to meet, live together, to fight, to talk, and, perhaps, to sympathize with each other.

Freedom to travel and to meet, the basics of communication, was, and is, inseparable from political freedom. Historians have certainly been aware of the equation between freedom and movement, but few have thoughtfully pursued it as a point worth considering in the colonial context in itself. For example, in Canada, royal officials introduced laws from the mid-seventeenth century to curb the freedom of movement of the coureurs de bois. Although historians tend to interpret these laws as economically motivated,[5] the regulations consistently emphasized the fear of moral decay inherent in mixing European and Native societies.[6] The historiography of slavery in the French Antilles offers further insight into the threat of travel and assembly as a means of building autonomy and even community within plantation slavery. Most historians have traditionally mentioned travel and assembly restrictions as a minor part of the overall portrait of the stifling and repressive nature of plantation society and the Code Noir.[7] However, an understanding of communication strategies is just beginning to be appreciated.

For example, Carolyn Fick noted that in pre-revolutionary Saint Domingue, voodoo "facilitated secret meetings ... [and] provided a network of communication between slaves of different plantations who gathered clandestinely to participate in the ceremonies, and secured the pledge of solidarity and secrecy of those involved in plots against the masters."[8] In Louisiana, Gwendolyn Midlo Hall found evidence that slaves used backwater cypress woods (*la cyprière*) as clandestine meeting places to plan insurrections and harbour escaped slaves, or maroons.[9] By concentrating on plantation slavery, historians have ignored the colonial towns, where slaves mixed easily and increasingly over the eighteenth century with far less supervision. One of the most eminent historians of French Caribbean slavery, Gabriel Debien, decided to forego analysis of town slaves, arguing that they composed only one-tenth of the overall slave population, and later historians have noted the inactivity of urban slaves at critical moments of rebellion.[10] Yet colonial authorities increasingly distinguished between the more spirited town and more docile plantation slaves, and noted the unsafe opportunities for mixing that towns offered. From wherever the marginalized members of colonial societies came, their ability to meet each other or form liaisons with the lower echelons of white colonial society both perplexed and frightened colonial authorities. This chapter considers, first, the role of soldiers and convicts in challenging the authorities, mainly of Canada and Louisiana, and how these authorities reacted to that challenge. It then explores the very different legally based suppression of communications inherent in the plantation slave society of the Îles du Vent, as prescribed by the Code Noir and local police regulations, and the efforts by slaves and free blacks to challenge or at least mitigate restrictions on travelling, meeting, and learning.

EMIGRATION AND EMPIRE

The state's control over the marginalized began on the shores of France. Historians have accepted until recently that metropolitan authorities controlled all aspects of migration from France to the colonies to preserve not only the purity of Catholicism, untainted by Protestant teachings, but the feudal traditions of the *ancien régime* itself. In the case of Canada, the best studied French colony, the meagre number of emigrants, which historians had estimated to number between 7,000 and 10,000 for the entire period, constituted the obvious proof of the success of state policy. However, Peter Moogk first challenged this idea and the number, arguing that the total was closer to 27,000, most of whom returned to France after a stint in "purgatory."[11] He discovered that not only did French authorities try very hard to entice settlers, but they also attempted unsuccessfully to promote migration of artisans by forcing colonial-bound ships to carry indentured servants from 1699 on.[12] Even in the case of forced passage for indentured servants, merchants were not above simply evading the law by falsifying embarkation and landing records.[13] In short, migrants were available, but after 1664 most simply did not desire to relocate to Canada. Leslie Choquette, using a very different data set, concluded that the number should be even higher, with a minimum number of 37,000 emigrants for both Canada and Acadia and possibly up to 67,000, about two-thirds of whom returned.[14] Choquette stressed the "modernity" of *ancien régime* migrants to Canada, noting that most were urban dwellers, drawn into the bustling Atlantic commercial world of Ponant France and Paris, who sought economic improvement. Despite differences, both scholars underscore a critical point: the state proved to be less restrictive, and less successful, in its ability to control and direct emigration.

The case of Louisiana is quite different, for great expectations and even enthusiasm accompanied the initial settlement from France by a state-supported monopoly, the Compagnie des Indes. Even before John Law made Louisiana the vehicle for wild speculation, Secretary of the State for the Marine Jérôme de Pontchartrain experienced difficulty generating enthusiasm among French intendants for emigration.[15] During the initial founding period of New Orleans (1718–23), privately funded police scoured the streets of Paris, Lyon, Orléans, and other cities for vagabonds to be transported en masse; some nine hundred actually arrived in the colony between 1719 and 1720.[16] Not surprisingly, excitement over Louisiana soured very quickly, and the colony became synonymous with desperate, disconsolate exile, as portrayed in Abbé Prévost's story *Manon Lescaut*.[17] Throughout the eighteenth century, the state could not overcome popular perceptions and recast migration patterns.

Emigration had a curiously "levelling" effect, as far as metropolitan attitudes might have been concerned: many elite officers and convicts were sent against their wills. Once they were in the colonies, a significant distinction over movement managed by the colonial government ensued. Elites enjoyed a wide range of personal freedom to travel. However, members of the very lowest ranks of colonial society – semiskilled apprentices, labourers, *engagés*, soldiers, *filles du roi*, and convicts – experienced the reverse: the state supported the migration of them to the colonies, but once they were there, their movements were supervised as closely as possible by colonial bureaucracies. A case in point is the story of Esther Brandeau.[18] A twenty-two-year-old originally from a Jewish bourgeois family in Bayonne, in France's extreme southwest corner, she had rejected Judaism and crossed gender lines in order to escape an impending marriage. Dressed as a common male labourer, she served as a ship's cook, tailor's apprentice, and soldier with regiments in Brittany and Poitou for five years before taking ship for Canada. Soon after her arrival she was discovered and brought before the intendant. Although she voluntarily entered a convent, she was expelled a year later and deported back to France in 1739, where she disappeared from the records. Her story alerts us to the ease for labourers (whether male or female) to migrate to the colonies and the low tolerance for social diversity on the part of colonial, though not necessarily metropolitan, authorities. This dichotomous system of migration filtered out potentially disruptive literate influences, but it also initially fostered the settlement of a highly diversified, generally young, largely male subclass in all colonies. This latter group had nothing to lose from severing ties with France and everything to gain by creating their own in the colonies. Metropolitan officials had no leverage with which to discipline this "third estate" as it did with nobles or merchants with property or kin in France.

Once in a colony, poorer whites and even many bourgeois artisans found it difficult to travel or return to France. The Marine officially encouraged migration between colonies, although colonial officials in each were loathe to see skilled whites and potential defenders leave their jurisdictions. Louisiana was in an especially precarious situation, for both Canada and the Îles du Vent denied permission to merchants and potential landowners to relocate there.[19] But in areas where movement was as handy as the nearest cart, horse, canoe, or *pirogue*, habitants and poor white planters (usually referred to as *petits blancs*) left without the approval of officials. For example, the sudden blight of cocoa trees on Martinique in 1726 forced many *petits blancs* on Martinique to dodge creditors by relocating to Dominica, Saint Lucia, or the Grenadines, where the king's law hardly reached.[20] Of course, the Marine regulated the transatlantic voyages of soldiers, allowing only those of good character (*gens sûrs*) to travel.[21] Mobility and regular contact over long distances therefore constituted important elite privileges as much as they were denied to commoners.

CAGING CONVICTS AND SEGREGATING SOLDIERS

According to Canada's authorities, the least trustworthy groups were convicts and soldiers. Neither group chose to come to the colony; both were sent mainly for security reasons, convicts to preserve France and soldiers to preserve New France.[22] Both groups were also recruited in part to make the colony more productive, by providing cheap labour to build infrastructure such as forts, walls, batteries, and roads. Vagabonds or petty criminals rounded up in Paris or the Ponant ports became soldiers; nearly six hundred convicted salt-smugglers (*faux-sauniers*) were sent to Canada alone between 1730 and 1743, an average of about forty-five per year.[23] It is these two groups that comprised two-thirds of all judicial cases brought before the courts in Canada.[24] But their independent and disruptive "spirit," stemming in most cases from maltreatment, poor or little food, cheating on pay, or a combination of all three, caused authorities grave concern. The actions of a few could have a major impact on colonial policy. For example, within a few months of their arrival, the salt smugglers were blamed for the sudden increase in petty crimes in Quebec and its surrounding countryside. By 1742 the militia in Canada routinely arrested beggars in order to halt robberies.[25]

All colonial leaders fretted over the disruptive influence of "idle" whites. In 1729, Governor General Jacques-Charles Bochart de Champigny authored a new ordinance to control the movement of wandering beggars, who displayed "a nonchalant, idle, libertine spirit" in the Îles du Vent. He believed that they cooperated with domestic slaves or free blacks in stealing and fencing stolen goods, since the whites could be easily observed "playing cards and drinking in the taverns and huts of mulattoes and free Negroes."[26] Soldiers were hardly better. Governor General Charles de Beauharnois complained that most of the soldiers under his command were "a motley collection of people, without heart and without honour."[27] Others preferred to use habitants as canoe paddlers because soldiers not only were slow to become inured to the hard work, but were also "highly seditious and poor subjects."[28] We can only guess how precarious royal authority seemed to colonial leaders with the defence of the colony depending on armed men who barely lived within the king's writ.

While there may have existed a cultural cleavage between French-born soldiers and Creoles, the authorities did what they could to encourage the split. In both Louisiana and Île Royale, the Marine stationed Swiss regiments. These soldiers, who were mainly German-speaking Protestants, were clearly appreciated by Canadian and Louisiana authorities. "They are useful on occasions of mutiny," wrote Governor Pierre de Vaudreuil-Cavagnial, in the same letter asking that their force be doubled to three hundred men.[29] However, Swiss and French soldiers also could join forces, as they did during the Christmas 1744 mutiny at Louisbourg.[30] While in France the billeting of soldiers proved to be an effective way of suppressing regional sedition, in French America it had the opposite affect. Most soldiers in Canada were billeted with private families until barracks were built in 1748.[31] The barracks were necessary, according to Governor General Beauharnois, because soldiers often caroused with their landlords by getting drunk on *guildive*, a rum-based liquor with a high alcohol content much cheaper than wine. Once the soldiers were intoxicated, Beauharnois charged, their Canadian landlords talked them into committing robberies, while the landlords resold the pilfered or stolen goods. Such liaisons were especially prominent in Montreal. Occasionally, small groups of drunken soldiers talked one another into "prendre canôt," literally stealing a canoe and departing south deep into the woods and lakes of the *pays d'en haut*. Sometimes, he complained, soldiers even ran through the streets of Montreal at night, drinking, cursing, and singing, terrifying residents behind their shuttered windows.[32]

Deserters, aided by urban inhabitants, challenged authorities in all three colonies. However, the low numbers seem out of proportion to the concern caused. In Canada, Jay Cassel calculated that an average of fifteen desertions per year occurred in the *troupes de la Marine*, a number that he found "astonishingly low," given their wretched living conditions. However, André Lachance has pointed out that the low number of convictions may in fact hide a high success rate of escapees, at least for the Montreal district on the doorstep of the *pays d'en haut*.[33] At any rate, colonial leaders found the supportive attitude taken by colonials the most frustrating and worrisome aspect. "Canadians think they are dishonoured if they have arrested a deserter," lamented Beauharnois in a 1736 report. He found that whenever orders were sent to militia commanders to arrest deserters known to be in each militia captain's district, the deserters were somehow never found.[34] Governor General Charles de Caylus levelled similar charges on militia commanders in the Îles du Vent. Noting that the "spirit of impudence has taken deep roots here," he found that when he sent the militia to arrest criminals or deserters, militia captains sent their own slaves ahead to warn the accused before their arrival. The captains could then say, quite truthfully, that they never saw the culprits.[35] Authorities read into these instances of mutual support the possibility of more widespread challenges to the social order.

To curb both stealing and desertion, officials in all three colonies advocated a variety of means to increase supervision over the comings and goings of ordinary soldiers. Constructing barracks proved to be the easiest way to segregate soldiers from the rest of the community and impose military order and supervision. Governor General Beauharnois over the years implored Maurepas to allocate money for their construction, which would make it considerably easier for officers to know where to find their men each morning.[36] The barracks were finally built in Quebec between 1748 and 1752.[37] Royal Engineer Gaspard Chaussesgros de Léry placed them on the edge of a cliff, within hailing distance of the intendant's palace, and incorporated large, open courtyards into the design, allowing officers to monitor their men's activity at a glance.[38] In Louisiana the central location of the barracks on either side of the *place d'armes* in the middle of town made soldiers highly visible, although whether this served to check them or cow the colony's lawless Canadian population is an open question. However, as New Orleans grew and the barracks fell into ruin, Governor Louis Billouart de Kerlérec advocated building at least one of the new structures at the edge of town, but with officers' quarters at either end.[39]

Throughout the Îles du Vent, controlling desertions and collusion prompted colonial leaders to increase recorded information on soldiers in order to track them more easily. Most troops outside Fort Royal lived in small, dilapidated quarters such as the fort at Saint Pierre, making desertion easier. Under the Regency, officials proclaimed a general amnesty for deserters from the colony's French regiment, the Compagnie franches de la Marine. But of the forty-five articles setting the terms of the amnesty, ten pertained to the use of more precise and extensive record-keeping to track each soldier's movement.[40] Supervisory actions included issuing permits for those travelling more than two leagues from camp, keeping records on those who escaped to foreign lands, and recording desertions and deaths in special registers, which were to be reported on a monthly basis to the Marine Council. The regulations even called for an early type of identity card, requiring the recording of physical details for each man, including his country of origin (presumably to determine accent or complexion), age, height, colour of eyes and hair (or of wig), and any visible marks or scars on the face or upper torso. Over thirty years later, the problem not only remained but had grown more acute with the advent of near-continuous war after 1744. Governor General Caylus in the Îles du Vent recommended the use of a mounted patrol, or *maréchaussée*, composed of French officers directing slave soldiers, to track down deserters. Such units had already been introduced into Saint Domingue as early as 1721.[41] The Marine acted on his recommendation very slowly, establishing a mounted patrol only after Great Britain restored Martinique and Guadeloupe to France in 1763. It is not clear why the Marine took so long, although it is tempting to speculate that before the British conquest, planters probably objected to the idea; when these same planters proved to be less loyal than the Marine had thought, the use of slaves on mounted patrols might even have been a veiled form of retaliation by the state.

Deserting sailors posed nearly as many problems in both the Îles du Vent and Louisiana. The end of war in 1713, the "golden age of piracy," and the general increase in merchant shipping to these two colonies allowed crews to jump easily from one vessel to sign on another for higher wages, actions that not only "ruined commerce" but supported lives as "libertines." Along with stiffer penalties, officials were ordered to keep records of sailors entering and leaving port.[42] Whether the regulations were enforced remains unclear for the French islands; they were definitely not enforced in Louisiana, a colony desperate to attract any skilled labourers it could. To carefully monitor such movement, the state would have had to invest more heavily in infrastructure, such as barracks, and clerks to keep records, a task that it had just begun to undertake in the 1750s.

Taverns clearly topped the list of officials' most socially dangerous community institutions. Alcohol fuelled much of daily colonial strife, and the literate elite widely believed that the unlettered were unrepentant drunkards.[43] But more than petty violence and irresponsible carousing was at stake. In Canada, Governor General Beauharnois originally intended to shut down the mess canteens run by sergeants for the soldiers in Quebec. But when he looked into the matter, he discovered that these same cabarets were the primary sources of support for the sergeants and their families.[44] Although he declined to obey Marine orders on humanitarian grounds, the discontent such action would have caused must also have been on Beauharnois's mind. One observer on Martinique recommended destroying cabarets altogether, for they were "the usual recipients of all escaped negroes, who find in their garrets a sheltered refuge from the pursuit of their Masters, and where sailors, soldiers, and deserters are sure to respect their asylum."[45] Foreigners who lodged at taverns were also watched.[46] Officials regularly attempted to limit the numbers of taverns in the Îles du Vent from 1658. But as early as 1713, nearly two hundred operated in Saint Pierre itself, although only about fifty were officially approved. Governor François de Fenélon limited their number to forty when he re-established French dominion over Martinique and Guadeloupe in 1763.[47]

Given their fears, officials strove to segregate soldiers, slaves, and white colonists from each other. Nowhere did colonial officials take the threat of collaboration among these groups more seriously than in Louisiana. Fights between soldiers and habitants were the ostensible grounds for first introducing laws separating the two groups in 1733, but subsequent laws substituted for the specific mention of fights the intriguingly vague "disturbances of good society." The laws remained unenforced in any event.[48] Governor Vaudreuil-Cavagnial introduced a stricter social code (*réglements de police*) in 1751 when he felt social order slipping beyond his grasp.[49] His motivations have been attributed by his best biographer, Guy Frégault, to a desire to refine the morals of the colony in general and its capital in particular, although historian Thomas Ingersoll suggests more realistically that they were promulgated in conjunction with a messy attempt by the governor and major of New Orleans to monopolize tavern-keeping.[50] In the preamble to the regulations, however, other motives are articulated. They first asserted the need to "correct base and debauched people" and, second, demanded the aid of law-abiding, settled colonists to support official efforts.

Not surprisingly, the first eight articles limited the operations of taverns. Only six were allowed to serve "moderate" amounts of liquor to voyageurs, the sick, and sailors. Soldiers, free blacks, black slaves, and members of Native tribes were barred from these taverns under penalty of a stiff fine on the first offence and sentenced to the galleys for life on the second. Soldiers were restricted to two mess canteens, one for regular troops and the other for the Swiss guards, thus ensuring religious segregation between Catholics and Protestants. Habitants were forbidden to approach either type of establishment, let alone be served there, and could consume liquor only in their own homes. Finally, the regulations called upon respectable habitants to report the existence of illegal, unlicensed taverns (*cabarets borgnes*), which had mushroomed on the outskirts of town. Operated by poorer whites and free blacks, they served a largely slave clientele and were believed to undermine slave loyalty to masters by encouraging theft and the fencing of stolen goods. Unlike in previous regulations, fights between slaves or between free blacks and whites were not mentioned. The unpopular nature of the regulations is indicated by the fact that Vaudreuil-Cavagnial had to postpone the announcement for over two months because the Superior Council feared a popular backlash.[51] While the code may have had a variety of motives, the desire to clearly demarcate boundaries between respectable society and the lowest social orders, and even between these humble groups, runs consistently through the whole document.

Despite the precautions, revolts by soldiers did occur. At the very least, white habitants or *petits blancs* seldom aided authorities; more often they supported or harboured the agitators. Most revolts were in the earlier part of the eighteenth century, when food and material shortages plagued officials, colonists, soldiers, and slaves alike. The difference in the military, of course, was that officials sometimes ate spoiled food and slept poorly, while soldiers and slaves went hungry and slept in the open. Several revolts and desertions accompanied the founding of New Orleans. In 1719, when France and Spain fought a brief war, fifty-six soldiers deserted during Governor Bienville's attack on Pensacola in Spanish Florida. Most were eventually pardoned after serving as convict labour, but Bienville had the two ringleaders executed. Four years later, in May 1723, sailors protesting poor pay and living conditions on shore revolted at Biloxi, which still served the colony as the main port.[52] This protest apparently sparked another barely a month later, when some forty soldiers demonstrated for three successive days in New Orleans before the house of the Superior Council's dean, Antoine Bruslé. They specifically protested against sleeping in the open, the lack of bread, and the limited opportunities to work for others than the Compagnie des Indes and thus earn higher wages. When the councillor chastised them for acting against the king's orders, they retorted that "had the king seen them, he would take pity on them." Their commander, Banes, even tacitly supported the soldier's actions by arguing that their conditions were undeniably wretched. To prevent a union between the garrison and the townspeople, who had similar complaints, the Superior Council rejected an earlier set of regulations limiting pay scales and increased wages for soldiers.

Louisiana's tinderbox reflected both the unrealistically high expectations held by white emigrants and poor planning. Soldiers shared the hopes of the former and certainly suffered from the latter. Of course, the greatest insurrection in the Îles du Vent, the Gaoulé of 1717, pitted colonial militia and some of the island's nobility against Governor General La Varenne and Intendant Ricouart. The majority of soldiers remained stationed in Fort Royal, and they did not fire on the nearly three thousand rebels as they passed a night on the beach adjacent to the fort.[53] Whether they would have if ordered to do so remains open to debate. The small number of soldiers – less than six hundred – in Saint Domingue during the uprising of 1722–23 ensured that they stayed safely tucked away in their small forts, although authorities believed that some of the *petits blancs* who took up arms and elected representatives were local deserters.[54] Because armed soldiers supported the colonial hierarchy, they could express dissatisfaction within certain bounds and have their demands respected by colonial authorities.

Another martial group who exercised even greater independence from colonial authority were the "mission" Iroquois. While not technically a part of French colonial society, since they lived apart in their own villages under the tutelage of Jesuit priests and met with Canada's governors as independent peoples, the mission Iroquois played a crucial role in the defence and economy of Canada. Their ambiguous role in French imperial policy and its far-flung communications network requires some explanation. After their first decade of missions in Huronia, the Jesuits decided at some point in 1640–41 to create several Catholic mission settlements where Christianized Native peoples could live beyond the reach of brandy-bearing French traders, yet be close enough to act as protective barriers against attack. Founded on the same principles as Jesuit *réductiones* in Paraguay, the most prominent *réserves* were the shifting settlement of Sillery, renamed Lorette, outside Quebec,[55] and two larger and more strategically placed settlements outside Montreal, one to the west on Lac des Deux Montagnes, guarding the Ottawa River route (near present-day Oka, Quebec), and another at Sault Saint-Louis as the first line of defence on the St Lawrence River opposite Lachine (now Kahnawake, Quebec). Montagnais and Algonquin peoples were first drawn to Sillery, where a Jesuit priest and several nuns preside over daily prayers and penance, and tried to convince male warriors to take a hand in plowing, a traditionally female occupation.[56] After the defeat by de Tracy's troops in 1665–66, the first wave of mainly Mohawk and Oneida Iroquois families escaping the brandy trade and attracted to Catholicism agreed to take up land at Sault Saint-Louis, and shortly after at Lac des Deux Montagnes.

Over the next ninety years, the villages became largely self-sufficient entities supported by hunting, agriculture, gifts of basic trade goods, and arms from New France's governor general but paid for by the Marine and packed in Rochefort. Although villagers appropriated some European clothing, regularly attended mass, joined choirs, and sought healing and spiritual guidance from a resident Jesuit priest, they did not, by and large, learn French, or accept European gender divisions, and they acknowledged acceptance of a priest by adopting him into a clan according to traditional Iroquois ritual.[57] They also travelled regularly to hunt or trade without any official supervision. Mission Natives actively pursued their own agendas: they acted on their own to persuade other villages or groups to join them, and they migrated, so that by the early 1750s a scattering of mission Natives, mainly converted Mohawk Iroquois, could be found in any number of cosmopolitan Native trading villages in the upper Ohio River valley.[58] Sault Saint-Louis's warriors ranged between New France and the upper New York colony to sell prime beaver pelts to Anglo-Dutch traders near Albany in exchange for cheaper English goods and rum. Many relied on their relatives still resident in the area to help them.[59] One byproduct of this contact was that parties of English and Dutch merchants travelled to Montreal on a regular basis from the mid-1720s to about 1740 to collect debts and coordinate deliveries with the French entrepreneurs who clandestinely supplied the mission traders.[60] The trade became so active and Canada's governors so exasperated with their known contacts with the enemy that by 1751 Governor General La Jonquière described the villages and their suppliers as forming a "semi-independent" empire.[61]

However, in return, the mission Natives provided a very important source of prized warriors and supplies. In 1757, for example, over eight hundred seasoned mission warriors accompanied the main body of French soldiers and Canadian militia in attacks on New York.[62] Raids sometimes pitted non-Christian Iroquois against mission Iroquois, which only complicated Native and French diplomacy.[63] Colonial officials relied heavily on mission Natives for valuable information. Mission chiefs regularly reported what they heard in conferences with British officials at Albany, and they warned French military officers of impending attacks by the British or hostile Native villages. For example, in early 1726, Tegaioguen, a leading warrior from Sault Saint-Louis, warned the king's lieutenant in Montreal that an attack on the newly planted post of Niagara would be carried out by Anglo-Americans that spring.[64] The ambiguous role of the mission villagers underscores the extent to which French colonial economic policy could bend to accommodate the realities of defence, and the gathering of information necessary for defence. They were not a part of the colonial social order, just its defenders and purveyors of information, a role that left them free from overt state influence.

ENCODING SLAVES

In the French Antilles, African slaves posed a far greater challenge to traditional French concepts of social order, precisely because they were integrated more closely into daily economic life. More than any other non-French or non-Catholic group, they represented a new class in French society that could not be incorporated into the traditional trinity of the three estates. The special status of slaves as outlined in the Code Noir of 1685 served to confirm metropolitan control over colonial actions. These regulations had been established with the Antilles in mind, and they were revised to introduce a harsher regime for Louisiana in 1724. Although officials never promulgated the Code Noir in New France, the approximately 2,500 slaves who lived in the colony throughout the French regime nominally came under its provisions.[65] Intendant Raudot allowed slaves to be held in 1709 and passed an ordinance permitting both the possession and the selling of slaves in 1713. Nearly two-thirds of the 4,000 slaves enumerated by Marcel Trudel in the Canadian records before 1800 were Natives, mainly Pawnee from what is now the region of Iowa and Nebraska. In fact, the French word for the tribe became synonymous with any Native slave. Of the remainder, about 1,400 were of West African descent, and the majority of these were introduced after the British Conquest of 1760. Black slavery also existed in Louisbourg. Ken Donovan has found records for at least 216 slaves who lived in the town between 1713 and 1758, virtually all of whom laboured as domestics for the wealthier inhabitants. In the first twenty years of Louisbourg's existence, most had been brought from Martinique, but by the 1730s a growing number were "Creoles" born in the port.[66] These slaves also came under the provisions of the Code.

Scholars have argued for years over the intent of the Code. Earlier historians building on the theories of Gilberto Freyre and, later, Frank Tannenbaum, portrayed it as a humanitarian document in comparison with the more restrictive and brutal measures adopted in the British and Dutch colonies.[67] At the same time other scholars, beginning with the great historian of the French slave trade, Gaston-Martin, have been quick to point out that regardless of the Code's intent, planters ignored the humanitarian impulses on a regular basis, exercising what Pierre Pluchon has called "domestic despotism."[68] Yet the Code can also be thought of as an attempt by metropolitan officials to legally and mentally incorporate a large group of people who had no previous social standing in the traditional division of the three estates. The Code Noir is crucial to understanding slavery in the French colonies, for although local colonial regulations and the interpretation of them varied considerably from colony to colony, as Thomas Ingersoll pointedly shows in comparing Louisiana and Saint Domingue,[69] the Code Noir nevertheless served as an ideal of individual conduct and social behaviour, as did so many *ancien régime* edicts and ordinances. Colonial officials cited the Code and commented on its applicability or shortcomings for specific problems.

Limitations on learning, travel, and assembly, all components of effective communications, comprised no less than twenty of the sixty articles comprising the Code of 1685 and twenty-one of the fifty-five included in the Louisiana Code of 1724.[70] Both codes clearly sought to eliminate the slaves' public voice and exposure to the world, and to circumscribe the range of people in whom slaves could place trust and affections. These clauses can be divided into five distinct groups: limitations on spiritual communication, restrictions on marriage and family relations, prohibitions on public gatherings, muting of a public voice, and punishment for desertion (*marronage*).

The first five articles of the Code Noir limited spiritual contact. Scholars have virtually ignored these articles, probably because they viewed them as dogmatic repetitions of professions of the faith in the latter days of Louis XIV's reign.[71] Yet they are arguably the most important regulations of all for limiting the most potentially disruptive contacts slaves could make. Their placement at the very beginning of the Code signifies the importance attached to the church's teachings as the only way to remake the slave in the French image. The Code Noir dictated insulating slaves from all contacts not supervised directly by church or state. As Yvan Debbasch has pointed out, fully subjugating a slave to a master helped reinforce both the pillars of traditional authority, since the master, who acted as a "good family father" to his or her slaves, also came under the same authorities.[72] Slaves were slotted into the prevailing paternalistic hierarchy at the level of the child. And like a watchful father who shields his children from corrupting influences, colonial masters isolated their slaves. The first article reiterated the ordinance of April 23, 1615, which expelled all Jews from the kingdom of France within three months. The second ensured that all slaves would be taught only Catholicism. The third explicitly banned any teachings other than those of the church, ruling that those who did so "should be punished as rebels and disobedient to our [the king's] commands." The fourth specified that all overseers must be Catholics, and the final article expressly forbade Huguenots from interfering with observance of Catholic rites.[73] This separation extended beyond life. Baptized slaves were segregated in their own cemeteries, unbaptized ones buried in fields at night (that is, in unconsecrated ground, without ceremony).

While the intent of the Code was undoubtedly to maintain a Christian sense of order, as Mathé Allain has suggested,[74] these five regulations also effectively sealed slaves off from ideas, education, and even fellowship not directly supervised by the church. In the context of the late seventeenth century, the regulations were absolutely necessary. The fire of the Counter-Reformation had burned low, allowing Huguenots and Jews to reclaim a more open and prominent role in commercial affairs. Although England had just allowed a Catholic king on the throne, his position was known to be very weak. Moreover, the French colonies were vulnerable to the fast-growing and belligerent English and Dutch settlements. Finally, metropolitan administrators had begun to realize that the intensive proselytizing by missionaries had largely failed. Both Native peoples and African slaves stubbornly preserved their own beliefs. Colonists in the tropics, who regularly dispensed with mass, seemed especially poor models of conduct.[75] While it is customary to twin the Code with the Revocation of Nantes suppressing Protestantism in France, issued later in the same year, it is also useful to recall that only in the late 1670s did the problems of managing large groups of imported slaves on sugar plantations in the Îles du Vent begin to occupy copious space in the letters of colonial officials sent back to Versailles. It is worth considering whether officials feared more from Islam, more localized tribal beliefs, or even Dutch Calvinism (for the many slaves still bought on Dutch islands) as means of creating an atmosphere of mutual support and cohesion among slaves, beyond their master's control.

Allied to spiritual belief were the articles governing marriage (articles 8–12). The original 1685 regulations did not explicitly ban interracial marriages, but efforts to suppress miscegenation became a cornerstone of the 1724 regulations for Louisiana.[76] The thrust of the 1685 laws seemed more to ensure that the church could police intimate contact, since they urged masters to act literally as fathers in order that their "children" more closely resemble a traditional French family. Even paternalism could extend only so far: because white planters raped their female slaves and many kept slave concubines, children of slave women were assigned their station in life according to their mother's condition.[77] Since many French *petits blancs* in both Martinique and early Louisiana lived in open concubinage with their female slaves, this rule closed the lid on the early emergence of a large, legalized mulatto population.[78] In an effort to curb miscegenation, the Dominicans regularly made pregnant or unwed female slaves with mulatto children do public penitence, thereby hoping to advertise the identity of the father. Governor François de Feuquières and Intendant Charles Besnard in the Îles du Vent contested the practice on the grounds that such public exposure introduced a custom not authorized by the Council of Trent, but they also admitted that doing away with the penitence would help diminish public "disorders," that is, reduce the numbers of battles in which male planters engaged with the Dominicans.[79]

A third set of clauses in the Code limited slaves' physical movement.[80] Those from different plantations or different masters were prohibited from associating, day or night, under any circumstances, including at weddings. For the first time, the Code detailed physical punishment for transgressors, including whipping and branding with a symbol of the fleur-de-lys for first-time offenders, more serious punishments dictated by a judge for a second infraction, and the death sentence for a third. Article 16 also identified masters' quarters, major roads, and isolated spots (*lieux écartés*) as the most dangerous sites for clandestine gatherings. Masters were heavily fined for allowing slaves to gather at such assemblies. In conjunction with movement, several articles limited the freedom to sell goods or produce in markets. The intent of articles 7, 28, and 29 may be construed solely as an attempt to hinder the ability of slaves to sell stolen goods.[81] However, these regulations were really a continuation of those prohibiting assemblies, since personal profit and ownership were prohibited elsewhere in the Code. Weekly markets are traditionally essential forums of information exchange and social interaction generally in agricultural societies, and still are so in Martinique's smaller centres. Here, male and female slaves of all ages from towns or large plantations mingled with slaves from the country or smaller plantations, or even from distant parts of the colony. They were bound to exchange news, gossip or, worse, swap grievances and voice discontent, while easily evading the ears of authority in the noise and bustle.

Articles 30, 31, and 32 of the 1685 Code muted the public voice of slaves. The first barred them from public office and from acting in a public capacity. Their depositions in trials were counted as "mémoires" to aid judges, but could not be accepted as proof. The second prohibited slaves from entering into contractual agreements. Yet the last clause allowed them to be tried, independent of the master's responsibility (unless the master was an accomplice). These articles are inconsistent, for the evidence of slaves was mistrusted because they lacked sufficient reasoning ability, while at the same time slaves could stand trial as reasoning and calculating beings. Since dispensing justice was not only the king's primary duty but also the primary framework within which communication with his subjects took place, banning slaves from public responsibility, entering into contracts, or supplying evidence removed them from conceptual foundations of the monarch-subject relationship. At the same time, being held accountable for one's actions (or sins) reflected the church's teachings supporting free will. The Code Noir, in short, could not escape the burden of contradiction that legally undermined the institution of slavery in the West.

The last set of regulations dealt harshly with the persistent problem of slave runaways, or *marronage*.[82] For the first absence, the ears were cut off and one shoulder branded with a fleur-de-lys; for the second, the hamstring cut and the other shoulder branded; execution followed the third attempt. The stipulation of absence beyond one month is very important, for it distinguished between the many temporary runaways (*fuites légères*, also *petit marronage*), who may have left the plantation for any number of reasons, and the smaller number of maroons who chose to live independently (*grand marronage*), outside their master's power, and hence that of the king. As Gabriel Debien has shown, temporary runaways occurred frequently and on all plantations, while permanent runaways were far fewer, but aroused considerable fear among planters.[83] Bodily mutilation served a grisly communications role, helping to identify first-time rebels to authorities and *petits blancs*, and to serve as a warning to other slaves.

STATE SUPERVISION AND LOCALIZED OPPRESSION

The Marine genuinely expected the Code to suffice for most problems. However, the greed of planters subverted whatever responsibilities or obligations the regulations outlined, and slaves themselves were adept at circumventing the limits imposed on them. If white colonists wished to preserve slavery, they had to go beyond metropolitan laws to contain the ever-constant threat of cooperation and union among slaves. From the moment that slaves arrived in the colonies, they were subjected to a regime of what communications theorist Cal Loque has called "enforced ignorance," which systematically limited their attempts to gain knowledge of their new surroundings.[84] Historians have rarely analyzed this aspect of containment, preferring to concentrate instead on the gruesome details of punishment, torture, and humiliation as means of social control. Over a long period, however, the systematic deprivation of knowledge may have accomplished more to maintain the stability (and profitability) of plantation slavery than subjugation by whipping, raping, branding, or garotting.

Limiting knowledge had become a well-entrenched custom, and even a system, by the late seventeenth century. According to Father Labat, newly acquired slaves were placed in the huts of Christian Creole slaves, but ate and slept apart until they began to take an interest in learning about Catholicism. Often an elderly black slave (usually a male) taught the new arrivals their catechism.[86] The acclimatization process was hardly easier than the brutal and harrowing voyage that deposited slaves on American shores. At least half of all new slaves in Saint Domingue died within their first three years, mainly from disease and the punishing environment of sugar-cane production. The death rate nearly approached the same number in the Îles du Vent, and did so in the first years of slave imports into Louisiana.[86] Few slaves ever fully learned French, and while this lack had the distinct advantage of keeping alive African dialects and culture, it also had the disadvantage of keeping slaves sealed off from the wider world of information provided by French and European knowledge generally.[87] Of course, white colonists and the clergy tacitly agreed not to teach slaves reading and writing. In Canada, Trudel found only nine slaves (eight of these of African descent) throughout the entire French regime who could sign their names.[88] There are no references to such teaching in the Îles du Vent, and even efforts to teach the catechism in creole dialects on Saint Domingue came under fire.[89] Instead, new slaves were often awed by the "magic" of French planters, who could make "paper speak." The *philosophe* Thibault de Chanvalon, who lived in Martinique in the 1750s, admitted with slight guilt that slaves' ignorance could be entertaining.[90] While whites recognized intelligence in individuals, contemporary observers believed slaves as a group to be irrational beings "who conducted themselves solely by fear, and understood only that which they could see."[91] In addition, slaves had few opportunities to explore their new environments. The work regimen was not only punishing and geared to producing profits, but allowed overseers to maximize supervision, while minimizing free time for slaves.

Nevertheless, slaves throughout the Îles du Vent and Louisiana consistently challenged the limits on communications imposed on them. Slave assemblies represented a continuing problem which local authorities policed as best they could. Segregation, a type of divide-and-control strategy, formed the basis of official laws and actions. In Louisiana the Superior Council issued a new ordinance reiterating articles 13 and 14 of the 1724 Code two years later when it noted that assemblies by both African and Native slaves continued unchecked.[92] Governor Étienne Périer in 1728 proposed a plan to halt the exodus of African slaves from New Orleans to the refuge of neighbouring Native tribes. In order to foment "misunderstanding" (*mésintelligence*) between them, he urged prohibiting French masters from taking African slaves to visit or live in Native camps or villages, ensuring that the two groups would have few opportunities to learn about each other.[93]

The 1751 regulations for Louisiana encompassed black slaves as well as white soldiers. In creating them, Governor Vaudreuil-Cavagnial and Louisiana's Superior Council introduced whipping for many transgressions and for the first time specifically prohibited any assembly inside New Orleans or in the vicinity. All slaves travelling on New Orleans's streets or on any roads or paths connecting with the city, whether on foot or horseback, were required to ask permission of any whites encountered to proceed, and any white could seize a horse ridden by a slave on any pretext. Other articles ordered slave owners to monitor the movements of their own slaves, noting that those from surrounding plantations met others who lived in town in order to "prowl, steal, and drink." Any slaves found outside their home plantations without notes from their masters were to be immediately secured and imprisoned. Finally, slaves could no longer socialize after church services.[94]

Any type of unsupervised travel caused planters anxiety. Masters on Martinique detested slave *corvées* because, aside from the loss of several days of their slaves' labour, public work gangs often incorporated people from different plantations over a whole region, mixing them together so that, "being no longer under the careful eye of their masters, [the slaves] might understand in this condition a gleam of liberty."[95] Only the Christmas holidays consistently opened the door to the greater Atlantic world for slaves on an annual basis.[96] They expected and received at least a week off from work, giving them a chance to visit other plantations or even nearby towns. Not surprisingly, the days between December 25 and New Year's Day were especially trying for whites in the Îles du Vent. At least three major conspiracy rumours circulated in Saint Pierre between 1717 and 1748. The most serious occurred in late 1727, causing both clerical and secular authorities to agree to limit slave holidays. Governor General Feuquières set a curfew for Saint Pierre and Fort Royal from December 17, starting at 8 p.m., and organized nightly patrols to enforce it.[97] Martinique's planters found it difficult to strike a balance between allowing their slaves too much and too little contact, since the potential for violence existed on either side of a narrow line. Significantly, it was left to colonial clergy, officials, and planters to negotiate the issue of holidays, for it lay outside the control, and comprehension, of metropolitan authorities.

Colonial port towns allowed slaves many more opportunities to circulate with minimal supervision. As in the case of soldiers, authorities focused on the busy taverns as hives of potential disorder. Gabriel Debien noted that colonial ports acted as magnets for escaped slaves since they could find shelter in taverns, blend easily into the bustling crowds, and always find work as labourers, peddlers, or sailors.[98] Regulations were passed in the Îles du Vent throughout the eighteenth century to exclude slaves and limit their use by free blacks, but to little effect. As one contemporary writer noted, the regulations were widely ignored since "only slaves ... frequented [free-black] taverns." By late 1763, fights regularly broke out in Saint Pierre's taverns between young whites and free blacks.[99] Charging free blacks with the vice of encouraging slaves to steal and live "scandalously" against church and king, the 1751 New Orleans regulations forbade them to serve liquor to slaves in their taverns. The penalty for an infraction was the loss of freedom, and all French whites found near such places were to be publicly whipped by the executioner and sent to the galleys.[100] In 1763, however, *commissionaire* Jean-Jacques-Blaise d'Abbadie reported that the town's militia needed to be augmented in order to combat an increasing number of street fights.[101] While it is not clear why authorities failed to enforce these regulations, it is evident that townspeople of all races found evading them useful and profitable. Such public indifference suggests a current of popular resistance to official attempts at segregation.

Aside from monitoring the actions of the slaves, major colonial officials also kept a close eye on tavern proprietors and even their own minions. On at least one occasion, officials accused white cabaret owners of using their slaves – or worse, the slaves of others – to purchase produce in the countryside, transport it to the towns, and sell it for up to four times the cost usually paid by townsfolk.[102] In 1761 the Superior Council of the Îles du Vent accused Intendant Paul-Pierre Lemercier de La Rivière's own secretaries of taking bribes to authorize a local dance organized by slaves and free blacks in Saint Pierre. The intendant complained of this usurpation of the council's authority, but the Creole dean of the council sidestepped the issue by emphasizing the French intendant's ignorance of slaves' true nature, which he depicted as diabolical and prone naturally to disorder.[103] Although the motivation for whites to work with slaves may have been monetary, the point here is that poorer white colonists, and even some metropolitan clerks on the king's business, pursued their own relations regardless of the state's wishes.

So long as slaves remained locked in American colonies, the Marine appeared content to let colonial officials interpret the Code Noir as they saw fit. The true challenge to metropolitan authorities began when a growing level of contact and prosperity between the tropical colonies and France allowed hundreds of retiring or absentee planters and even royal officials to travel and live in France with domestic slaves purchased in the Antilles.[104] At first, metropolitan officials acceded to planters' requests to bring their slaves to France, allowing them to land without their "property" being able to declare their freedom. Some French members of the provincial parliaments had cited laws dating from the early fifteenth century which stated that a slave touching French soil instantly obtained freedom regardless of the circumstances.[105] Historian Sue Peabody has traced the development of laws governing slavery in France in the eighteenth century and found that claims for freedom beginning in the 1690s led eventually to the Edict of 1716, which allowed slavery in France on the condition that masters brought slaves to be educated in Christianity or in a useful trade. However, each provincial parliament handled the edict differently, so that, for example, the Paris parliament did not register it, leaving slaves who lived under its jurisdiction – about one-third of the enslaved population in the kingdom – in legal twilight. After 1763 the black population in France, though minuscule, began to grow quickly (in Bordeaux from 14 to 121 in fourteen years), leading to very strict segregation laws by 1777.[106] Meanwhile, from across the Atlantic came other pressures. As early as 1727, Governor General Champigny alerted Secretary of State Maurepas to a serious problem, complaining that when slaves returned from France, they became unmanageable. From the colonial planter's viewpoint, removing skilled or potentially trainable slaves harmed the colony in two ways. First, so few slaves returned that they deprived the colonies of cheap but sorely needed skilled and semi-skilled tradesmen. Secondly, those slaves who did return attained such a level of worldliness that they became very difficult to control.

In 1752, at the height of the Îles du Vent's golden age, the governor and the intendant penned a joint letter that faithfully echoed the planters' sentiments. It warned Secretary of State Rouillé that returned slaves from France "acquired knowledge which they might well use to their advantage," adding, "Nearly all leaders of the revolts and the very worst subjects among the negroes or mulattoes are to be found among those who have been in France."[107] The administrators sent a list stretching back twenty years of slaves who had not returned, and they promised to keep the minister updated every six months. This transatlantic recrossing by slaves points to a small but consistent traffic that threatened to bring the repugnant plantation regime into the heart of France. While perhaps four thousand slaves may have resided in France at any one time by the 1770s,[108] a cursory glance at the ships' papers recorded in the port of Bordeaux in 1740 shows a steady entry of about twenty annually.[109] Of course, at least some of these slaves stayed only temporarily and were dragged back to the Antilles when their masters had settled affairs; but a small number stayed in the port cities. Metropolitan authorities in the colonies also objected to the importation of slaves from British and Dutch Caribbean ports. Initially, the reports mentioned only fears over disease, but increasingly the complaints centred on the debased morals and independent spirit of the slaves.[110] Travel evidently opened up a new world to slaves, for a variety of reasons, upon which we can only speculate. Of course, the importation of slaves who had lived in non-French colonies created the possibility of expanding non-Catholic influences, although colonists did not voice concern over this matter.

While no major slave revolt occurred on Martinique or in Louisiana during the *ancien régime*, it would be mistaken to conclude that slaves integrated peacefully into French colonial communities. The few who are mentioned in the official correspondence are most likely only those who became publicly known. Local officials wished to appear in control at all times, and news of revolts or large escapes tarnished their image. Slaves normally chose two paths of escape on Martinique: either by ship or into the mountainous interior. In 1717, during the Gaoulé, for example, five slaves seized a small schooner from a local merchant in Saint Pierre and eventually sailed to Antigua.[111] An increase in this form of escape is indicated by the introduction of new measures in 1743 which increased the penalties against slaves hijacking boats or found on foreign vessels.[112]

The existence of maroon communities greatly alarmed colonial officials for a number of reasons. Maroons found refuge in the rugged interiors of both Martinique and Guadeloupe, well beyond the reach of sugar plantations and the parties of soldiers sent to capture them. With the expansion of small cocoa plantations in the islands' hills, beginning in the late 1690s, and coffee plantations from the late 1720s, even these areas of safety began to evaporate. As late as 1710, two "cabals" of fugitive slaves living in the forested bluffs immediately above Saint Pierre cooperated to prepare an attack on the port. One group supposedly maintained close links with sympathetic African slave domestics and free blacks in town.[113] When officials and white planters learned of the preparations, they moved quickly and captured many of the fugitives. Punishment was swift, brutal, and temporarily effective. Of the twenty-eight slaves arrested in the incident, one was burned alive, nine broken on the wheel, and seven hanged. The eleven remaining slaves were severely whipped and branded with the fleur-de-lys, and Governor General Phélypeaux boasted of a return to "tranquility" among the slaves. Perceptions of danger differed greatly between metropolitan officials and creole planters, hindering attempts at a united response to *marronage*. Debien argued that planters seldom worried about most runaways, even long-term ones, partially because they were too costly and time-consuming to track down, while colonial leaders instead insisted that they were desperate bands whose example of free living and hunting dangerously communicated the impotence of royal authority, presumably not just to slaves but to "libertines" as well.[114] Colonial leaders passed further regulations in 1743 to control them on both Martinique and Guadeloupe, and resilient communities of maroons, estimated by officials at over three hundred on Martinique alone in 1769, continued to pose a threat to social peace. Each time, they found little material support among planters to help them.[115] Maroons also lived within the vicinity of New Orleans, although their presence there is less well documented. Official documents record a low but consistent number of escapes into the cypress swamps, by boat to Spanish Pensacola, and, on at least one occasion, to Spanish Havana.[116] To what degree the existence of maroons fuelled plans by some slaves to seek freedom and offered some intangible hope to those who stayed is impossible to know, at least from official documents. But from the point of view of royal authority, concern turned not so much on a fear of a general uprising as on a comment on official impotentcy. *Marronage* appeared to be a kind of insult hurled in the face of a supposedly all-powerful state and its economic underpinnings.

SLAVES AND INFORMATION CONTROL: THE NEW ORLEANS "CONSPIRACY" OF 1731

The New Orleans slave conspiracy of 1731 dramatically illustrates the importance of freedom of communications, specifically movement, and the state's use of isolation as a powerful means to control slaves. The most detailed account has been left by Antoine Le Page du Pratz, a minor nobleman who managed the king's brickworks where the slave conspiracy was hatched. While historians contest the accuracy of du Pratz's story, because of the gratuitous, self-aggrandizing role he gave himself, or whether any conspiracy actually existed other than in the minds of officials, his account is in accord with the major events mentioned in official documents.[117] The conspiracy began in the immediate aftermath of the Natchez massacre, when French colonists in New Orleans expected a larger and more ferocious assault by the surviving Natchez and their much larger ally, the Chickasaw nation.[118] Many recently arrived slaves, especially those of the large contingent from the Bambara nation, hoped to take advantage of the confusion and uncertainty to win their own freedom.

One afternoon a female slave owned by the Compagnie des Indes and attached to its brickworks was struck by a soldier in what can only be construed as a failed rape attempt. In her anger and defiance, she let slip that the French would not be striking slaves much longer. Brought before Governor Périer and du Pratz, she said nothing; du Pratz volunteered to investigate. Late that night he and a young male slave (apparently an interpreter) stole into the slaves' compound. They overheard several men gathered around a concealed fire discussing plans for a revolt. Nothing could begin, the slaves decided, until the annual flour convoy from the Illinois country arrived in a few days' time, since many of the paddlers were relations and therefore dependable. Du Pratz reported his findings to the governor and suggested a plan, which he believed very clever, to capture the conspirators without raising a general alarm among other slaves. A few days later du Pratz arranged for each of the six conspirators to be assigned to a different work detail. While the gangs laboured, he called each one aside on a pretext, escorting him to tool shed located some distance away. Once inside, a team of concealed soldiers bound and gagged each slave then smuggled them all across the river, hidden in boats, to the prison in New Orleans. Each slave was kept separated from the others, and beaten and tortured for information. They revealed nothing, but du Pratz, with evident satisfaction, thought that by breaking all six on the wheel in public for the crime of slandering in jest (*badiner*) and hanging the bondswoman, the executions would wring acquiesence from other slaves throughout lower Louisiana.

If it is accepted that the details of the narrative are largely accurate, even if the specific role played by du Pratz is not, it is clear that authorities took advantage of slaves' limited options to communicate with one another to defeat the conspiracy. The slaves could organize only in secret at night while they were locked in a compound, while du Pratz and his slave enjoyed complete freedom of movement. Du Pratz and the soldiers devoted an extraordinary amount of time and energy to keeping secret the arrest, transportation, and torture of the conspirators, so as not to arouse an immediate and spontaneous uprising by public displays. Officials separated the supposed leaders, the easier to instill fear from isolation and to corroborate stories. Finally, it is evident that a sense of common interest did not unite the slaves. Du Pratz could apparently rely on the loyalty of his own slave, however gained or extracted, and the conspirators could only count on the loyalties of their own language group. The role of the well-travelled Illinois boatmen is important. They may have possessed knowledge of the territory and had access to transportation essential to the success of the revolt.[119] The secrecy and the use of isolation to cut communication between slaves described by du Pratz are reminiscent of methods used by totalitarian regimes to "disappear" their opponents.

Slaves bore the brunt of two overlapping species of authoritarian government: that imposed by the metropolitan state and that enacted by local authorities, usually in consultation with the plantocracy. But the application of power was never uniform or wholly successful, especially in colonial ports. In Canada the relatively smaller size of the marginalized estate translated into easier control. By contrast, the majority enslaved population and their economic centrality in the Îles du Vent led to a far greater response by the state to control their movements and communication. As a colony of a colony, Louisiana occupied a unique situation where initially soldiers, Canadians, convicts, and slaves offered a variety of opportunities for combining to resist colonial leaders. Although the American "Jim Crow" segregation laws date from the late nineteenth century, segregation itself is rooted in the earliest years of colonial Louisiana. Desertions and the freedom of travel enjoyed by most Native peoples demonstrated, however, that the authorities could only control movement in cooperation with colonists. But for the large numbers of slaves, where all whites and free blacks were potential slave owners, colonial authorities could count on a far broader range of support in proscribing movement, daily contact, and education. From the moment of a new slave's arrival to his or her death, and often that of a free black's as well (as the trial of Étienne La Rue suggests), officials forbade every slave from ranging over both the geographic and the intellectual landscape available to even the poorest whites. The limitations on travel interfered with the ability to gather knowledge, to give voice to anger, to find common cause, and to seek common redress. But the two levels of authority did not always share the same perceptions, or pressures, and were at times at odds. In that space between regulation and practice, the people of the marginal estate began to meet, to talk, to trust, and sometimes to plan.

CHAPTER SIX

Merchant Networks and Imperial Dependence

Toward the end of the War of the Austrian Succession, one of Saint Pierre's larger shippers informed his agent and friend in the French port of Marseilles of changes in his operations. Henceforth, his sugar, coffee, and bills of exchange would be shipped via the neutral Dutch islands of Saint Eustatius and Curaçao and channelled through an agent of their mutual acquaintance in Amsterdam. Increasing numbers of British privateers and warships had forced Martinique's authorities to turn a blind eye to what had been considered smuggling during peace. The shipper specified that the profits in his forthcoming ventures be transferred to Marseilles, where he could build a small capital base to weather any potential disasters. With either complete or partial stakes in some seventeen ships sailing to France, Canada, Havana, and even Brazil, he fretted over the safety of his cargoes. He closed his letter with the usual warm words of *politesse* that characterized the period, assuring his friend of "the joy that I would have if my position would enable me to be of some use to you, to better convince you of my esteem and friendship."[1]

This letter is typical of the thousands that crossed the Atlantic between France and its colonies every year. It is an intriguing document for several reasons. For one thing, it clearly indicates how French colonial merchants utilized an extensive circuit of international shipping and correspondence routes by the mid-eighteenth century to circumvent the dynastic wars of the period. The control of their own ships allowed merchants to bend rigid metropolitan regulations far enough to turn a profit. The assurances of respect and mutual interest display the high degree of trust and intimacy fostered by regular contact, which in turn grew from the ceaseless crossing of the Atlantic by merchant vessels.

The letter is most remarkable in quite another respect: its author. The Saint Pierre shipper was no ordinary *commissionaire*, but in fact

Charles de Thubières, Marquis de Caylus, governor general of the Îles du Vent.[2] The authorization to trade with the Dutch originated from his desk. He regularly used a small number of discrete Saint Pierre agents to hide his commercial activities at a time when trade and discussions over money still sent shivers down the spines of the French nobility.[3] Pierre-Honoré Roux Pepin, the influential Marseillais merchant to whom Caylus wrote, must have smiled when he read the governor general's closing offer to be of "some use" in Martinique.

Close contact between colonial officials and merchants was part of the larger, long-term trend of integrating the wealthier bourgeoisie into the traditional French elite. Transoceanic trade brought merchants and state officials into close and mutually profitable cooperation and social intercourse. Nevertheless, historians have traditionally viewed the relations between the French state and its merchants as a battle between a quasi-totalitarian Goliath and a spunky, laissez-faire David.[4] However, since the appearance of Jean Tarrade's work, *Exclusif mitigé* (1972), they have gradually accepted the existence of a complex interplay of special interests, bourgeois enterprise, and *philosophe* theories of the state in the formulation of *ordonnances* and *lettres patentes* touching colonial trade.[5] In part, the meeting of minds, money, and manners between ennobled officials and wealthier merchants can be seen as a natural outgrowth of what historians now identify as two largely independent French economies. The port cities and larger riverine towns of France emerged as glittering gems of long-range, mercantile capitalist economies from the larger soil of nearly stagnant, localized, and even subsistence-level agricultural economies of the country's interior.[6] Until recently, French historians have seldom examined the role of communications in bringing merchants and officials together. If the subject is mentioned at all, discussions of communications are limited to technological advances or geographic constraints, such as the building of canals or post roads and the impediments of riverine transportation, and are linked to the weak growth of national, integrated markets.[7]

In the eighteenth century, successful merchants had not only to master different forms of communication but also to nurture and reap the fruit of continuous contact. Historians of the Anglo-American world have recognized, at least since Bernard Bailyn's work on New England merchants, that place of business and the cultivation of contacts were at least as important as literacy and accounting skills.[8] French historians such as Paul Butel have observed that "the postal wagon, the horse and the stables which lodged them, also compose the instruments of business."[9] In placing communications at the heart of commercial life, Dale Miquelon has observed, "The merchant was always a writer and a traveller, a specialist in communication."[10] But the role of kinship and co-religionist ties in cementing transatlantic commerce as well as frontier commercial exchange has increasingly received greater scrutiny.[11] J.F. Bosher has taken the study of kinship networks farther by tracing the ties between co-religionists in western European and colonial ports. He distinguished between a commerce-oriented Protestant "Atlantic trading society" and a clerical, professional, and venal office-holding Catholic "Bourbon official society." Both groups included merchants, but merchant networks were at the financial and social heart of the "Protestant International," creating a more unified and cosmopolitan identity.[12] In raising the question of religion in determining commercial activity, Bosher challenges the larger link between modernity and the emergence of an Atlantic world. If the Atlantic world is a transition between the medieval world and global contact based on notions of individualism, the nation-state and capitalism, where do kinship networks fit? What conditioned their willingness to work with or against the state? Did the state attempt to control merchants in the French Atlantic world, and if so, how? The preponderance of overseas kin relations in commercial enterprises also raises difficult questions about the relation of overseas commerce to emergent forms of imperial government in the seventeenth and eighteenth centuries. Where did merchants place their loyalties? The ubiquitous nature of smuggling in all French colonies clearly demonstrates that colonial needs and desires were often at odds with imperial policies and resources.

This chapter examines the influence of long-distance merchants in altering the parameters within which the state functioned in the colonies. Through ships and the correspondence carried by ships, the great merchants (*négociants*) of the French ports enjoyed access to a very large and diverse matrix of resources, talents, and contacts. For those in France with the right connections, any amount of credit, any personnel, and all types of goods or produce could be summoned from nearly any point in Europe north of the Danube and west of the Oder, and sent to any location frequented by European merchant ships, whether in the Americas, sub-Saharan Africa, or South and East Asia. The Marine would have found it hard to make quite so extensive a claim. While it maintained a monopoly on raising and allocating military force across the Atlantic and in the colonies, it found its ability to support that force – whether transporting men, sending supplies, or transmitting orders and reports – limited by financial resources, court politics, and foreign intervention. Most of all, it had to rely on merchants to succeed. The state could fully extend its grasp overseas only by recourse to the commercial networks of merchants in the French

Atlantic ports. Where merchants were least important to the state's needs, such as in Canada, their impact on royally sanctioned colonial policies tended to be less. But where the state consistently relied on merchants and their ships, such as in the Îles du Vent and Louisiana, merchants gained a greater weight in colonial affairs, simply avoided state regulations through smuggling, or more often, piloted some course between these two. This reliance upon merchants and shipping is best demonstrated in the economicaly dynamic Îles du Vent, which will receive the bulk of attention in this chapter.

MERCHANTS AND COSMOPOLITAN NETWORKS

Two basic types of merchants handled transatlantic trade in the port towns. The first were representatives of established merchants or mercantile partnerships based in the major French trading cities of Bordeaux, La Rochelle, Nantes, or Marseille. Often they were brothers, sons, nephews, and sons-in-laws of prominent merchants or, more rarely, family friends or simply trusted employees. These merchants might trade only for the duration of a voyage, as many ship captains did, or establish themselves locally, acquire land, a spouse, and a family, and settle permanently in America, as did Paul Rasteau when he came to New Orleans in 1736.[13] Until 1763 these metropolitan merchants dominated all French-American trading activity, since they possessed a full-fledged purchasing and marketing system through their families that in turn opened large credit pools within France.[14] The second group were colonial-born (Creole) merchants, often artisans, local merchants in a specialized trade such as furs or indigo, or small ship captains who gradually expanded their operations. More rarely, planters in the French Antilles or Louisiana might market their own produce. While these merchants dominated more local trade, they were limited by having poorer access to credit and knowledge and contacts about marketing colonial products in France. Moreover, most were prohibited, or at least officially discouraged, from pursuing direct trade with France; authorities opened only intercolonial trade to Creoles. They formed a merchant "underclass" within the larger body. As Dale Miquelon aptly noted of Canada, "While many Canadians were at the top, only Canadians were at the bottom."[15] However, Kathryn Young has suggested that the two types of merchants in fact were closely allied and formed a single collective identity.[16] In a sense, the division between metropolitan and Creole merchants reflected the dichotomous Atlantic world/localized economies of France, and the limits on Creole activity enhanced the imperial privileges of metropolitan merchants. Regardless of origins or length of residence, the most powerful merchants, colonial or metropolitan, were those with the most extensive and reliable transatlantic contacts.

However, a third type of merchant lived in the French Caribbean, and in Saint Pierre in particular. Historians of the region dutifully mention a powerful group of colonially based commercial agents, or *commissionnaires*. They were generally acknowledged to be cunning and highly self-interested, men who amassed "questionable, but considerable fortunes," and who "took their toll of the feckless planters and had many of them in their debt."[17] Yet all references to the *commissionnaires* are derived either from complaints by royal officials such as Caylus, who were themselves suspect, given their activities, or from the complaints of the Nantes Chamber of Commerce in the 1720s, the most outspoken voice against English slave-smuggling.[18] The *commissionnaires* as an identifiable group remain elusive. We do not know who they were, to whom they were married, how many existed, how much capital they controlled, and exactly how they operated.[19] It is striking that these shadowy merchants, so vilified in the official sources, are rarely identified as individuals. Equally striking is the fact that they represented the only wealthy and literate residents in the islands who were not directly dependent on royal patronage dispensed through local officials. Further, it is not all clear that relations with the plantocracy were always antagonistic. In 1730, naval captain Rossel outlined the advantages that planters derived from selling their sugar to Saint Pierre's *commissionnaires*: a single location, ease of finding a plurality of buyers at any time, leading to shorter stays in port and more competitive prices, prompt payment in cash, and a wide variety of goods to choose from.[20] Both groups stood to profit from smuggling, which would make them material and even ideological allies, not enemies. Nor is it clear that metropolitan merchants were in open competition with the *commissionnaires*, since onerous laws regulating commerce applied to both, and since the slight evidence there is suggests that *commissionnaires* formed partnerships with resident metropolitan merchants.[21] In short, the *commissionnaires* appeared to have been vilified precisely because they had carved out a significant territory of operations beyond effective imperial control.

Wherever their place of residence or the types of goods they bought and sold, all merchants relied heavily on writing and keeping accounts as the key to open the Atlantic world. The time and energy devoted to tracking information and keeping contacts alive via letter-writing cannot be overemphasized. The mundane aspects of keeping track of bills of lading, sales, customs slips, various authorizations, and other ships papers required an enormous amount of concentration, education, and time. In Canada, agents of Rouen's Dugard and Company, François

Havy and Jean Lefebvre, recorded all their documents in triplicate. At the end of each season, the daily entries of goods received and payments made were transferred to a ledger then "condensed" to a current accounts book in order to send notices for debt payments.[22] Ship captains had to keep similar extensive account books. They often doubled as merchants, and so also had to organize information, keep records, and be accomplished and reliable letter-writers. The ship's papers of the *L'Hirondelle*'s Captain Grenouilleau included an account book with sales grouped by like items, another account book of daily expenses, and a daybook of current accounts (*livre de brouillard*), which listed daily debit and credit balances. Entries covered forty to fifty pages in each book for the duration of a single voyage.[23] One twelve-month voyage in 1750–51 to Léogane on Saint Domingue (probably a slave-trading venture) generated forty letters and copies of accounts by the ship's captain, Raymond Gaultier, which he sent from a number of French Antilles ports back to the ship's owner in Bordeaux.[24] Frequent lawsuits created even more paperwork. In one documented instance from 1719, damages suffered by a ship from Quebec while in the port of Louisbourg generated thirty-eight separate written legal documents in the course of one month, all of which were copied for the local admiralty court. Twelve of the longer pieces were also copied for Île Royale's Superior Council. In 1738 another accident resulting in a damaged ship in Louisbourg produced 166 folio pages of written depositions in six weeks.[25] Merchants handled this paperwork themselves or employed young clerks, who either were hired from local families or were young members of the merchant's own extended family. A culture of careful documentation and extensive recording of information was therefore not the provenance of the state alone. Merchants and ship captains had to be trained purveyors and recorders of information, and they formed their own mini-bureaucracies to administer their domains.

Regular correspondence demanded even greater effort. To summon resources and credit, the larger French merchants in Europe with colonial operations relied on a vast and geographically diverse network of correspondents. A few examples will suffice to show their impressive reach. From his riverfront home in Bordeaux, Jean Pellet received letters not only from his brother Pierre in Saint Pierre but from associates and agents in Marseille, Toulouse, Bayonne, Rouen, and Troyes in France; from London and Cork, Ireland; from Amsterdam, Rotterdam, and Middleburg in Holland; from the German principality of Hamburg; from Geneva, Switzerland; and from other agents in Cadiz, Bilbao, and La Coruña in Spain.[26] Although situated in the Mediterranean, merchants of Marseille entered easily into transatlantic shipping. In addition to contacts in Holland, through whom he communicated with Governor General Caylus, Honoré Roux regularly corresponded with agents throughout Provence, in six different ports in northern Italy as far as Livorno, and in Bordeaux (the embarkation port for many of his colonial ships), and with an agent in London before and during the Seven Years War.[27]

The best-connected French Atlantic merchants of the mid-eighteenth century may well have been the Jewish family of Gradis from Bordeaux.[28] Abraham Gradis's only surviving letterbook indicates that his communications network rivalled and possibly surpassed that of the Marine itself. In this letterbook, his secretaries wrote 569 letters, totalling 980 folio pages, in the eleven months from May of 1756 to March of 1757 just to agents and contacts in France and neighbouring countries. These included letters to other merchants and many royal officials in forty-four French locations, including Angoulême, Auxerre, Bayonne, Blois, four different correspondents in Brest, Calais, Candiac, Chataigneraye (?), Havre de Grace, Hendaye (on the Spanish border), La Rochelle (including to ships anchored in its harbour waiting to sail), Le Havre, Laudernau (?), Le Mans, L'Isle d'Aix (an anchorage favoured by naval vessels and convoys), Lille, Lyon, Marseille, Montabaun, Morlaix (Brittany), Mornas (near Orange on the Rhône), Nantes, Nérac (in Guyenne), Nîmes, Niort, Orleans, fourteen different correspondents in Paris, Pau, Périgeuex, Preignac (near Bordeaux), Puy, Rochefort, Rouen, Saint Denis (outside Paris), Saint Étienne, Saint Jean d'Angély (east of Rochefort), Saint Malo, "Saint Siumphorieun de Laye" (Saint Symphorien-en-Leyre, wine merchants south of Bordeaux), Toulon, Toulouse, Tours, Vannes, and nine addresses "à la Cour," as well as to Saint Sebastian and Cadiz in Spain and to agents in the major European entrepôts of London, Amsterdam, and Lisbon.[29] Gradis's correspondents also included the keeper of the seals and the foreign minister at Versailles, the new governor general of New France, Pierre de Vaudreuil-Cavagnial, and the disgraced secretary of state for the Marine, Jean-Frédéric Phélypeaux, Comte de Maurepas.

In Martinique the family established two family connections in Saint Pierre by 1727, and at the same time sent goods to another nephew in Léogane, Saint Domingue.[30] In the 1730s and early 1740s, Abraham Gradis also corresponded directly with Intendant Jacques Pannier d'Orgeville and Martinique's local governor, André Martin de Poinsable.[31] In the 1750s he aided the botanical interests of the Marquis de La Galissonière, the former interim governor of New France, by sending crates of seeds and young trees to Canada for planting experiments.[32] Gradis also established firm contact with the secretary of state for war, and later for the marine, Étienne-François, Duc de

Choiseul. After an exasperating meeting held with Marine officials to work out the details for supplying the Antilles in September of 1761, Choiseul confided to Gradis that "it is you with whom I am well at ease." In their correspondence, the duke adopted a far less formal style, addressing Gradis as "My dear friend," an uncharacteristic mark of friendship.[33]

This astonishing range of contact, we might note, relied in part on Gradis's familiarity with enlightened administrative officials such as La Galissonière and Choiseul. Even more than Roux, he could depend on his London connections to arrange for wheat to be sent to Canada during peace and to release the crews of his ships when they were imprisoned during war.[34] Although Guy Frégault, in his penetrating study of Canada's last intendant, François Bigot, condemned the "Israelite" Gradis family as the prime culprits in the graft and corruption scandals known collectively as the *l'affaire du Canada*,[35] it is at least as important to recognize the essential reliance by the Marine's upper echelon upon Abraham Gradis. Given the near-universal contacts and the resources they could summon, it should not be surprising that the Marine turned repeatedly to members of the Gradis family to support its projects in North America.

Extensive geography did not guarantee strong connections if they were not constantly refreshed. While it is very difficult to estimate the regularity of mercantile contact and gauge the exchange of information among merchants, either across the Atlantic or within a colony, the small number of individual examples we have suggests some general patterns. In Quebec the frequency of mercantile contact proved to be indistinguishable from that of officials, since both were limited by climatic constraints. Like Marine dispatches, letters from metropolitan merchants arrived in a single bundle, and their colonial agents tried to send their responses back on the same ship.[36] In Louisiana the meagre production of the colony and problems associated with securing return cargoes appears to have similarly affected both merchants and administrators alike. But the Îles du Vent, and the port of Saint Pierre in particular, offered far greater possibilities for year-round contact. For example, from mid-1718 to early 1720, Bordeaux's Jean Pellet received seventy-five letters from his brother in Saint Pierre. During the era of their busiest shipping operations to Martinique, which lasted from 1721 until 1732, Pierre averaged between thirty and forty letters per year, not including duplicates.[37] The level of return correspondence is harder to determine, although Pierre Pellet occasionally acknowledged receiving three to five letters per month, spaced evenly apart, during the height of Saint Pierre's shipping season. Over the course of the year, then, the volume of letters sent from Bordeaux roughly equalled the number received from Saint Pierre.[38] In the 1720s the large number of ships calling at Saint Pierre allowed Jean Pellet in Bordeaux to receive news six to ten weeks old from Saint Pierre on a continual weekly basis, an advantage not enjoyed by merchants on nearby Guadeloupe.[39]

More importantly, Pellet received responses from his brother to specific inquiries within sixteen to twenty-one weeks (four to five months) after first writing about them.[40] Any pressing matter, such as the bankruptcy of a major debtor, received three complete inquiry-response rounds within twelve to fourteen months, within the chronological period of most long-term loans or credit extensions. To increase the chances that important letters got through safely, merchants sent as many as four different copies of documents by different ships, a procedure also occasionally practised by the Marine.[41] In comparison, the Marine could usually rely on two complete inquiry-response rounds from its officials at the very best. If it depended only upon its own vessels, then it possessed no more than two opportunities per year to send instructions and receive reports. By contrast, Jean Pellet in Bordeaux averaged one such opportunity every two weeks, that is, about twenty-five to thirty such opportunities in a year, a ratio of at least twelve to one. While it is true that royal ships on special assignments increased the contact somewhat more, such voyages were haphazard and often consisted of merchant vessels ferrying supplies. Unlike in either Canada or Louisiana, then, merchants in the French Caribbean could enjoy a tremendous advantage over the state in terms of keeping informed and making transatlantic decisions. In order to match mercantile connections in the Caribbean, the Marine had to avail itself of merchant ships to transport information between France and the Îles du Vent.

THE HIDDEN ROLE OF LETTERS: SECURITY AND TRUST

The content of mercantile correspondence is of special interest because important aspects of it have been overlooked or dismissed by current historians of colonial commerce. Not surprisingly, merchants routinely discussed prices and cargo compositions at some length in their letters. As early as 1727, Jean Pellet began to send his brother Pierre a printed form that listed 120 different French goods and colonial items, including twelve different types of coarse and refined sugar.[42] The intendants of the Îles du Vent provided the same service for the secretary of state and the chief clerks of the Marine, although such lists, if they were sent with official dispatches, arrived only two to three times per year. This information helped merchants on both sides of the Atlantic to adjust outgoing cargoes to take advantage of market conditions. Debt and credit flows were equally important. Discussions of amounts owed, the timing of payments, and the results of the latest lawsuits often filled up more space than any other single item of business.[43] This mundane information formed the vital blood of commercial circulation in the Atlantic World.

Two other types of mercantile information that have not received adequate attention are ship movements and assurances, or reiterations, of trust. Yet eighteenth-century French merchants considered them so crucial that most letters contained both. Ship movements – arrivals, departures, and the correspondence carried on them – arguably addressed merchants' single greatest anxiety about the safety of cargoes, and they invariably appeared as the first item of business. Put another way, a critical role of transatlantic mercantile communications concerned the method of communication itself. On the eve of the Seven Years War, the agent of Bordeaux merchant Dufons fretted that no ships had arrived for a month, and that ships currently in port were reluctant to leave, having just learned of the capture of eleven ships out of Saint Pierre a few days earlier. However, he reported that one ship captain had decided to brave the privateers within the week. The arrival of this letter itself is the proof that this ship captain successfully completed the crossing.[44] Letters could also be used to track down the whereabouts of ships. Rochellais merchant Étienne Belin wrote to his agents in Saint Pierre, Brétonnière and Guesdon, to gather what news they could of his slave ship *La Fidèle*, bound for Saint Domingue, by questioning other slave captains who might arrive in port as to whether they had sighted the vessel.[45] Even news of anticipated ship arrivals could greatly influence short-term commercial affairs. In early 1752, trading virtually halted at Saint Pierre during its normally busy season when news reached the town that a large number of ships was expected to arrive within a few weeks from Bordeaux. Merchants limited their dealings in anticipation of the flood of goods and lower prices.[46] While the evidence here is culled from merchants in the Îles du Vent, an impressionistic look at correspondence for Canada (Havy and Lefebvre) and Louisiana (mainly Paul Rasteau) shows the consistent inclusion of the same two types of information.

War presented more formidable logistical problems and increased anxieties about ship safety. Late in the War of the Austrian Succession, a Saint Pierre *commissionaire* by the name of Aquart forwarded a detailed advisory on vessels loaded with cargoes owned by Dufons of Bordeaux. He advised Dufons of the recent safe arrival of a shipment of ship's cordage, that he would forward the bills of sale on the first available ship for Bordeaux, and finally, that he had divided three lots of coffee, and the requisite paperwork, among three different ships (including the names of the ships, their captains, and their home ports) in order to cushion any possible loss from capture. Aquart provided this information so that Dufons could arrange insurance for the cargoes in Bordeaux.[47] Another major source of shipping news during war was truce ships (*parlementaires*). Aside from supplying general news and the observations of prisoners, these ships, because of their frequent passage, allowed colonially based merchants to track their losses and adjust their business accordingly. In 1746 Aquart advised Dufons that a British truce ship carrying French prisoners from Antigua had brought news that one of Dufons's ships had been captured by a 28-gun British frigate about 120 miles from Saint Pierre, but it had unfortunately sunk because of a leak in the hull (all the crew had been rescued).[48] While the news was bad, it undoubtedly allowed Dufons time to adjust his shipping operations or even curtail activities, as he apparently chose to do.

Through regular contact, colonial merchants were able to earn the crucial capital that made French business run: mutual trust and a good reputation, which contemporaries termed *avoir de crédit*.[49] Regular contact allowed Saint Pierre's *commissionnaires* to explain and defend their conduct whenever breaches were suspected. One *commissionnaire*, mortified by accusations of financial misconduct, wrote his to Bordeaux employer, "The Confidence which you have yourself entrusted in me should calm my fears and place me beyond reproach, being persuaded that I will never abuse it."[50] At the same time, the circulation of news increased the awareness of dealings on both sides of the Atlantic. When Jean Pellet discovered from other Bordeaux merchants that his brother in Saint Pierre had explored the possibility of forming a partnership with a Marseillais merchant, he bitterly accused him of duplicity. In turn, Pierre scolded Jean that "you must not be scandalized if I receive certain letters from France and which I choose not to relate to you ... it must suffice for you to know that I have refused them."[51] With the air cleared, the brothers continued their partnership (in association with a local *commissionnaire*) for another decade. The reliance on regular correspondence effectively extended the mental world of the French ports, expanding the geographic domain in which trust could germinate and flower. Considered together, ship movements and assurances of trust established the basic framework within which overseas merchants could effectively operate. Merchants constantly needed to verify ship safety and itineraries in order to take advantage of market opportunities and absorb losses, and in a world of extended credit, they had to negotiate with others with the confidence that their own resources were secure. Through such items, they adjusted their mental construct of acceptable speeds of communication to match wind, current, and the fortunes of conflict, and judged character on consistent and reliable correspondence.

TRANSATLANTIC SHIPPING

Correspondence by itself represented at best only half the mercantile communications system. Letters required ships, and close contact by letter could be only as good as shipping connections allowed. The Marine varied little in its shipping operations, sending one ship to each colony and usually two to the Îles du Vent and Saint Domingue in peacetime. However, the patterns of mercantile shipping differed enormously between the French American colonies. Quebec's have been the object of several good studies,[52] while Louisbourg and New Orleans have received some attention. Shipping operations to the ports of the Îles du Vent, including Saint Pierre, Fort Royal, Trinité, Basse-terre, and Le François, have not been studied at all. Yet Canada's shipping patterns were in many ways the exception. The volume and rhythm of contact provide an idea of the reliability and steadiness of contact that merchant shipping provided even for the most anemic port, New Orleans. We are handicapped in ascertaining ship movements, since they rely entirely on those prepared by the king's Domaine and port captain or pilot. While these summaries (*états*) appear for the most part to be reliable for Canada, they are haphazard for many other colonies, such as Louisiana, and were certainly inaccurately reported, if not falsified outright, by officials and clerks in the Îles du Vent. However, if we accept patterns, rather than exact numbers, we can at least garner some idea of the relative availability of contact at different chronological periods for each colony.

The trends in Canada's seaborne traffic are well known and can be reviewed briefly here. Virtually all transatlantic ships called at Quebec, a fact that aided in the keeping of records. Quebec had four distinct periods of metropolitan contact in the eighteenth century: a short era of neglect during the War of the Spanish Succession; an era of stable if minimal, arrivals largely from La Rochelle until the early 1730s; the replacement of La Rochelle by Bordeaux after 1742, with a slightly higher number of shipping arrivals and departures, and the emergence of Louisbourg as New France's main contact; and a final period characterized by an influx of military-related shipping from 1752 to 1758, mainly from Bordeaux and Rochefort[53] (see table 6.1). Although the large French military buildup in Canada prior to the Seven Years War has been attributed to strictly military and strategic factors, it is never-

Table 6.1
Ship arrivals in Canada, 1700–1758

Year	*La Rochelle*	*Bordeaux*	*Marseille*	*Other French*[1]	*Louisbourg*	*Martinique*	*Total*
1715	5	1		1		1	8
1720	3	1		1		2	7
1725	4	4	2	2	12	2	26
1730	5	2	-	1	31	16[2]	39[2]
1735	4	1	2	2	22	2	34
1740	3	6	-	6	17	6[2]	32[2]
1745	3	6	1	-		-	10
1750	11	12	-	-		-	23
1755	8	32	2	3		-	45
1758	7	38	2	9		-	56

SOURCES: For columns 1–5 from Pritchard, "Ships, Men, and Commerce," 489–96, tables 2–10, and from Pritchard, "Pattern of French Colonial Shipping to Canada before 1760," tables 2, 4, 5. For Martinique, from Mathieu, *Commerce Entre nouvelle-France et les Antilles*, table on 226–7. Lowest figures are used, except for 1755 and 1758.

[1] Comprising Saint Malo, Rouen/Le Havre, and Nantes.
[2] = estimate.

theless striking that the increased traffic from Bordeaux, and the consequently larger attention that Canada received from its merchants, preceded the strategic re-evaluation of Canada by the Marine.

However, metropolitan contact tells only a part of the story. From the early 1720s, Quebec also began to receive a trickle of ships from the West Indies. By 1730, their numbers compared favourably with French arrivals. The War of the Austrian Succession halted such movements; although shipping subsequently resumed, it was erratic in the 1748–55 period.[54] More importantly, the 1724–43 period witnessed a leap in ship traffic to and from Louisbourg. As we saw in chapter 3, this port also served as a magnet for New England's fishermen and smugglers and for returning West Indian ships.[55] For a period of approximately fifteen years (c. 1728–43) and again briefly from 1750 to 1756, Quebec truly became a cosmopolitan colonial port through Louisbourg, immersed in both the regional and the wider Atlantic trading worlds.

One indication of how this link helped expand Quebec's potential news sources is provided by a rare document listing the arrival of vessels at the beginning of the port's navigation season in 1743. After the opening of the harbour in the first days of May, a total of nineteen ships dropped anchor in the next seven weeks, including eleven from

France (nine from Bordeaux alone), a schooner from Labrador, another from the northern St Lawrence shore, two ships from Saint Pierre (Martinique), one from Saint Domingue, and two from Louisbourg, both of which carried West Indian products. One of the French ships originated in Saint Malo but carried New England flour freighted by Intendant François Bigot in Île Royale at the request of Intendant Hocquart to avert famine in Canada.[56] In a little more than month, Quebec could therefore potentially learn of events from Saint Domingue, the eastern Caribbean, New England, the northern reaches of Canada, southwestern France, and Normandy, and of course, about any major developments in court. Merchant shipping to Quebec provided a wide variety of news long before the royal ship carrying dispatches from France brought the latest news and confirmed what the colony already knew. What is unique about Quebec's shipping patterns is what is missing. It was the only French colonial port not to have direct regular seaborne smuggling contacts. Its merchants and seafaring population were overwhelmingly French or Canadian, creating a marginally less cosmopolitan atmosphere than even smaller French fishing ports.[57] Contacts centred squarely on French merchants and remained dependent on state shipping contracts. Not surprisingly, such contacts cemented strong ties to metropolitan society (in comparison, for example, to Montreal) and weakened the access of Canadian merchants with fewer ties to credit sources. Shipping patterns ensured that Quebec's merchants lived in a transplanted corner of the Ponant.

From the viewpoint of seaborne contact, Louisiana and the Îles du Vent exemplified commercial environments more representative of Atlantic trade than that found in Quebec. The greatest era of metropolitan contact for New Orleans, parallel to Quebec's experience in the 1750s, endured no longer than the last years of the Regency (1720–23). French merchants rarely ventured up the Mississippi until the 1750s.[58] Contacts with Saint Domingue, as we have seen, assumed a far larger role during this same period (see table 6.2). The expanded world of merchant contacts was based on a growing trade of construction and food supplies with Saint Domingue and the Îles du Vent, on a smaller scale, and with Spanish Havana. The re-export of French manufactured goods and luxuries to Havana after 1748 substantially broadened the town's economic base, and therefore its communications network, despite Spanish officials' view that New Orleans existed merely as a haven for smugglers.[59] During the Seven Years War, when British privateers cut contact with France after 1755, regional mercantile connections provided the only source of news on European events. For example, when a small vessel from Le Cap brought the news that Commissary Rochemore's arch rival, Governor Kerlérec,

Table 6.2
Arrival of legitimate shipping in Louisiana, 1715–1764

Year	*L'Orient*	*La Rochelle*	*King's*	*Bordeaux*	*FWI*	*Other*	*Total*
1715[1,2]	2						(2)
1720[1]	21		8				(29)
1725[1]	7						(7)
1730[1]	6						(6)
1735		5	4	3		1	13
1740		4	3	0	5	4	16
1745		3	2	3	(10)		17
1750		2	1	2	(10)	4	22
1755		5	2	2	(10)		19
1764		3	1	1	4	9	21

SOURCE: Clark, *New Orleans, 1718–1812*, tables 1 (37) and 3 (83); also 38–9, 71–3, 82–4.

KEY: L'Orient = Compagnie des Indes port in Brittany; King's = king's ships, most of which were probably loaded at La Rochelle before 1739 and in Bordeaux thereafter; FWI = French West Indies (mainly Saint Domingue); Other would include vessels from other French ports and Spanish-American ships; ( ) = estimates.

[1] Ships arriving in 1715 would have anchored at Île Dauphin, and those in 1720 would have anchored both there and at Île aux Vaisseaux off Biloxi. By 1730, virtually all ocean-going ships anchored at New Orleans.
[2] Departures from destinations other than France not recorded.

was about to be recalled, Rochemore's attitude toward the governor became noticeably more bellicose, allowing him to make accusations of graft under Kerlérec.[60] In competition with these largely European and mercantile-dominated communications network there arose a land-based and Native-dominated communications system. As Daniel Usner has shown, New Orleans emerged as the centre of a far-flung frontier exchange economy through its outlying posts along the Mississippi, Mobile, and Red River systems.[61] Contacts reached west to Los Adages in Spanish Texas[62], north to the Illinois posts and from there to the Great Lakes, and as far east as British Charleston. Nevertheless, neither sea or land was reliable: slow development hindered the former, and nearly continual Native-European or inter-tribal warfare the latter.

As the commercial entrepôt for the entire Îles du Vent, Saint Pierre's connections were necessarily seaborne. Unlike that of either Quebec or New Orleans, the dimensions of its trade have not been analyzed, even though the scent of sugar attracted merchant ships like honeybees to a

Table 6.3
Arrival of legitimate shipping at Martinique, 1715–1765

Year	*France*	*Afr.*	*SpM*	*NF/IR*	*StD*	*Lou.*	*StE*	*Cur.*	*DWI*	*Other*	*Total*
1715	59			1							60
1733	147	4	26	18	2					1	198
1737	153	9	32	0							194
1745	76	7	6	12			13	18	3	9	144
1752	165	0	32	72	1	4					274
1758	2	0	0	1		0	89	1	0	1	94
1765	153	6	96	-	1	12		100		109	476

SOURCES: 1715 (January–June 1715 only): AC, C8A, 20, Record of merchant ships trading in Martinique, June 10, 1715; 1733: ibid., C8B 17, Record of ship arrivals, nos. 12–28, May 15, 1734; 1737: ibid., Record of ships for 1737, nos. 45–51, June 20, 1738; 1745: ibid., 21, Records of commerce for 1745, nos. 17–34, August 12, 1746 [another 7 came from Holland, 1 from Ireland (Cork), and 1 from Bermuda, all to exchange prisoners]; 1752: ibid., Records of commerce for 1752, nos. 61–72, October 25, 1753; 1758: ibid., 22, [Monthly] Records of commerce for 1758, nos. 11–27 [for eight months only; one ship from Demerara]; 1765: ibid., 21, General record of commerce in Martinique for 1765, no. 75, March 30, 1773. The category of "Other" included 92 ships from the British colonies and 17 from Cayenne.

KEY: Afr. = African slave ships; SpM = Spanish Main (Venezuela and Cumana); NF/IR = New France/Île Royale; StD = Saint Domingue; Lou. = Louisiana; StE = Dutch Saint Eustatius; Cur. = Dutch Curaçao; DWI = Danish West Indies (Saint Thomas, Sainte Croix); Other = mainly Rhode Island, New York, Bermuda, Barbados.

hot summer meadow. While ships from all over France dropped anchor, those from the ports of Nantes, Bordeaux, and later Marseille dominated. This variety of traffic offered merchants a wide range of potential news sources and carriers from all corners of the kingdom. Even more impressive is the volume of shipping reaching Saint Pierre. As early as 1715, sixty ships came from France in the first six months, in comparison with seven for Quebec and four for New Orleans for the entire year.[63] Jean Cavignac estimated that up to eighty ships visited Saint Pierre annually in the 1720s, and at least double that number by 1740. The trade statistics for this period bear him out[64] (see tables 6.3 and 6.4). The diverse ports of origin and high volume combined to offer Saint Pierre's merchants a stable, year-round choice of ships on which to send their correspondence.

Saint Pierre's trade connections extended even further. The northwest-southeast axis of shipping routes described in chapter 3 invited ships from all parts of the eastern Caribbean and the North American Atlantic seaboard. There was no dearth of reports by exasperated offi-

Table 6.4
Departure of legitimate shipping from Martinique, 1733–1765

Year	*France*	*Afr.*	*Cd'E*	*NF/IR*	*StD*	*Lou.*	*StE*	*Cur.*	*DWI*	*Other*	*Total*
1733	148		29	18	31					6	232
1736	146		44	13							203
1745	98		19	9		2	13	18	3	9	171
1752	167		37	45		1				2	250
1760							46	9		10	65
1765	133		31	-	28	9		90		109	400

SOURCES: 1736: AC, C8B 17, Record of ships departing in 1736, nos. 38–44, June 15, 1737; 1760: (for Saint Pierre only) ibid., C8B 22, Record of commerce for 1760, nos. 36–9, April 17 and December 10, 1760. For other years, see table 6.3.

KEY: Afr. = African slave ships; Cd'E = Côte d'Espagne [Spanish Main] (Venezuela and New Granada); NF/IR = New France/Île Royale; StD = Saint Domingue; Lou. = Louisiana; StE = Dutch Saint Eustatius; Cur. = Dutch Curaçao; DWI = Danish West Indies (Saint Thomas, Sainte Croix).

cials on the colonists' predilection for dealing in smuggled goods and slaves. In 1714 Intendant Vaucresson reported that his rigid measures to prevent smuggling had merely forced daytime landing into a night-time activity in Saint Pierre. The captain of a royal ship reported in 1730 that while every beach on Martinique was the scene of clandestine trade, Saint Pierre remained the centre of trade, an accusation echoed by Neuville, the director of the Domaine in Saint Pierre, nine years later.[65] As Governor General Caylus's letters show, illegal contacts proved too tempting for many, if not most, French officials. The problem appears to have been especially acute on Martinique, in large measure because of the volume and bustle of shipping, which in turn hindered detection. But the most famous case probably concerned Father Antoine Lavalette, *procureur* for the Jesuit mission in Saint Pierre and later its superior. The spectacular bankruptcy of his illegitimate shipping operations triggered the investigation into the French Jesuits and led to their banishment from France in 1762.[66] From about 1756 onwards, Lavalette had shipped sugar and coffee to Dutch Saint Eustatius using the same agent as Caylus used, Teminck, and working through Saint Pierre *commissionaires* Rachon and Cartier. From there the cargoes went either to Amsterdam or to Cadiz, to be re-exported by his agents Lioncy and Gouffre in Marseille.

Before 1744, Martinique boasted a greater range of contacts than any French colony, Saint Domingue included. These contacts can be traced largely through the trade goods reaching or leaving the Îles du

Vent. Since the Dutch grew a minuscule amount of tropical produce on their Caribbean islands for export, we know that most of the sugar, coffee, indigo, and cotton they exported came from either the British or the French islands. Saint Eustatius, a mere "rock" in the arc of the Lesser Antilles, grew in the late seventeenth century as a favoured exchange site, as did Curaçao even earlier for trade to the Spanish Main. Wim Klooster's work on the Dutch entrepôts in the seventeenth and eighteenth centuries has shown that the Îles du Vent sent 39 per cent of all Curaçao's sugar exports in the late 1720s. War increased this traffic further, and its planters shipped between 9 and 16 per cent by value of all Curaçao's coffee exports during the War of the Austrian Succession. Saint Eustatius absorbed a large but unspecified amount of sugar and coffee from the French Windward Islands, and this value also probably jumped during war years.[67] French authorities confirmed the Dutch trade connection. In 1747 Intendant Ranché reported that some forty Dutch vessels alone had anchored at the island in the first five months of the year, and this number, if anything, was probably too low.[68] During the Seven Years War, trade with Saint Eustatius kept Martinique's economy alive after 1758, when contact with France had virtually ceased. According to official records for the eight months reported in 1758, two ships arrived from France, and eighty-nine either left for or arrived from Saint Eustatius (the *état* grouped arrivals and departures together).[69]

While officially encouraged, direct trade with Spanish American ports on the Venezuelan coast for tobacco, leather goods and mules for the island's sugar mills sputtered during the first half of the eighteenth century.[70] British and Anglo-American traders nabbed the major share of trade and supplied Martinique's planters with construction supplies, food, horses, tools, and, above all, slaves. Prior to 1718, relations between Saint Pierre and Antigua merchants had been close enough for merchants to journey back and forth to collect debts or repossess ships taken by runaway slaves.[71] Although the number of smugglers is impossible to determine, the size of the English traffic is suggested by shipping statistics of 1765, when restrictions were temporarily lifted. Of all the *états* of the period, this single one is probably the most accurate, since an entire corps of new officials had replaced the disgraced group of wartime, and the new officials had much to gain by showing the negligence of their predecessors. The Duc de Choiseul, in part on advice from his new Martinique-born chief clerk, was also anxious to accurately gauge the extent of foreign commerce in order to create a new free port system (see tables 6.3 and 6.4). The results from the survey of 1765 are therefore highly informative. Of the 109 ships listed as "other," a total of 92 sailed from New York, Rhode Island, Barbados, or Bermuda.

Part of the difficulty in determining the extent of smuggling is the exact role played by the "neutral Islands" of Dominica and Saint Lucia. In 1730 Lieutenant Rossel reported that up to fifteen or twenty English ships could be found at any one time at the "Carénage" of Saint Lucia (Castries) trading with creole ships.[72] These traders exchanged not only food, dry goods, and slaves, but undoubtedly news and rumours as well.[73] While many of these ships plied the eastern Caribbean, some ventured as far as the Portuguese Cape Verde Islands.[74] The largest number of illicit traders may indeed have come from the Îles du Vent. In 1751, colonial officials reported that more than two hundred vessels based largely in Saint Pierre sailed in the inter-island trade. For this reason, Governor General Bompar and Intendant Hurson objected to a new ordinance that stipulated where these small ships could land. Not only would it prove impossible to enforce, they argued, but if successfully applied, the regulations would strangle the colony's economy by choking off the clandestine trade in construction supplies, food, and slaves.[75] Smuggling undoubtedly supplied news that lay beyond the control of the Marine in the colonies or the state in France. This illegal trade provided the material foundations upon which colonists both in the Îles du Vent and on Saint Domingue could develop a more independent and critical view of colonial administrations. As we will see in chapter 7, the state linked smuggling, weak loyalty, and the quick surrender of Martinique together in the aftermath of defeat in 1762.

PRIVATE CONTACTS AND PUBLIC USES

The Marine availed itself of the great web of mercantile ship movements to keep informed of colonial events. Many examples are scattered throughout the official correspondence. Secretary of State for the Marine Maurepas first learned of *commissaire-ordonnateur* François Clairambault d'Aigremont's death in Montreal from La Rochelle merchant Antoine Pascaud in June 1729, several months before the king's ship officially brought the news.[76] Natural disasters might spread the net farther and bring traditional enemies together to exchange news in order to help. For example, Canadian authorities determined that *Le St. Jérôme* of Quebec had been wrecked on Sable Island in 1714 by piecing together reports obtained from New England fishing boats that had forwarded the information to Île Royale's governor.[77] In the Îles du Vent, a ship freighted with supplies to rebuild Saint Pierre after the 1738 fire first brought news of the disastrous hurricane that levelled much of Guadeloupe in September of the same year. Grateful officials went so far as to reward the captain, who had cut short loading to bring news of the disaster, 100 livres on the king's account.[78] Even smugglers were accepted as legitimate information providers. The news of the death of Louis XIV in September 1715 reached Cayenne in January 1716 from a Boston ship trading horses for sugar. The governor believed the news trustworthy, although he prudently asked for confirmation from the Marine. Of course, the Boston ship did not inform him that the secretary of state to whom he wrote the letter, Jérôme de Pontchartrain, had already been dismissed from office.[79]

Merchants were especially valuable to colonial officials during wartime. The French policy of using small and lightly armed escorts to convoy merchant ships helped keep the colonies current with information in the first years of war in 1744–45 and 1756–58.[80] Of course, the military buildup in Canada during the first three years of the Seven Years War led to the closest, most consistent contact with France ever, when some twenty-nine naval ships were sent to Quebec.[81] However, Louisiana lived throughout the Seven Years War awash in rumours. Cut off by Jamaican privateers, the colony was severed from court news for more than two and a half years at the beginning of the war. In 1757 Governor Kerlérec had been without news from court since the last letter dated July 15, 1755; royal ships only reached the colony again with a few official dispatches in September 1758. In the meantime, he complained bitterly that 160 of his own letters, sent by various means since hostilities had begun, remained unanswered.[82] Regional contacts provided news, and any news magnified colonist's sense of vulnerability. In July 1762, when a small French privateer brought news of the British siege of Havana, Kerlérec prepared New Orleans for an attack believed to be only weeks away.[83]

The enemy might also provide important information, albeit in a roundabout fashion. For example, in August 1747 a Quebec ship entered Boston harbour to exchange prisoners; among its return cargo were recent issues of Boston newspapers, whose contents were carefully perused by Governor La Galissonière and reported back to France.[84] We can only speculate on whether reports from Guadeloupe during its sudden rise to sugar-producing wealth after the British conquest of 1759 dampened the will of Martinique's planters to resist enemy forces in January of 1762.[85] As a result of Martinique's unique position as a crossroads, news sometimes reached the Îles du Vent by the most bizarre routes. In 1742 a Nantes slave-ship captain recently arrived from Barbados brought news of British warship movements to Governor General Champigny. Champigny discovered that the captain had reached the British island after escaping in a skiff, alone, from a slave revolt on board his ship in the Bight of Benin off the West African coast, working his way first to Portuguese São Tomé, from there presumably north to the Portuguese Azores, and then taking passage on an English ship, which eventually landed in Barbados. It is not clear how he reached Martinique from Barbados, but Champigny trusted him enough to deduce (erroneously) that Great Britain had just declared war against France, and he ordered defensive preparations.[86] Considered together, this collection of examples during peace and war captures the vast number and haphazard origins of opportunities available to officials who tapped into merchant-supplied news.

Recognizing the value of merchant vessels as carriers of dispatches and providers of colonial news, the Marine tried to systematize the sending and receiving of transatlantic information by issuing periodic orders for updates on port arrivals and departures. In 1712 Secretary of State for the Marine Jérôme de Pontchartrain complained to Intendant François Beauharnais at Rochefort that he was unable to send dispatches as often as he wished to the colonies, for he had no idea when merchant ships departed. Henceforward, monthly reports were to be submitted which listed the names, destinations, complement, and home ports of all ships ready to sail in a month's time.[87] The Marine issued a similar directive to Nantes shippers in 1726.[88] When war threatened in the early 1740s, Maurepas distributed a circular letter announcing new regulations for the reception of colonial dispatches, noting that too many had been lost by merchant ship captains. He ordered what amounted to the creation of a rudimentary postal system, where the commissaries of the Marine in French and colonial ports would keep records of every packet sent and received and issue receipts to the captains responsible. These were to be gathered together and shipped back to the Bureau of Colonies every three months in France, every six months from the Antilles and Louisiana, and every year from Canada.[89] The plan does not seem to have been implemented. It is doubtful that such a labour-intensive scheme would have found favour with overburdened port intendants and their clerks. Such examples illustrate the circuitous routes that information often took to reach colonial officials, and they help explain officials' desire to tap all possible sources. In the gathering of such information, the hierarchical reporting structure of absolutism vanished, replaced by a kind of meritocracy of information suppliers. And as colonial leaders could only be acutely aware, its effectiveness depended on mercantile contacts, whether state-sanctioned or not.

THE PRESSURE PRINCIPLE

Merchants made the short but significant leap from news suppliers to policy advisers quickly, and from advisers to critics even faster. There existed several mechanisms that colonial *négociants* and metropolitan merchants and captains could use to make their opinions known to the state. Merchants with strong metropolitan connections used captains to carry complaints about colonial leaders, about regulations, or about other merchants back to the chambers of commerce in French ports. These reports were used as a basis for propaganda pieces that circulated among chambers of commerce and leading merchants.[90] When these complaints concerned colonial officials, and they often did, the *premier commis* sorted through the maze of accusations and countercharges brought forward by both sides to present an abstract to the secretary of state to decide. Individual or small groups of merchants and shopkeepers also had the ear of the colonial intendant, and the intendant's letters to the Marine regularly touched upon complaints and concerns expressed by merchants.

Collective action by merchant assemblies also provided a formal means to voice concerns. Canada officially banned all assemblies as early as 1677, but allowed irregular meetings of a merchants' syndic in Quebec to continue.[91] As trade increased after 1713 and the merchant community grew, the need for concerted action became more evident. However, the establishment of formal syndics in Quebec and Montreal in 1717 represented the vestige of past power, rather than a mark of an emerging representative institution. These two syndics addressed their grievances to the governor and the intendant in fawning deferential language that contrasts clearly with the polite but firm rhetoric of the French chambers of commerce. Nonetheless, collective meetings by merchants led at times to direct influence on state policy. A presentation by the syndic of Quebec merchants in late 1744 demonstrates the vast information base that merchants could draw upon to offer informed advice to the state. Worried over the safety of their ships after predations by New England corsairs during the summer shipping season of 1744, the Quebec syndic compiled reports from three different Saint Malo fishermen (made, presumably, first in Louisbourg), a Quebec schooner from Quirpon on the Petit-Nord fishing coast, local ships from Louisbourg, missionaries at Saint Augustin on Baie Phélypeaux, and several Saint Malo fishermen who had escaped from a Guernsey-based privateer to outline the patterns of corsair sailings. After citing several problems with the last convoy, the merchants then proposed their own convoy system, naming the four Saint Malo captains they wished to see appointed to direct it. Secretary of State Maurepas acknowledged the presentation but made no formal answer. Nevertheless, he organized a convoy the following year which followed the general outline of the syndic's plan.[92]

In another incident after the war, Governor General Jacques-Pierre de La Jonquière could not comprehend why complaints over fur-post licences were not made to him directly, since his audiences were public and he listened to "all the people from all the Estates together."[93] The subtle infusion of republican behaviour is suggested by the fact that the governor general of New France willingly treated all three social orders together (*indistinctement*) as a kind of collective. Whether or not internal divisions separated the mercantile community, its members could act in unison to criticize officials when their larger interests required it. By controlling their own means of transport, merchants in all three colonies exerted their influence by circulating "general complaints" over officials' conduct. This subtle shift from merchants acting as a corporate body to express collective grievances within established channels to merchants advising the state when they (merchants) saw fit to do so is contemporary with the kind of critical public that Jurgen Habermas ascribed to the metropolitan bourgeoisie engaged in aesthetic criticism as a prelude to political criticism. However, it would seem that, under the pressures of long-distance trade and war and with the self-interested help of at least some colonial leaders, merchants made the leap faster.

The merchants of Nantes were especially critical in the 1720s of their treatment by colonial officials in the Îles du Vent. In 1726 the city's merchants sent one of their members to seek a royal audience on the dangerous conduct of the Superior Council of Martinique. This body had inexplicably (in their view) freed several English ships caught smuggling at Saint Lucia and taken to Saint Pierre as prizes.[94] Later, in 1730, Governor Champigny and Intendant Jacques Pannier d'Orgeville defended permissions granted to ships from Barbados and New England to import slaves and food, noting that the Compagnie des Indes ships had abandoned their responsibilities. If they thought that Saint Pierre's metropolitan merchants would be thankful, they were sorely disappointed, for they noted that "in the place of thanks, [Maurepas has] received only complaints." They singled out the "false reports" of another Nantes merchant, de Launay-Montaudoüin, whom they tried to discredit by accusing him of engaging in smuggling. Champigny and d'Orgeville finished their letter by calling for captains who started such rumours to be punished for damaging commerce and not bringing their accusations to the colonial authorities designated to handle the problem in the first place.[95]

In order to stem further criticism, the two leaders held a meeting of all bourgeois in the port, including French ship captains, resident metropolitan merchants, and *commissionaires*, asking them to freely offer their own observations on the problems of smuggling.[96] The meeting may have been called to smother the voices of Nantes merchants, who stood most to lose from the smuggling of slaves from the British islands. Champigny and d'Orgeville reported that the merchants had little to say, in any case, suspecting that most were too heavily involved in smuggling to speak. Although the Îles du Vent's merchants and planters established the most ambitious and best organized scheme by creating a combined colonial chamber of commerce and agriculture, the representation on it by merchants was in fact limited (see chapter 7). The association pressured the Marine successfully into allowing neutral traders to supply slaves. Not surprisingly, the French chambers of commerce viewed the upstart with alarm.[97] Whether or not the leaders' motives were honest, the fact that they felt compelled to defend their actions publicly attests to the strength of commercial interests in colonial issues. Colonial-based merchants also became critics in Louisiana, although much later. In New Orleans, Governor Étienne Périer urged the Compagnie des Indes to allow the port's merchants to organize their own syndic, since "tumultuous" ad hoc assemblies of the people were the only alternative.[98] The town's merchants still engaged in collective action more than thirty years later, taking Governor Kerlérec's side in his disputes with Intendant Rochemore by demanding the immediate recall of the colony's *commissaire*.[99]

The diverse range of mercantile contacts in French America presented a considerable challenge to state control. The problem is easier to understand if we take seriously officials' unease, in the examples cited above, over the ability of merchants to circumvent traditional channels of information provision and advice. Smuggling, for example, did not only mean lost revenue and vociferous complaints from French merchants, but represented unrestricted circulation, which struck at the heart of the French state's role as final arbitrator of communal (and often competing) interests. The state attempted to assert control over commercial contacts in two distinct ways. First, it simply limited the contact that merchants could have either between themselves or with others. These efforts, mostly in the form of various edicts on commerce, have received the most attention by historians. Secondly, the state increased its collection of data about, and records of, mercantile movements in order to restrict unapproved transactions. These efforts mainly introduced some type of permit system.

SETTING BOUNDARIES

From 1713 to the de facto acceptance of free trade by neutral merchants in 1756, there is a subtle, yet unmistakable trend by the state toward loosening restrictions on commercial exchange in general and shipping to the French Antilles in particular.[100] After a period of some confusion between the end of war in 1713 and the acceleration of the sugar exports from the French Windward Islands in the mid 1720s,[101] a definitive statement on state policies appeared in the form of the letters patent of October 1727, which remained the basic document governing colonial commerce until the end of the Seven Years War.[102] These regulations expanded commerce and commercial communications by guaranteeing the right of fifteen French ports to engage in overseas commerce, by removing limitations on ports of origin, including Spanish ports in the circuits of French shipping, and by, for the first time, allowing direct trade between Ireland and the Antilles. Also for the first time, French and foreign smugglers were identified as enemies of French commerce, and several articles concerned the capture and prosecution of smugglers. As Bernard Vonglis has pointed out, the regulations were aimed primarily at reinforcing metropolitan control over sugar production. However, lost in many assessments is the significant emphasis on freer trade *within* France by extending trade privileges to more French ports. In essence, the 1727 edict guaranteed freer metropolitan commerce in order to circumscribe colonial clandestine trade.

However, the new rules did not altogether lessen contact. Despite the crusade against smuggling, they allowed a most important loophole to what would otherwise appear to be draconian measures. Foreign ships damaged by storms or needing water were allowed to dock in thirteen major French Antilles ports that kept king's garrisons, including Fort Royal, Saint Pierre, La Trinité, and Basse-terre, for a limited period of time. While cash was preferred for the funding of repairs or to obtain supplies, foreign captains were allowed to land part of their cargoes to pay for labour, parts, and food, so long as they obtained permission from local authorities.[103] Foreign merchants, especially English captains from Barbados and Antigua, swiftly took advantage of the loophole. Storms suddenly increased markedly in the eastern Caribbean, at least on paper, and "hurricaned" English ships dropped anchor in many towns throughout Martinique and Guadeloupe, even outside the normal limits of the hurricane season.[104] Colonial officials carefully submitted the appropriate paperwork, but they could not disguise their complicity from metropolitan merchants, who protested vehemently to Maurepas.[105] A further unknotting of restrictions followed the 1727 rules, allowing salt beef from Ireland from 1728 (which permitted the import of some English goods), trade with Cadiz in 1737 and with the Portuguese Cape Verde Islands in 1740, and butter and cheese from Denmark (which effectively legalized trade with Danish Saint Thomas) in 1741.[106] The advent of nearly twenty years of war and brittle peace, beginning in 1744, demolished any pretence on the part of authorities to regulating colonial trade. Despite widespread opposition from merchants in the French ports, neutral ships from Holland and Denmark were allowed free trade in 1756. French chambers protested that this freedom would only act as a "subtle poison [which] will creep into the hearts of our fellow citizens, only to bring discouragement, consternation, and despair."[107] With this move, the secretary of state simply "approved" what the French Navy could neither halt nor hinder on the eve of war. The subsequent reorganization of the French colonies following the Treaty of Paris in 1763 included legitimizing a large number of free ports in the French Caribbean. Not surprisingly, these ports were all well-established smugglers' harbours, such as the Cul-de-Sac (Castries) on Saint Lucia, Point-à-Pitre on Guadeloupe, and Môle Saint Nicholas on northern Saint Domingue.

The second method the state used to control mercantile commercial contact relied upon increased efficiency in record-keeping. Since patrols by land and sea were expensive, and only marginally effective when used, the Marine simply employed more clerks and customs officials to track a greater number of records. This approach also had the distinct benefit of increasing the number of entry-level colonial patronage positions. The certificates issued to slave ships calling at in the French Caribbean ports provides a good example of how authorities tried to make the system work and how merchants evaded it. In 1716 the Marine issued an ordinance that essentially disbanded the slave trade monopoly but also firmly subordinated the slave trade to metropolitan control. The system demanded that certificates for the value of the slaves landed be filled out in order to claim a lower duty on the colonial products purchased from the sale of slaves. The Law fiasco interrupted smooth operation of the new laws until they were applied in earnest starting in 1724. By 1731 the director of the *fermes* at Nantes began to reject the certificates because they were not properly signed by the intendants on Saint Domingue and Martinique; instead, their clerks had been forging the intendant's signature, which the director detected.[108] In addition, and rather incredibly, the regulations did not require the recording of the numbers of slaves landed, only the amount of merchandise traded for them. This oversight made it impossible to ascertain the claims made by ship captains.[109] In 1734 the Marine issued a new ordinance, which outlined how the forms should be filled out by captains.[110] Clerks were to make at least three copies of each document, one to be kept by the intendant, one by the captain, and the last deposited with the *ferme*'s office in the French port of origin. Officials constructed the process so that authorities could track any given ship's cargo on either side of the Atlantic by comparing copies from one office with those deposited in the other. The system was simple but, given that ships' invoices often covered between five to twenty full pages, highly labour-intensive.

In practice, slavers used a variety of simple means to circumvent the reporting. A scandal erupted on Martinique in 1741 when the Marine discovered that clerks in Intendant de Lacroix's office at Saint Pierre had issued false trade certificates for Saint Domingue.[111] In other cases, captains sought to avoid paperwork entirely. Slave ship captains hid illegal trade by making it appear that all goods and produce loaded had originated from the sale of slaves, whether they had or not. Since such goods were charged only half the regular customs according to the 1716 regulations, captains could pocket substantial sums on each voyage. In another practice, slave ship captains would sell a part of their human cargo clandestinely in Saint Pierre, load more slaves at Saint Thomas or Saint Eustatius up to the number just sold, and arrive at Saint Domingue with the numbers complete and their papers in legal order.[112] Recognizing the abuses, the *fermes générales* issued new regulations and new forms in 1742. Only the intendant's clerks were allowed to write on the required papers, and the forms were designed so that individual slave sales corresponded directly to an equivalent amount in produce or merchandise.[113] The slave traders of Nantes protested immediately, calling the quest for more detailed information "ridiculous" and adding indignantly, "It is with this measure that the *fermier* has begun to usurp the scruples of his Majesty."[114] The next set of regulations dropped the extraneous records, and this time it was printed in order to better police the authorization process; for the first time, the Nantes Chamber of Commerce approved.[115] Nevertheless with their strong regional connections, merchants in the French Caribbean continued smuggling slaves into the 1760s. As noted in chapter 5, ship captains carrying indentured servants also falsified their records in order to escape what they considered an additional tax. The point here is that Marine officials believed that more careful documentation could diminish the use (and cost) of force, such as the employment of customs cruisers, to limit smuggling.

COMMUNICATIONS ENTREPRENEURS: PRINTING, POST, AND PACKET

The Marine arguably pursued a third way of controlling mercantile activity, this one quite different from the first two. The state consistently supported the creation of ventures aimed at communications, so long as they were heavily regulated and supervised. In effect, it offered to form partnerships with individuals, who would enjoy state protection of their privileges, a form of chartering monopolies similar to the initial trading companies of the seventeenth century. The weak attempts to introduce printing and postal services in all three colonies provide good examples of how this process worked. Printing has perhaps the most curious history, and the slow French advance of printing requires some explanation. After all, British and Spanish colonies had freely imported such technology into their colonies, even if they used it in different ways. In New France, printing operations did not ever develop. Only late in the French regime did Governor La Galissonière and Intendant Bigot in Canada briefly consider introducing a press (1749). The former imagined the advantages of reproducing official documents, the latter the tighter control over card money. The Marine rejected financing either proposal, but would consider any should a printer apply for a licence.[116] However, a printer did build a print shop at the very end of Louisiana's French administration. Denis Braud, a merchant of New Orleans, had sought a licence as a bookseller for some time before purchasing a press and importing type from France in the spring of 1764. Ironically, the first printed broadside issued from his press announced the cession of the colony to Spain in the summer of 1764.[117] In either case, merchants held the initiative.

Only in the Îles du Vent and Saint Domingue did printers operate prior to 1763. In 1726, colonial authorities awarded a monopoly to one Devaux, who established himself in Fort Royal as a colonial printer and bookseller. The Marine clearly worried over the possibility that he might print unmonitored material, and it ordered colonial leaders to "supervise [the operation] with very close attention."[118] Within a few years, Devaux received a warrant (*brevet d'imprimeur*) to publish royal ordinances and colonial factums and to import and sell any books approved by the intendant.[119] Part of the reason for the quick procurement of the licence may have been a warning by Champigny and d'Orgeville that merchants received a continuous flow of all types of unapproved books and "public news" from undisclosed sources. The licence changed hands over the next thirty years, passing to Joachim Boy, then to Henri Sinson de Beaulieu from 1742, and finally to Pierre Richard in Saint Pierre by 1750, but the business never grew beyond the modest production of officially approved documents.[120] Officials recognized the need for printing, but conceived of it as an appendage to royal operations and privilege. The widespread use of a colonial press dates almost immediately from the British occupation of Martinique in February of 1762. In fact, the first widely printed work that has survived was the articles of capitulation, printed at Saint Pierre by Richard.[121] Only after the restoration of French rule in July 1763 did locally printed documents begin to appear regularly, perhaps continuing an operation found useful under the occupation. Metropolitan officials decried the expenditure and urged colonial leaders to seek funding from interested individuals instead. That the operation of a press amounted to a patronage appointment is not unusual, for in France, England, and the British colonies, printers sought backing from the wealthy or operated the press as an adjunct to other positions, usually as postmaster.[122] Economics and not censorship dictated whether printers would prosper.

More ambitious plans were formulated for postal systems in each colony. Although the crown granted monopolies and even published royal ordinances announcing their establishment, none ever functioned prior to 1763. In Canada the postal system was twinned in 1721 with the private development of a road to connect Quebec with Montreal. The man who held the rights, Nicolas Lanoullier de Boisclerc, a clerk attached to Intendant Bégon, ran into financial troubles. The document specified that, in light of the high cost of sending letters by canoe, Boisclerc was to receive a twenty-year monopoly to operate three postal bureaus "as they are in France," in return for building roads and bridges connecting Quebec, Trois-Rivières, and Montreal. The plans were reintroduced after the Conquest.[123] Louisiana's even smaller population base, weak economy, and diffused network of posts and settlements along a few major riverine arteries discouraged the contemplation of any such proposals.

Efforts to establish a postal system on Martinique date as far back as 1701. In that year a Saint Pierre merchant named Repaire de Nayat contacted Secretary of State Pontchartrain directly about establishing a small office to efficiently exchange inter-island letters. Pontchartrain asked Intendant François Roger Robert for his opinion. The intendant dismissed the proposal as "impracticable," noting that only Nayat ever complained of misdirected letters. He added his expectation that in future Nayat and merchants like him would refrain from contacting Pontchartrain directly on such matters.[124] In 1738 the royal judge stationed at La Trinité, Nicolas Lavasseur, revived the idea with the support of Intendant d'Orgeville. The plans were impressively detailed, clearly centred on Saint Pierre and not Fort Royal, and allowed royal correspondence to move free of charge. Most important of all, the system would depend upon a high degree of coordination and cooperation among habitants in the countryside to collect and distribute mail, thus incorporating the militia groups, albeit as a means of lowering expenses. The cost would range from one *sol marquée* for a single letter to the expensive seven and half *sols* for a small package. Ship captains would deliver and receive inter-island and transatlantic mail at a main office located in Saint Pierre. Lavasseur envisioned that mail between any part of the island would take no longer than twenty-four hours for delivery, and inter-island routes a week.[125] However, the system never got off the ground. His original supporter, d'Orgeville, was transferred to Saint Domingue and the new intendant, de Lacroix, turned from supporter to enemy when Lavasseur ran afoul of one of the intendant's secretaries in early 1739.

That colonial officials saw the need for a postal system is demonstrated by the serious consideration given to a plan submitted to Governor Bompar and Intendant Hurson by the new secretary of state for the Marine, Rouillé, in 1752.[126] We lack the details of this plan, but do know the response to it. While acknowledging that the efficient distribution of letters, including royal dispatches, remained a serious problem, the two officials rejected the metropolitan-devised plan as too expensive, unsupervised, and subject to misuse by merchant captains and a potential source of many lawsuits for the island's already inundated courts. Instead, they submitted their own plans, which suggested that postal distribution would be managed more efficiently by a tax collector resident in France. Again, nothing came of the proposal. The first operational postal system sprang up briefly under Governor La Touche's initiative during the British siege of 1762, but disappeared with the occupation. After another false start in 1765, colonial officials established a viable system in 1766 based in Saint Pierre. A contemporary observer remarked that this government-run system offered many advantages, including the sharing of ideas and "views" among all islanders, and relieved militia officers from an overreliance on slaves to deliver letters and messages.[127] Neither the Marine nor colonial authorities envisioned using these services to ease the work of the colonial bureaucracy and to enhance the state's presence in the daily lives of the colonists. This is not to fault colonial authorities with being unable to grasp the obvious. Throughout the seventeenth and eighteenth centuries, printing and postal services were continually evolving, and the extent of their uses and influences was slowly realized through trial and error.

A final effort to tie the colonies more closely to the state began with plans to introduce a packet service in the summer of 1763. With the interruption of merchant traffic during the Seven Years War, swift-sailing corvettes from Rochefort had shuttled dispatches and small amounts of scarce war supplies to the Caribbean colonies.[128] However, the irregularity of departures demonstrated desperation rather than a conscious reformulation of policy. After France reoccupied the Îles du Vent in July 1763, the Marine circulated a printed ordinance announcing the new packet service "to deliver more promptly to the King's colonies the orders he deems convenient to make, and to thereby allow the return of the letters and responses of his Governors and Intendants." Nine corvettes, stationed at Rochefort and commanded by king's officers, were to depart without fail on the tenth of each month, sailing to Cayenne, Fort Royal on Martinique, and Le Cap on Saint Domingue before returning to Rochefort, anchoring no more than five days in each colonial port. The plan called for the agent to forward all mail, regardless of whether it listed a "distinguished address" or not.[129] The idea was hardly new, for the British crown had already sponsored a similar service sixty years previously during the War of the Spanish Succession.[130] However, within the French Atlantic the service represented a bold move to replace state reliance on mercantile networks with a state-supervised service. Choiseul's distrust of merchants was so great that he dismissed an offer put forward by a private company to operate a packet service, calling it "the most contrary to our wishes of all the aforementioned [proposals]."[131] However, the packet service operated haphazardly for only a few years. Like printing and postal services, packet boats fell into the chasm between plan and implementation, as entrepreneurs and the state sought some type of mutually comfortable working relationship. In all three areas of technological improvement in the communications infrastructure, the involvement of the state dated from 1763 and remained incompletely realized under the Duc de Choiseul.

The ability of merchants in the French Antilles to establish trading links beyond the control of metropolitan and colonial authorities did not threaten the social order in the same manner as slave revolts did. The long-term consequences, however, must not be underestimated. The Marine needed French merchants in all colonies at all times; the reverse was seldom true, with the notable exception of Canada in war. Royal officials took advantage of merchants' transatlantic connections, but at a price. Given their wide spectrum of international contacts and their control of shipping, and given the inability of colonial administrators to supervise and efficiently tax the high volume of traffic, merchants in effect established their own postal systems and their own educational institutions (based on apprenticeships of kin) and, most importantly, developed their own means of collecting and gathering information. Particularly in the Îles du Vent, metropolitan and colonial merchants began to criticize the state, even while planters and local colonial merchants evaded state supervision. Within this colonial world, the nobility and the wealthier bourgeois mingled socially, discussed options, argued, and shared investment opportunities. After 1763, it would become increasingly difficult to tell them apart.

CHAPTER SEVEN

Authority's Fragmented Voice

Conspiracy and rebellion hung in the heavy air of New Orleans in June 1759. War raged all across the world, but had not yet touched Louisiana. But other trouble was brewing. On the afternoon of June 23, two loyal inhabitants brought word to Governor Louis Billouart, Comte de Kerlérec that a "cabal" composed of several officers, including Captain d'Erneville, a man whom Kerlérec had praised and even promoted less than two years earlier, was meeting in the house of his enemy, *commissaire-ordonnateur* Michel-Vincent Gaspard de Rochemore. He guessed that they were doing nothing short of plotting his overthrow and the destruction of the king's authority in the colony, using the pretext of the visit of a small, 15-ton English neutral flag sloop. The vessel, *The Three Brothers*, had anchored that morning. A small guard of French soldiers personally loyal to Kerlérec brought its captain, Joseph Bull, to the governor's house. Kerlérec quickly discovered that, although Bull grasped a commission from the governor of Rhode Island in his hand and he had a cargo of desperately needed food on board, he had not actually brought any French prisoners with him. With no British prisoners then in New Orleans, Bull's trip was futile. Kerlérec therefore courteously bid the captain to "go as he had come." Bull returned to his ship and prepared to sail.

But the conspirators used the arrival of *The Three Brothers* as a pretext to strike. They first spread rumours through the town that the English were actually spies and that Kerlérec, the personal representative of the king, had refused to imprison them. That night, Captain d'Erneville convened a clandestine meeting with most of Louisiana's officers in his own home; with no breeze to prod the evening stillness, the neighbours heard everything. He drafted a written statement actually condemning Kerlérec, his own commander, for showing a lack of resolve in letting the captain and his crew go free; d'Erneville then raced to the governor's house at dawn and, in a loud and impudent manner, waved the document and challenged the bleary-eyed governor to take action. Kerlérec, trying to buy time, hurriedly agreed to arrest the English captain. D'Erneville then tried another tack and called a meeting the next day of three junior officers known to be supporters of the governor. He tried at first to trick and then to bully them into signing a copy of the letter condemning the governor. This would show that the governor had no support at all in the colony, and he could be removed with impunity by the *commissaire* and his allies among the officers and the Superior Council. But the three young officers stood fast and refused. Apprised of their determination, Governor Kerlérec took heart and seized the initiative. He called a meeting of all New Orleans and asked the assembled throng whether they wanted to buy the food offered by the English ship, which the colony so desperately needed. The townsfolk replied with a resounding round of cheers for the governor and the king. Alarmed at the governor's daring and popular support, d'Erneville and Rochemore backed down. The conspiracy had failed and the king's authority had prevailed.[1]

New Orleans, again in June 1759. The sloop *The Three Brothers* lay tied up before the town, under guard by a French captain and four soldiers.[2] Captain Joseph Bull, a former prisoner of war in the colony, had returned in the small sloop laden with manufactured goods and a few barrels of flour. Governor Kerlérec ordered his arrest, but inexplicably, he then quietly ordered Bull and his small crew (two young men and two teenaged boys) released and free to leave. But several people saw Bull being escorted into the governor's private vessel and rowed to his ship. Rumours circulated immediately. Several officers, including two long-serving captains, de Reggio and d'Erneville, were incensed that a British ship captain, who they were sure had visited a British privateer cruising off the Mississippi's mouth and known to have taken five French vessels destined for the colony, sat comfortably in the governor's own boat with his muddy boots on the king's arms.

That night, the officers met informally at d'Erneville's house to discuss the issue, and they nominated the captain, a man whom Governor Kerlérec had recently promoted and whom the governor seemed to trust, to "humbly" present their petition. D'Erneville consented and arrived at the governor's residence at the first light of dawn, since the governor had asked that he be awakened early anyway. Governor Kerlérec heard him out, thanked him courteously, and agreed that Bull should be arrested as a precautionary measure. He ordered Captain de Reggio to pursue the English boat, which had sailed the night before.

De Reggio caught up with it downriver, rearrested Bull and his crew, and placed the king's seals back on the ship's goods. The governor complimented de Reggio for his swift work. Within a week, the colony's court, the Superior Council, found Bull guilty of smuggling, and ordered the ship condemned and the cargo sold. Upon hearing the news, Kerlérec acted swiftly. He convoked a town assembly at his own residence within three days of the judgment after high mass and presented a petition from several merchants to the assembled crowd asking free entry for the English ship. When no cries of support were heard, the governor's own men, who had been carefully planted among the assembly, began to cheer their approval; the rest of the crowd sullenly followed suit.[3] Governor Kerlérec then wrote to Rochemore and ordered him to release the captain, crew, and ship and let them sell their cargo in peace. Rochemore complied, but under mild protest. When Captain de Reggio later asked the governor why he had initially approved of his conduct in arresting the English, Kerlérec answered that he did not recall ever having done so.

These two versions of the exact same events reached the Marine in the spring of 1760. They would at first appear to be yet another example of the traditional belief that relations were strained between sword and robe nobilities. A proud and haughty military governor would naturally be in conflict with a civil commissary who poured over account books. Such personal battles are etched into the earliest histories of every French colony and have supplied many tantalizing stories for scholars. As Paul Roussier observed, "disagreement was virtually a law in the colonies, as in France, between governors and intendants, possessors of equal powers in fact and in law, and moreover, forced to work closely in order to supervise and balance each other."[4] However, a closer look at the *Three Brothers* affair reveals a more complicated series of interactions. The split within the military corps into pro- and anti-governor factions, the amiable treatment of the enemy, the negation of the Superior Council's decisions, the mutual support demonstrated between the governor and New Orleans's merchants, and the use of rumours and meetings to enlist the support of "the people," by both the governor and the officers suggest a more complex factional battle between colonial elites that cannot be strictly accounted for by robe and sword antipathy. The *Three Brothers* incident is more than another example of how to weigh conflicting sources, and it is more than a story about two scorpions fighting in a nearly forgotten part of an old colonial empire. The example points up one of the most critical problems in French overseas administration. Since all law and authority emanated from the king, the king's decisions as to what should be done and how to best accomplish his goals could only be as solid and binding as those who reported to him. But whom should the Marine believe? How could personal jealousies be separated from the perceived good of the colonists? What if a minor official exposed graft or the incompetence of his superiors, people proposed and protected by the upper echelon of Marine bureaucrats and endorsed by the Marine minister himself: who should be blamed for their failure? The *Three Brothers* affair points to the need to reconceptualize robe-sword conflict, and it raises different questions about the state's relations with governing elites in its colonies. Who were the elites who enjoyed close contact with the French court through the secretary of state for the Marine? How does an exploration of communications help us understand the relationship between the state and colonial elites? What caused disunity among those elites?

We must first understand the composition of colonial elites and their relation to a centralized administration. This relationship differed fundamentally from the model of "co-option" of local rulers and leaders by the state described by William Beik for France, or from aid in overseas government described for the Anglo-American Atlantic world in separate works by Elizabeth Mancke and Michael Braddick.[5] In these examples, the state organized an almost naked contractual arrangement that tapped into existing provincial, local, or mercantile leadership, augmenting the power of local actors in exchange for wringing secure tax revenues (at least in France) and supporting and enforcing state policies. In the French Atlantic, as we have seen in chapter 1, local elites had arisen before 1664, but these had always been closely tied to powerful factions at court from the very beginning of settlement. After the direct imposition of royal authority in 1664, these elites were directly incorporated into the Marine's administration. Both theoretically and in fact, a single chain of patron-client relations linked officials from the lowest post in the colonies to the secretary of state for the Marine at Versailles. In their official capacities, local governing elites did not have a separate local identity and power base: they might be Canadian-born commanders of lucrative fur posts, great Creole planters, or energetic and respected members of Louisiana's Superior Council, who had never seen France, but they were all clients of more powerful agents and owed their position ultimately to the king.

The exact nature of patron-client relations even in *ancien régime* France remains elusive. The great French historian Roland Mousnier identified two types of patron (or master)-client relations: a feudal, more formal, emotional relationship between a noble and an underling predicated on unquestioned devotion (*fidelité*) by the latter and a more reciprocal and less emotionally binding type between administrators.

Sharon Kettering, in a critique of Mousnier's work, stressed self-interested reciprocity in all patron-client relations, at least by the late seventeenth century. The nature of these relations is hard to determine, since they were not always recorded, and even if they were, Kettering believes that "patrons and clients sometimes wrote one thing and did another."[6] However, the demands of new colonial environments and transatlantic contact superimposed another type of relationship, that of cultural broker.[7] Colonial elites, who were for the most part also royal officers, functioned as the sole mediators between the Bureau of Colonies, most of whose personnel had never crossed the Atlantic and who therefore lacked first-hand experience with the places that were the focus of their professional lives, and the highly complex, dynamic, and often explosive mix of wealthy and poor white colonists, non-French (or non-Catholic) residents, African-born, Creole, or Native slaves, and a galaxy of Native allies. In their capacity as cultural brokers, colonial officers provided two invaluable services to their patrons in the Marine: they furnished reliable information based on their position in the colonial hierarchy, explaining their free, unfree, and Native alliance constituencies, as well as the "new world" of what is now called the Atlantic economy, to the secretary and the clerks in the Marine.

In return, the Marine allowed colonial officials the right to wield and disseminate the king's authority. This right was publicly displayed through a variety of means. These can be collectively referred to as promotions and marks of esteem (medals, admission to specific orders), and they functioned as the true wages of the king's service. They conferred prestige and power by demonstrating the relationship of the recipient to the king, and since distance from the king determined one's standing in *ancien régime* hierarchy, only those who could make a strong claim on having his attention, no matter how low, could take a seat at the table of power. This exchange – information for promotions and honours – formed the primary basis upon which the Marine managed all of France's overseas possessions. So long as the exchange operated smoothly and the reporting hierarchy remained respected, the king's authority appeared strong. But this rigid structure could be undermined in a variety of ways. From the perspective of colonial authorities, any disunity, or even appearance of it, among the king's officers and the upholders of the social order could lead to a serious challenge to their authority.

THE COLONIAL INFORMATION ELITE

From the standpoint of communications, the state largely rearranged the governing elite in each colony to be different from that in France.

In contrast, most historians of New France have assumed that, with the exception of a poor seigneur here and a crafty merchant there, colonial societies replicated the traditional three estates of France, and that there existed a close correlation between social and political influence.[8] And most works agree that a major influence of colonial life lay in the transforming affect of commerce on nobility in the colonies, which muddied the relations between large-scale merchants, wealthy seigneurs, and planters, although the same can be said for France at the time.[9] But in the colonies the state placed very specific demands for information procurement and distribution upon those it chose to govern, and these demands helped rearrange the traditional hierarchy in subtle ways.

The greatest differences can be glimpsed in the slightly redefined roles of three segments of the colonial elites: colonial nobility, the enhanced position of clerks, and the clergy. In regard to the nobility, two "types" appear to have co-existed in the French Atlantic world, each with little connection to the other: an older nobility, principally based on land ownership in France and secondarily on land ownership in the colony, and a second type, of colonial origin stamped in part by land ownership but especially by service through the extended patron-client network of the Marine. The state ensured that a large overseas-born imperial nobility would not arise, for the granting of noble status became restricted in New France after 1680 and prohibited in the Îles du Vent from 1730 (a solid analysis of Louisiana remains to be undertaken).[10] Thus nobles not employed in the king's service, few though these were, retained great prestige locally, but were not important suppliers of official information. Conversely, non-noble underlings or lower-echelon nobles occupying strategic positions could substantially enhance their power. For example, S. Dale Standen has shown that in Canada private secretaries attached to governors or intendants could develop their own enterprises and profit from their positions as what communications theorists might call "gatekeepers" to colonial leaders, and that they even generated distrust and antagonism in otherwise solid working relationships between governors and intendants.[11]

Finally, we must note the diminished stature of the clergy in most colonies, including Canada, the seat of the bishopric for all New France. The clergy enjoyed considerable power in rural France, but experienced great difficulty finding enough recruits and funds to place priests in most colonial rural parishes. Furthermore, both the regular clergy and lay orders were denied the important role of announcing royal edicts and regulations after 1717,[12] and were consequently in most colonies regarded as useful but not critical gatherers of information and disseminators of the king's word. Unlike in France, with its traditional estates of clergy, nobility, and bourgeois/commoner, colonial hierarchies might be thought of as representing a musical chord with four descending strings: governors, intendants, superior councils, and the clergy. When tuned properly, the four worked harmoniously; but disagreement created shrill dissonance.

At the apex of the colonial communications hierarchy stood the governor general, the king's personal representative. He reported to the Marine on matters touching war, diplomacy, and the nobility, drawing upon the experience and information supplied by a pyramid-like structure of subordinate officials: governors of the smaller military districts, king's lieutenants, majors and assistant majors in the larger towns or forts, the royal engineer, the king's physician, and the company captains of the regular troops (*troupes de la Marine*), who numbered between twenty-eight and thirty in Canada and about thirty-seven in Louisiana.[13] All these potential information suppliers were also part of the governor's patronage positions, approximately forty in total. In addition, there were the commanders of the Protestant Swiss Kerrer regiments (Hallwyl after 1752) and the militia captains for each parish. While these were not patronage positions per se, governors could recommend honours and thus exert tremendous influence on their fortunes. Colonial governors spent much of their time scrutinizing the behaviour of their underlings, as well as of the colonial nobility generally, a fact reflected in the large amount of space devoted to reporting on the elites in official correspondence.[14] The core of this work involved judging candidates by the length of their career, displays of valour, exemplary leadership, gentlemanly conduct, zeal for the king's service, socially acceptable marriage, and disinterest in commercial activity at the level of retail buying and selling.[15] Governors also gathered information on the backgrounds of colonial nobles in order to filter out any former domestics or skilled workers,[16] supervised the conduct of errant sons of noblemen,[17] and advised the Marine about the sons of officers when approving *congés* for return voyages to France,[18] especially if they were enrolling as naval cadets in the prestigious Rochefort corps.[19] As well, governors controlled other exclusive domains of information gathering. For example, in North America, they hosted yearly conferences with up to ten or twelve Native nations at either Montreal (for Canada) or Mobile (for Louisiana). The conferences with Native peoples in particular served to renew old alliances or forge new ones, functioned as a kind of court where cross-cultural transgressions could be openly settled, and yielded highly detailed accounts of war, migrations, and trade in the *pays d'en haut*.[20] In the French Antilles, governors were more limited in their contact with their counterparts in the Spanish, British, or Dutch islands.[21] Unlike the

North American governors, those in Saint Domingue and the Îles du Vent also toured the coasts or individual islands extensively, gruelling expeditions that consumed a minimum of five weeks in the eastern Caribbean.[22]

Intendants and *commissaires-ordonnateurs* formed a second pole of authority, patronage, and information gathering and transmission. The Marine required two basic types of information from these officials: progress reports on projects initiated by the Crown, and more basic statistical measurements of demographics and economic growth. For example, in 1716 the instructions for Intendant Louis-Balthazar de Ricouart in the Îles du Vent asked for information on the efforts by the Spanish to expand their bishopric on Hispaniola to include the French islands; crown propositions to limit buying and selling produce by the clerical orders and the size of plantation profits of the four religious orders (Jesuits, Dominicans, Carmelites, and Capuchins); whether new converts were instructing their children in Catholicism; funding irregularities for the new hospital at Fort Royal; a report on efforts to allow vessels to call only at the quarantine port of La Trinité if the "illness of Siam" (yellow fever) reappeared (an outbreak in fact occurred later that year); and the demographic and gender balance on each island, supplemented with a feasibility study on whether the French population could be augmented by encouraging young French men and women to marry early (eighteen and fourteen respectively). These were only about half the items and were limited to Martinique and Guadeloupe; reports more limited in scope were required for six other islands. The crown also demanded annual statistical accounts of goods in the king's storehouses, weapons and military supplies sent from France, including cannon and carriages, copies of general expenses and revenues, and after 1720, annual statistical tables, or *états*, of ship arrivals and departures, the number of slaves imported, the number and kinds of plantations, and prices for colonial products, including five types of raw and semi-refined sugar.

To help gather this information, intendants drew upon a hierarchy of officials similar in number to that of the governor in both Canada and the Îles du Vent, about forty. These ranged from the commissaries in the major towns and forts, to officials in each colony's courts and taxing offices (superior, Admiralty, king's Domaine), and a hierarchy of clerks.[23] All these officials above the grade of regular clerk could, and occasionally did, send letters and requests of their own to the secretary of state for the Marine. In addition, the intendant had daily contact (and probable collusion) with colonial merchants, which opened further avenues for acquiring valuable information.[24] Finally, the intendant, like the governor, observed his own robe nobility underlings, noting such qualities as diligent work habits, sobriety, and penmanship.[25]

The third branch of the colonial information elite consisted of the members of the Superior Council. These bodies originated as appellate courts, although they all inherited informal traditions of advancing some legislation.[26] Starting with New France in 1703, Louis XIV reconstituted the courts from "sovereign" to "superior" councils, underlining the message of subservience to royal authority. Although councillors theoretically represented all free (and Catholic) colonists, the governor and the intendant jointly chose them all with approval from the Marine, ensuring that only the most prominent colonists with proven records of service to the crown would represent the colony. For this reason, Superior Councils never emerged as bastions of independent aristocratic influence, as the *parlements* continued to be in France until 1789. And unlike governors and intendants, Superior Councils were officially charged only with top-down information flow, distributing royal ordinances and edicts. In the late seventeenth century, only handwritten copies of ordinances were sent out to the colonies, but by the 1720s printed copies (*exemplaires*) were sent to the Îles du Vent. From 1730, printed copies were also sent on a regular basis for all royal *arrêts* and ordinances. The Marine's clerks placed edicts and letters in sealed bags or envelopes and forwarded them to the governors and intendants, who in turn distributed them to councillors, militia officers, seigneurs, and influential habitants.[27] Information and regulations intended for public knowledge were first registered by the Superior Council in each colony in order for them to become law; in effect, the very recording of the document gave it the force of law. The actual announcement to the public followed the traditional practice of being "registered, promulgated, and published [i.e., distributed]." Upon receipt of a royal decree, the intendant (as "president" of the Superior Council) usually ordered the document read aloud at one of the regular meetings of the council. Once it was read, the council's clerk, or *greffier*, affixed the king's seal, and dated and signed the document. This process constituted registration. Although Superior Councils enjoyed a theoretical right of remonstrance, the presence of at least one of the king's highest officers turned these into de facto *lits de justice*, a royal session in a French *parlement* in which the king's edicts were automatically registered.[28] Once registered, the court clerk or his assistants wrote out several copies by hand, dated and signed them, filed at least one copy in the colony's archives, and then sent the rest to the king's attorney (*procureur du roi*). These minor officials in turn ensured their delivery to the court bailiffs (*huissiers*) who served in each military district. At first, the bailiffs passed these documents to the local clergy to read after mass, but increasingly the responsibility fell to secular authorities, either to the bailiffs themselves or to notaries and militia captains.[29]

This very brief overview obscures several important differences between the traditional roles of Superior Councils in each colony. In Canada, advancement through the king's service, combined with the rewards of the fur trade, appear to have siphoned off the more talented and ambitious,[30] rendering the council a weak and barely competent institution of royal authority.[31] In contrast, greater wealth, common cause over freer trade, and the irregular presence of the king's officials in the Îles du Vent's council meetings combined to create a tradition of agitation against royal officials, a situation similar to that in Saint Domingue. Only in those colonies relying heavily on state support for defence and the economy, such as Louisiana and Île Royale, did the Superior Council become an effective organ of state rule. Even there, factional battles mitigated the appearance of elite solidarity.

The role and information networks of the fourth and last elite group, the clergy, is the most difficult to assess. Not only did each colony have a different assortment of regular orders, but also the scarcity of priests in parishes undermined the clergy's influence. Although a chain of spiritual command existed from God's representative on earth, the pope, down through the bishop or provincial of each order, to the priests and curés officiating at mass in each colonial parish,[32] in all colonies the state paid the clergy's bills and influenced the appointment of the major clerical leaders. Religious personnel were useful but not indispensable members of the colonial information gathering and disseminating network. Aside from announcing royal edicts until 1717, priests regularly used the pulpit to support state policies, especially during times of war. The clergy also recorded vital statistics and births, information increasingly crucial to the formulation of policies, as Charles O'Neill has pointed out for early Louisiana.[33] The same applied to Canada and the Îles du Vent. The travels of Jesuit Pierre-François-Xavier de Charlevoix from Quebec to New Orleans in 1720–22 and of the Dominican Jean-Baptiste Labat in the West Indies from 1694 to 1706, to name but two of the best-known among many, became authoritative sources on the overseas colonies for the French reading public in the mid-eighteenth century. Both authors were staunch supporters of aggrandizing France's overseas possessions and suggested how to guide them toward greater economic productivity.[34] Other clerics were used primarily as explorers, such as the accomplished Jesuit geographer Antoine Laval, sent to the Gulf coast in 1720 to make astronomical observations and find suitable harbours along the marshy coastline.[35] French clerics also understood the need to act in concert with the state's agenda. Pierre de La Rue, Abbé de L'Isle-Dieu, who acted as the official agent for the bishop of Quebec in Paris, proclaimed in his first letter on New France to the new secretary of state for the Marine, Antoine-Louis Rouillé, that for nearly twenty years "I have always attended carefully to the thinking of the Court."[36] L'Isle-Dieu used his position to the benefit of New France's clergy, although not always with tangible results.

This brief outline of the four major branches of the "information elite" in each colony – the governor general and his staff, the intendant and his staff, the Superior Councils, and the clergy – suggests a well-articulated, integrated, and hierarchical organization in each colony to ensure the smooth collection and distribution of information and knowledge. However, the existence of so many competing voices could also cloud the reception and use of this information. Disagreement between the elites communicated royal weakness, and nowhere is the problem of the fractured 'royal voice' more evident than in the rewards for supplying information.

THE SINEWS OF PATRONAGE: PROMOTIONS

In order to keep the colonial bureaucracy functioning efficiently and the information flowing, the Marine needed to continually reward and promote its colonial officers. This proved to be a complex and difficult task during prolonged periods of peace, when the officer corps became glutted. The Marine always tried to reinforce the power of both the governor and the intendant by sending all promotions and honours to them for distribution in their respective departments.[37] Colonial leaders normally presented a short list of two to four candidates, being sure to indicate their top choice.[38] Advancement could positively reinforce elite esprit de corps, and the intense competition among officials to display their zeal (*zèle*) for the king's service sharpened their work habits. As Intendant Hocquart in Canada observed in the case of royally bestowed awards such as royal *brevets* (warrants for the king's service) for his clerks, "they continually have their attention employed elsewhere, and thus become less attentive and subordinate; a *brevet* removes all their anxieties, binds them more fully to the service, and flatters their pride, more so by the hopes that they shall thereby advance."[39] Efficient transatlantic communications thus ensured the regularity and even the fairness of promotions, and these in turn were the glue that bound colonial officers and their families more firmly to metropolitan authority.

Winning promotion not only bestowed public recognition on the man who achieved it but also signified the level of influence held with the secretary of state, and ultimately with the king, of the man who conferred it. In this way, promotions acted as a kind of communication device, advertising the relative standing of the recipient in the colonial hierarchy. While such control strengthened the Marine's hand in patronage, it tended to sow disagreement among the growing number of officers competing for the relatively static number of positions in peacetime between 1713 and 1743.[40] Intendant Hocquart made this point when he advised Maurepas in 1731 that the Marine's commissary in Montreal should be admitted to the Superior Council's meeting at Quebec in order to establish his position in the imperial hierarchy. The commissary's current inferior position behind the king's lieutenant undermined the importance of the post, and Hocquart observed that "his Majesty has accorded to this position honours and privileges the extension of which imprints and enforces respect for the authority of those who hold it."[41] In Louisiana, French-born officers bristled with indignation at the favouritism shown to "servile" Canadian officers by Governor Bienville. One officer wrote, "[Bienville] believes that only Canadians understand his instructions; they are the only ones he patronizes and protects, in such a servile manner, and to the point that there is not one capable [officer] among them."[42]

French Antilles officials were especially sensitive on this point, given the considerable financial opportunities offered in the plantation colonies. For example, in 1727 Intendant Blondel urged the secretary of state to award a *brevet* and the status of council member to the new royal surveyor, for otherwise the colonists would ignore his demands for slave *corvées* to repair the roads.[43] In another incident, Governor General Champigny complained to Maurepas in 1735 that passing up the son of one Sieur Mullevaud for an appointment in the naval cadets at Rochefort had a terrible effect on his own credibility among people who were "continually occupied with knowing what occurred at Court as concerned their superiors." Such actions made it difficult to win people over, particularly when war threatened, and Champigny urged the secretary of state not to squander such opportunities to augment his authority.[44] He complained again in 1741 when Maurepas passed over his candidate for governor of Martinique, Lonvilliers de Poincy, in favour of André Martin de Poinsable. The governor general portrayed de Poincy as a broken man, "morose" and "mortified," who was forced to return to his plantation in disgrace.[44] Nine years later, Poinsable, now governor of Martinique, observed that promotions were not to be made lightly. Since returning from France, he had discovered that "Envy and Jealousy have reach their peaks, and it will be difficult to soften the heart of some of our islanders when all that they covet remains in the hands of others ... authority thereby is little respected by the lack of examples."[46] He then hinted to the newly appointed secretary of state, Rouillé, that the public knowledge of his own recent lack of advancement compared to the promotions of others would have a "poor effect" on his ability to carry out his duties.[47] With so many officers in the Îles du Vent, there were bound to be winners and losers in the competition for promotions. Significantly, governors and intendants often expressed the fear that ignoring their own candidates not only diminished the power of their subordinates but also opened the door to broader social disorder. The omnipotence of Martinique's ruling elite appeared so brittle that any cracks threatened the whole structure.

Of all the honours granted by the king, two alone significantly enhanced political clout. The court dangled the attainment of noble status as a means of reinforcing colonial loyalty.[48] The practice, introduced in the early years of Louis XIV's reign, proliferated to such a degree that in 1730 Maurepas notified Governor General Champigny and Intendant d'Orgeville that the inheritance of nobility for children of ennobled Creole planters in the Îles du Vent would henceforth cease. The two leaders objected to the decision, pointing out that conferring nobility afforded the best incentive for improving the work of Superior Council members. Otherwise, they noted, "this grace will become useless for the object which we have at heart, which is to inspire the Officers to their work, and assure us of their loyalty." They assured the secretary of state that only men of outstanding ability were included on their recommendation lists.[49] Military commanders received a further coveted honour which, above all else, signalled full confidence from the king: the Croix de Saint-Louis. In Canada it was deemed essential for the governor general to be awarded one. In recommending Governor -General Beauharnois for the Croix in 1731, Intendant Hocquart may have simply been trying to return a favour for his own recent promotion. Nevertheless, he couched his plea for the honour in terms of its value for the whole colony, for it would greatly increase respect for the position of governor general, particularly as a badge of distinction worn at Native conferences.[50] In the Îles du Vent, Governor General Champigny showed himself either particularly sensitive or anxiously vulnerable about the Croix. After he had pressed for its bestowal on six officers for several years, word finally reached the island in late 1741 that they had in fact gained the distinction. But the crosses and printed commissions themselves had not yet arrived, and the officers still awaited the actual medals in mid-1742. Champigny warned Maurepas that the tardiness would have a bad effect, making it appear that the governor general lacked the secretary of state's full confidence.[51]

The Marine influenced colonial elites in other ways, such as providing the salaries, supplies, and even trade goods that (clandestinely) supported the lifestyle of most, although, as Catherine Desbarats has recently pointed out, state funding as the basis of Canada's economy prior to 1755 may not have been as large or crucial as previously assumed.[52] Information gathering, recording, and distribution for the Marine consumed an enormous amount of time, energy, and cost for the elites, and may be said to have formed the basic core of their relation to the state. In return, the state, through the Marine, dispensed patronage in the form of appointments and honours, communicating to the holder, but especially to those under his authority, an achievement recognized ultimately by the king. This "information-patronage system" remained fragile in the imperial context and subject to cracking under stress. Nothing was more stressful than war, and it was during war that the system proved to be most fragile. The Seven Years War provides several striking examples of how breakdown in the information-patronage system created serious fissures among colonial elites.

CANADA: CULTURE WARS

Historians since Francis Parkman in the nineteenth century have been fascinated by the clash between Canadian governor general Pierre de Vaudreuil-Cavagnial and French general Louis-Joseph de Montcalm. Most accounts focus on the personalities of the "hot-tempered, supercilious" Montcalm, who "continually fumed over slights," and the "resentful, vain," and insecure Vaudreuil-Cavagnial.[53] Clearly, personal animosity poisoned their relationship. Other accounts emphasize the animosity between the 3,200 French officers and soldiers and the equally large number of *troupes de la Marine* and Canadian militia.[54] While a complete reassessment of the Montcalm-Vaudreuil conflict within the sweep of the entire North American theatre of war is outside the scope of this study, we can detect some ways in which information exchange and the concomitant role of patronage adversely affected the ability of its top military commanders to conduct war. It is useful in this context to consider Montcalm and Vaudreuil-Cavagnial as cultural brokers and patronage dispensers in direct competition over two scarce resources: the portrayal of reality and the winning of public recognition.

From the outset of war, the secretary of state for the Marine uncategorically assured Vaudreuil-Cavagnial that any French army commander would work directly under his authority.[55] Both officials in turn repeatedly assured their superiors in France, the ministers of the

Marine and of War, of the "perfect cooperation" that existed between them, a belief repeated by other Canadian "experts" such as the Abbé de L'Isle-Dieu.[56] As late as the summer of 1757, Montcalm wrote a letter to Secretary of State for the Marine Jean-Baptiste de Machault that portrayed both Vaudreuil-Cavagnial and Intendant François Bigot sympathetically, at least for Montcalm. He described Bigot as a "man of spirit and intelligent" and portrayed Vaudreuil-Cavagnial as a "decent man, mild, but with no character, surrounded by men who seek to erode the confidence he might have for [me]," although Montcalm took an early dislike to Vaudreuil-Cavagnial's younger brother, the "dim-witted" François-Pierre de Rigaud de Vaudreuil, governor of Trois-Rivères and commander of the Marine troops and militia.[57] The Marine at first accepted these assurances.[58] However, by the spring of 1758 the split had become the subject of common knowledge, and officials such as Bigot were alarmed over an impending explosion that would lose the colony. The split was so well known that Montcalm reported to his horror that it had been the subject of several accounts in New York newspapers, increasing the morale of the enemy. No amount of conciliatory oratory could fool the colonists.[59] By the fall of 1758 Vaudreuil-Cavagnial warned the Marine not to accept any observations by two returning officers (André Doreil and Louis-Antoine de Bougainville), since they were blind to the colony's true interests and mere sycophants of Montcalm's. In turn, Montcalm reported that the Canadians had become "discouraged" and had no confidence in their colonial leaders.[60] The Marine could only respond with a series of bland pronouncements urging each to work with the other. However, the head of the Marine, Machault, did send Montcalm a special cipher to allow him to "give free reign to any observations he might make on military and administrative matters in the colony."[61] It was in this acerbic atmosphere of distrust and disparagement that the Marine had to judge the commanders of the war effort and make decisions about the North American theatre of war.

In the midst of the summer campaign of 1757, it became painfully clear that the division between Vaudreuil-Cavagnial and Montcalm rested on more than vanity. The leaders argued over military strategy, and their division rested directly on different types of geographic knowledge and training gained in the field. As a young cadet during his father's tenure in 1721, Vaudreuil-Cavagnial had travelled Lake Ontario, meeting with Seneca and Onondaga leaders. As governor of Louisiana, he had mastered an entirely new set of Native alliances, although within a familiar geographic and cultural setting.[62] Once back in Canada, he worked hard to keep the traditional Native alliance system functioning, and even succeeded for a time in strengthening it.

Vaudreuil-Cavagnial saw Lake Ontario both as a key to maintaining Native alliances and as a corridor for raiding Anglo-American settlements deep in New York and potentially as far as Pennsylvania and Virginia. Recognizing the necessity of keeping these lines of communication open, he rushed four ships to completion at Fort Frontenac by the summer of 1756 to ensure French dominance of the lake.[63]

Montcalm, on the other hand, with solid experience on the farmlands and cultivated highlands of central European battlefields in 1744–48, had little use for an inland sea and deplored ambushes in the forest. By 1757 he had "renounced" any intention of fortifying the Lake Ontario area, while the governor general in turn insisted he was "determined to never abandon the Lake ... and [moreover] decided to re-establish a small navy to ensure our superiority."[64] Montcalm took his case to the Minister of the Marine, observing that the presence of large, professionally trained European armies in North America completely altered the tactics necessary. In a famous passage, he proclaimed that "the nature of the war in this colony had radically changed ... Our principles of war considering our inferiority, ought to be to contract our defensive, in order to preserve, at least, the body of the colony."[65] In other words, he advocated a temporary return to the old "compact colony" policy of Pontchartrain in 1700. After two years of indecision, the Marine fully endorsed his strategy by early 1759.[66]

As for Native alliances, Vaudreuil-Cavagnial insisted on their necessity as much as Montcalm decried their uselessness and savagery.[67] Of course, Canada's Native allies in the Ohio valley and among the Iroquois pursued their own strategic policies, which revolved around neutralizing both the French and the British in the eastern Great Lakes.[68] Colonial military commanders considered Native allies, and the mission Iroquois in particular, essential to Canada's war effort. French officers, on the other hand, insisted that the Natives were true "savages" who only half-heartedly supported the war. One official, André Doreil, asserted in a long dispatch to the Marine that the Iroquois allies had fooled the governor general into believing they would send warriors to aid French forces in Lake Ontario.[69] The matter came to a climax in the summer of 1757 after the successful siege of Fort William Henry, along the Lake Champlain border. The French accepted the surrender of about 2,400 British soldiers and colonial militiamen if they took an oath not to again bear arms; they did so and were marched south to the nearest British fort to be discharged. Shocked by this illogical military move, warriors (apparently Abenaki from Maine and not Iroquois) nabbed nearly 300 hundred soldiers en route, and executed and scalped at least 30 before Montcalm and several of his officers personally intervened to stop the bloodshed.

Disgusted with messy American guerrilla war and its grisly trophies, Montcalm ignored orders from Vaudreuil-Cavagnial to complete the sweep of British forts in the region.[70] He also sent copies of the governor general's letters on Native allies to the minister of War to demonstrate the governor's inability to be reasonable on the matter.[71] For their part, Native leaders were so disgusted with Montcalm's conduct that they sent emissaries to complain bitterly to Vaudreuil-Cavagnial. The next year, in reporting the victory at the Battle of Carillon, in a wartime "letter" printed and circulated in France to publicize the victory, Montcalm again demeaned the Native allies by noting that this "great action" was the first won according to proper tactics and without Savages.[72] The Canadian Iroquois, Algonquians, Abenaki, and others, on their part, again denounced Montcalm to Vaudreuil-Cavagnial, and only some strenuous efforts by the Chevalier de Lévis, Montcalm's second-in-command, persuaded some of them to stay.[73] In responses on the Native allies, the Marine once again walked a fine line. In letters to the governor general, it expressed great trust in his ability to direct Native allies, but also chastised him for his "lenient" handling of Natives in general and the Iroquois in particular. To Montcalm it stressed that a firm hand and patience were needed in equal measure to tolerate their "odd pleasures," carefully laying blame on Montcalm's subordinates for rash behaviour.[74]

Most of all, Montcalm and many of his subordinate French officers disliked Canada and mistrusted Canadians. From the outset, French officers made no secret of their disgust with the Canadian-stationed *troupes de la Marine* and especially with the Canadian militia. The distaste of Montcalm and his officers was not unusual; at least since the early eighteenth century, newly arrived French nobles were shocked by the lack of respect shown them by the habitants.[74] The antipathy ran deep: according to a French engineer, commenting on the attitudes of Canadians, "in this country, the Original Sin is to be French."[76] Added to this antipathy in the Seven Years War was the lack of communication and accommodation between two very different military cultures. French soldiers were trained in the complicated manoeuvring of sieges and massed troops on European battlefields. Most French officers complained that Canadians closely copied the combat of Native warriors, opting for hit-and-run-style raids, whooping when they attacked, and boasting of their exploits afterwards.[77] In addition, French officers were horrified by the unprofessional military habits of the Canadian militia: the impossibility of organizing them into proper ranks or drilling them in precision marching; the sloppy care they exhibited for their arms and shot; their insistence on sleeping in birch-thatched huts instead of proper tents; their annoying familiarity with their own commanders; their irritating habit of leaving campaigns early to return home and get the harvest in.[78] The second-in-command under Baron de Dieskau, the Comte de Montreuil, derided Canadians in a typical fashion when he dismissed them as "very brave behind a tree and very timid when not covered."[79] In order to improve the conduct of, and instill respect in, the Canadian militia, one memorandum advocated the need to organize the militia into grades, merge most with the French or Canadian *troupes de la Marine* ("since they pass winters together and so know and like each other"), and authorize the governor general to issue royal commissions to militia officers who distinguished themselves in combat.[80] The Chevalier de Lévis proved to be a unique exception to the generally negative attitude harboured by French officers. Not surprisingly, he enjoyed the respect of Vaudreuil-Cavagnial, who welcomed the change in command upon Montcalm's death at Quebec in 1759.

Montcalm's own attitudes on the militia were more nuanced, but nonetheless reflected an even more patronizing perception of colonists. "Canadians," he said, "[are] basically spirited and courageous but up to the present nothing animates this machine nor serves to develop the seeds which have been planted."[81] The use of the word "machine" (*machine*) is particularly revealing. In the eighteenth century, the term suggested a logical arrangement or organization found in Nature, the ultimate goal of which lay hidden from human understanding. For Montcalm, Canadians appeared to exist in a type of Newtonian void, an organic body of latent power, but whose universal laws of action remained obscured from rational inquiry. He tried to remain tactful in his official pronouncements, in part because the Marine insisted on the centrality of the Canadian militia and the Native allies.[82] In the same report that took a swipe at the Native allies, Montcalm twice mentioned the "heroics" of both the militia and the Canadian *troupes de la Marine*. However, Vaudreuil-Cavagnial complained that Montcalm still publicly attributed victory to the French troops and minimized the role of the Canadians.[83] As if to prove the governor correct, Montcalm proceeded to antagonize several distinguished Canadian officers in the aftermath of Carillon by assigning them to serve as subordinates under French officers of the same rank. They angrily resigned their commissions.[84]

On his side, Governor General Vaudreuil-Cavagnial consistently promoted the "good will and zeal" of the Canadians, who supplied the needs of the French army with food and graciously shared their lodgings during winter, and he complained of Montcalm's continual disparagement of their efforts.[85] In late 1758 he scoffed at French artillery officers, who "displayed an unbounded revulsion to serving with the colonial troops," and who, he believed, wished for nothing else but to "return [to France] and enjoy their promotions."[86] In another instance, the governor general insisted on paying Canadian officers the same living allowance as the French, since they toiled in the most "exposed positions" but did not "complain like the others."[87] The Marine responded by sending credit notes totalling 12,000 livres, one half to be distributed by Vaudreuil-Cavagnial to the Canadian officers and the other by Montcalm to the French.[88] Significantly, as the war dragged on, French officers appeared to ameliorate their earlier views. Military historian Martin Nicolai believes that it took several years of trial and error to integrate the very different fighting skills of Canadians and French regular troops into a coherent whole, a task that Lévis achieved by early 1760, after he had assumed command upon Montcalm's death.[89] But by then the British Navy had beaten the French in the race to secure the St Lawrence, making any further defence futile.

Both Vaudreuil-Cavagnial and Montcalm, as autonomous leaders of sizable military forces until 1759, also acted as patrons to layers of subordinate officers and even regular soldiers. In their letters and comments, each commander clearly saw himself as the guardian not only of a specific people but also of a distinctive and honourable military tradition. Integrating the two opposing cultures, which had been built up over generations in radically different geographic and social contexts, proved far too ambitious and difficult within the space of a few years and under the pressures of war. The Marine further suffered from having a series of inexperienced ministers guiding its affairs. It could only offer platitudes in place of policies and firm commitments.

ÎLES DU VENT: BIRTH OF A REPUBLIC?

Unlike Canada, the Îles du Vent experienced no direct threat during the first few years of the war, but it did suffer severe economic problems and food shortages. The economies of the sugar islands had bounced back with great vigour after 1748, and they grew rapidly in the brief interwar period; even Guadeloupe began to emerge from Martinique's shadow. As we saw in chapter 6, however, French commercial shipping ground to a halt by early 1757, and the Caribbean islands survived economically only by their re-exports through neutral Dutch and Danish entrepôts. Meanwhile, Saint Pierre's corsairs again prowled Caribbean waters, seizing British merchant ships by the score every month. Nevertheless, by early 1759, feeding both the free and unfree populations had emerged as a major concern, and colonial authorities, unlike their Canadian counterparts, did not receive a heavy infusion of supplies, recruits, and credit. After the occupation of Guadeloupe, authority began to be more openly contested.

Even before the war began, Governor General Maximin de Bompar and Intendant Charles-Morin Hurson began on poor terms with the colony's Superior Council. In 1751 Intendant Hurson created a new post, backed by the governor, but three council members (one noble and two ennobled after the war) sought to expand its area of competence by making the appointment. The intendant secured censure for the three by the Marine, which publicly banned them from attending council for six months.[90] By the end of Bompar's tenure, the council had offended the departing governor by refusing to assign even a small deputation to attend his formal farewell. In explaining its conduct to the Marine, the council ingeniously adopted a narrow interpretation of a 1721 royal ordinance forbidding special recognition of officers without the king's express consent.[91] An undercurrent of metropolitan-colonial hostility persisted between other members of the elite and further contributed to tarnishing the orderly conduct and unity of colonial authority. For example, in Lamentin, a town on Martinique northeast of Fort Royal, a French-born Capuchin priest aggressively promoted a young French novice over an older Martinique-born cantor and sacristan, leading to a long battle with his parishioners. When Governor General François de Beauharnais became involved, the priest gave the prie-dieu reserved for the governor to the young novice, symbolically reasserting the primacy of church over state.[92] Such incidents serve as a reminder that metropolitan-Creole conflict often expanded into a triangular set of combatants, where one metropolitan authority would protect Creole members against another metropolitan authority. As the new governor general, Beauharnais would have had occasion not only to placate his Creole constituency but also to use the incident to keep the clergy firmly in check.

Metropolitan-colonial relations reached its nadir under Beauharnais's tenure. In ways reminiscent of the Marquis de Montcalm, he continually made plain his deep distrust of the colonists to the Marine. Initially, the governor appeared to be well disposed to the white colonists generally and their commanders in particular. His official report on the British attack of January 15, 1759, on Martinique presented a straightforward narrative of events, noted the competent work of Creole officers, and praised their "ardour and desire to battle," noting courageous action by militia commanders on two separate occasions and "the most pronounced zeal" even of the merchant-composed militia of Saint Pierre in defending the port.[93] But instead of forging pride and a harmonious bond, the victory brought resentment into broad daylight. Immediately after Guadeloupe's fall, which occurred four months after the attack on Martinique, Beauharnais's letters struck an ominous tone. He accused the Guadeloupe colonists of surrendering in order to escape paying their debts and asked the Marine to send 1,500 more French troops to keep Martinique's planters from delivering the island to the enemy.[94] At the same time, the Superior Council addressed a letter to Beauharnais which outlined the colony's distress, blamed his predecessor, Bompar, for the corrupt misuse of shipping permissions, and proclaimed the loyalty of all colonists, even slaves, to the king despite the threat of famine, all as a means to pressure Beauharnais to open island shipping to free commerce with neutral ports, even those of the "regicides," a reference to the English islands.[95] To worsen matters, Martinique's governor, Rouillé de Raucourt, forwarded the letter on behalf of the Superior Council to the Marine. This action could only have infuriated Beauharnais, who not only had adopted Bompar's autocratic governing style but had continued farming out valuable trading permits to favoured merchants.

Guadeloupe's surrender sent a tidal wave of fear and not a few shivers of joy through planters on neighbouring French islands. The British commander, John Barrington, conquered the island by systematically burning plantations and marching captured slaves into the holds of British ships, all as a policy to weaken the commitment of the island's only main force, the militia. But the terms of the capitulation were very generous: they pledged low taxes, allowed retention of religious worship and French law, and best of all for the planters, guaranteed easy access to cheaply priced slaves and British markets. Within the year, Guadeloupe suddenly emerged as a sugar-producing giant. We do not know how closely colonists on other islands were able to follow events on the island, but regular inter-island contact existed, and it seems to have softened the resolve of other militias. Shortly after Guadeloupe's capitulation, nearby Marie-Galante surrendered easily, after the British commander offered similar terms.[96] To the south on Saint Lucia, Lieutenant Longueville reported trouble, squelching hopeful rumours that the island would be the next target for the British Navy. He also stressed an increasingly shrill theme taken up later by Intendant La Rivière, that the court had been mislead into thinking the islands could defend themselves, and he pleaded for more soldiers to ensure loyalty.[97] Some officers around Beauharnais began to complain openly of their poor relations. Rouillé de Raucourt, who had helped the Superior Council, took to writing directly to the chief bureaucrat of the colonies, Accaron, to lament that "Monsieur the General hardly ever consults me," a situation he believed all colonists knew about except those with connections to court. The royal engineer, Picaudeau des Rivières, also notified the Marine about a recent quarrel with Beauharnais over road repairs. "It is devastating," he wrote, "having served with honour to my age, [to be] treated like rot, a Slave made to support his master."[98]

With the regard for state authority reduced in the remaining islands, the new minister of War and soon to be the new minister of the Marine, the Duc de Choiseul, acted to shore up colonists' confidence. Some four hundred French grenadiers arrived in the colony in March 1761, suggesting not only more help but also that metropolitan authorities were finally taking the colony's plight seriously. More importantly, news arrived that Beauharnais had been recalled in late 1760, to be replaced by a new, Creole governor, Louis-Charles Levassor de La Touche, a member of one of Martinique's most illustrious families. He also carried exceptional credentials as an ardent representative of the Creole elite, since his grandfather had been a major leader of the 1717 Gaoulé revolt.[99] In making the appointment, the Marine ignored its own recent ordinances barring leading officials from serving in the same colony as their kinsmen; in effect, Versailles virtually confessed that the colony was slipping beyond the grasp of metropolitan authority. While it might be argued that the appointment demonstrated, as La Touche's commission stated, the king's "satisfaction with [the colonists'] valour and loyalty,"[100] such a move by mid-1761 appears more likely a desperate attempt to reassert royal control and marshal confidence under the name of a respected Creole family. In a sense, the metropolitan-Creole relationship was subtly reversed: instead of Creoles looking to the state to enhance their local authority, the state now appeared to need the respect of Creole society to polish its tarnished image.

La Touche went to work immediately after his arrival on Martinique in February 1761. He made several inspection tours of the island's batteries and small forts, began desperately needed road repairs, and incessantly urged officers and militia captains in their districts to prepare for a certain British attack. For the first time, he ordered the distribution of printed ordinances to ensure that the king's word was seen in every corner of the island. Few of these latter documents have survived, but they indicate a hint of independent patriotic themes mixed with the more traditional concept of "zeal" for the king's service. For example, in September 1761 La Touche proclaimed:

> In the different orders which it has pleased His Majesty to give us, he is "highly satisfied with the patriotic sentiments that the loyal subjects of Martinique have demonstrated, and he counts equally upon their valour and their actions

to destroy the unjust enterprises of his enemies"; a mark so flattering, so precious, for the whole colony could only produce in the heart of his people the strongest impulses to further heighten the esteem he has had of them for all time. It hardly need be added that their lives, their fortunes, their honour are in *their* hands; that all France, and even all Europe, will watch carefully the destiny they are going to pursue ... that by the proof of their valour which they will show on every occasion, they will gladly cover themselves with glory, or lose everything they have worked to achieve until today [italics added].[101]

La Touche then addressed colonists directly, calling on officers and militiamen to put aside petty squabbles and "work toward the well-being and glory of the colony by the most perfect union."[102] The theme of Martinique's destiny, so reminiscent of an earlier vision of a "city upon a hill" in colonial Massachusetts, may have been a simple, if stirring, rhetorical device, but it clearly appealed to the emotional dimension of self-determinism, meeting it at least halfway.

The growing rift between metropolis and colony also heightened between 1760 and 1761 with the introduction of a new institution: the Combined Chamber of Agriculture and Commerce. The Superior Council had taken advantage of the victory over the British in January to apply to the king for his permission to form the chamber in mid-1759; Louis XV signed the request into law in December, and it met for the first time on May 17, 1760. The chamber's charter stipulated that it possessed the right not only to advise colonial officers in commercial and agricultural affairs but also to send representatives to the King's Council on Trade in France. It was supposedly composed of four "habitants," or planters, and four merchants nominated by the Superior Council, and it provided a more direct arena for presenting the views of colonists, albeit those wealthy enough to serve without needing a salary.[103] In reality, four of the six members whose origins are known were French who had emigrated to Martinique, and three of the four merchants had retired from commerce to become plantation owners. As Bernard Vonglis has pointed out, the Superior Council had revived an idea dating back to the 1720s, but squashed as too "republican" in the aftermath of the 1717 Gaoulé.[104] The association acted on a variety of fronts and did so with some effect: as noted in chapter 6, it pressured the Marine successfully into allowing neutral traders to supply slaves, an activity that several French chambers of commerce strenuously objected to. Its latent role as an independent authority emerged quickly. In May 1761 the chamber began to convene without dutifully advising the governor, holding meetings that spilled over several days. Alarmed, Intendant La Rivière not only complained of the meetings but, worse, he had obtained the memorandum sent to court in October of the previous year, which he and the new governor, La Touche, had found "vicious [and] base in form, sound and style."[105] While battles with the Superior Council seemed to have diminished by 1761, those with the Combined Chamber appear to have warmed up.

After a second British naval force captured Martinique in January 1762, the Combined Chamber emerged as a bona fide representative institution. The British, better prepared, larger, and undoubtedly profiting from experience gained in Guadeloupe, routed Martinique's half-hearted defenders in less than three weeks, a defeat that brought renewed hand-wringing at court and another official inquiry. Once again, the surrender terms were favourable to Martinique's planters and to the clergy, but this time they were especially supportive of the Superior Council and the Combined Chamber. Suddenly, the island's colonial institutions found themselves with fewer limits: they were supposed to actively represent the colonists to their British overlords. The Combined Chamber, in particular, changed from an economic advisory body into an administrative organization. The chamber's members created a system of forty-eight commissioners to run affairs in each of the island's twenty-eight parishes, under the supervision and with the approval of the British occupation governor. Two of the chamber's deputies even journeyed to London to present petitions and requests to King George III later in the year.[106] The British, then, acted exactly as the ally that planters in the Îles du Vent hoped they would be. When Governor François de Fenélon re-established French dominion in July of 1763, he first expelled the merchants from the chamber, supposedly to halt bickering between them and the planters, then dissolved the commissioner system altogether. The speed with which French metropolitan officials acted suggests that they recognized a serious and entrenched threat to re-establishing royal authority over the colonists. The Duc de Choiseul subsequently recruited the chamber's Parisian deputy, Jean Dubuc, into the Marine's service as *premier commis* of the Bureau of Colonies.[107] Regardless of Dubuc's personal talents, the move could not have been a more symbolic demonstration of the Marine's desire to learn from past mistakes and integrate colonial voices and experience into the highest echelons.

Although La Touche had failed to prevent a British victory in February 1762, he did rally the colonists to defend the island at a critical moment, a point the Marine noted in its own investigation of his conduct.[108] Neither he nor any major Creole officer was saddled with any serious accusations of neglect of duty. This outcome should not be surprising, since a contrary conclusion would have been a direct criticism of Choiseul's actions. What did come under fire were the colony's two local institutions. Both the Superior Council and then the Combined Chamber had pursued agendas of political criticism, acting in a manner that the state could only perceive as quasi-autonomous, circumventing the dictates of royal governors and addressing the crown directly, scheduling its own meetings, and actively cooperating with an enemy when the opportunity to do so arose. While the experience of the Îles du Vent differed in many obvious ways, there is one significant similarity: metropolitan-colonial conflict also pervaded the political structure, and the effort to synthesize the needs and concerns of each into an imperial whole came too late to prevent defeat and occupation.

LOUISIANA: ISOLATION AND FACTIONAL REFORMATION

Unlike either residents in the embattled Canadian heartland or those facing the slow picking off of the Îles du Vent, Louisiana's inhabitants held their breath for several years over an invasion that never came, only to be captured by a peace treaty after they had exhaled. No major military help from France arrived until mid-1762, when the Marine sent ten incomplete companies of troops to the colony; in the end, the vastness of Louisiana's territory and its isolation proved to be its best defence. Governor Kerlérec, beneficiary of two savvy Canadian governors before him (Bienville and then Vaudreuil-Cavagnial), kept the Native alliance system in the southeast intact, with help from British traders who had cheated and mistreated enough Cherokee, Choctaw, Alabama, and others to ensure that French diplomacy held for the duration of the war.[109] He also used his diplomatic talents to diffuse potential factional problems in 1753, when both Canadian and French-born officers in Louisiana feared losing their seniority because of an influx of older officers from Louisbourg and Saint Domingue.[110] He and *commissaire-ordonnateur* Michel worked well together, putting an end, temporarily, "to the division that has reigned at different times between the leaders of the Colony."[111] Population grew, albeit marginally; some shortages occurred, but did not reach the near-famine level experienced in the French islands of the eastern Caribbean. The only major problem, and one that potentially carried serious repercussions in factional disputes, involved the persistent issue of redeeming worthless colonial money.[112] Nevertheless, French Louisiana appeared to be safely tucked away, awaiting only the outcome of war. Yet the war produced what appears to have been one of the most internally turbulent eras politically ever experienced by any French colony prior to 1791, although noticed by few historians.

While it is clear from the correspondence that a personality conflict embittered the governor and the *commissaire-ordonnateur*, it is not clear why, for the first time, charges of sedition within the elite arose. What went wrong?

French colonists in Louisiana maintained two basic types of contact that brought European news. Trade relations with Havana, Pensacola, and the Illinois posts and a small but consistent intercolonial trade with Saint Domingue, not to mention visits by Anglo-American ships, kept the colony informed of events during the war, as we saw in chapter 3. However, French colonial leaders required more than general news of events to make decisions. Since all major policy and administrative decisions emanated from the king, loss of contact with France meant that official colonial society became severed from its political foundation. Of course, officials could, and certainly did, make decisions on their own; even so, when regular correspondence resumed, and when officials returned to France, they understood that either the Marine or independent commissions of inquiry would pass judgment on their actions. The most difficult questions would pertain to whether they had usurped the prerogatives of royal authority, especially in military conduct, financial affairs, promotions, and punishments. French Louisiana provides an excellent example of one of the most basic tensions inherent in the *ancien régime*, the necessity of asserting claims to complete control and of compromise during insecure circumstances. The rupture of regular contact both froze and liberated the colonial elites at the same time, throwing them into desperate attempts to claim the ghost of a royal authority that had effectively deserted the colony.

From mid-1756, direct contact with France and with the other French Caribbean colonies virtually evaporated. The Marine scaled back its own shipping operations, sending vessels to Louisiana only in even years: one in 1756, none in 1757, two travelling together in 1758 (bringing the new *commissaire-ordonnateur*, Rochemore), none in 1759 (although the king's dispatches were carried on at least one merchant vessel), one in 1760, none in 1761, and two merchant vessels in 1762, freighted with supplies and nearly five hundred soldiers on the king's account.[113] The increase of British mastery over the Caribbean from Guadeloupe's fall in 1759 not only hindered inter-Caribbean French commerce, but also forced British privateers to seek what few prizes there were off the Mississippi's mouth, further shutting down arrivals and departures at New Orleans. The volume of the Marine's correspondence fell accordingly. It had ranged between 44 to 54 folio pages between 1755 and 1758, dropped to 33 in 1759, and to only 3 (all circular letters) in 1760, remained low at 4 (half of which were circular letters) in 1761, and crept back to 30 only in the second half of 1762. As early as September 1758, Governor Kerlérec complained that the Marine had not responded to a single one of the 162 letters he had sent in the eighteen months ending in the spring of that year.[114] It is also far from clear that all letters written from France actually reached Louisiana, or that Louisiana officials had an accurate idea of the swift rise and fall of naval ministers during the Seven Years War. But it is clear that the Marine did not appreciate the rise of two embittered factions, one centred around Governor Kerlérec, comprising an assortment of family relations, merchants, and officers connected to the interior post trade, and a second surrounding *commissaire-ordonnateur* Rochemore, containing his relations, merchants, and disaffected officers not involved with or frozen out of the interior post trade.

The problem of intermittent communication undermined royal authority in two distinct ways. First, it complicated the ability of officials to plead their cases and seek redress. For example, in May 1759 both Governor Kerlérec and Captain d'Erneville wrote to Le Normant de Mézy to sway opinion over the developing feud, the former to warn Le Normant against interfering too strongly (since he enjoyed the support of Secretary of State Massiac), the latter urging him to act quickly. But Le Normant, a former *commissaire ordonateur* of Louisiana who had risen to the post of intendant general of the Marine and the Colonies in the summer of 1758, had already retired from service under pressure by November of the same year.[115] Both sides learned of this development only later, by December of 1759. Uncertainty over who might direct the Marine led each faction to proceed carefully against the other, while documenting absolutely every encounter to explain its actions and expose the allegedly incriminating behaviour of its rival. Second, the lack of news directly undermined the ability of a king's official to establish discipline among others or enlist the trappings of authority by delaying rewards for service. Rochemore attracted to his clique disgruntled military officers in New Orleans in part because they had not received any news of their promotions for several years. Kerlérec complained to the Marine that if he tried to punish these officers, they intentionally misinterpreted his orders, and he made the connection that lack of news from France diminished their fear of rebuke from the Marine.[116] This intermittent communication helps to explain, in part, why both factions engaged in a circuitous war against subordinates and foreigners for over four years without taking any decisive action. It is against this backdrop of intermittent royal communication across the Atlantic that the Kerlérec-Rochemore conflict must be understood.

Poor communications led to a variety of stratagems to connect with France, or failing that, to censure what came from France. Governor Kerlérec had the upper hand in this regard. According to his enemies, he ordered the commander at La Balize to scour incoming ships, including any merchant vessel, remove their letter packets, and send them directly to him. In this way, he opened and read all mail from the court addressed to him and Rochemore jointly, and even managed to acquire personal letters of Rochemore and his followers.[117] In return, the governor charged at least one merchant captain in association with Rochemore with opening some of his official mail from court and spreading news of it in Saint Domingue.[118] Both Kerlérec and Rochemore also sent personal representatives back to France to make their cases at court. Kerlérec, early in the dispute, sent his personal secretary, Thiton de Silègues, in March 1759. Once in France, Silègues lobbied for the governor, but sent back very few letters to apprise him of the court's positions. Kerlérec followed this mission with a second, sending his nephew Dessalles and another young ensign, La Frenière (two of the three officers who had rejected d'Erneville's entreaties). In turn, Rochemore sent the king's physician for Louisiana, Sieur Fontenette, to represent his interests. Kerlérec had issued a warrant for the physician's arrest, but Rochemore's accomplices smuggled him aboard a small Saint Domingue coasting vessel by hiding him between two mattresses.[119]

The trickle of contact with France created an intensely partisan situation. Each side manoeuvred to discredit the other, but because of the few letters and orders received, could not be sure which actions would bring dismissal, rebuke, or reward. The factions did not divide along any easily identifiable lines. Each side placed and promoted relatives to important posts within its functional spheres of influence, in part to bolster its security. For example, Governor Kerlérec created a new military detachment composed of young artillery ensigns and appointed his nephew, Dessalles, to lead them. Rochemore, on his part, championed his brother-in-law, Sieur Normant (also related to former intendant Le Normant de Mézy), as the new king's storekeeper because, he explained, the young man was trustworthy, and anyway "such close affinities between *commissaire* and storekeeper were often found in France."[120] As supreme commander over Native alliances, Kerlérec cultivated fort commanders and the commissaries who actually managed the king's storerooms in the *pays d'en haut* posts, or he placed his own relations in significant posts. He drew several of New Orleans's major merchants to his side, such as Chantalou (also spelled Chantillon), a representative of Bordeaux's Jung family, Caminada (arguably the colony's richest merchant in the

1750s), Lassize, and the father-and-son team of the Raguets.[121] Several of these merchants also served on Louisiana's Superior Council, a fact that in part explains the strained relations between this body and the *commissaire ordonateur*. As noted above, many senior officers in New Orleans had settled in the colony and developed strong family connections and plantations in the vicinity.

The inconsistent contact with the Marine encouraged a growing reliance on using "the public" as a means to justify conduct or reinforce the severity of charges. Recourse to "the public" or the needs or desires of "the public" appears in virtually every letter written by both factions, a phenomenon not seen in either Canada or the Îles du Vent. These references were more than rhetorical devices. There were three basic ways the "public voice" made an appearance in the official correspondence. First, there were the specific identifiable publics, such as merchants, who forwarded correspondence under the sponsorship of one or the other party. In the wake of the seizure of the British neutral-flag ship *The Texel* in March 1759, three months prior to *The Three Brothers*, a group of eighteen prominent merchants and some twenty-five planters (including at least five officers) signed a petition to allow the ship to trade in New Orleans, pleading, in rather bland terms, that the "[n]eed and want is greater than ever. Rich residents are forced to mix their own bread [i.e., with rice or corn]. The misery of the people is too great to give you details of it." The merchants sent a second petition two months later (signed by at least ten of the original signatories), and the churchwardens of New Orleans sent a third directly to the Marine in May. This last petition complained of graft under Rochemore and his secretary (Bellot), and described the necessity of the neutral-flag trade: "The habitants, fatigued by a bloody war ... thanked the Governor and Intendant for the help they have procured ... [in the meantime] there arrived an English *parlementaire* laden with provisions and dry goods, both useful to the colony, the first so that we need not take food from out of the mouths of our Negroes, the second to dress them."[122] The *aide major* dismissed the petitions by noting that the merchants who signed it were the same as those engaged in the neutral-flag trade.[123]

Kerlérec continued sponsoring similar petitions to denounce Rochemore for the next three years.[124] In a very different vein were several petitions submitted to the Marine by officers. Since they represented the social and even economic core of the colony, their words carried great weight. Several protests were made to authorities, not all of them over the issue of the neutral-flag trade. While some officers banded together to protest Kerlérec's admission of English vessels, many of the same signers also protested against abuses by Rochemore over payments for clothing.[125] The fact that officers assembled at all automatically gave them an ominous collective identity in the eyes of the governor, even if they did not explicitly attack him.

The "public" appeared in a second way: as vaguely sculpted participants in the see-saw contest for supremacy. Of course, officials construed their behaviour to suit the needs of their reports, often to show a negative or positive response to their own actions. There were thus "scandalized" publics, "suffering" publics, and publics that served as mute witnesses to a humiliating action. The Rochemore faction appeared to pepper its correspondence with many brief references to a public shocked, dismayed, or even gripped with near panic by the actions of its opponents. For example, Rochemore explained Kerlérec's surprise reversal to rearrest Captain Bull by noting that "the said Joseph Boull [*sic*] came here only to obtain knowledge about the Colony ... [and] the people were greatly alarmed by this." [126] In another example, Rochemore characterized the effect of the governor's policing of mail this way: "The public often mistrusts this manner of acting and considers it like a sort of inquisition."[127] On his side, Kerlérec took the moral high ground and often presented himself as the sole resource for a public oppressed by Rochemore. At the height of the dispute over *The Texel*, the governor wrote the *commissaire*:

> Monsieur, Let us rejoice for our colonists and let us enjoy being the servants, of deriving sweet satisfaction from bringing to their attention that we know how to obtain aid even from our enemies.
>
> Do you believe, Monsieur, that such circumstances might not be able to soothe their unhappiness and re-animate their zeal for the orders that we can give them, each one, in his way, in the service of the king?
>
> Yes, Monsieur, when you know the inhabitants of this Colony, you will grant that they have spirit and feeling, and you will see that they are sensitive to signs of kindness that one shows them, and that they feel, in the same way, the indifference you seem to have toward their situation.[128]

The governor carefully forwarded such letters to the Marine as well. Rochemore, perhaps wisely from the point of view of the later investigation, did not answer, only annoying Kerlérec further. When he announced the sale of *The Texel*'s goods, Kerlérec proudly recounted that he heard "a general cry in all the streets, 'Long Live the King and his Governor.'"[129] As described at the beginning of this chapter, the governor called a meeting of the public to make a similar announcement for the sale of *The Three Brother*'s cargo, exclaiming, "You demand, my children, that *parlementaires* have free entrance to the ports, [so] that they might make their sales tranquilly?"[130] If accurately reported, this unabashed mixture of paternalism and free enterprise suggests that Louisiana, perhaps because of its precarious isolation, had evolved in a manner quite opposed to the Marine's policies, where a governor might carve out his own domain, and support his own version of free trade.

Finally, a third type of "mute public" was cited as a witness to elite humiliation and served as a constant backdrop. For example, Governor Kerlérec lamented in one long, melancholy letter that his authority had sunk so low that he had become the target of songs "the most indecent and the most foul, composed, they say, by Madame de Rochemore, corrected by Monsieur [de Rochemore], and enriched by the Sieur Normant [the storekeeper], brother of Madame."[131] Rochemore, writing at the same time, complained that the governor, having read Marine letters intended for Rochemore, relished telling everyone of the Marine's poor opinion of the *commissaire*, and he warned that the "breach" not only affected him personally, but undermined the "consideration that the public should have for the position which I occupy."[132] When Rochemore finally received official censure for his conduct, he fought back by exposing cosy corruption practices under Kerlérec. The governor had demanded a hefty share in all *pays d'en haut* trade, levied a private fee of 10 per cent on the value of all smuggled goods from British ships (upon his arrival, Kerlérec had offered Rochemore a cut of 5 per cent, the same split he had provided Rochemore's predecessor, but Rochemore reported that he had refused), and given the concession of valuable land within New Orleans to his son, nephew, half-brother, and unspecified, favoured "others."[133] While historians have tended to accept the assessment of Villiers du Terrage (a descendant of Kerlérec's) that Rochemore played the role of "villain," it is more likely that both leaders had carved out their own self-enrichment arrangements and were battling desperately to preserve these and to promote their own clients in the process. The dearth of news and regular contact created in Louisiana a kind of power vacuum that the two different factions scrambled to fill. It is most striking that immediately after the reappearance of regular contact and royal authority under *commissaire* d'Abbadie in 1763, and with the spectre of a more stringent Spanish rule hanging over the heads of New Orleans's merchants, the colony proved to be remarkably free of factional battles. However, these energies would shortly turned into a patriotic rebellion when Spanish rule finally arrived in 1768.

The diversity of power relations in each colony demanded administrative flexibility on the part of an increasingly centralized state. Each colony proved to be different from France, and vastly different from the others. Yet the Marine negotiated these distinctions with some success. In both Canada and Louisiana the heavy military expenditures and reliance on Native diplomacy strengthened the position and patronage network of the governor, while in the Îles du Vent the commercial importance of plantation products and the physical presence of much of the bureaucracy in the major port of Saint Pierre appears to have favoured the intendant's position and patronage system. The governor could profit and win promotion only as the protector of merchants, not as a diplomat or a commander of posts. In New France the creation of a bishopric and its associated institutions supported a relatively strong presence by the lay religious orders and cooperation with the regular clergy, and this in turn helped foster a strong patriarchal form of social order. But it also provided an independent power base to report on and even critique official actions. In all three colonies the Superior Councils were officially merely transmitters of the laws and decrees of the metropolitan state. But in actual practice these councils enjoyed varying degrees of autonomy, which were inversely linked to state spending. As I have suggested, the weaker the economic presence of the state, the more the colonial councils voiced concerns or even challenged the state's other officials.

What undermined the functioning of any of these three groups of elites, but especially of the first – the governor and the intendant – were disruptions in the reporting hierarchy. Independent reports by underlings or other elites cracked a myth of monolithic authority just as much as delays or denials of advancement or honours by the Marine. Throughout the first half of the eighteenth century, the Marine showed a clear preference for assessments of colonial situations by its metropolitan officials, rather than from the Creoles in subordinate positions who chose to expose or criticize them. In this way, for example, the victory at Carillon under Montcalm became a victory by the French in America, not the French of America, and Creoles or habitants were quick to realize the slight. The Marine remained reluctant to address the problem of ultimate command from 1755 until early 1759. While it is true that the importation of European armies, logistics, and battle tactics revolutionized the Seven Years War in North America, it is equally plausible that the encroaching subordination of Canadian traditions of warfare to European ones constituted a revolution in its own right. By accepting the assessments of Montcalm – that is, privileging European experience over Canadian – the Marine, we should note, placed Canada in the position of engaging in the type of conflict it could not hope to win. Years of cultivating misleading reports also fostered a belief within the Marine that the Îles du Vent not only could defend itself but would remain staunchly loyal during any attack. Finally, the lack of communication by the Marine with top officials in Louisiana exacerbated factionalism and invited, at the very least rhetorically, a laissez-faire economy with overtones of democratic participation. We return to the question posed at the beginning of the chapter: whom could the Marine believe? The answer, of course, proved to be no one. In this respect, the greatest hindrance to open communication and close elite cooperation may have been competition and cultural perceptions, not distance or difficulty of travel. Within this dilemma of determining truth in transatlantic information lay the problem of bureaucratic confusion and inertia, the key weakness in the administration of the French Atlantic in the eighteenth century.

Conclusion

The first French colonizers were met with a hard land. Cold that inflicted pain, sickness that killed. Around them the unknown forest, a vast wild solitude. And along with those uncertain beginnings, the constant fear of the Iroquois, who had no intention of letting themselves be despoiled. Fortunately the palisade was there, reassuring.

Some among us inherited from that time a siege mentality.

Daniel Poliquin, *In the Name of the Father*

The rain washed down the timbers, the sails, the rigging; it made the black spot marking where they had put the piece of sheet metal even more obvious ... You could still see the thick remains of blood that were around it. Because rebels had been made to dance to the rhythm of the fire on the hot metal whenever they refused to walk during the half hour of exercise on deck. And the metal itself was there, twisted, humpbacked, blackened, bloody, and the rainwater striking it with a cheerful patter could not wash away the thickly aggregated soot of burned blood and rust.

Édouard Glissant, *The Fourth Century*

[T]hrough this medley of languages and colors, were the people of the port, the sailors of the ships, who came in great waves to spend their money in the cabarets, to buy for the night the beautiful women both dark and light ... to crowd the narrow streets on the way to the old French Opera House and the Théâtre d'Orléans and the St. Louis Cathedral, from whose open doors came the chants of High Mass over the crowds of Place d'Armes on Sundays, over the noise and bickering of the French Market, over the silent, ghostly drift of the ships along the raised waters of the Mississippi, which flowed against the levee above the ground of New Orleans itself, so that the ships appeared to float against the sky.

This was New Orleans, a magical and magnificent place to live

Anne Rice, *Interview with the Vampire*

The former French colonies of Canada, the Îles du Vent, and Louisiana are now the very different province of French-speaking Quebec in Canada, the French Overseas Departments (DOM) of Martinique and Guadeloupe (with the same territorial boundaries determined in 1763), and the American state of Louisiana, the eighteenth to join the union and one of the first to leave it in 1861. The three quotations above capture something unique to each of the former colonies: cultural survival in Quebec, the violence of slavery in Martinique and Guadeloupe, and the exotic appeal of Louisiana and especially of New Orleans. Even more striking is the fact that the quotation for each place might also be applicable to the other two. Each former colony is perceived to have a political culture under siege, has a long and bloody history of human endurance after forced dislocation or separation and often under searing violence, and is regarded by the larger political units to which it belongs as enticingly unusual, mysterious, perhaps even faintly decadent. More than two centuries after its political death, the legacy of the French Atlantic lives, barely perceptible through the separate evolutions of the three former colonies. While this book has highlighted the many differences between these colonies, it is useful to briefly review the continuities, beginning with the political culture inherited by each from *ancien régime* France.

The early modern French state emerged over the course of the sixteenth and seventeenth centuries with a distinctly territorially based administration rooted in traditions of medieval kingship and divine-right hierarchy. In the 1660s Louis XIV and Jean-Baptiste Colbert secured control over most of France, most of the time, by creating a permanent and mainly centralized bureaucracy charged with governing a distinct geographic space. The state used an increasingly more complex information gathering and analyzing corps of officials to investigate the provinces, compile statistics, censor subversive tracts, project royal authority through public ceremonies, and manage information flows through an efficient postal system and a steadily improving road system. However, these new methods of centralized power could be applied only incompletely and incrementally in France. But the overseas colonies offered a far less developed terrain where traditional institutions and infrastructure in the form of buildings, defence works, roads, and improved harbours were almost wholly lacking and could be refashioned more completely by the state, and in the state's new image. The overseas colonies were an extension, then, of a new and very authoritarian state, which used one of its most important monopolies, that of information, to try to create a new kind of social order.

In reality, France's far-flung colonial possessions offered too many challenges to the state and its control over communications. From inception to implementation, the efficient use of information could be compromised at seven critical junctures. First, efforts to rationally coordinate the regular sailing of officials and official dispatches could only be accomplished with great effort and at high costs, and could never be foolproof. Once official dispatches or officials themselves left the coast of France, they entered a world of sea, winds, currents, and seasons, where the labour and knowledge of seafarers predominated. Second, once in the Americas, information moved only with the cooperation of early settlers, who had gained extensive knowledge of natural conditions and had adapted their lives to the new environments. A third factor was that royal officials had to negotiate with colonists to pay for and build the principal seat of protection, glory, and royal information dissemination, the king's town. Towns offering strong defence and a secure harbour, such as Quebec, merited full attention from the crown; those lacking these natural features, such as Saint Pierre, were dismissed as unsuitable sites to project the king's power. Fourth, state-sponsored ceremonies that celebrated battles, royal births, and restorations to health were far fewer in the colonies and were adapted to colonial traditions, ritual calendars, and political needs. Fifth, although the state used its official monopoly over information to instill social order in colonial societies, it found controlling the lower social echelons of defenders, prisoners, and enslaved labourers, who together constituted the most marginalized of colonial society, the most difficult. Fearing collusion between these groups and the poorer habitants or the *petits colons*, the state actively manipulated the environment of information exchange in order to divide and regulate their behaviour.

At a sixth juncture, the state could not do without the extensive contacts and information gathering provided by merchants and their ships; colonial officials turned a blind eye to smuggling not only because of the profits it brought but also because the "new world" of intercolonial commercial and information exchange proved too vast to control and too useful to suppress. The state increasingly came to rely upon merchants as information carriers and providers, and in turn, merchants cast a more critical eye on officials' conduct and on state policies. Finally, the facade of elite unity, so vital for authoritarian governments to ensure social order, suffered continual erosion. Although the state's colonial officials were seemingly well integrated into metropolitan patron-client networks and appeared to be closely monitored, the plurality of information suppliers, combined with the officials' incessant demands for promotions and honours as badges of royal favour and approval, undercut the rigid reporting hierarchy and led to public disputes among leaders or a public loss of face by officials. Colonial leaders constantly fretted that such incidents diminished their power and left open the very real possibility of disobedience and even revolt. The greatest fissures were cultural, erupting between metropolitan and Creole leaders, and war exacerbated these tensions further. The French overseas possessions created a "new world" of information exchange and knowledge, yet the early modern state found that authoritarian control could not be exercised as thoroughly or adjusted quickly enough to effectively construct or patrol the colonies.

This study poses many unanswered questions and leaves many avenues open to exploration that are applicable either to these colonies or to others. A systematic study of Saint Domingue, unique and ultimately so influential among all the *vieilles colonies*, needs to be undertaken. A study of communications would be valuable to enhance our understanding, for example, of the transatlantic transmission and interplay of Enlightenment ideals and West African political traditions in the pre-revolutionary decades. The role of women in keeping alive transatlantic community deserves attention, as does the transmission of heritage and information in creating an Afro-Caribbean culture. The formation of American-based identities would benefit from a closer analysis of transatlantic education (formal and not), personal transoceanic contacts, informal news exchange, availability of print and reading patterns, and the impact of highly cosmopolitan sites of interaction among both free and unfree colonists or between European colonies. The work of the various religious orders would prove critical in this last respect. Finally, the exchange between the Old World and the New ran in both directions, as J.H. Elliott and Alfred Crosby recognized many years ago. Tracing the impact of knowledge about the colonies or derived from them on, say, individual French *philosophes* and regional academies in the Ponant would throw open many new windows on the Enlightenment.

While it is beyond this study to trace the direct links between the eighteenth-century political culture and the present, there are intriguing similarities which are interesting in their own right, and which might form a profitable basis of future contact and cooperation in the surviving regions of francophone America. There is the obvious: all three former French colonies – Quebec, Martinique and Guadeloupe, and Louisiana – are now parts of much larger political entities. All three share a French linguistic heritage, and civil law codes continue to be of paramount importance as defining cultural references. Like metropolitan observers in the eighteenth century, the larger political units to which the three former colonies now belong view them as exotic, freer, and even hedonistic destinations. As the travel brochures describe them, they are inherently "Other," whether a "slice of old

Europe" (Quebec), all-inclusive resorts serviced by the heirs of slavery (the DOM), or the infectious home of jazz and zydeco, the carefree venue of Mardi Gras, and the supernatural realm of vampires (Louisiana). Like the resource-rich *vieilles colonies*, economically all three remain strikingly tied to resource exploitation. Despite the impact of an industrial revolution that remained limited to greater Montreal, iron ore and nickel, hydroelectricity, forestry products, and tourism (which shares characteristics with resource-based export industries) continue to form the backbone of Quebec's exports. The economies of Guadeloupe and Martinique are dominated by tourism, bananas, and rum, and the privileged position of these products or services is increasingly undermined by competition from the newer members of the European Union. Louisiana relies on sulphur, oil, and again tourism. In Quebec, manufacturing persists through government-supported efforts, not unlike those of eighteenth-century Canada and Louisiana or the mono-production of the eighteenth-century Îles du Vent. All three now rank among the poorer political units of their respective countries, and unemployment is high, critically so in Martinique and Guadeloupe, as of this writing. All three have a pattern of electing strong, often populist leaders who emerged from within the government bureaucracy, such as the notorious Huey P. Long in Louisiana and Maurice Duplessis in Quebec, or the advocates of ethnic/racial pride and independence, such as Aimé Césaire in Martinique or René Lévesque in Quebec. Here again, there are parallels with the autocratic governors such as Vaudreuil, Champigny, and Kerlérec in the eighteenth century. The relations of these former colonies to their larger political configurations remain highly contentious issues for Quebec and Martinique-Guadeloupe. Both are desperately searching for new definitions of freedom, whether as independent states or by renegotiating their links to Canada and France respectively.

Efforts by the early modern French state to control communications helped forge the political culture shared by all three colonies. The state used control over communications to divide as much as to unite; not surprisingly, the chase for empire left colonial societies stranded and as divided from the metropolis as they were from one another. The challenge of open communications remains at the heart of any future resolution of sensitive issues with their larger political units or in forging new links among themselves. These ghostly ties are another reminder of the complex, deep, and still troubled world of the French Atlantic.

Appendices

APPENDIX A

Secretaries of State for the Marine

1669–83	Jean-Baptiste Colbert
1683–90	Jean-Baptiste Antoine Colbert, Marquis de Seignelay
1690–99	Louis Phélypeaux, Comte de Pontchartrain
1699–1715	Jérôme Phélypeaux, Comte de Pontchartrain
1715–23	Council of the Marine (during the Regency); Louis-Alexandre de Bourbon, Comte de Toulouse, chief
1723	Charles-Jean-Baptiste Fleuriau, Comte de Morville
1723–49	Jean-Frédéric Phélypeaux, Comte de Maurepas
1749–54	Antoine-Louis Rouillé, Comte de Jouy
1754–Feb. 1757	Jean-Baptiste de Machault d'Arnouville
Feb. 1757–June 1758	François-Marie de Peirenc de Moras
June–Oct. 1758	Claude-Louis de Massiac, Marquis de Massiac
Nov. 1758–61	Nicolas-René de Berryer
1761–66	Etienne-François Choiseul, Duc de Choiseul

APPENDIX B

Governors General and Intendants of New France

Governors General

1665–72	Daniel de Rémy, Seigneur de Courcelle
1672–82	Louis de Buade, Comte de Frontenac
1682–85	Joseph-Antoine Le Febvre de La Barre
1685–89	Jacques-René de Brisay de Denonville, Marquis de Denonville
1689–98	Comte de Frontenac
1698–1703	Louis-Hector de Callière
1703–25	Philippe de Rigaud de Vaudreuil, Marquis de Vaudreuil
1725–26	Charles Le Moyne, Baron de Longeuil[1]
1726–47	Charles de Beauharnois de La Boische, Marquis de Beauharnois
1747–49	Roland-Michel Barrin de La Galissonière, Marquis de La Galissonière[1]
1749–52	Jacques-Pierre de Taffanel de La Jonquière, Marquis de La Jonquière
1752–55	Ange Duquesne de Menneville, Marquis Duquesne
1755–60	Pierre de Rigaud de Vaudreuil de Cavagnial, Marquis de Vaudreuil (known as Vaudreuil-Cavagnial)

Intendants

1663	Louis Fortel de Robert[2]
1665–68	Jean Talon
1668–70	Claude de Boutroue d'Aubigny
1670–72	Jean Talon
1675–82	Jacques Duchesneau de La Doussinière et d'Ambault
1682–86	Jacques de Meulles
1686–1702	Jean Bochart de Champigny
1702–05	François de Beauharnois de la Chaussaye, Baron de Beauville
1705–10	Jacques Raudot and Antoine-Denis Raudot
1710–26	Michel Bégon de la Picardière[3]
1724	Edmé-Nicolas Robert[4]
1725	Henry de Chazel[4]
1725–28	Claude-Thomas Dupuy
1729–48	Gilles Hocquart[5]
1748–60	François Bigot

[1]Interim.
[2]Did not take up post.
[3]Arrived Sept. 1712.
[4]Died en route.
[5]Interim from 1729; appointed intendant 1731.

APPENDIX C

Governors General and Intendants of the Îles du Vent

Governors-General

1667–77 Jean-Charles de Baas-Castelmore
1677–90 Charles de La Roche Courbon, Comte de Blénac
1690–92 François d'Alesso, d'Eragny
1692–96 Comte de Blénac
1696–1700 Thomas-Claude Renart de Fuchsamberg, Marquis d'Amblimont
1700–01 Charles de Peychpeyrou-Commingue de Guitaud[1]
1701 Charles, Comte d'Esnotz de Forbonest[1]
1701–02 De Guitaud[1]
1702–03 Nicholas de Gabaret[1]
1703–09 Charles-François Machault de Belmont
1709–10 Nicolas de Gabaret[1]
1710–13 Raymond Balthazar de Phélypeaux du Verger
1713–15 Georges-Robert Cloche de Mont Saint-Rémy de La Malmaison[1]
1715–17 Abraham de Belleprat de Duquesne-Guitton
1717 Antoine d'Arcy de La Varenne
1717–27 François du Pas de Mazencourt, Marquis de Feuquières
1727–44 Jacques-Charles de Bochart, Marquis de Champigny
1744–50 Charles de Thubières, (also Taubière) Marquis de Caylus

Intendants

1679–82 Jean-Baptiste Patoulet
1682–85 Michel Bégon
1684–95 Gabriel du Maitz de Goimpy
1695–1704 François Roger Robert
1704 Croizet[3]
1704–06 Jean-Jacques Mithon de Senneville[2]
1706–16 Nicolas-François Arnoul, Seigneur de Vaucresson
1716–17 Pierre de Marseille[4]
1717 Louis-Balthazar de Ricouart, Seigneur d'Hérouville[5]
1717–18 Constant de Silvecane
1719–22 Charles Besnard
1722–26 Charles-François Blondel de Jouvancourt
1728–37 Jacques Panier d'Orgeville
1737–44 César-Marie de Lacroix
1744–49 Jean-Louis de Ranché[6]
1749–54 Charles-Marin Hurson
1754–57 Antoine Lefebvre de Givry
1759–62, 1763–64 Paul-Pierre Lemercier de La Rivière, Baron de St-Médard

1750–57	Maximin, Comte de Bompar
1757–61	François, Marquis de Beauharnais de Beaumont
1761–62	Louis-Charles Levassor de La Touche
1759–60	Byam Crump (British; Guadeloupe)
1760–63	Campbell Dalrymple (British; Guadeloupe)
1762–63	William Rufane (British; Martinique)
1763–64	François-Louis, Marquis de Salignac de Lamotte-Fénelon (Martinique)
1763–64	François-Charles de Bourlamaque (Guadeloupe)

[1]Interim, holding rank as lieutenant-general.
[2]Interim, serving in the capacity of intendant.
[3]Did not take up post.
[4]Dean of the Superior Council, serving as Marine *commissaire*.
[5]Removed during the Gaoulé of 1717.
[6]Interim from 1744; appointed intendant in 1746.

APPENDIX D

Governors and Commissaires-Ordonnateurs of Louisiana

Governors

1701–03	Jean-Baptiste Le Moyne de Bienville[1]
1703–06	Pierre Le Moyne d'Iberville[2]
1707–08	Nicolas Daneau de Muy[3]
1707–13	Le Moyne de Bienville
1710–16	Antoine Laumet de Lamothe Cadillac[4]
1716–17	Jean-Michel l'Épinay de Longueville
1717-1725	Le Moyne de Bienville
1723–25	Pierre Sidrac Dugué de Boisbriant[5]
1725–25	Antoine Le Moyne de Châteauguay
1726–32	Étienne Boucher Périer de Salvert
1732–43	Le Moyne de Bienville
1743–52	Pierre de Rigaud de Vaudreuil de Cavagnial, Marquis de Vaudreuil (known as Vaudreuil-Cavagnial)
1752–63	Louis Billouart, Comte de Kerlérec de Kervasegan
1763–65	Jean-Jacques-Blaise d'Abbadie[6]

Commissaires-Ordonnateurs

1707–11	Jean-Baptiste-Martin Diron d'Artaguiette[7]
1712–16	Jean-Baptiste Dubois Duclos
1716–20	Marc-Antoine-César-Anne Hubert
1720–21	Michel-Léon Duvergier[7]
1722–24	Savoy[7] and Jacques de La Chaise
1724–26	Jean Perreault[7] and Jacques de La Chaise
1726–30	Jacques de La Chaise
1731–44	Edmé-Gatien Salmon
1744–48	Sébastian-François-Ange Le Normant de Mézy
1748	Vincent-Guillaume Le Sénéchal d'Auberville[7]
1748–52	Honoré Michel de La Rouvillière de Villebois
1752–57	Le Sénéchal d'Auberville[7]
1757–58	Jean-Baptiste-Claude Bobé-Descloseaux[7]
1758–62	Michel-Vincent Gaspard de Rochemore
1762–65	Jean-Jacques-Blaise d'Abbadie

[1]Commander of Mobile post.

[2]Appointed first governor but non-resident; functions *sur terre* carried out by Bienville.

[3]Died en route.

[4]Arrived 1713.

[5]Interim governor.

[6]Appointed *commissaire-ordonnateur*, 1762, then director-general of colony in 1763, effectively combining military and police powers.

[7]Not commissioned; serving as Marine *commissaire*.

Notes

ABBREVIATIONS

AC Archives des Colonies (in the Archives Nationales, Paris, and in CAOM, Aix-en-Provence)
ADCM Archives Départementales de Charente-Maritime (La Rochelle)
ADG Archives Départementales de Gironde (Bordeaux)
ADLA Archives départementales de Loire-Atlantique (Nantes)
AM Archives de Marme (in the Archives Nationales, Paris)
AMN Archives Municipales de Nantes
AN Archives Nationales (Paris)
Beinecke Walter Beinecke Lesser Antilles Collection, Hamilton College (New York)
BMLR Bibliothèque Municipale de La Rochelle
BN Bibliothèque Nationale (Paris)
BRH Bulletin des recherches historiques
CAOM Centre des Archives d'outre-mer (Aix-en-Provence)
CCLR Archives de Chambre de Commerce et de l'Industrie de La Rochelle
CCM Archives de Chambre de Commerce et de l'Industrie de Marseille
DCB *Dictionary of Canadian Biography*
DFC Dépôt des Fortifications des Colonies (in CAOM, Aix-en-Provence)
JR *The Jesuit Relations and Allied Documents*
MG Manuscript group (for NA)
MPA *Mississippi Provincial Archives: French Dominion*
NA National Archives of Canada (Ottawa)
NMC National Map Collection (in NA)
NYCD *Documents Relative to the Colonial History of the State of New York*

PAC Public (now National) Archives of Canada
RAPQ *Rapport de l'Archiviste de la Province de Québec*, 1920–61
Rochefort 1E Archives Maritime de Rochefort, sous-série 1E (in NA, MG 6, C1)
RSC "Records of the Superior Council [of Louisiana]"

INTRODUCTION

1 AC, C11E, Account of the advantages and disadvantages for each parish in New France, compiled by Monsieur Collet, attorney general for the Superior Council of Quebec, ff. 65–231, 1721.
2 Resbecq, "Administration centrale," 427–8, 451–2.
3 Miquelon, *New France, 1701–1744*, 234; Jaenen, *Role of the Church in New France*, 90.
4 Pagden, *Lords of All the World*, esp. 66–73.
5 Brewer, *Sinews of Power*, 120–6, 167–78 (economy and imperialism), and chap. 8 (information and administration); Rediker, *Between the Devil and the Deep Blue Sea*, chap. 1; Hancock, *Citizens of the World*, chap. 1; Gould, *Persistence of Empire*, 35–69. On Greater Britain, see the relevant articles by Armitage, "Greater Britain," and Landsman, "Nation, Migration, and the Province," and the fascinating counterpoint offered by Pocock, "New British History in Atlantic Perspective."
6 See, for example, Curtin, *Rise and Fall of the Plantation Complex*; the essays in Solow, *Slavery and the Rise of the Atlantic System*; Gilroy, *Black Atlantic*; Thornton, *Africa and Africans in the Making of the Atlantic World*; Gerzina, *Black London*; Eltis et al., *Rise of African Slavery in the Americas*.
7 AC, C11A 87, ff. 264–7, La Galissonière to Maurepas, October 24, 1747; ibid., 96, ff. 248–71, Memorandum on the Colonies of France in North America, December, 1750 [unsigned but replicating the earlier document]; see also Lamontagne, *La Galissonière et le Canada*, chap. 6].
8 Price, *France and the Chesapeake*, 1: 78.
9 Most historians refer to variations on "la France coloniale," "les vieilles colonies," "Les Nouvelles Frances," or simply "France (or the French) in America." See Julien, *Français en Amérique*; Pagden, *Lords of All the World*, 136–7; Eccles, "Fur Trade and Eighteenth-Century Imperialism," and *France in America*; Boucher, *Nouvelles Frances*. For a more popular history, see Quinn, *French Overseas Empire*.
10 Miquelon, "Envisioning the French Empire," quote 671.
11 Marzagalli, "French Atlantic," 71.
12 Braudel, *Mediterranean*, esp. 1: chaps 2 and 3; Godechot, *Histoire de l'Atlantique*; Liss, *Atlantic Empires*; Butel, *Atlantic*; Chaudhuri, *Trade and Civilization in the Indian Ocean*.

13 Pérotin-Dumon, "French America," 552–4.

14 Elliott, *Imperial Spain*, 167–78; McAlister, *Spain and Portugal in the New World*, 186–97, 435–9.

15 Bodin, *Six Books of the Commonwealth*, 1–7, 115–28; Bossuet, *Politics Drawn from ... Holy Scripture*, 41–7, 173; Louis XIV, *Mémoires for the Instruction of the Dauphin*, 63, 140, 144, 155, 247; also Hanley, "Engendering the State"; Phillips, "Family and Political Ideology"; Merrick, "Patriarchalism and Constitutionalism."

16 Many now support some variation of David Parker's earlier contention that "absolutism was always in the making, but never made" (Parker, *Making of French Absolutism*, quote xvi, also 125–35). See also Mousnier, *Institutions of France*, esp. 2: 99–136; Beik, *Absolutism and Society*, 3–17, 182–96; Kettering, *Patrons, Brokers, and Clients*; Collins, *Classes, Estates, and Order*, esp. chap. 7; Durand, "What Is Absolutism?"; Bonney, *Political Change in France*, 450; Mettam, *Power and Faction*, 10–24; Farge, *Dire et mal-dire*, 43–56.

17 Ranum, *Paris in the Age of Absolutism*, 272–82.

18 Kettering, *Patrons, Brokers, and Clients*; Beik, *Absolutism and Society*; Major, *From Renaissance Monarchy to Absolute Monarchy*.

19 Innis, *Bias of Communications*, and *Empire and Communications*. Assessments of Innis's influence include Patterson, *History and Communications*, 3–20; Westfall, "Ambivalent Verdict"; and Carey, *Communication as Culture*, 142–72. For a highly critical stance, see Eccles, "Belated Review of Harold Adams Innis," 61–78.

20 Habermas, *Structural Transformation of the Public Sphere*, 16–27, 38–43, 67–70.

21 Chartier, *Cultural History*, 7–9, and "Texts, Printing, Reading," 163–6, 171–4.

22 Headrick, *Tools of Empire*, 129–208.

23 McQuail, *Communication*, 3–5, 25–6; Severin and Tankard, *Communication Theories*; Mattelart and Mattelart, *Rethinking Media Theory*, chap. 4.

24 Carey, *Communication as Culture*, 14–21, quotes 20–1.

25 Herman and Chomsky, *Manufacturing Consent*, 1–36; Peters, *Speaking into the Air*, 1–31.

CHAPTER ONE

1 For recent attributions, see Pagden, *Lords of All the World*, 47; Quinn, *French Overseas Empire*, 12.

2 For overviews on sixteenth-century French maritime and settlement ventures, see Morison, *European Discovery: Southern Voyages*, 585–95, esp. note 594, and *European Discovery: Northern Voyages*, 339–454;

Quinn, *North America from the Earliest Discovery*, chap. 8; La Morandière, *Histoire de la pêche française*, vol. 1; Meyer, "Des origines à 1763," 56–71; Vergé-Franceschi, "Amirauté de France," and *Marine et éducation*, 7–18; Van Ruymbeke, "Charlesfort, Fort Caroline"; Cabantous, *Dix mille marins*, 129–41; Boucher, *Nouvelles Frances*, chaps 1–2; Trudel, *Beginnings of New France*, 11–53; Harris, *Historical Atlas of Canada*, plates 19–22. On the French Wars of Religion, see especially the essays in Davis, *Society and Culture in Early Modern Franace*; Le Roy Ladurie, *Carnival in Romans*; Diefendorf, *Beneath the Cross.*

3 Bodin, *Six Books of the Commonwealth*, bk 1 (9–18), bk 4 (133–45).

4 Boucher, *Nouvelles Frances*, 17–22; Droulers, "Saint-Louis-du-Maragnan," 88–9.

5 Meyer, "Des origines à 1763," 62–3; Trudel, *Beginnings of New France*, 73; Cole, *Colbert and ... Mercantilism*, 1: 68–75.

6 Griffiths, "1600–1650: Fish, Fur and Folk"; Trudel, *Beginnings of New France*, 71–92; Eccles, *France in America*, 14–19.

7 Trudel, *Beginnings of New France*, 93–9; Eccles, *Canadian Frontier*, 23–6.

8 Trudel, *Beginnings of New France*, 99–101.

9 Dessert, *Royale*; Major, *From Renaissance Monarchy to Absolute Monarchy*, 220–1, 289–94.

10 Collins, *State in Early Modern France*, 31, 58–60.

11 Cole, *Colbert and ... Mercantilism*, 1: 197–204.

12 Ibid., 1: 199–200; Major, *From Renaissance Monarchy to Absolute Monarchy*, 231–5.

13 Cole, *Colbert and ... Mercantilism*, 1: 164–94.

14 Hausser, *Pensée ... du Cardinal de Richelieu*, 127–34, 193.

15 Collins, *State in Early Modern France*, 51–5.

16 Ibid., quote 91; Cole, *Colbert and ... Mercantilism*, 1: 19–26, 209–34, 335–55. A solid and succinct discussion can be found Miquelon, *New France, 1701–1744*, 7–9.

17 *Traicté de l'oeconomie politique* (1615), cited in Cole, *Colbert and ... Mercantilism*, 1: 83–100; quote 96; on Richelieu, 144–53.

18 Mims, *Colbert's West India Policy*, 14–21.

19 Ibid., 22–9; Cole, *Colbert and ... Mercantilism*, 1: 185–91; Butel, *Atlantic*, 117–21.

20 Debien, "Engagés," especially chaps. 4 and 6.

21 May, *Histoire économique de la Martinique*, 87; Mims, *Colbert's West India Policy*, 31–3.

22 May, *Histoire économique de la Martinique*, 87–90. On the sugar-slavery relationship, see Dunn, *Sugar and Slaves*, 188–262; Curtin, *Rise and Fall of the Plantation Complex*, 73–110; Thornton, *Africa and Africans*, 162–77.

23 May, *Histoire économique de la Martinique*, 53–6; Eccles, *Canadian Frontier*, 38.
24 Trudel, *Beginnings of New France*, 169–72.
25 Eccles, *France in America*, 35–7; Greer, *Peasant, Lord, and Merchant*, 11–15; Harris, *Historical Atlas of Canada*, plates 51–2.
26 Trudel, *Beginnings of New France*, 108–36.
27 Ibid., 230–45; Trigger, *Children of Aataentsic*, 476–616; Eccles, *France in America*, 39–45.
28 Trudel, *Beginnings of New France*, 187–90.
29 For an overview, see Beik, *Urban Protest*, chap. 2; Collins, *State in Early Modern France*, 62–78.
30 Eccles, *Canadian Frontier*, 52–6; Trigger, *Children of Aataentsic*, 653–64, 725–82; White, *Middle Ground*, 2–6, 29–34.
31 Eccles, *France in America*, 38–9; and *Essays on New France*, 110–12.
32 Cole, *Colbert and ... Mercantilism*, 1: 241–4.
33 Esquemeling, *Buccaneers of America*, 9–13; Butel, *Caraïbes*, 67–72, 167–70.
34 Esquemeling, *Buccaneers of America*, 39–42.
35 Butel, *Caraïbes*, 160–79.
36 Cole, *Colbert and ... Mercantilism*, 1: 248–9; Boucher, "Shadows in the Past," 13–26.
37 Géraud-Llorca, "Coutume de Paris outre-mer."
38 Dessert, *Royale*, 21; also Meyer, *Colbert*, 274–5.
39 For example, see Cole, *Colbert and ... Mercantilism*, 1: 278–84, 332–5.
40 Meyer, *Colbert*, 12, 164–81, 230–60; Dessert, *Royale*, 22–33; Vergé-Franceschi, *Marine française*, 34–43.
41 Dessert, *Royale*, 24.
42 Vergé-Franceschi, *Marine et éducation*, 61.
43 Cole, *Colbert and ... Mercantilism*, 1: 450–73, 2: 333–49; Meyer, *Colbert*, 260–95; Dessert, *Royale*, 22–33.
44 Dessert, *Royale*, 19 and appendix 11; Meyer, *Colbert*, 270–1.
45 Isambert, *Recueil*, no. 981, "Ordinance of the Navy," August 1681.
46 Meyer, *Colbert*, 272.
47 Cole, *Colbert and ... Mercantilism*, 1: 342–7; Meyer, *Colbert*, 232–8.
48 For an overview, see Ly, *Compagnie du Sénégal*, 113–204; Cole, *Colbert and ... Mercantilism*, 2: 117–31; Crété, *Traite des nègres*, 20–4. For the most accurate recent assessment of the number of slaves transported, see Geggus, "French Slave Trade."
49 Eltis et al., *Trans-Atlantic Slave Trade.*
50 Crouse, *French Struggle*, 6–12; Frostin, *Révoltes blanches*, 78–81; Eccles, *France in America*, 65–6.
51 Eccles, *Canadian Frontier*, 107, 109.

52 Ibid., 112–13; Dechêne, *Habitants et marchands*, 173–80; Miquelon, *New France, 1701–1744*, 159–64.
53 Frostin, *Les Révoltes blanches*, chap. 1; Butel, *Caraïbes*, 167–8.
54 Butel, *Caraïbes*, 169–70; Price, *France and the Chesapeake*, 1: 83–93.
55 See Bézard, *Fonctionnaires maritimes*, esp. 22–105, 157–204.
56 Ibid., 34–60.
57 Ibid., 157–204; Vergé-Franceschi, *Marine et éducation*, 156–7.
58 Bézard, *Fonctionnaires maritimes*, 176.
59 Ibid., 100–5.
60 Vergé-Franceschi, *Marine française*, 62–3.
61 MacKay and Scott, *Rise of the Great Powers*, 41–50.
62 Griffiths, *Contexts of Acadian History*, xix, 34–45; Brière, "Pêche et politique."
63 Miquelon, *New France, 1710–1744*, 11.
64 Johnston, *Control and Order*, 8–12.
65 Pluchon, "Économie d''Habitation,'", 198–9, quote 198.
66 Frostin, *Révoltes blanches*, 137–42; Butel, *Atlantic*, 123–6.
67 Poussou, *Bordeaux et le sud-ouest*, 343–86.
68 Roche, *France in the Enlightenment*, 109–73; Collins, *State in Early Modern France*, 176–84; Léon and Carrière, "Appel des marchés"; Léon, "Réponse de l'industrie," 217–66.
69 Butel, *Atlantic*, 132–8.
70 AMN, HH-228, no. 3, p. 3, Memorandum on Nantes's commerce and the means to augment it ..., 1714.
71 May, *Histoire économique de la Martinique*, 97–9.
72 Clark, *New Orleans, 1718–1812*, 52–9.
73 Crowley, "'Thunder Gusts,'" 13–15; Greer, "Mutiny at Louisbourg," 70–110.
74 Crowley, "'Thunder Gusts,'" 118–19.
75 Frostin, *Révoltes blanches*, 166–265, esp. 242–59.
76 Petitjean-Roget, *Gaoulé*, 324–62.
77 Tarrade, *Commerce colonial*, 1: 85–95; see also Dessalles, *Annales du Conseil souverain*, 4: Vonglis, 26–30n3.
78 Butel, *Atlantic*, 131–2.
79 Nash, "Irish Atlantic Trade," 342–8; Filion, *Pensée ... de Maurepas*, 139–41, 419–22.
80 On debts, see also Morineau, "Vraie nature des choses," esp. 12–14.
81 Butel, *Atlantic*, 162–4.
82 Gaston-Martin, "Nantes et la Compagnie des Indes," 433–5, and *Histoire de l'esclavage*, chap. 4; Berbain, *Comptoir français*, 34–46; Stein, *French Slave Trade*, table A1, 207–8; Eltis et al., *Trans-Atlantic Slave Trade*.
83 Girod de Chantrans, quoted in Butel, *Atlantic*, 158.

84 Based on Frostin, *Révoltes blanches*, 32–3; Schnakenbourg, "Statistiques pour l'histoire ... de plantation," table 3.1, 85–6.
85 Mathieu, *Commerce entre la Nouvelle-France et les Antilles*, 122–3; Miquelon, *New France, 1701–1744*, chaps 7–8.
86 Miquelon, *New France, 1701–1744*, 179–86.
87 Moore, "Other Louisbourg"; Balcom, "Cod Fishery of Isle Royale."
88 Short description, Clark, *New Orleans, 1718–1812*, 16–20; comprehensive version, Giraud, *History of French Louisiana*, vol. 3.
89 Vergé-Franceschi, *Marine française*, 84–101, 114–15 (budgets).
90 Merrick, *Desacralization of the French Monarchy*, 32–48, 122–4.
91 Collins, *State in Early Modern France*, 199–204.
92 Pritchard, *Louis XV's Navy*, 7–33, 71–88, 126–42.
93 See especially Gould, *Persistence of Empire*, 30–69.
94 Montesquieu, *Spirit of the Laws*, bk 3 passim, 238–41, 149–64.
95 Voltaire, *Candide*, 92.
96 Pritchard, *Anatomy of a Naval Disaster*.
97 AC, C11A 96, ff.248–71, Memorandum on the colonies of France ..., December 1750; Lamontagne, *La Galissonière et le Canada*, chap. 6; Savelle, *Origins of American Diplomacy*.
98 McKay and Scott, *Rise of the Great Powers*, 171–7; Savelle, *Origins of American Diplomacy*.
99 Griffiths, *Contexts of Acadian History*, 89–90.
100 Steele, *Guerillas and Grenadiers*, 111–28.
101 Smelser, *Campaign for the Sugar Islands*, 15, citing Julian Corbett.
102 Meyer, "Des origines à 1763," 112.
103 Ibid.
104 Eltis et al., *Trans-Atlantic Slave Trade*.
105 AC, C8A 65, ff. 27–8, Fénélon and La Rivière to Choiseul, August 4, 1763.
106 Pares, *War and Trade*, 181–2.
107 Meyer, "Des origines à 1763," 137–47.
108 Aldrich, *Greater France*, esp. chap. 1.

CHAPTER TWO

1 Saint-Simon, *Mémoires*, 4: 628, 1347.
2 AN, K 1719/11, "Report on the proclamation of peace by the king," May 22, 1713 [signed Montjoye St. Denis].
3 Ibid.
4 Isherwood, *Music in the Service of the King*, 89, 250–1.
5 Saint-Simon, *Mémoires*, 4: 628. For other occasions, see AN, K 1719, 30/8, "Birth of Monseigneur le Dauphin" [September 9, 1729]; ibid., 15/12, *Relation des Cérémonies de la Paix qui doivent s'observer à la*

publication qui se sera à Paris le 12 février 1749 ... [printed January 30, 1749].

6 AC, C8A 19, ff. 217–18, Phélypeaux to Pontchartrain, September 10, 1713. See also chapter 4.

7 AC, B 35, ff. 524, Pontchartrain to Phélypeaux, April 21, 1713; ibid., ff. 526–6v., King's orders, May 22, 1713.

8 Ibid., ff. 270–70v., King's orders [New France], May 22, 1713; ibid., ff. 354–4v., King's orders [Louisiana], May 22, 1713.

9 AC, C13A 3, ff. 437v.–38, Cadillac to Pontchartrain, February 20, 1714.

10 Juchereau, *Histoire de l'Hôtel-Dieu de Québec*, 503–4.

11 AC, C11A 34, f. 41, Vaudreuil to Pontchartrain, September 8, 1713; ibid., f. 4v., same to same, November 15, 1713.

12 Savelle, *Origins of American Diplomacy*, 125–44; McKay and Scott, *Rise of the Great Powers, 1648–1815*, 58–66; and Vries, *Economy of Europe in an Age of Crisis, 1600–1750*, 125–44. For Canada, see Miquelon, *New France, 1701–1744*, chapter 3. For Louisiana, see Giraud, *History of French Louisiana*, 1: chaps 6 and 7.

13 AC, B 34, ff. 185v.–6, Pontchartrain to Vaudreuil, August 9, 1712; ibid., ff. 186v.–7, same to same, August 31, 1712.

14 AC, C8A 19, ff. 2, 16v.–17v., Phélypeaux to Pontchartrain, January 10, 1713.

15 Ibid., C11A 34, ff. 34–5v., Vaudreuil to Pontchartrain, February 11, 1713.

16 Ibid., B 35, f. 353, Pontchartrain to Cadillac, March 12, 1713.

17 See Giraud, *History of French Louisiana*, 1: 249–54.

18 Saint-Simon, *Mémoires*, 4: 628 and 1347n3.

19 Petitot and Monmerqué, *Collection des mémoires*, 224.

20 Tessier, *Diplomatie royale française*; Antoine, *Conseil du roi*, 543; Mousnier, *Institutions of France under the Absolute Monarchy*, 2: 235–44; Bosher, *French Finances, 1770–1795*, 34–6.

21 Mousnier, *Institutions of France under the Absolute Monarchy*, 2: 235–39; Antoine, *Conseil du roi*, 544–56; Frégault, *XVIIIe siècle canadien*, 168.

22 Bosher, *French Finances, 1770–1795*, 36.

23 Mousnier, *Institutions of France under the Absolute Monarchy*, 2: 240–2; Tessier, *Diplomatie royale française*, 298–303.

24 Term used in AC, C8A 19, f. 205, Phélypeaux to Pontchartrain, August 12, 1713; see also Strayer, *Lettres de Cachet and Social Control*, 1–3.

25 AC, B 35, ff. 44–5, Louis to M. l'Evésque de Québec, May 31, 1713.

26 Ibid., f. 271, Pontchartrain to Vaudreuil, May 31, 1713; ibid., ff. 271v.–2, Pontchartrain to Bégon, May 31, 1713; ibid., ff. 272–3, Louis to M. l'Evésque de Québec, May 31, 1713; ibid., ff. 273–3v., Louis to Bégon, May 31, 1713. See also for Plaisance (Placentia), ibid., ff. 273–3v; Louisiana, ibid., ff. 354–5; and the Îles du Vent, ibid., ff. 526–7.

27 Boulle, "French Colonies and the Reform," 28–50; Deschamps, *Méthodes et les doctrines coloniales*, 35–7; Duchêne, *Politique coloniale de la France*, 30–9; Rule, "Colbert de Torcy"; Symcox, "Navy of Louis XIV," 132–5.
28 Schaeper, *French Council of Commerce*, 242–6.
29 Meyer, "Decideurs," 81–97.
30 Bosher, "Treasurers of the Navy and Colonies," 327–48; Mousnier, *Institutions of France under the Absolute Monarchy*, 2: 144–5, 172–9; Duchêne, *Politique coloniale de la France*, 37; Frégault, *XVIIIe siècle canadien*, 165–7.
31 Duchêne, *Politique coloniale de la France*, 39–42.
32 AC, B 35, f. 225, Pontchartrain to Fontanieu, August 2, 1713.
33 Pritchard, *Louis XV's Navy*, 22.
34 AC, B 35, f. 254, Pontchartrain to Vaudreuil, March 29, 1713.
35 Figures based on Rochefort 1E, vols. 81–3, 1713.
36 Steele, "Moat Theories and the English Atlantic," 25 and note 38 (note computational error); also *Politics of Colonial Policy*, 7–9, 142–3; and Baugh, *British Naval Administration*, 35, 61–3.
37 Memain, *Marine de guerre sous Louis XIV*, 287–91.
38 Arbellot, "Grande mutation des routes," 765–6; Livet, "Route royale et la civilisation française," 63–5; Trénard, "De la route royale à l'âge d'or des diligences," 102–3; Lepetit, *Chemins de terre et voies d'eau*, chap. 1; Beik, *Absolutism and Society*, 99–100.
39 AC, B 35, ff. 30v.-31, Pontchartrain to Valminière, February 8, 1713.
40 Vaillé, *Histoire générale des postes françaises*, 4: 83–92; 5: 8–29, 231–8, 292–300.
41 *Almanach royal*, 176, 180, 182; Arbellot, "Grande mutation des routes," 765, 790.
42 Vaillé, *Histoire générale des postes françaises*, 5: 227–32.
43 AC, B 35, f. 125v., Pontchartrain to Beauharnais, July 8, 1713.
44 Mémain, *Marine de guerre sous Louis XIV*, 287.
45 Beik, *Absolutism and Society*, 100.
46 Mémain, *Marine de guerre sous Louis XIV*, chap. 1; Acerra, "Rochefort: l'arsenal, l'eau, et les vaisseaux"; Lavedan, *Histoire de l'urbanisme*, 2: 213–16.
47 Accera, "Rochefort: l'arsenal, l'eau, et les vaisseaux," 55.
48 Quoted in Pritchard, *Louis XV's Navy*, 91.
49 Accera, "Rochefort: l'arsenal, l'eau, et les vaisseaux," 52–3; Giraud, "France and Louisiana in the Early Eighteenth Century," 659; and Bosher, *Business and Religion*, 294–5.
50 AC, B 35, f. 524, Pontchartrain to Phélypeaux, April 21, 1713; ibid., ff. 524–5v., same to same, April 26, 1713.
51 Ibid., C8A 10, ff. 239–49, d'Amblimont to Pontchartrain, July 10, 1698; ibid., 13, ff. 305–6v., Observations of America made by the Sieur Lainé, royal pilot ..., February 1701; also Stein, *French Sugar Business*, 60–4.

52 Giraud, *History of French Louisiana*, 1: 62–5.
53 Pritchard, "Ships, Men, and Commerce," 39.
54 AC, B 35, ff. 4–5v., Pontchartrain to Beauharnais, January 20, 1713 [marked January 30 in inventory].
55 Rochefort 1E/81, 46–9, La Maignière to Pontchartrain [sent February 1713]; AC, B 35, f. 30v., Pontchartrain to Beauharnais, February 7, 1713. On the lawsuit, see Bosher, *Business and Religion*, 296–302.
56 Rochefort 1E/342, 23–5, Beauharnais to Pontchartrain, February 14, 1713; AC, B 35, ff. 39v.–40v., Pontchartrain to Beauharnais, February 22, 1713.
57 Rochefort 1E/342, Beauharnais to Pontchartrain, February 9, 1713; AC, B 35, ff. 39v–40v, Pontchartrain to Beauharnais, February 22, 1713.
58 Ibid, f. 34, Pontchartrain to Beauharnais, February 10, 1713; Rochefort 1E/342, 35–41, Beauharnais to Pontchartrain, February 25, 1713.
59 AC, B 35, f. 40v., Pontchartrain to Beauharnais, February 22, 1713.
60 Rochefort 1E/81, 137, Pontchartrain to Beauharnais, April 19, 1713; AC, C8A 19, ff. 151–1v., Phélypeaux to Pontchartrain, June 20, 1713.
61 Rochefort 1E/81, 139–40, Pontchartrain to Beauharnais, April 22, 1713.
62 AC, C8A 19, Phélypeaux to Pontchartrain, June 20, 1713.
63 Ibid., B 35, f. 525v., Pontchartrain to Phélypeaux, May 8, 1713; ibid., C8A 19, f. 204v., Phélypeaux to Pontchartrain, August 12, 1713.
64 Ibid., C8A 19, ff. 416–16v., Vaucresson to Pontchartrain, September 1, 1713; ibid., f. 217, Phélypeaux to Pontchartrain, September 10, 1713.
65 Ibid., B 35, vol. ff. 7–7v., Pontchartrain to Duclos, January 27, 1713; Ibid., ff. 39v.-40v., same to Beauharnais, February 22, 1713; ibid., C13A 3, ff. 319–20, Beauvais to Crozat, January 18, 1713; and ibid., ff. 343–5, Crozat to Pontchartrain, May 18, 1713.
66 Rochefort 1E/342, 93–6, Beauharnais to Pontchartrain, June 12, 1713; ibid., 109–13, same to same, August 31, 1713.
67 AC, B 35, ff. 153–3v., Pontchartrain to Desmarest, September 8, 1713; ibid., f. 178v., same to Laudreau, October 25, 1713.
68 Ibid., ff. 70–1, Pontchartrain to Beauharnais, March 22, 1713; ibid., f. 86v., same to Besnard, April 10, 1713; ibid., ff. 86–6v., same to Beauharnais, April 10, 1713, ibid., ff. 95v.–6, same to same, May 10, 1713.
69 Ibid., ff. 254–8, Pontchartrain to Vaudreuil, March 29, 1713; ibid., ff. 265v.–6, same to same, April 18, 1713; ibid., ff. 320v.–7v., same to same, July 4, 1713.
70 Ibid., ff. 107v.–8v., Pontchartrain to Beauharnais, May 31, 1713.
71 Rochefort 1E/342, 91–2, Beauharnais to Pontchartrain, June 6, 1713; AC, B 35, ff. 120v.–1, Pontchartrain to Beauharnais, June 14, 1713; ibid., C11A 36, ff. 198–9, Sieur Faures Grivollière [*sic*], 1716.
72 Ibid., B 35, ff. 275v.–86, Memorandum from the king to Vaudreuil and Bégon, June 25, 1713; ibid., ff. 320v.–7v., Pontchartrain to Vaudreuil, July 4, 1713; ibid., f. 125v., same to Beauharnais, July 8, 1713.

73 AC, C8A 19, ff. 217–20, Phélypeaux to Pontchartrain, September 10, 1713; and ibid., ff. 416–18v., Vaucresson to Pontchartrain, September 1, 1713; Dessalles, *Histoire générale des Antilles*, 3: 406–8.
74 AC, C8A 19, f. 205, Phélypeaux to Pontchartrain, August 12, 1713.
75 Ibid., ff. 204–5v.
76 Petitjean Roget, *Gaoulé*, 199–200.
77 AC, C13A 3, ff. 437v.–8, Cadillac to Pontchartrain, February 20, 1714; also RSC 16: 305–7, Duclos to Pontchartrain, October 25, 1713, 17: 282–3, 287, Memorandum of M. Duclos, October 1713.
78 AC, C11A 36, ff. 198–9, Sieur Faures [de la] Grivollière [*sic*], 1716; ADCM, C 157/62, Marine Council to Beauharnais, June 10, 1716.
79 Rochefort 1E/342, 107, Beauharnais to Pontchartrain, August 26, 1713; AC, B 35, ff. 128v.–9, Pontchartrain to Buisson, July 19, 1713; ibid., ff. 156–8v., same to Beaumanoir, September 19, 1713.
80 AC, C11B 1, ff. 30–7, Costebelle to Pontchartrain, August 10, 1713.
81 Ibid., B 36, ff. 362–2v. 375, Pontchartrain to Bégon, March 22, 1714; ibid., ff. 375–5v., king's Letter for singing the Te Deum, April 19, 1714; and ibid., ff. 376–76v., Letter of the king for singing the Te Deum for the Peace of Rastatt [*sic*], April 19, 1714.

CHAPTER THREE

1 Charlevoix, *Histoire et description générale de la Nouvelle France*, first two quotes 51, third 58, fourth 47.
2 Miquelon, *Dugard of Rouen*, 55.
3 Braudel, *Mediterranean and the Mediterranean World*, esp. 1:1.
4 Proulx, *Between France and New France*, quote 13; see also Meyer, "Des origines," 13–20.
5 Butel, *Négociants bordelais*, 119–21; Cavignac, *Jean Pellet*, 49–50; Carrière, *Négociants marseillais au XVIIIe siècle*, 177–83, 605–20; Dardel, *Navires et marchandises*, chap. 1.
6 Bosher, *Canada Merchants*, and "Huguenot Merchants and the Protestant International"; Young, "Crown Agent – Canadian Correspondent." On the Anglo-American colonies, see, for example, Bailyn, *Peopling of British North America*, esp. chap 1.
7 Steele, "Moat Theories and the English Atlantic"; see also Steele, *English Atlantic*, 5–10.
8 Steele, *English Atlantic*, quote 5, and 276.
9 Ibid., 97–108.
10 On the northern route, see Mathieu, *Commerce entre la Nouvelle-France et les Antilles*, 80–4; Miquelon, *New France, 1701–1744*, 124; Pritchard, "Ships, Men, and Commerce," 29–36; and Proulx, *Between France and New France*, 47–64, 76–80. For the gulf route, see Giraud, *History of*

French Louisiana, vol. 1: 62–8; and Hall, *Africans in Colonial Louisiana*, chap. 3 passim.

11 Hachard, *Voyage des dames religieuses Ursulines*, 40–5; Pritchard, "Ships, Men, and Commerce," 29.

12 AM, 4JJ, 29/50, *L'Orox*, observations of August 12 to September 10, 1737.

13 AC, C11A 36, ff. 198–9, Deposition of Sieur Faures Grivollière [*sic*], 1716.

14 AM, 4JJ, 34/4 bis, *Le Borée*, observations of January 26 to February 23, 1741; ibid., 34/8, *L'Hirondelle*, observation of March 16, 1763; Carrière, *Négociants marseillais au XVIIIe siècle*, 1:184–92, 2:614–15.

15 Steele, *English Atlantic*, 23, 49, 86.

16 Based on AM, 3JJ, vol. 271, Report on the means for assuring navigation to the River of Quebec, November 24, 1725 [signed Captain Voutron]; AC, C11A 67, ff. 209–11v., Hocquart to Maurepas, September 2, 1737 [voyage of *Le Jason*]; NA, MG 18, J 5, "Detailed remarks on the shores and rivers of Canada" [*L'Héros*'s log of 1712]; Lahontan, *Nouveaux voyages*, 1: 257–63; Charlevoix, *Histoire et description générale de la Nouvelle France*, 3: 47–80; J.C.B. Bonnefons, *Voyage au Canada*, 17–28; Dargent, "Relation d'un voyage de Paris à Montréal en Canada en 1737"; Pagés, "Relation d'un voyage de Paris en Canada" [1741]; and Pellegrin, "Mémoire sur la navigation du Canada" [1757], 1–4. For secondary descriptions, see note 10.

17 J.C.B., quoted in Moogk, *Nouvelle France*, 126.

18 Pritchard, "Ships, Men, and Commerce," 35–7.

19 Lafrance, *Épaves du Saint-Laurent*, 159–60.

20 Gosselin, *L'Instruction au Canada*, 330–44, citing Rochemonteix.

21 Quoted in Pritchard, "French Charting of the East Coast of Canada," 121.

22 Gosselin, *Instruction au Canada*, 330–44; Pritchard, "Ships, Men, and Commerce," 22–5.

23 AM, 3JJ/271, "Report" [Captain Voutron]; Pritchard, "La Richardière," *DCB* 3: 620–2; and Pritchard, "French Charting of the East Coast of Canada," 122–3.

24 AC, C11A 104, ff. 3–4v., Vaudreuil and Bigot to Berryer, October 22, 1759.

25 Ibid., ff. 446–8, Dubois to Berryer, February 22, 1759; PAC 1905:7, Levis to Dumas, May 27, 1760.

26 Charlevoix, *Histoire et description générale de la Nouvelle France*, 3: 71; Kalm, *Travels in North America*, 2: 434.

27 AC, A 24, ff. 14–15, Ordinances for the king's ships, 1681.

28 Asselin, "Louis Prat," *DCB* 2: 531–2; Pritchard, "La Richardière," *DCB* 3: 620–2; and Pritchard, "Pellegrin," *DCB* 4: 619–21.

29 AC, C11A 51, ff. 103–6v., Beauharnois and Hocquart to Maurepas, October 25, 1729. See also Pritchard, "Ships, Men, and Commerce," 45, and Mathieu, *Commerce entre la Nouvelle-France et les Antilles*, 120–1; Pritchard, "La Richardière," *DCB* 3: 620–2.

30 AC, C11A 36, ff. 176–7, Prat to Marine Council, November 15, 1716; ibid., 46, ff. 317–18, same to Maurepas, October, 1724; ibid., 48, ff. 99–102v., Beauharnois and Dupuy to Maurepas, October 30, 1726.

31 Ibid., B 53, ff. 467–7v., Maurepas to Beauharnois and Hocquart, March 22, 1729; ibid., C11A 79, f. 277v., Hocquart to Maurepas, September 15, 1743; Brisson, *Charpentrie navale à Québec*, 44–62.

32 Pritchard, "Pellegrin," *DCB* 4: 619–21.

33 Miquelon, "Havy and Lefebvre of Quebec." On monetary confusion, see AC, C11A 75, ff. 10v–12v., Beauharnois and Hocquart to Maurepas, September 8, 1741. On port activity, see Mathieu, *Commerce entre Nouvelle-France et les Antilles*, 120–1; Pritchard, "Ships, Men, and Commerce," 37–9.

34 AC, C11A 52, ff. 42–9, Description of events in Quebec on the occasion of the Dauphin's birth, [signed Beauharnois and Hocquart], October 15[?], 1730; ibid., 77, f. 277, Hocquart to Maurepas, June 11, 1742.

35 Ibid., 104, ff. 451–3v., Dubois to Berryer, 1759.

36 Moore, "Other Louisbourg," 235–7; McLennan, *Louisbourg*, 221–2.

37 Mathieu, *Commerce entre Nouvelle-France et les Antilles*, 88–9; McNeill, *Atlantic Empires of France and Spain*, 181–90; Moore, "Other Louisbourg," 79–96.

38 Mathieu, *Commerce entre Nouvelle-France et les Antilles*, 86–9, 121.

39 Malartic, *Journal des campagnes*, 163–4.

40 Drawn from AM, 3JJ, 261/4, Remarks and observations for navigating from France to Martinique [1733]; ibid., 261/9, Different routes and navigational methods to gain the Spanish Main and the American islands, n.d.; ibid., 278/3, Observations from the voyage of the *La Gironde* [1735]; ibid., 4JJ, 29/39, *La Baleine*, observations, September 20 to December 16, 1735; ibid, 29/42, *L'Orox*, observations, October 31 to December 18, 1736; ibid., 34/5, *La Galattée*, observations January 11 to October 23, 1750; ibid., 34/7, *Le Parham*, observations January 12 to June 5, 1753 [incorrectly noted as 1763]; ibid., 34/8, *L'Hirondelle*, observations, February 24 to September 21, 1763; Labat, *Nouveau voyage aux isles de l'Amérique*, 1: 8–21; Cavignac, *Jean Pellet*, 50–5; Miquelon, *Dugard of Rouen*, 91; Petitjean Roget, *Société d'habitation*, 1: 211–22.

41 Petitjean Roget, *Société d'habitation*, 1: 211.

42 Ibid., 1: 219–22.

43 AM, 4JJ, 27/3, *Le Maréchal d'Estrée*, observation of February 6, 1724; ibid., 34/5, *La Galattée*, observation of July 16, 1750.

44 Stein, *French Slave Trade*, 96–7; AM, 4JJ 27/4, observations for *La Mutine*, June 5 to July 2, 1723.
45 AM, 4JJ 27/3, *Le Maréchal d'Estrée*, observations of July 13 to October 23, 1723.
46 Labat, *Nouveau voyage aux isles de l'Amérique*, 1: 22; Cavignac, *Jean Pellet*, 53–5; AM, 3JJ, vol. 279/9, Report on the Spanish Main, islands, harbours, and bearings of America, n.d.
47 Thibault de Chanvalon, *Voyage à la Martinique*, 150–2.
48 AC, DFC, 15/191B, "Plan of the City of St. Pierre and its surroundings" [signed Thomas Scott, 1763].
49 AC, C8A 28, ff. 64–7, Feuquières and Besnard to Council of the Marine, May 30, 1720; ibid., C8B 4, nos. 50, Pau to Council of the Marine, June 16, 1716.
50 Dessalles, *Annales du Conseil souverain*, 1: 320–1.
51 AC, C8A 10, ff. 240–40v., d'Amblimont to Pontchartrain, July 10, 1698; ibid., 13, ff. 305–6v., Observations on America made by Sieur Lainé, royal pilot ..., February 1701; Labat, *Nouveau voyage aux isles de l'Amérique*, 1: 25–6.
52 AC, C8A 13, ff. 305–6v., Observations on America by made Sieur Lainé ..., February 1701.
53 May, *Histoire économique de la Martinique*, 230–7.
54 AC, C8A 39, ff. 343v.–6, Report on the coasts of the Îles du Vent, [signed Blondel], December 6, 1728.
55 Ibid., 39, ff. 97–100, Champigny and Blondel to Maurepas, May 19, 1728.
56 Ibid., 49, ff. 356–7, La Croix to Maurepas, December 10, 1738.
57 Ibid., C8B 11 no. 7, Bart to Choiseul, [n.d., after March 1762].
58 For example, ibid., B 35, ff. 156–8v., Pontchartrain to Chevalier de Beaumanoir [Sailing instructions for Antilles], September 19, 1713; ibid., C8A 50, ff. 79–80v., Champigny and de la Croix to Maurepas, July 10, 1739.
59 AM, 4JJ, 29/39, Log of *La Baleine*, 1736; ibid., 29/42, Log of *L'Orox*, 1736; ibid., 29/55, Log of *Le Fleuron*, 1740–41.
60 For example, see ibid., 54, ff. 230v.–1v., Champigny to Maurepas, August 21, 1742. On the comparable relationship of Barbados and Antigua to Jamaica, see Steele, *English Atlantic*, 29–31.
61 AC, C8B 17, no. 12, Record of French ships leaving Martinique, and those arriving from France, [1733]; ibid., 21, no. 61 and 62, Record of French ships arriving in and departing from Martinique [for the year 1752, signed Intendant Hurson, October 25, 1753]; Stein, *French Sugar Business*, 60–4.
62 On climate, see Watts, *West Indies*, 13–25.

63 AM, 4JJ, 34/5, *La Galattée*, observations, May 27 to June 12, 1750.
64 See, for example, ADLA, C-735, ff. 5–5v., "Letter from a merchant in Martinique to another in Marseille," October 2, 1727.
65 AC, C8A 21, ff. 61–3v., Vaucresson to the Marine Council, February 4, 1716; ibid., 47, f. 125, Champigny to Maurepas, December 20, 1736; May, *Histoire économique de la Martinique*, 138, 147–53.
66 Ibid., B 35, ff. 32–2v., Pontchartrain to Beauharnais, February 10, 1713; ibid., C8A 49, ff. 269–70, de la Croix to Maurepas, June 6, 1738.
67 AM, 4JJ, 34/4, *Le Gliton*, observations of December 19 to 27, 1733; see also AC, C11A 85, ff. 38–41, Extract of minutes from the Court of Admiralty ... of Fort Royal, [signed de Salaberry], April 2, 1746; Pritchard, "Salaberry," *DCB* 3: 582–3.
68 AM, 4JJ, 15/21 bis, *Le Courier de Bourbon*, log of 1723; and ibid., 19/81, *La Fortune*.
69 Maupassant, "Armateurs bordelais," 170–5.
70 Based on AC, C13A 7, ff.7–20, de la Chaise to Marine Council, September 6, 1723; ibid., C13C 1, ff. 90–8., Memorandum to aid in the Development of Louisiana, [n.d., but 1750–60]; Ibid., 4, ff. 73v.–8, Memorandum of services rendered by the Sieur Beranger for the province of Louisiana from 1697 until 1722; AM, 4JJ, 15/19, *La Galattée*, observations March 24 to May 2, 1723; Ibid., 18/66, *Le Somme*, observations, February 16 to March 14, 1741.
71 Giraud, *Histoire de la Louisiane française*, 3: 312–15, 327–38.
72 Delanglez, "Louisiana in 1717," 103–6.
73 *MPA* 3: 504.
74 AC, C13A 15, ff. 185–6, Salmon to Maurepas, December 14, 1732.
75 Charlevoix, *Histoire et description générale de la Nouvelle France*, 3: 443; AM, 4JJ, 18/66, *Le Somme*, observation of March 14, 1741.
76 Frégault, *Iberville le conquerant*, 313.
77 Surrey, *Commerce of Louisiana*, 76–81; O'Neill, *Church and State in French Colonial Louisiana*, 201; Giraud, *History of French Louisiana*, 5: 146.
78 Le Page du Pratz, *Histoire de la Louisiane*, 1: 261.
79 AC, C13A 7, f. 21, La Chaise to company, September 6, 1723; ibid., C13A 8, ff. 61, Fiou to company, May 1724.
80 AC, C13A 14, ff. 21–3, Périer and Salmon to Maurepas, April 1, 1732; ibid., 18, ff. 95–6, Bienville and Salmon to Maurepas, August 9, 1734.
81 Ibid., C13A 6, ff. 339–41, de la Tour to Marine Council, September 13, 1722; ibid., 26, ff. 127–30, Salmon to Maurepas, March 8, 1741; Surrey, *Commerce of Louisiana*, 50.
82 AC, C13C 1, ff. 93–4v., Memorandum to aid in the development of Louisiana, [n.d., c. 1750–60].

83 Giraud, *History of French Louisiana*, 5: 173–4; Surrey, *Commerce of Louisiana*, chap. 20.

84 Giraud, *History of French Louisiana*, 5: 120–1.

85 AC, C13A 26, ff. 127v.–8, Salmon to Maurepas, March 8, 1741; ibid., 28, ff. 276–8, Le Normant to Maurepas, October 4, 1744.

86 Cole, *Colbert and … Mercantilism*, 1: 308–9, 374–83.

87 Nordman and Revel, "Formation de l'espace français," 83.

88 Roche, *France in the Enlightenment*, 44–9, quote 47.

89 Surrey, *Commerce of Louisiana*, 33–4.

90 Bolster, *Black Jacks*, 47–62; see also Thornton, *Africa and Africans*, 37–8.

91 Innis, *Fur Trade in Canada*, 23–6, 43–83 passim; Eccles, *Canadian Frontier*, 106–11, 145–7; Lunn, "Illegal Fur Trade Out of New France"; Harris, *Historical Atlas of Canada*, plates 37–40.

92 Charlevoix, *Histoire et description de la Nouvelle-France*, 3: 192–3; see also Cassel, "*Troupes de la Marine*," 272–5; Dechêne, *Habitants et marchands de Montréal*, 130; Eccles, *Canadian Frontier*, 203n22; Innis, *Fur Trade in Canada*, 20, 60.

93 Kalm, *Travels in North America*, 2: 551.

94 Bougainville, "Mémoire sur l'état de la Nouvelle-France," 44–5.

95 Bougainville, *Ecrits sur le Canada*, 103–4.

96 Parent, *Histoire … des chemins sous l'ancien régime*, 1–3, 80.

97 Ibid., 66.

98 Glazebrook, *History of Transportation*, 97–104.

99 Parent, *Histoire … des chemins sous l'ancien régime*, 9 (table 1), 26, 57.

100 AC, C11A 58, f. 245v., Hocquart to Maurepas, October 10, 1732; ibid., 60, ff. 80–4, Same to same, October 14, 1733; ibid., ff. 178–81, Lanoullier to Maurepas, October 17, 1733; Parent, *Histoire … des chemins sous l'ancien régime,* 19–29; Horton, "Lanoullier de Boisclerc," *DCB* 3: 350–2.

101 AC, C11A 62, ff. 302–5, Lanoullier to Maurepas, October 10, 1734.

102 Ibid., 64, f. 264, Same to same, October 31, 1735.

103 Ibid., C11A 58, f. 245v., Hocquart to Maurepas, October 10, 1732; ibid., 60, f. 82, Same to same, October 14, 1733; ibid., 64, f. 97, same to same, October 15, 1735.

104 Giraud, *History of French Louisiana*, 1: 92, 344–5.

105 Surrey, *Commerce of Louisiana*, 35–40, 42–6, 75–6; NA, MG18, J 14, Duverger, "Relation d'un voyage," 80–2.

106 NA, MG18, J 14, Duverger, "Relation d'un voyage," 75–6; C13A 7, ff. 10–21, La Chaise to Marine Council, September 6, 1723; ibid., C13A 30, f. 248v., Anonymous memorandum, [post-1746]; ibid., C13A 34, f. 118v., Michel to Maurepas [Rouillé], August 12, 1749.

107 Usner, *Indians, Settlers, and Slaves*, 228–30.
108 AC, A 23, f. 120v., Ordinance on the repair of roads, September 15, 1735 (see marginalia).
109 Ibid., C13A 41, f. 159–60, Vezin to minister, September 15, 1758 [joined to letter of Rochemore to Machault, January 3, 1759].
110 Ibid., C13A 26, ff. 117–18, Salmon to Maurepas, March 6, 1741.
111 Walthall and Emerson, "French Colonial Archaeology," 1–13, esp. map, 9; Keene, "Fort de Chartres," 39 (map).
112 Bougainville, *Ecrits sur le Canada*, 108–11.
113 Charlevoix, *Histoire et description générale de la Nouvelle France*, 108–438 passim.
114 NA, MG18, J 14, Duverger, "Relation d'un voyage."
115 For a diverging view, see Cassel, "*Troupes de la Marine*," 280–5.
116 ADG, 7B 1828, J. Pellet to P. Pellet, August 19, 1724.
117 For example, see AC, C8A 45, f. 317, Statement of general expenses, June 30, 1735; ibid., 59, f. 413, King's Domaine ... Statement of Supplementary expenditures, October 10, 1753.
118 Ibid., C8B 9, no. 104, General summary of expenses and receipts [for 1732, signed d'Orgeville, December 31, 1734]; ibid., C8A 49, f. 435v., General summary of expenses [for 1739, signed La Croix], March 18, 1740.
119 Labat, *Nouveau voyage aux isles de l'Amérique*, 1: part 1, 65–6;part 2, 76–8.
120 Chauleau, *Société à la Martinique*, 113.
121 Chanvalon, *Voyage à la Martinique*, 132–4.
122 On black sailors, see Linebaugh and Rediker, "Many-Headed Hydra"; Scott, "Afro-American Sailors"; and Bolster, *Black Jacks*, chap. 6.
123 May, *Histoire économique de la Martinique*, 191–5.
124 Ibid.
125 AC, C8A 27, ff. 22–22v., Feuquières and Besnard to Marine Council, April 8, 1720; Dessalles, *Annales du Conseil souverain*, 1: 533–7; Daney, *Histoire de la Martinique*, 2: 58–60; May, *Histoire économique de la Martinique*, 193.
126 AC, C8A 38, ff. 250–3v., Blondel to Maurepas, August 6, 1727.
127 Ibid., ff. 93–102, Abridged report on the inspection of the island, [signed Joncheray], April 4, 1727.
128 May, *Histoire économique de la Martinique*, 194.
129 AC, ff. 256v.–7, Blondel to Maurepas, August 6, 1727; ibid., 39, ff. 346v.–7v., Memorandum on the Windward Islands of America, [signed Blondel], December 6, 1728.
130 Ibid., 50, ff. 394–95v., Nadeau de Treuil to Maurepas, April 10, 1739.
131 Dessalles, *Annales du Conseil souverain*, 1: 482.

CHAPTER FOUR

1 AC, C11A 52, ff. 42–9, Report of events at Quebec, Canada, the capital city of New France, on the birth of His Lordship the Dauphin, [dated October 15, 1730].
2 Davis, *Society and Culture*, 208.
3 Kertzer, *Ritual, Politics, and Power*, 9.
4 Ibid., 3.
5 Ibid., 24–34.
6 Burke, *Fabrication of Louis XIV*, 6–8, 43–4.
7 Darnton, *Great Cat Massacre*, chap. 3, quote 120; Bercé, *Fête et révolte*, 13–16, 89, 103; Vovelle, *Métamorphoses de la fête en Provence*, 66–77; Quéniart, *Culture et société urbaines*, 457–68.
8 Fogel, *Cérémonies de l'information*, 18, 247–8.
9 Ibid., 247.
10 Louis-Sebastien Mercier, cited in Farge, *Fragile Lives*, 175, also 170–283.
11 Coates, "Authority and Illegitimacy," 65–90, quote 90.
12 Coates, "Representations of Authority," 8. I am indebted to Professor Coates for allowing me to see and quote from his paper before publication.
13 Lebrun, "Calendrier agro-liturgique," 347–51; table in Rombouts, "Celebration of Public Events in Eighteenth-Century France," 61.
14 Johnston, *Religion in Life at Louisbourg*, 14–19, especially table 2.
15 Juchereau, *Histoire de l'Hôtel-Dieu de Québec*, 488.
16 ADG, 7B 1205, P. Chety to F. Chety, August 18, 1749.
17 RSC 5: 400 and 8: 500.
18 Labat, *Nouveau voyage aux isles de l'Amérique*, 2: 326–8.
19 Ibid., 327.
20 Ibid, 326.
21 Kalm, *Travels in North America*, 2: 467.
22 Quéniart, *Culture et société urbaines*, 133.
23 Fogel, *Cérémonies de l'information*, appendix 2, 448–50.
24 Ibid., 252–66; table, 254.
25 AC, C8A 56, f. 245, Champigny and Ranché to Maurepas, March 15, 1745; ibid., f. 257, Champigny to Maurepas, February 7, 1745; ibid., 57, f. 53, Caylus to Maurepas, February 26, 1746; ibid., C13A 33, f. 55, Vaudreuil to Maurepas, August 26, 1749.
26 AC, A 24, f. 149v., King's declaration, August 2, 1717; Dessalles, *Annales du Conseil souverain*, 1: 472–3 [Îles du Vent]; *Édits, ordonnances royaux*, King's declaration, August 10, 1717 [New France]; O'Neill, *Church and State*, 235–6 [Louisiana].
27 AC, C8A 60, f. 207, General Rates, [signed Bompar and Hurson], February 1, 1754; Lanctot, "Régime municipal en Nouvelle-France," 272.

28 Moogk, "'Thieving Buggers' and 'Stupid Sluts,'" 531; Dessalles, *Annales du Conseil souverain*, 1: 386–9.
29 AC, C13A 35, f. 52v., Regulations on public order for the province of Louisiana, March 1, 1751.
30 Ibid., A 24, ff. 983–9v., Regulations on precedence, September 30, 1713; ibid, vol. 21, ff. 57–8v., Regulations on rank in the churches of Canada, April 27, 1716 [also ibid., C11A 106, ff. 377–80, same date]; and ibid., vol. 23, ff. 115v.–16, King's ordinance of August 17, 1734, concerning the rank and placement [of officials] in churches and public ceremonies.
31 This unique example for Louisiana can be found ibid., C13A 15, f. 241, Plan of the Building of the Parish Church, July 29, 1732.
32 Ibid., A 24, Regulations on Precedence, September 30, 1713.
33 For a brief survey of his life, see Lamontagne, *La Galissonière et le Canada*.
34 AC, C11A 88, ff. 36–8, Report on the Comte de La Galissonière in New France, September 19, 1747.
35 Moogk, *Nouvelle France*, 160–70.
36 Kalm, *Travels in North America*, 2: 464–5; AC, C13A 37, ff. 34v.–5, Kerlérec to Rouillé, March 8, 1753.
37 AC, C13A 37, ff. 34–8, Kerlérec to Rouillé, March 8, 1753.
38 Ibid., f. 35v., same to same.
39 Ibid., ff. 39–39v., Response of Monsieur de Kerlérec to the clergy ... on the day of his reception, February 9, 1753.
40 Ibid.
41 Ibid., ff. 40–1, Response of Monsieur de Kerlérec to the gentlemen of the Grand Council ... February 9, 1753.
42 Ranum, *Paris in the Age of Absolutism*, 276–8.
43 McKay and Scott, *Rise of the Great Powers, 1648–1815*, 127–30; ADG, C-3619, Report of the festival given by the city of Bordeaux upon the birth of His Lordship the Dauphin, September 1729, quote 1.
44 AN, K 1719, 30/2, Louis to His Lordship the Archbishop of Paris, September 4, 1729.
45 From ADG, C-3619, Report of the festival given by the city of Bordeaux upon the birth of His Lordship the Dauphin, September 1729. This report includes identical handwritten and printed copies.
46 Ibid., 2.
47 Ibid., 3.
48 Ibid., 4.
49 AC, B 53, f. 306, f. 373v., ff. 456–7; ff. 576v.–7, 616–16v.; AN, K 1719, 30/2, Louis to His Lordship the Archbishop of Paris, September 4, 1729.
50 AC, B 53, ff. 344–4v., King's letter to the Marquis de Champigny, September 4, 1729.

51 Ibid., C8A 40, ff. 123–4, Champigny to Maurepas, December 5, 1729; ibid., f. 202v., same to same, December 15, 1729.
52 Ibid., f. 123v., same to same, December 5, 1729.
53 Ibid., f. 124., same to same, December 5, 1729.
54 Haan, "Covenant Chain: Iroquois Diplomacy," 202–10; Standen, "Charles, Marquis de Beauharnais," 106–46, 257–68; Eccles, *Canadian Frontier*, 142–5; and Banks, "Culture and Communications," 92–105.
55 Miquelon, *New France, 1710–1744*, 140–2.
56 Dubé, "Dupuy," DCB 2: 207–13; Dubé, *Claude-Thomas Dupuis*, chap. 4.
57 Jaenen, *Role of the Church in New France*, 56–9.
58 Miquelon, *New France, 1701–1744*, 126–44, 166–79; Standen, "Charles, Marquis de Beauharnais," 180–97, 227–33; Dubé, *Claude-Thomas Dupuy*, 238–44, 258–74; Lunn, "Economic Development in New France"; and Reid, "Development and Importance of ... Quebec," chaps 6–9.
59 Based on AC, C11A 52, ff. 42–9, Report of events at Quebec, Canada, the capital city of New France, on the birth of His Lordship the Dauphin, [dated October 15, 1730].
60 On *L'Héros*, see Proulx, *Between France and New France*, 133.
61 Roussier, "Fètes d'autrefois à la Martinique," 221.
62 Isherwood, *Music in the Service of the King*, chap. 6.
63 Quéniart, *Culture et société urbaines*, 464–6.
64 Fogel, *Cérémonies de l'information*, 133–5, 154–5.
65 Ibid., 154–63, 169–72, 187–91.
66 Ibid., 154–6; AN, K-1719/34, Pastoral letter of His Lordship the Archbishop of Paris, [1746], 6.
67 The entire French text reads:

Nous vous louons, ô Dieu! nous vous bénissons, Seigneur.
Toute la terre vous adore, ô Père éternel!
Tous les Anges, les Cieux et Toutes les Puissances.
Les Chérubins et les Séraphins s'écrient sans cesse devant vous:
Saint, Saint, Saint, est le Seigneur, le Dieu des armées.
Les cieux et la terre sont pleins de la majesté de votre gloire.
(Fogel, *Cérémonies de l'information*, 155)

68 Ibid., 156.
69 AC, C11A, f. 45v., Report of events at Quebec, Canada ... [dated October 15, 1730]. French text:

La fable peint l'amour dans Sa minorité
chés elle cet Enfant ne quite point cet âge
Notre Amour cher dauphin a Seul cet avantage
qu'il est a vôtre Égard dans Sa majorité.

70 "Utriusque franciae Spes et amor." I am indebted to Professor R.S. Kilpatrick, Queen's University, for help in translating these inscriptions.

71 "Dominabituo a mari usqué ad maré [*sic*]."
72 "Sunt munera Divum."
73 Kalm, *Travels in North America*, 2: 422, 540–2, 578.
74 AC, C11A 52, f. 47, Report of events at Quebec, Canada, the capital city of New France, on the birth of His Lordship the Dauphin, [dated October 15, 1730].
75 Johnston, *Religion in Life at Louisbourg*, 18.
76 AC, C11A 52, ff. 42v.–43, Report of events at Quebec, Canada, the capital city of New France, on the birth of His Lordship the Dauphin, [dated October 15, 1730].
77 ADG, C-3619, Report of the Feast ..., 3.
78 Ibid., Chauvelain to Boucher, September 26, 1729; see also Quéniart, *Culture et société urbaines*, 459.
79 Abbadie, "Journal," 99, 103–4, 115, 116, 118–20, 126.
80 Johnston, *Religion in Life at Louisbourg*, 15, 18.
81 Roussier, "Fêtes d'autrefois à la Martinique," 223.

CHAPTER FIVE

1 Drawn from Dart, "Criminal Trial in Louisiana," 377–90.
2 Lachance, *Marginaux*, 153–4.
3 Ménétra, *Journal of My Life*, 288–9.
4 Choquette, "Corporatism or Physiocracy?" quote 11.
5 Eccles, *Canadian Frontier*, 7–9, 109–13; Miquelon, *New France, 1701–1744*, 154–5; Dechêne, *Habitants et marchands de Montréal*, 220–6; White, *Middle Ground*, 58. On Louisiana, see Usner, *Indians, Settlers, and Slaves*, 6–8. For a counterpoint emphasizing liberty, see, for example, Parkman, *France and England in North America*, 2: 607.
6 *Édits et ordonnances*, 1: 341, Ordinance of March 1714; 350, Letters patent of March 1716; 551, Declaration of the king April 1737.
7 Martin, *Histoire de l'esclavage*, 28; Gisler, *Esclavage aux Antilles françaises*, 97–8; Fick, *Making of Haiti*, 21.
8 Fick, *Making of Haiti*, 41–5, 57–60, quote 59.
9 Hall, *Africans in Colonial Louisiana*, 202–7; see also Craton, *Testing the Chains*, 163–4.
10 Debien, *Esclaves aux Antilles françaises*, 85; see also Pérotin-Dumon, "Cabotage, Contraband, and Corsairs," 58, 61; Geggus, "Major Port Towns of Saint Domingue," 110–11.
11 Moogk, "Reluctant Exiles," quote, 463.
12 Ibid.; see also Moogk, *La Nouvelle France*, 100–3, 110–12.
13 Moogk, "Reluctant Exiles," 491–6.
14 Choquette, *Frenchman into Peasants*, 2–22.
15 Allain, "French Emigration Policies," 110–11.

16 Hardy, "Transportation of Convicts"; Conrad, "Emigration forcée," 125–9.
17 Ingersoll, *Mammon and Manon*, xxvii, 10–11.
18 AC, C11A 70, ff. 129–30, Deposition of Esther Brandeau, September 15, 1738; Tisdel, "Brandeau," *DCB* 2: 95–6; also in Choquette, *Frenchmen into Peasants*, 137–9.
19 AC, C11A 65, ff. 128–8v., Beauharnois to Maurepas, October 13, 1736; ibid., C13A 36, ff. 272–2v., Michel to Rouillé, September 23, 1752.
20 Pares, *War and Trade in the West Indies*, 195–202.
21 See, for example, AC, C11A 77, ff. 123–4v., Beauharnois to Maurepas, September 28, 1742.
22 Proulx, "Soldat à Québec"; Cassel, "*Troupes de la Marine*," 94.
23 Paquin, "Revol," *DCB* 3: 554–5.
24 Lachance, *Marginaux*, 153–60.
25 AC, C11A 65, ff. 60–1, Beauharnois and Michel to Maurepas, October 1736; ibid., 69, ff. 217–19, Hocquart to Maurepas, July 12, 1738; ibid., 77, ff. 135–6v., Beauharnois to Maurepas, October 27, 1742.
26 Ibid., A 25, ff. 134–4v., Ordinance of M[essieur]s de Champigny and d'Orgeville, March 14, 1729.
27 Ibid., C11A, 67, f. 176v., Beauharnois to Maurepas, October 15, 1737.
28 Ibid., 95, f. 55–6, La Jonquière and Bigot to Rouillé, October 8, 1750.
29 Ibid., C13A 35, ff. 33–3v., Vaudreuil to Rouillé, May 22, 1751.
30 Greer, "Mutiny at Louisbourg," 70–110.
31 Proulx, "Soldat à Québec," 550; Cassel, "*Troupes de la Marine*," 391.
32 AC, C11A 67, ff. 176–8v., Beauharnois to Maurepas, October 15, 1737; ibid., vol. 77, ff. 323–5, Beauharnois to Maurepas, September 12, 1742.
33 Cassel, "Troupes de la Marine," 127–30, quote 128; Lachance, "Désertion et les soldats déserteurs," 151–61.
34 AC, C11A 65, ff. 127–31v., Memorandum to Maurepas, October 13, 1736.
35 Ibid., C8A 58, ff. 140–4, Caylus to Maurepas, November 7, 1748, quote f. 140v.
36 Ibid., C11A 67, ff. 177–8, Memorandum to Maurepas, October 15, 1737; ibid., 69, ff. 113–14v., Beauharnois to Maurepas, October 3, 1738; ibid., 77, ff. 323–25, same to same, September 12, 1742.
37 Cassel, "*Troupes de la Marine*," 397–401.
38 AC, C11A 93, ff. 37–9v., La Jonquière and Bigot to Maurepas, October 7, 1749; ibid., 95, f. 84v., same to same, October 18, 1750; Proulx, "Soldat à Québec," 550.
39 Ibid., C13A 37, ff. 14–17, Kerlérec, Vaudreuil, and d'Auberville to Rouillé, April 28, 1753.
40 Ibid., A 25, ff. 117–24, Ordinance of the king for the Compagnie franches de la Marine, [n.d., but included in 1717 material].

41 Ibid., C8A 58, f. 142v., Caylus to Maurepas, November 7, 1748; Frostin, *Révoltes blanches*, 222n5.
42 AC, C8B 8, no. 90, Ordinance of the king, May 22, 1719; ibid., A 25, ff. 152v.–3v., Ordinance on the subject of deserting sailors in the colonies, December 23, 1721; ibid., A 23, ff. 134–4v., Ordinance of the king, February 13, 1743.
43 Ibid., C11A 67, f. 95v., Memorandum, [anonymous], 1737; Seguin, *Civilisation traditionnelle*, 90–1.
44 AC, C11A. 77, ff. 27–8, Beauharnois and Hocquart to Maurepas, September 21, 1742.
45 Dessalles, *Annales du Conseil souverain*, 1: 184.
46 AC, A 25, ff. 132–4, Ordinance of M[essieur]s Champigny and d'Orgeville, March 14, 1729.
47 Chauleau, *Société à la Martinique*, 161; Dessalles, *Annales du Conseil souverain*, 1: 180–4, 376–80; Daney, *Histoire de la Martinique* 2: 130, 146–7.
48 AC, A 23, f. 114v., Ordinance on cabarets, December 19, 1733; RSC 16: 509, August 24, 1746; Dart, "Cabarets of New Orleans."
49. Ibid., C13A 35, ff. 39–52v., Regulations for Good Order for the Province of Louisiana, February 18, 1751.
50. Frégault, *Le Grand marquis*, 409–10; Ingersoll, *Mammon and Manon*, 104–07.
51 AC, C13A 35, ff. 37–8, Vaudreuil and Michel to Maurepas, May 27, 1751.
52 Ibid., C13A 7, ff. 164–6, de la Chaise to Marine Council, June 5, 1723; Heinrich, *Louisiane sous la Compagnie des Indes*, 57 and note 3.
53 Petitjean-Roget, *Gaoulé*, 318–26.
54 Frostin, *Révoltes blanches*, 189–90, 203–6.
55 Jaenen, "Some Unresolved Issues," 114–18.
56 Axtell, *Invasion Within*, 61–2.
57 Ibid., 84, 124–5.
58 White, *Middle Ground*, 193, 220; also *JR*, 68, Father Nau to Madam Aulneau, October 2, 1735, and 69, same to same, October 3, 1741.
59 Lunn, "Illegal Fur Trade Out of New France," 61–76.
60 On Anglo-Dutch trade, see AC, C11A 55, ff. 166–9, Hocquart to Maurepas, October 15, 1731. References to fur smuggling are voluminous. For examples, see ibid., 41, f. 105, Extract of memorandum to the king, July 1718 [dated October 26, 1719]; ibid., 53, f. 215, Hocquart to Maurepas, October 10, 1730; ibid., 67, ff. 128–32, Beauharnois and Hocquart to Maurepas, 1737; ibid., 77, ff. 352–4, Hocquart to Maurepas, September 22, 1742.
61 Ibid., 97, ff. 173–4, La Jonquière to Rouillé, November 1, 1751.
62 Axtell, *Invasion Within*, 277.

63 See, for example, AC, C11A 77, f. 170, Onondaga [sachems] to Beauharnois, July 6, 1742.
64 Wraxall, *Abridgment*, 151; AC, C11A 48, ff. 161–2, Noyan to Beauharnois, September 22, 1726; *NYCD* 9: 1110–11, Beauharnois to Maurepas, October 29, 1744.
65 Trudel, *Esclavage au Canada français*, 163, and *Dictionnaire des esclaves*, xv–xxvii; also Lachance, "Esclaves," 201–8 (based mainly on Trudel's work).
66 Donovan, "Nominal List of Slaves," 151–62, and "Slaves and Their Owners."
67 Tannenbaum, *Slave and Citizen*, 165n153, also 46, 98–9; Davis, *Problem of Slavery*.
68 Pluchon, *Nègres et Juifs*, 178–83, quote 178; Gaston-Martin, *Histoire de l'esclavage*, 28–9; Gisler, *Esclavage aux Antilles françaises*, 6–11, 26, 32–3; Cohen, *French Encounter*, 52–8. For Louisiana, see Allain, "Slave Policies in French Louisiana"; and Brasseaux, "Administration of Slave Regulations."
69 Ingersoll, *Mammon and Manon*, 135–43.
70 *Code noir*, 28–58 (1685) and 281–315 (1724).
71 Debien, "Christianisation des esclaves," 525–5.
72 Debbasch, "Au coeur du 'Gouvernement des esclaves,'" 31–53; *Code noir*, 54.
73 *Code noir*, 30–1, 36.
74 Allain, "Slave Policies in French Louisiana," 128.
75 AC, C8B 11, no. 22, Memorandum in response to the proclamation of October 20, 1763; Debien, *Esclaves aux Antilles françaises*, 269–71.
76 *Code noir*, 33–5.
77 Article 13 in 1685 Code, article 10 in 1724 Code.
78 Labat, *Nouveau voyage aux isles de l'Amérique*, 1: pt 2, 32–3, 37.
79 AC, C8B 8, no. 123, Judgment rendered by the governor and intendant of the islands of America, October 10, 1722.
80 Articles 16 and 17 of 1685 Code, 13 and 14 in 1724 Code.
81 Daney, *Histoire de la Martinique*, 2: 137.
82 Articles 38 and 39 in the 1685 Code, 32–4 in 1724 Code.
83 Debien, *Esclaves aux Antilles françaises*, 413, 422, 443.
84 Loque, "Transcending Coercion," 33–5.
85 Labat, *Nouveau voyage aux isles de l'Amérique*, 2: 48–9; Debien, *Esclaves aux Antilles françaises*, chap. 3.
86 Debien, *Esclaves aux Antilles françaises*, 83–4.
87 Ibid., 41–51; Hall, *Africans in Colonial Louisiana*, 187–93.
88 Trudel, *Esclavage au Canada français*, 167.
89 Debien, *Esclaves aux Antilles françaises*, 283–4.
90 Thibault de Chanvalon, *Voyage à la Martinique*, 65.

91 AC, C8B 11, no. 22, Memorandum in response to the promulgation of October 20, 1763.
92 Ibid., A 23, ff. 68–8v., *Arrêt*, July 7, 1726.
93 Ibid., C13A 11, ff. 97–100, Périer to Maurepas, August 18, 1728, quote f. 97v; Hall, *Africans in Colonial Louisiana*, 99–102.
94 AC, C13A, 35, f. 48, Regulations for good order for the province of Louisiana, February 18, 1751.
95 Dessalles, *Annales du Conseil souverain*, 1: 482.
96 Debien, *Esclaves aux Antilles françaises*, 154–7, 461.
97 AC, C8A 39, ff. 185v.–8, Blondel to Maurepas, January 13, 1728; ibid., 24, ff. 80–4, Feuquières to Marine Council, January 12, 1718; and ibid., 58, ff. 242v.–3, Caylus to Maurepas, January 14, 1749.
98 Debien, *Esclaves aux Antilles françaises*, 453.
99 Dessalles, *Annales du Conseil souverain*, 180–4, quote 183; AC, C8A 66, f. 346, Fenélon to Elva [Martinique governor resident in Saint Pierre], February 19, 1764.
100 Ibid., C13A 35, ff. 38–52v., Regulations for Good order for the Province of Louisiana, February 18, 1751.
101 Abbadie, "Journal," 119.
102 AC, C8A 24, ff. 61–2, Feuquières and Silvecane to Marine Council, September 10, 1718.
103 Ibid., 63, f. 404, La Rivière to M. Assier, January 28, 1761; ibid., f. 405, Assier to La Rivière, January 30, 1761.
104 Pluchon, *Nègres et Juifs*, 127–35.
105 "Edict of the king concerning the negro slaves of the colonies, October 1716," *Code noir*, 169–81.
106 Peabody, *"There Are No Slaves in France,"* 11–22, 106–20; ADG, 3669, no. 24 "Statement on the number of blacks and slaves of both sexes, 1777."
107 AC, C8A 59, f. 296, Bompar and Hurson to Rouillé, July 28, 1752.
108 Peabody, *"There Are No Slaves in France,"* 3–4.
109 For examples, see ADG, 6B 45–53, Passports of Catholicism, including 6B 49, f. 13v., Deposition of Pierre [slave travelling on own], January 19, 1740; ibid., f. 21, Deposition of Sieur Dubarry, April 20, 1740; ibid., f. 24, Deposition of Sieur de Champigny, May 25, 1740.
110 AC, F3 259, f. 287, Massiac to Beauharnais, March 10, 1758.
111 Ibid., 23, ff. 47–55, Feuquières to Marine Council, December 21, 1717; Debien, *Esclaves aux Antilles françaises*, 454.
112 AC, A 25, ff. 271v.–3, Declaration of the king concerning the disciplining of the Negroes, February 1, 1743; Hall, "Maritime Maroons."
113 AC, C8A 17, ff. 361–5, Vaucresson to Pontchartrain, August 30, 1710.
114 Debien, *Esclaves aux Antilles françaises*, 465–6.

115 Daney, *Histoire de la Martinique*, 2: 102–3; AN, Mi 1, no. 299, Census of the island of Martinique, 1769.
116 Hall, *Africans in Colonial Louisiana*, 146–8.
117 Le Page du Pratz, *Histoire de la Louisiane*, 3: 303–17; Dumont, *Mémoires historiques*, 20–8; AC, C13A 13, ff. 87–7v., Movements of the savages of Louisiana, July 21 and 28, 1731; ibid., ff. 200–200v., Beauchamp to Maurepas, November 5, 1731; Hall, *Africans in Colonial Louisiana*, 106–8; Giraud, *History of French Louisiana*, 5: 415; Usner, *Indians, Settlers, and Slaves*, 74–5.
118 Giraud, *History of French Louisiana*, 5: 407.
119 Usner, *Indians, Settlers, and Slaves*, 230, 232–3.

CHAPTER SIX

1 CCM, L9/690, Caylus to Roux, August 16, 1747.
2 Daney, *Histoire de la Martinique*, 2: 119–26; Pritchard, "Naval Career of a Colonial Governor," 12–23.
3 See, for example, Doyle, *Oxford History of the French Revolution*, 26–30; Chaussinand-Nogaret, *French Nobility in the Eighteenth Century*, 86–113.
4 Hauser, *Pensée ... du Cardinal de Richelieu*, 128–34, 189–91; Cole, *Colbert and ... Mercantilism*, 2: 553–8; Clark, *La Rochelle and the Atlantic Economy*, 17–18, 227; Schaeper, *French Council of Commerce*, 9–13; Boulle, "French Colonies ... during and following the Seven Years' War," 344–53, 394–408; on mercantilism, see Miquelon, *New France, 1701–1744*, 6–12.
5 Tarrade, *Commerce colonial de la France*, 55–85.
6 Goubert, "Tragique dix-septième siècle," 331, 346; Léon and Carrière, "Appel des marchés," 167, 177; Davis, *Rise of the Atlantic Economies*, 230–5.
7 Braudel, *The Identity of France*, 1: 268–72.
8 Bailyn, "Communications and Trade"; Steele, *English Atlantic*, 214–27; Hancock, *Citizens of the World*, 86–113.
9 Butel, *Négociants bordelais*, 167.
10 Miquelon, *Dugard of Rouen*, 73.
11 Menkis, "Gradis Family," 151–77; Bédard, "Présence protestante," 325–49; Petitjean-Roget, "Protestants à la Martinique," and "Juifs à la Martinique"; Lafleur, "Juifs aux îles françaises." On frontier exchange, see, for example, Dechêne, *Habitants et marchands de Montréal*, 91–4, 212–15, 220–6; Usner, *Indians, Settlers, and Slaves*, 210–18, 277–8.
12 See Bosher, *Canada Merchants*, 115–17, 168; "Famille de Fleurance," 173–202; "Quebec Merchant's Trading Circles," 372–98; "French Protes-

tant Families," 438–63; and "Huguenot Merchants and the Protestant International," 99–100.

13 Clark, *New Orleans, 1718–1812*, 93–9; see also Miquelon, "Havy and Lefebvre."

14 Cavignac, *Jean Pellet*, 151–63.

15 Miquelon, *New France, 1701–1744*, 131.

16 Young, *Kin, Commerce, Community*, 5, 82–3.

17 ADLA, C-735, Memorandum of the Sieur de Rousel ... for Monseig[neu]r le Comte de Maurepas, December 1730, 2 [first quote]; Pares, *War and Trade in the West Indies*, 187–9, 290; 187 [second quote].

18 Pares, *War and Trade in the West Indies*, 187–9, 290; Miquelon, *Dugard of Rouen*, 92; May, *Histoire économique de la Martinique*, 217–18; Gould, "Trade between the Windward Islands," 481–3.

19 The destruction of Saint Pierre's notarial records in the tragic eruption of Mount Pelée in 1902 eliminated the most valuable records for studies such as those made by historians about merchants in other colonial ports.

20 ADLA, C-735, ff. IV., 3V.–4V., Memorandum of the Sieur de Rossel, December 1730.

21 Ibid., Ordinance of the king to counter the captains or factors of merchant vessels who trade illegally, November 26, 1719.

22 Miquelon, *Dugard of Rouen*, 81.

23 ADG, 7B 1484; Meyer, *Armement nantais*, 137–42; Miquelon, *Dugard of Rouen*, 101–2, 197–201.

24 ADG, 7B 1207, Letterbook of Captain Raymond Gaultier.

25 Mathieu, *Commerce entre la Nouvelle-France et les Antilles*, 57–8.

26 Cavignac, *Jean Pellet*, 163–5; Miquelon, *Dugard of Rouen*, 49.

27 CCM, L9/689, Barral to Roux, March 18, 1762; ibid., same to same, October 20, 1762.

28 Maupassant, *Grand armateur de Bordeaux*; Menkis, "Gradis Family," 117–39; Bosher, "Shipping to Canada in Wartime," 464–86.

29 Gradis Archives, Letterbook for 1756–57.

30 Menkis, "Gradis Family," 173–77.

31 ADG, Fonds Gradis, microfilm 1 Mi 112 B8, D. Gradis to David Mendes, March 28, 1733; M. Depas to A. Gradis, April 25, 1741.

32 Ibid., 130, La Galissonière to A. Gradis, March 29, 1751, and December 9, 1752; and ibid., 163, same to same, May 20, 1754.

33 Ibid., microfilm 1 Mi 112 B4, A. Gradis to David Gradis, September 11, 1761; ibid., 218, Choiseul to A. Gradis, March 10, 1763; ibid., same to same, September 12, 1763; Boulle, "French Colonies and the Reform of Their Administration," 530n58.

34 ADG, Fonds Gradis, microfilm 1 Mi 158, Rouillé to A. Gradis, December 17, 1751; ibid., same to same, December 30, 1752; ibid., 112 B2, A. Gradis to Mendes Dacosta [in London], November 27, 1759.

35 Frégault, *François Bigot*, 1: 283–95, 391–3.
36 Miquelon, *Dugard of Rouen*, 73.
37 ADG, 7B 1826–32 [1718–32], Fonds Pellet.
38 Ibid., 7B 1828, P. Pellet to J. Pellet, letters of April 24, July 9, August 19, and October 21, 1724.
39 Ibid., 1303, Duveau to Dufons, August 1, 1753.
40 Ibid., 1828, Pierre Pellet to Jean Pellet, letters of April 24, July 9, August 19, October 21, and November 28, 1724; ibid., 1830, Pellet and Larroque to Jean Pellet, letters of May 21, May 31, July 15, September 2, 1727.
41 CCM, L9 689, Barral to Roux, February 20 and October 1, 1756; ADG, 7B 1205, Chety senior to Chety junior, n.d. [between 1754 and 1755], and ibid., 1828, P. Pellet to J. Pellet, April 24, 1724.
42 ADG, 7B 1830, P. Pellet to J. Pellet, May 31, 1727; also ibid., 7B 1303, Lamy to Dufons, July 30, 1743; BMLR, MS 1992/1, Bretonnerie and Guesdon to Belin, August 3, 1751; ibid., 1992/5, same to same, April 20, 1752.
43 BMLR, MS 1992/1, Bretonnerie and Guesdon to Belin, April 3, 1751; ibid. same to same, March 23, 1753; ADG, 7B 1322, Mertens to Dulorie, October 8, 1749. On debt and letters of credit, see Cavignac, *Jean Pellet*, 105–21; Clark, *La Rochelle and the Atlantic Economy*, 140–5, and Meyer, *Armement nantais*, 215–25.
44 ADG, 7B 1303, Dutasta to Dufons, January 7, 1756; ibid., same to same, March 3, 1756.
45 BMLR, MS 1992/5, April 20, 1752; ibid., 1992/7, May 18, 1752.
46 ADG, 7B 1303, Barbazont Lafont to Dufons, March 2, 1752.
47 Ibid., Aquart to Dufons, March 15, 1747.
48 Ibid., Aquart to Dufons, April 18, 1746; ibid., same to same, June 8, 1746.
49 Ibid., 1322, Mertens to Dulorie, November 15, 1749.
50 Ibid., 1303, Lamy to Dufons, July 30, 1743; ibid., same to same, April 17, 1744; ibid., same to same, January 10, 1751 [quote].
51 Ibid., 1828, P. Pellet to J. Pellet, August 19, 1724.
52 Pritchard, "Ships, Men, and Commerce," and "Pattern of French Colonial Shipping"; Mathieu, *Commerce entre la Nouvelle-France et les Antilles*; Bosher, *Men and Ships in the Canada Trade*.
53 See tables 1–17 in Pritchard, "Ships, Men, and Commerce," 196–9, 487–502; Mathieu, *Commerce entre la Nouvelle France et les Antilles*, 151–62, appendix A; Cassel, "*Troupes de la Marine*," 259, 264–8.
54 Mathieu, *Commerce entre la Nouvelle-France et les Antilles*, 151–62.
55 Moore, "Other Louisbourg"; Butel, *Négociants bordelais*, 36–7; Mathieu, *Commerce entre la Nouvelle-France et les Antilles*, 3, 84–7; Miquelon, *Dugard of Rouen*, 93–9. On smuggling, see McNeill, *Atlantic*

Empires of France and Spain, 188–90; Chard, "Price and Profits of Accommodation," 209–27; and Crowley, "Government and Interests," 92–9.

56 AC, C11A 80, ff. 303–3v., List of ships arrived at Quebec, June 25, 1743.

57 Cabantous, *Dix mille marins face à l'océan*, 129–41.

58 *MPA*, 3: 571–3, Instructions to Bienville and Salmon, February 2, 1732.

59 Moore, "Cypress Lumber Industry"; Gould, "Trade between the Windward Islands". On Havana, see AC, C13A 28, ff. 62–3v., Vaudreuil to Maurepas, July 26, 1743; ibid., 42, f. 85, Kerlérec to Berryer, December 21, 1760; NAC, MG 18, G 2/19, Vaudreuil Papers, Vaudreuil to the court, November 10, 1748; Clark, *New Orleans, 1718–1812*, 86–90; Surrey, *Commerce of Louisiana*, 390–5, 404–6, 431–41.

60 AC, C13A 42, f. 131v., Rochemore to Berryer, December 1, 1760.

61 Usner, *Indians, Settlers, and Slaves*, chap. 3.

62 La Vere, "Between Kinship and Capitalism."

63 AC, C8A 20, ff. 443–4v., Statement of merchant ships engaged in commerce at Martinique, July 10, 1715; also Pritchard, "Ships, Men, and Commerce," table 10.

64 Cavignac, *Jean Pellet*, 176.

65 AC, C8A 20, ff. 48–5–?, Vaucresson to Pontchartrain, April 11, 1714; ibid., 50, ff. 412–20v., Neuville [director of king's domaine in Saint Pierre] to Maurepas, November 17, 1739; ibid., 60, ff. 225–8, Bompar and Hurson to Rouillé, March 6, 1754; ADLA, C-735, f. 2, Memorandum of Sieur de Rossel, December 1730.

66 Rochemonteix, *Père Antoine Lavalette*, 136–7, 149–50, 165–6.

67 Klooster, *Illicit Riches*, 89–98 and appendices 5, 9–10.

68 ADLA, C-735, Copy of a letter written to Monseigneur le Comte de Maurepas by the Chamber of Commerce of La Rochelle July 22, 1747; May, *Histoire économique de la Martinique*, 141.

69 AC, C8B 22, Statement of Commerce, no. 11–27, 1758.

70 Ibid., C8A 39, Memorandum on ... the Windward Islands, ff. 367–8v., [signed Blondel], December 6, 1728; ibid., F3 256, f. 672, Maurepas to de la Croix, October 20, 1738; May, *Histoire économique de la Martinique*, 147–53; Duviols, "Côtes du Venezuela," 5–9.

71 AC, C8A 23, ff. 47–55, Feuquières to Marine Council, December 21, 1717.

72 ADLA, C-735, f. 6, Memorandum of Sieur de Rossel, December 1730.

73 Pares, *War and Trade in the West Indies*, 195–216.

74 ADG, 7B 1828, P. Pellet to J. Pellet, May 31, 1727.

75 AC, C8A 59, ff. 158–62, Bompar and Hurson to Rouillé, November 14, 1751.

76 Ibid., B 53, ff. 162–3, Maurepas to Beauharnais, June 7, 1729.

77 Ibid., C11A 35, ff. 3–5, Ramezay and Bégon to Pontchartrain, September 13, 1715.
78 Ibid., C8A 49, ff. 70–1, Champigny and de la Croix to Maurepas, September 13, 1738; ibid., f. 435, General accounts of receipts, March 18, 1740; ibid., 54, f. 231v., Champigny to Maurepas, August 21, 1742.
79 Ibid.,, C14A 9, f. 136, d'Albon to Pontchartrain, January 21, 1716. I am indebted to James Pritchard for this citation.
80 Buchet, *Lutte pour l'espace caraïbe*, 1: 578–84.
81 Proulx, *Between France and New France*, 135–6.
82 AC, C13A 39, ff. 277–8v., Kerlérec to Machault, October 21, 1757; ibid., 40, f. 62, same to same, September 17, 1758.
83 Ibid., C13A 43, f. 90–1v., Kerlérec to Choiseul, July 26, 1762.
84 Ibid., C11A 87, ff. 129–30, La Galissonière and Hocquart to Maurepas, October 12, 1747.
85 Pares, *War and Trade in the West Indies*, 190–1, 236–7.
86 AC, C8A 55, ff. 160–2, Champigny to Maurepas, January 11, 1742; see also ibid., 54, f. 231v., same to same, August 21, 1742; ibid., 55, f. 87, same to same, n.d. [1743?].
87 Ibid., B 34, f. 198, Pontchartrain to Beauharnais, July 26, 1712.
88 Ibid., B 49, ff. 111v.–12, Maurepas to Renaud, October 15, 1726.
89 Ibid., B 72, f. 55–55v, Circular letter for the colonies, June 7, 1741; ibid., f. 65, Maurepas to Hocquart, May 26, 1741; Bosher, "Shipping to Canada in Wartime," 468n1.
90 See, for example, ADLA, C-735, Letter of M. "X," merchant in Martinique, to M. "Y," merchant in Marseille, October 2, 1727; compare with CCM, H20, The judges and consuls of Nantes to those of Marseille, February 14, 1726.
91 *RAPQ*,1927–28, Ordinance of M[onsieur] de Frontenac prohibiting *habitants* from assembling without permission, [March 23, 1677]; cited in Choquette, "Corporatism or Physiocracy?" 7–10 and note 44.
92 AC, C11A 82, ff. 338–43, Presentation made by the merchants and bourgeois of Canada to Monseigneur Maurepas, October 30, 1744; ibid., B 82, ff. 8–9, Maurepas to Beauharnois and Hocquart, March 31, 1745.
93 Ibid., C11A 97, f. 132–4, La Jonquière to Rouillé, October 19, 1751.
94 AMN, HH 228/8, Memorandum [de Vallincourt?], September 8, 1727; ibid., HH 228/9, January 22, 1728.
95 AC, C8A 41, ff. 73–8, Champigny and d'Orgeville to Maurepas, October 19, 1730; quotes ff. 73v. and 78 respectively.
96 Ibid., C8B 9, no. 87, d'Orgeville to Maurepas, December 12, 1730.
97 ADG, C-4323/20, [Perdrigeon?] to their honours at the Chamber of Commerce of Bordeaux, June 6, 1760.
98 AC, C13A 11, ff. 100–1, Périer and La Chaise to the Directors of the Company, August 18, 1728.

99 Ibid., F3 25, ff. 101–6, Letter from the merchants of New Orleans, May 6, 1759.

100 Tarrade, *Commerce colonial ... à la fin de l'ancien régime*, 1: 83–112.

101 For earlier regulations, see AC, A 25, ff. 51–6, Letters patent of the king, April 1717.

102 Ibid., ff. 83v.–90, Letters patent of the king, October 1727; see analysis by Vonglis in Dessalles, *Annales du Conseil souverain*, 2: 2n3, 26–30.

103 AC, A 25, ff. 83v.–90, Letters patent of the king, October 1727, articles 11–16.

104 See, for example, AC, C8A 42, ff. 210–12v., d'Orgeville to Maurepas, June 8, 1731; quote f. 211v.

105 Ibid., 41, ff. 73–8, Champigny and d'Orgeville to Maurepas, October 19, 1730.

106 AC, A 25, ff. 143–3v., *Arrêt* of December 19, 1728; ibid., ff. 240–40v., *Arrêt* of September 30, 1737; ibid., ff. 258, *Arrêt* of December 27, 1740; ibid., f. 258v., *Arrêt* of February 7, 1741.

107 CCLR, 24/8534, p. 8, Bordeaux Chamber of Commerce to garde des sceaux, March 23, 1756.

108 ADLA, C 741/62, Copy of observations ... made by the controller-general in regard to representations made by the Council of Nantes, September 27, 1733.

109 Ibid., C 741/28, In regard to the certificates for merchandise derived from the sale of blacks ..., February 17, 1731; ibid., C 741/11, Ordinance of the king regulating the style of certificates for the trade of Negroes in the French islands of America, July 6, 1734.

110 Ibid., C 741/11, Ordinance of the King ..., July 6, 1734.

111 Beinecke NCH 1/76, ff. 18–19, Memorandum of M. de Lacroix, February 25, 1741.

112 AC, C8A 50, ff. 134–6v., Champigny and Lacroix to Maurepas, November 6, 1739.

113 ADLA, C 741/89, Ordinance of the king concerning the exemption accorded to merchandise derived from the trade in Negroes ..., March 31, 1742.

114 Ibid., C 741/92, Observations of the guinea merchants of Nantes ..., March 8, 1742.

115 Ibid., ADLA, C 741/90, Copy of a letter written by the judges and consuls of Nantes ..., March 4, 1744.

116 AC, C11A 92, f. 117, Bigot to Maurepas, October 25, 1748; ibid., B 89, ff. 270–70v., Maurepas to La Jonquière, May 4, 1749.

117 Ibid., C13A 44, ff. 47–8, d'Abbadie to Choiseul, April 10, 1764; Jumonville, "Frenchmen at Heart."

118 AC, B 51, ff. 279v.–80, Maurepas to Champigny and d'Orgeville, August 10, 1728.

119 Ibid., C8A 39, ff. 165–7, Champigny and d'Orgeville to Maurepas, October 10, 1728; Ibid., A 25, ff. 116–16v, Warrant as orinter and bookseller for the Windward Islands, February 8, 1729; ibid., B 53, ff. 236–6v., Maurepas to Champigny and d'Orgeville, February 15, 1729; Ibid., B 52, f. 302–2v., same to same, August 30, 1729.

120 Ibid., C8A 54, ff. 27–8, Champigny and de Lacroix to Maurepas, [April?] 1742.

121. Ibid., C8A 64, ff. 148–51, "Articles of capitulation for the island of Martinique ...," February 13, 1762.

122 Censer, *French Press*, 140–9; Black, *English Press*, 145–51, 288–9; Clark, *Public Prints*, 23–6, 92–5, 178–84.

123 *Édits et ordonnances*, 455–6, *Arrêt* of January 27, 1721; Keyes, "Commis des Trésoriers Généraux."

124 AC, C8A 13, ff. 156–6v., Robert to Pontchartrain, July 14, 1701.

125 Ibid., F3 256, f. 697–9, Announcement of new postal system, January 18, 1739; Ibid., C8A 50, ff. 426–7v., Lavasseur to Maurepas, March 25, 1739; ibid., ff. 428–9v., same to same, April 8, 1739; ibid., ff. 432–3, same to same, May 22, 1739.

126 Ibid., C8A 59, ff. 315–23, Bompar and Hurson to Rouillé, September 6, 1752.

127 Dessalles, *Annales du Conseil souverain*, 2: 227–8.

128 AC, C8A 61, f. 331, Beauharnais and Givry to Berryer, October 24, 1758.

129 Ibid., F3 259, ff. 857–62, Ordinance of the king regulating packetboats destined for the colonies, July 31, 1763.

130 Steele, *English Atlantic*, 173–83.

131 AC, C8B 11, no. 26, Proposition for Establishing a number of ships ... to be sent from French ports for America ..., February 12, 1764.

CHAPTER SEVEN

1 Based on AC, C13A 41, ff. 478v.–81v., Summary of the extract of the investigation into the Louisiana affair (1764); ibid., ff. 89–98v., Kerlérec to Berryer, 13 July 1759; ibid., ff. 252v.–9, Procedure followed in the confiscation of the English schooner *The Three Brothers* (various copied documents from 20 April to 20 July 1759).

2 Drawn from de Reggio to Berryer, October 14, 1759, cited in Nasatir and Mills, *Commerce and Contraband*, 159–61; also AC, C13A 41, ff. 478v.–81v., Summary of the extract of the Louisiana affair (1764); and ibid., ff. 252v.–9, Procedure followed in the confiscation of the English schooner *The Three Brothers*, (various copied documents from 20 April to 20 July 1759).

3 Nasatir and Mills, *Commerce and Contraband*, 160, de Reggio to Berryer, October 14, 1759.
4 Roussier, "Instructions donnés à l'intendant des Îles françaises du Vent," 69–72; Frégault, *XVIIIe siècle canadien*, 177–8; Crowley, "Government and Interests," 34, 50–60, 278; Standen, "Politics, Patronage, and the Imperial Interest"; Ingersoll, *Mammon and Manon*, 40.
5 Beik, *Absolutism and Society*, 234–81, 332; Mancke, "Another British America," 1–36; Braddick, *State Formation*, chap. 9, esp. 397–8.
6 Mousnier, *Institutions of France*, esp. 2: 99–107; Kettering, "Patronage in Early Modern France," quote 851.
7 Kim, "Theorizing Intercultural Communications," 11–21; Singer, *Intercultural Communication*, 2–19.
8 Miquelon, *First Canada*, 1–3, 37–47; Eccles, *France in America*, 118–20; Dechene, *Habitants et marchands*, 402–13.
9 Nish, *Bourgeois gentilshommes de la Nouvelle-France*; Chaussinand-Nogaret, *French Nobility in the Eighteenth Century*, chap. 5.
10 Gadoury, *Noblesse de Nouvelle-France*, 29–37 and appendix 2; Petitjean-Roget, *Gaoulé*, 33–4.
11 Standen, "Politics, Patronage, and the Imperial Interest," 31–3; Keyes, "Commis des trésoriers généraux"; see also the list of secretaries in New France and their financial dealings in *BRH* 41: 74–107.
12 See, for example, *Édits, ordonnances royaux*, 2: 333, Ordinance prohibiting persons to receive *arrêts* of the Superior Council without the express permission of Governor Beauharnois ..., March 27, 1728.
13 Chartrand, *French Soldier in Colonial America*, 16–18; Hardcastle, "Military Organization of French Louisiana," 350–1.
14 Pritchard, *Louis XV's Navy*, 59–60.
15 See, for example, AC, C13A 16, ff. 226–6v., Bienville to Maurepas, May 18, 1733; ibid., 37, ff. 126–9v., Kerlérec to Rouillé, November 27, 1753.
16 Ibid., C8A 27, ff. 173–8, Feuquières to the Marine Council, July 30, 1720; ibid., B 57, f. 802v., Orders of the king, September 2, 1732.
17 Ibid., C8A 41, ff. 160–60v., Champigny to Maurepas, December 22, 1730.
18 Ibid., C13A 17, ff. 238–40, Louisiana – Specific Requests, September 5, 1733; ibid., C11A 77, ff. 123–4v., Beauharnois to Maurepas, September 28, 1742; ibid., C8A 53, ff. 339–9v., Champigny to Maurepas, July 12, 1741.
19 Ibid., C8A 46, f. 103v., Champigny to Maurepas, July 1, 1735; ibid., C13A 17. ff. 238–9, Louisiana – Specific Requests, September 5, 1733.
20 On the value of Franco-Native conferences, see Banks, "Culture and Communications on the Lake Ontario Frontier." On the structure of Iroquois councils, see Druke, "Iroquois Treaties," and "Linking Arms," 29–39; Foster, "On Who Spoke First"; Fenton, "Structure, Continuity,

and Change in the Process of Iroquois Treaty Making"; Crane, *Southern Frontier, 1670–1732*, 69–70, 172; Woods, *French-Indian Relations*, 10, 18, 103, 115, 148, 161–2; Usner, *Indians, Settlers, and Slaves*, chaps 2 and 3.

21 AC, C8A 46, ff. 144–6, Champigny to Dottin [governor of Barbados], December 20, 1735; ibid., 51, ff. 1–3v., Conference of Champigny with E. Hawke [commander of an English warship] ..., February 3, 1740.

22 Ibid., C8A 17, ff. 404–11, Le Bègue to Pontchartrain, October 20, 1710; ibid., 39, ff. 7v.–8, Memorandum of the king, April 27, 1728; ibid., 42, ff. 2–3, Champigny and d'Orgeville to Maurepas, February 7, 1731; Beinecke NCH 1/83, ff. 11–15, Memorandum, [signed Poinsable], July 29, 1743.

23 AC, C11A 78, ff. 42v.–4, Hocquart to Maurepas, October 8, 1742; Vachon, *Administration de la Nouvelle-France*, 75–81, and for the Admiralty office, 69–71, 81–5; Mathieu, *Le Commerce entre la Nouvelle-France et les Antilles*, 40–2. For Louisiana, see AC, C13A 28, ff. 360–5, Statement of [salary] accounts ... for Louisiana during the year 1744, n.d., [signed Le Normant]. For the Îles du Vent, see, for example, ibid., C8A 53, ff. 468–75, Statement of expense of salaries for officers and others ..., December 31, 1740.

24 Horton, "Gilles Hocquart," 6.

25 Ibid., C11A 51, f. 267, Hocquart to Maurepas, October 25, 1729; ibid., 77, ff. 332–7v, same to same, September 17, 1742.

26 On New France, see Vachon, *Administration de la Nouvelle-France*, 47–9, 85; Cahall, *Sovereign Council of New France*, 161, 168–9; Reid, "Development and Importance of ... Quebec," 272–3. For the Îles du Vent, see Hayot, *Officiers du Conseil souverain*, 12–14; Banbuck, *Histoire politique de la Martinique*, chap. 9; Chauleau, *Société à la Martinique*, 80–6. On Louisiana, see Dart, "Legal System of Louisiana"; Hardy, "Superior Council," 88–9.

27 AC, C8A 35, f. 127–7v., Feuquières and Blondel to Maurepas, September 1, 1726.

28 Hanley, "*Lit de Justice*," 341–4.

29 Cahall, *Sovereign Council of New France*, 181–2.

30 See Allaire, "Officiers et marchands."

31 AC, C11A 67, ff. 115–17, Response to king's memorandum, 1737, [signed Hocquart]; Ibid., C11A 99, ff. 87–7v., Bigot to Rouillé, October 12, 1753; ibid., B109, ff. 6–6v., Berryer to Bigot, January 8, 1759.

32 Jaenen, *Role of the Church in New France*, 40–2, 58–64; O'Neill, *Church and State in French Colonial Louisiana*, 133.

33 O'Neill, *Church and State*, 235–8. For Île Royale, see Johnston, *Religion in Life at Louisbourg*, 14.

34 Labat, *Nouveau voyage*, 1: 225–56, 323–54; Charlevoix, *Histoire et description générale*, 3: 77–80, 437–42.

35 Delanglez, *French Jesuits in Colonial Louisiana*, 83–90; O'Neill, *Church and State in French Colonial Louisiana*, 9, 130.

36 RAPQ 1935–36: 294, L'Isle-Dieu to Rouillé, April 1, 1750.

37 AC, C13A 16, ff. 227–8v., Bienville to Maurepas, May 18, 1733.

38 Ibid., C8A 59, ff. 350–3v., Bompar to Rouillé, March 8, 1752; response, ibid., B 97, pt. 1, f. 1–2v., Rouillé to Bompar, [date illegible]; ibid., C13A 37, ff. 126–9v., Kerlérec to Rouillé, November 27, 1753; response, ibid., B 99, f. 283, Rouillé to Kerlérec, November 23, 1754; and Ibid., C11A 99, ff. 273–81, Duquesne to Rouillé, October 10, 1754; response, ibid., B 101, ff. 131–2, Machault to Duquesne, March 25, 1755.

39 Ibid., C11A 77, ff. 333–6v, quote 336–6v., Hocquart to Maurepas, September 17, 1742.

40 Eccles, *France in America*, 164n18.

41 AC, C11A 55, f. 365–6, Hocquart to Maurepas, October 21, 1731.

42 Ibid., C13A 23, ff. 186–7, d'Artaguiette to Maurepas, December 14, 1738 [quote f. 186v].

43 Ibid., C8A 38, ff. 248–9, Blondel to Maurepas, August 6, 1727.

44 Ibid., 46, ff. 132–3, Champigny to Maurepas, October 19, 1735.

45 Ibid., 53, ff. 364–5, Champigny to Maurepas, December 14, 1741.

46 Ibid., 59, f. 24v., Poinsable to Rouillé, January 26, 1750.

47 Ibid., ff.26–6v.

48 Gadoury, *Noblesse de Nouvelle-France*, 29–33, 42; Moogk, *Nouvelle-France*, 178–9.

49 AC, C8A 41, f. 17v., Champigny and d'Orgeville to Maurepas, February 27, 1730; Ibid., ff. 88–92, same to same, November 23, 1730.

50 Ibid., C11A 55, f. 164, Hocquart to Maurepas, October 15, 1731.

51 Ibid., C8A 53, ff. 364–5, Champigny to Maurepas, December 14, 1741; ibid., vol. 54, ff. 209v.–10, same to same, June 30, 1742.

52 Desbarats, "Deniers du roi."

53 Stanley, *New France*, 164–6, 177; quotes from Eccles, *Canadian Frontier*, 175–6 and note 32; Frégault, *François Bigot*, 2: 145–52.

54 AC, C11A 103, ff. 210–19, Reflections for M. de Vaudreuil, [signed Montcalm], 1758; ibid., 104, ff. 157v.–9, Montcalm to Belle-Isle, April 12, 1759. Eccles suggests upward of 16,000 men combined in 1756, see *France in America*, 200.

55 Eccles, *France in America*, 199.

56 NAC, MG 8 A1, 12: 59–63, Vaudreuil-Cavagnial to Minister of War, June 8, 1756; AC, C11A, 102, ff. 428–30, Pontbriand to Abbé de L'Isle-Dieu, October 30, 1757.

57 AC, C11A 101, ff. 3–4, Vaudreuil-Cavagnial to Machault, June 16, 1756; ibid, 102, ff. 197–9, Montcalm to Machault, July 11, 1757.

58 See, for example, ibid., C11A 102, ff. 270–3, Statement by the king, October 7, 1757.
59 Ibid., C11A 103, ff. 391–2, Bigot to Machault, August 13, 1758; ibid., ff. 138–9v., Montcalm to Vadureuil-Cavagnial, August 2, 1758; ibid., ff. 456–8, Summary of events in New France, [Bougainville?], December 28, 1758.
60 Ibid., C11A 103, ff. 274–5v., Vaudreuil-Cavagnial to Machalut, November 3, 1758; ibid., C11A 104, ff. 157–60, Montcalm to Belle-Isle, April 12, 1759.
61 Ibid., B 103, ff. 21–21v., Minister to Vaudreuil-Cavagnial, May 27, 1757; ibid., ff. 24–6, same to Montcalm, May 27, 1757; ibid., B107, ff. 17–18v., Minister to Vaudreuil-Cavagnial, February 14, 1758; ibid., B107, ff. 27–7v., Minister to Montcalm, March 3, 1758; ibid., B107, ff. 49–9v., Machault to Vaudreuil-Cavagnial, September 23, 1758; ibid., ff. 50–50v., Machault to Montcalm, September 23, 1758.
62 Frégault, *Grand marquis*, 90, 141–2; Graham, "Lawrence," *DCB* 3: 362–3; Eccles, "Rigaud de Vaudreuil," *DCB* 4: 660–74.
63 Gwyn, "Whitmore," *DCB* 3: 663; Stanley, *New France*, 138–41; Eccles, "Rigaud de Vaudreuil," *DCB* 4: 660–74.
64 AC, C11A 103, ff. 257–61v., Vaudreuil-Cavagnial to Machault, November 1, 1758.
65 Quoted in Stanley, *New France*, 221.
66 AC, B 109, f. 339, Berryer to Montcalm, January 26, 1759.
67 Ibid., C11A 103, ff. 138–9v., Montcalm to Vaudreuil-Cavagnial, August 2, 1758; Ibid., 104, ff. 478–82, Memorandum, [n.d. but post-1760]
68 White, *Middle Ground*, 240–56; Jennings, *Ambiguous Iroquois Empire*, chap. 1, 18, and *Empire of Fortune*, chap. 6.
69 AC, C11A 103, ff. 423–6, Doreil to Machault, August 31, 1758.
70 Ibid., C11A 102, ff. 278–8v., Report to the king on Fort Lydius [Fort Edward], November 1, 1757.
71 NA, MG 8, A1 14, pp. 223–4, Montcalm to Belle-Isle, August 1758.
72 AC, C11A 103, ff. 372–5, "Account of the English Attack in Canada," 1758.
73 Ibid., ff. 159–61, Speech of the domiciled natives, July 30, 1758.
74 See, for example, ibid., B 103, ff. 30–30v., Minister to Vaudrueil-Cavagnial, August 6, 1757; ibid., B 103, ff. 25–6, Minister to Montcalm, May 27, 1757; also ibid., B107, ff. 17–18v., Minister to Vaudreuil-Cavagnial, February 14, 1758.
75 Moogk, *Nouvelle France*, 143–5.
76 AC, C11A, f. 406v., de Pontleroy to Berryer, December 1, 1758.
77 Stanley, *New France*, 138–63.

78 AC, C11A 103, ff. 382–2v., Vaudreuil-Cavagnial to Montcalm, July 21, 1758; ibid., ff. 460–1v., Memorandum on the Canadian militia, [Bougainville?], 1758.
79 Montreuil to d'Argenson, 12 June 1756; cited in Nicolai, "Different Kind of Courage," 58.
80 AC, C11A 103, f. 461v., Memorandum on the Canadian militia, [Bougainville?], 1758.
81 AC, C11A 102, ff. 197–9, Montcalm to Machault, July 11, 1757.
82 On Montcalm's reactions to the Marine's policies, see, for example, ibid., 102, ff. 198–200, Montcalm to Machault, July 11, 1757.
83 Ibid., C11A 103, ff. 3340–1v., Report on the Battle of Carillon [observations by Vaudreuil-Cavagnial], 1758.
84 Ibid., C11A 102, ff. 175–6, Vaudreuil-Cavagnial to Moras, November 2, 1757; ibid., 103, ff. 145–5v., same to Berryer, August 4, 1758; ibid., f. 228v., same to same, October 25, 1758.
85 Ibid., C11A 104, ff. 128v.–9, Vaudreuil-Cavagnial to Berryer, November 28, 1759.
86 Ibid., C11A 103, ff. 228–9, Vaudreuil-Cavagnial to Machault, October 25, 1758 [first quote]; ibid., ff. 299–300, same to same, November 4, 1758 [second quote].
87 Ibid., C11A 103, ff. 301–6, November 4, 1758.
88 Ibid., B 109, f. 19v., Berryer to Vaudreuil-Cavagnial and Bigot, January 20, 1759. On the Marine's search for advice on handling such disputes, see ibid., B106, f. 33, Minister to M. Paulmy, April 2, 1758.
89 Nicolai, "Different Kind of Courage," 70–1.
90 Dessalles, *Annales du Conseil souverain*, 2: 66–9.
91 Daney, *Histoire de la Martinique*, 2: 150–3; Dessalles, *Annales du Conseil souverain*, 2: 70–3.
92 AC, C8A 61, ff. 199–206, Beauharnais and Givry to Moras, July 23, 1757.
93 Ibid., C8A 62, ff. 1–13, Account of actions in Martinique ..., [signed Beauharnais], January 15, 1759.
94 Ibid., ff. 97v.–9, Beauharnais to Berryer, May 17, 1759.
95 Ibid., 62, ff. 259–70, Superior Council memorandum, copy submitted to Beauharnais, March 7, 1759; also Dessalles, *Annales du Conseil souverain*, 2: 83–91, 91–2.
96 AC, C8A 62, ff. 185, La Chassaigne to Beauharnais, May 18, 1759.
97 Ibid., ff. 334–6, Longueville to Berryer, August 5, 1759; ibid., f. 437v., La Rivière to Berryer, January 20, 1760.
98 See, for example, ibid., f. 127, Beauharnais to Berryer, May 17, 1759; ibid., f. 253–3v., Rouillé de Raucourt to same, January 30, 1759; ibid., ff. 281–4, same to Accaron, May 20, 1759 [first quote f. 281]; ibid., ff. 247–50v., Picaudeau des Rivières to Berryer, December 16, 1759 [second quote f. 247].

99 Daney, *Histoire de la Martinique*, 2: 155, 185–6; Dessalles, *Annales du Conseil souverain*, 2: 73, 103, 119–20nn3–4.
100 Dessalles, *Annales du Conseil souverain*, 2: 186.
101 AC, C8A 64, ff. 153–7, General order ..., September 20, 1761 [quote f. 157].
102 Ibid.
103 Ibid., F3 259, f. 583, Extract of the registers from the deliberations of the Chambre mi-partie d'agriculture et de commerce, May 27, 1761; Daney, *Histoire de la Martinique*, 2: 176–9; Dessalles, *Annales du Conseil souverain*, 2: 93–102.
104 Vonglis, in Dessalles, *Annales du Conseil souverain*, 2, pt 2: 108–9n1.
105 AC, C8A 63, ff. 79–80, Levassor de La Touche to Berryer, May 30, 1761 [quote f. 79]; also Daney, *Histoire de la Martinique*, 2: 170–5; Anon., *Lettres sur la prise de la Martinique*, 7–9.
106 Dessalles, *Annales du Conseil souverain*, 2: 160–1, 165–73, and 177–94 passim; Boulle, "French Colonies and the Reform of Their Administration," 608.
107 AC, C8A 65, ff.144v.–5, Fenélon to Choiseul, July 26, 1763.
108 Ibid., 64, ff. 277–9, Judgment of M. Choiseul, November 14, 1762.
109 Usner, *Indians, Settlers, and Slaves*, 94–6.
110 AC, C13A 37, ff. 124–5, La Houssaye to Rouillé, November 26, 1753.
111 Ibid., B 95, pt 6, f. 14, Memorandum of the king to the S[ieur]s Kerlérec ... and Michel, October 20, 1752.
112 Clark, *New Orleans, 1718–1812*, 107–25.
113 Maupassant, "Armateurs bordelais au XVIII siècle," 159–78.
114 AC, C13A 40, ff. 62–3v., Kerlérec to minister, September 17, 1758.
115 Nasatir and Mills, *Commerce and Contraband*, 92, Kerlérec to Lenormand [*sic*], May 4, 1759; ibid., 99, Derneville [*sic*] to Le Normand [*sic*], May 7, 1759; Pritchard, *Louis XV's Navy*, 34–5.
116 AC, C13A 42, ff. 254v.–5, Summary of abuses which have occurred at Louisiana ..., December 12, 1761, [signed by Thiton de Silègues].
117 Nasatir and Mills, *Commerce and Contraband*, 179, Madame Rochemore to Choiseul, June 23, 1763.
118 AC, C13A 42, ff. 76–6v., Kerlérec to Accaron, December 21, 1760.
119 Ibid., C13A 41, ff. 224–6, Rochemore to Berryer, April 28, 1759 [also in Nasatir and Mills, 70[; Nasatir and Mills, *Commerce and Contraband*, 105, Kerlérec to Massiac [Berryer], May 20, 1759; ibid., 180, Madame Kerlérec to Choiseul, June 23, 1760.
120 AC, C13A 42, ff. 102–2v., Rochemore to Berryer, June 22, 1760.
121 See Clark, *New Orleans, 1718–1812*, chap. 5.
122 AC, C13A 41, ff. 384–8, Merchants to minister, May 4, 1759 [second quote, with some flourishes, from Nasatir and Mills, *Commerce and Contraband*, 94]; ibid., 37–9, Petition of the merchants and inhabitants

to Kerlérec, April 5, 1759 [first quote 38]; and ibid., 116–17, Memorandum of the merchants to Kerlérec, June 25, 1759.

123 Ibid., 47, Bellile [*sic*] to minister, April 21, 1759.

124 See AC, C13A 43, f.20, Kerlérec to Choiseul, June 21, 1762.

125 Ibid., ff. 117–18, Representations of the officers to Kerlérec, June 25, 1759; ibid., ff. 178–81v., Rochemore to Massiac [Berryer], March 7, 1759.

126 Ibid., C13A 41, ff. 251–2v., Kerlérec to de Reggio, [June 27, 1759].

127 Nasatir and Mills, *Commerce and Contraband*, 112, Rochemore to Le Norman[t], May 22, 1759; see also ibid., 99, d'Erneville to Le Norman[t], May 7, 1759.

128 Nasatir and Mills, *Commerce and Contraband*, 55–6, Kerlérec to Rochemore, April 24, 1759.

129 Ibid., 90, Kerlérec to Massiac [Berryer], May 3, 1759.

130 Ibid., 160, de Reggio to Berryer, October 14, 1759.

131 AC, C13A 42, f. 74v., Kerlérec to Accaron, December 21, 1760.

132 Ibid., 42, ff. 104v.–7, Rochemore to Berryer, June 22, 1760 [quote 104v]. For other examples, see ibid., 41, ff. 91–1v., Kerlérec to Berryer, July 13, 1759; ibid., ff. 224–7, Rochemore to Berryer, April 28, 1759; Nasatir and Mills, *Commerce and Contraband*, 113, Rochemore to Le Norman[t], May 22, 1759.

133 AC, C13A 42, ff. 110–18, Rochemore to Berryer, June 22, 1760.

Bibliography

MANUSCRIPT SOURCES

France

ARCHIVES DE CHAMBRE DE COMMERCE ET L'INDUSTRIE, MARSEILLES

H: Archives de la Chambre de Commerce – Commerce général

H 20, Martinique, 1726–91

H 26, Louisiana, 1718–77

L: Fonds privés

L9, Fonds Roux, 1728–1843, bundles 1–1, 318; Bundles 688–700, Correspondence from Martinique, 1734–1809; bundle 1317, Diant family (Martinique), Correspondence and business papers, 1751–88

ARCHIVES D'ENTREPRISES (IN ARCHIVES NATIONALES, PARIS)

Series 62 AQ, Fonds Dugard, Ship's account books, vol. 42 (Martinique, 1734–60)

ARCHIVES DÉPARTEMENTALES DE BOUCHES-DES-RHONE, MARSEILLES

B: Cours de l'Amirauté

9B, vols. 243, 245, 256, 258, 259, 261 (including permissions granted for slaves to migrate to France)

ARCHIVES DÉPARTEMENTALES DE CHARENTE-MARITIME, LA ROCHELLE

B: Fonds de l'Amirauté de la Rochelle

B 5743, Printed ordinances on maritime commerce, 1717–61

C: Intendance

C 157, item 62, Damages to *Le Prince*, 10 June 1716

E: Papiers de famille

E 486–7, Account books of Dupont and Rasteau families

E 512, Papers of slave ship *Le Bellone*, 1741–42
E: Supplemental
E (supp.) 154, Public ceremonies (expenses)

ARCHIVES DÉPARTEMENTALES DE GIRONDE, BORDEAUX
B: Fonds de l'Amirauté de Guienne
6B 26–27, Ships' registrations
6B 49, Catholic passports
6B 88, Captains' declarations
6B 360–70, Crew lists
7B: Fonds principaux des négociants
7B 1205–10, Fonds François Chety (1741–56) 1205 (Correspondence from Martinique); 1207–10 (Ships' papers and accounts)
7B 1303–1305, Fonds François Dufons (1746–63), (Correspondence and miscellaneous papers, Antilles)
7B 1322–1326, Fonds Pierre Dulorie (1734–50), (Correspondence and miscellaneous papers, St. Pierre)
7B 1467, 1477–8, 1484–5, Fonds Jacques Grenouilleau (1755–69): 1467 (Daily sales); 1477–8 (Receipts); 1484 (Miscellaneous); 1485 (Great account book)
7B 1826–35, 1851, 1869–70, 1872 Fonds Jean Pellet (1718–58): 1826–35 (Correspondence from Saint Pierre); 1851 (Copy book, Martinique); 1869–70, 72 (Ships' accounts)
7B 2816, Fonds Jean-Baptiste Montuy (1708–33), (Correspondence from Saint Pierre)
7B 2407, Fonds divers: Cornier (1712–1716)
7B 3099, Mélanges coloniales (1747–90), (Miscellaneous bills of exchange)
C: Fonds de l'Intendance
C-3388, 3421, 3619, 3667, 3669, 4252, 4256, 4262, 4269, 4323
Fonds Gradis
Microfilm 1 Mi (Correspondence): 112 (Correspondence of Abraham Gradis); 125 (Marriage contract, D. Lindo and E. Depas); 130 (Letters from La Galissonière); 143 (Marriage contract, B. Gradis and E. Gradis); 147, 158 (Letters from Rouillé); 162 (transcripts on relations with Père Lavalette); 163 (Letters from La Galissonière); 174 (Letters from de La Porte); 179 (Letters from Berryer); 189 (Letters to Mme Beaucourt); 217–18 (Letters from Choiseul); 229 (Various letters)

ARCHIVES DÉPARTEMENTALES DE LOIRE-ATLANTIQUE, NANTES
C: Chambre de Commerce de Nantes
C 735 Various documents, including reports from Martinique, 1670–1789
C 741 Slave trade, 1688–1789

ARCHIVES GRADIS (PRIVATE), PARIS

Copybook of Abraham Gradis, 1756–57

ARCHIVES MUNICIPALES DE NANTES

HH 144, Police and censorship, 1713–89

HH 228, Correspondence of Councillor Mellier on Antilles, 1709–29

ARCHIVES NATIONALES, PARIS

État générale des fonds

Series G, Postal service and messengers, vol. 124

Monuments Historiques

Series K, section 8, Colonies 16th to 18th centuries, vols. 1231, 1232

Series K, section 10, Ceremonies, vols. 1712, 1716, 1719

Military orders, hospital orders, and miscellaneous

Series M, Affaires Maritimes, 17th to 18th centuries, vol. 662

Microfilm

Microfilm 299 Mi 1, Recensement de l'Isle de la Martinique, 1769

Fonds de la Marine

Series B3, Correspondence with the Marine, vol. 207

Series 3JJ, Scientific and geographic observations, vols. 260, 261, 271, 276–80, 282, 284, 286

Series 4JJ, Ships' logs, vols. 15, 18, 19, 27, 29, 34

Fonds des colonies

Series A, Royal acts and ordinances, vols. 21–6

Series B, Letters sent from the Colonial Office, vols. 34–118 (1712–63)

Series C8A, General correspondence (Martinique), vols. 3–66 (1676–1765)

Series C8B, Supplementary correspondence (Martinique), vols. 4, 9, 10, 11, 17–23 (Commercial états)

Series C11A, General correspondence (Canada), vols. 34–106 (1713–60)

Series C11B, General correspondence (Île Royale), vol. 1

Series C11E, Boundaries and posts, North America, "Règlement des districts de paroisses, 1721" (Mémoire by Collet)

Series C13A, General correspondence (Louisiana), vols. 3–44 (1713–64)

Series C13B, Supplementary correspondence (Louisiana), vol. 1

Series C13C, Diverse correspondence (Louisiana), vols. 1, 4

Series F3, Collection Moreau de St. Méry, vols. 9–11 (Canada), vols. 26–8 (Martinique, varia, including navigation), vol. 39 (Martinique, descriptions), vol. 126 (Chambre de Mi-partie de Commerce et d'Agriculture, Martinique), vols. 252, 255, 256, 259, 263 (Code Martinique, 1720–63)

Series G1, Registers of civil censuses and varia, vols. 460–2

Series F5A, Religious missions, vols. 5, 6, 27–8

ARCHIVES PRIVÉS (IN ARCHIVES NATIONALES, PARIS)

Series AP 294, cartons 1–2, d'Andlau Papers (Martinique, 1655–1754)

Series AP 354, Lobel-Maby Papers, Dossier Jacques Touzay de Chencteau (Martinique, 1738–42)

BIBLIOTHÈQUE MUNICIPALE DE LA ROCHELLE

Mss. 1424–5, Rasteau family, business papers

1938, Various colonial commercial affairs, 17th to 18th centuries

1949, Van Hoogwerf family, 1738–91

1955, Various commercial documents, 17th to 18th centuries

1960, Rasteau family and Canada, 1760–65

1992, Miscellaneous merchants' correspondence, 1751–1850 (including some letters to merchants Belin, Arnault, Charruyer, Rasteau, Dupont, Van Hoogwerf, Admyrault)

BIBLIOTHÈQUE NATIONALE, PARIS

Nouvelles acquisitions françaises

Mss. 21, 261, "Principes des Ministres sur la Marine depuis 1669 jusqu'à 1723," by Pidansat de Mairobert

CENTRE DES ARCHIVES D'OUTRE-MER (CAOM), AIX-EN-PROVENCE

Dépôt des Fortifications des Colonies

Portfolio 15:104c, Plan du Fort-St-Pierre, 1702

142B, Plan de Réduit de St Pierre, 1727

149B, Plan de l'Isle de la Martinique, 1734

150B, Plan de la ville et rade du Fort Saint-Pierre, 1740

191B, Plan de la ville de St Pierre et de ses environs, 1763

Carton 47: 147, Relation exacte de la destruction des Nègres, révoltés de l'Isle de St. Jean, 1733; 178, Différentes lettres au sujet de l'entreprise des Anglais sur la Martinique (January 1762)

Carton 48: 202, Lettre au ministre sur la ville de St. Pierre, November 5, 1763, (signed Rochemore, royal engineer)

CHAMBRE DE COMMERCE DE L'INDUSTRIE DE LA ROCHELLE

Carton 22, Correspondence with various chambers of commerce (items nos. 7377–812)

Carton 24, Correspondence with Chamber of Commerce at Bordeaux (items nos. 8335–739)

Canada

NATIONAL ARCHIVES OF CANADA, OTTAWA

Microfilmed sets from the Archives Nationales, Paris, Fonds des Colonies,

series A, B, C8A, C11A, C11E, C13A/B/C, F3, F5A, G1
MG 6, A1, Archives Maritime Rochefort; Sub-series 1E, Correspondence of port intendants and secretary of state for the Marine, vols. 81–3, 342–3 (transcripts)
MG 18, E 22, Miniac Papers
MG 18, G 2, Vaudreuil-Cavagnial Papers (microfilmed from the Loudoun Collection at the Huntington Library, San Marino, Calif.)
MG 18, G 9, Hocquart Papers
MG 18, H 27, Félix Martin Papers
MG 18, J 5, "Remarques Particuliers des côtes et riviere [*sic*] du Canada" [photocopy of Canadian portion of *L'Héros*'s log of 1712]"

National Map Collection
NMC 1596, Plan de Quebeck, ville capitale de la nouvelle France [1716?]
NMC 1598, Veüe de la Ville de Quebec [1734?]
NMC 1736, [Plan of Quebec], 1709
NMC 133349, A Plan of Quebec, 1759
NMC 7154, Carte de la Route Tenuée L'Escadre du Roy En 1707
NMC 7608, Plan de la ville de la Nouvelle Orléans, May 1728
NMC 7613, Plan de la Nouvelle Orléans, 1731
NMC 7615, Plan de la Nouvelle Orléans, 1764
NMC 7701, A Plan of St. Pierre Bay, 1777

United States

WALTER BEINECKE LESSER ANTILLES COLLECTION, HAMILTON COLLEGE, NEW YORK
NCH Ms 55, 68–9, 74–6, 83–5, 88–9, 93, 97, 100, 120, 129, 140, 151–3, 155–6, 204, 216

PRINTED PRIMARY AND SECONDARY SOURCES

Abbadie, Jean-Jacques-Blaise, d'. "Journal." In *A Comparative View of French Louisiana, 1699 and 1762: The Journals of Pierre Le Moyne d'Iberville and Jean-Jacques-Blaise d'Abbadie*, edited and translated by Carl A. Brasseaux. Lafayette: Center for Louisiana Studies, 1979.
Abenon, Lucien René. *La Guadeloupe de 1671–1759: Étude politique, économique et sociale*. 2 vols. Paris: Éditions l'Harmattan, 1987.
– and John Dickinson. *Les Français en Amérique: Histoire d'une colonisation*. Lyon : Presses universitaires de Lyon, 1993.
Acerra, Martine. "Rochefort: l'arsenal, l'eau, et les vaisseaux." In *Les Marines de guerre européennes, XVII-XVIIIe siècles*, edited by Martine

Acerra, José Merino, and Jean Meyer, 51–61. Paris: Presses de l'Université de Paris de Sorbonne, 1981.
– and Jean Meyer, *La grand époque de la Marine à voile*. Rennes: Éditions Ouest-France, 1987.
Aldrich, Robert. *Greater France: A History of French Overseas Expansion*. New York: St. Martin's Press, 1996.
Allain, Mathé. "French Emigration Policies: Louisiana, 1699–1715." In *The French Experience in Louisiana*, edited by Glenn R. Conrad, 106–114. Lafayette: Center for Louisiana Studies, 1995.
– *"Not Worth a Straw": French Colonial Policy and the Early Years of Louisiana*. Lafayette: Center for Louisiana Studies, 1988.
– "Slave Policies in French Louisiana." *Louisiana History* 21 (1980): 127–37.
Allaire, Gratien. "Officiers et marchands: Les sociétés de commerce des fourrures, 1715–1760." *Revue d'histoire de l'Amérique française* 40 (1987): 409–28.
Almanach royal pour l'an mille sept cens treize. Paris: Laurent d'Houry, 1713.
Anderson, Benedict. *Imagined Communities: Reflections on the Origin and Spread of Nationalism*. Rev. ed. New York: Verso, 1991.
Anderson, Fred. *Crucible of War: The Seven Years' War and the Fate of Empire in British North America, 1754–1766*. New York: Vintage Books, 2001.
Andrews, Kenneth R. *Trade, Plunder and Settlement: Maritime Enterprise and the Genesis of the British Empire, 1460–1630*. Cambridge: Cambridge University Press, 1984.
Anonymous. *Lettres sur la prise de la Martinique par les Anglais en 1762*. Copy in Bibliothèque Nationale, Paris.
Antoine, Michel. *Le Conseil du roi sous le règne de Louis XV*. Geneva: Droz, 1970.
Aquila, Richard. *The Iroquois Restoration: Iroquois Diplomacy on the Colonial Frontier, 1701–1754*. Detroit: Wayne State University Press, 1983.
Arbellot, Guy. "La grande mutation des routes de France au milieu du XVIIIe siècle." *Annales: Économies, sociétés, civilisations* 28 (1973): 765–90.
Armitage, David. "Greater Britain: A Useful Category of Analysis?" *American Historical Review* 104 (1999): 427–45.
Axtell, James. *The Invasion Within: The Contest of Cultures in Colonial North America*. New York and Oxford: Oxford University Press, 1985.
Bailyn, Bernard. "Communications and Trade: The Atlantic in the Seventeenth Century." *Journal of Economic History* 13 (1953): 378–87.
– "The Idea of Atlantic History." *Itinerario* 20 (1996): 19–44.
– *The New England Merchants in the Seventeenth Century*. New York: Harper, 1955; reprint, 1964.

– *Voyagers to the West: A Passage in the Peopling of America on the Eve of the Revolution.* New York: Random House, 1986.
Baker, Vaughn B. "Cherchez les femmes: Some Glimpses of Women in Early Eighteenth-Century Louisiana." *Louisiana History* 31 (1990): 21–37.
Baker, William. *Colonial Vessels: Some Seventeenth-Century Sailing Craft.* Barre, Mass.: Barre Publishing, 1962.
Balcom, B.A. "The Cod Fishery of Isle Royale, 1713–1758." In *Aspects of Louisbourg*, Edited by Eric Krause, Carol Corbin, and William O'Shea, 169–97. Sydney, NS: University College Press of Cape Breton, 1995.
Banbuck, C.A. *Histoire politique, économique et sociale de la Martinique sous l'Ancien Régime (1635–1789).* Paris: Marcel Rivière, 1935; reprint, Fort-de-France: Société de Distribution et de Culture, 1972.
Banks, Kenneth. "Culture and Communications on the Lake Ontario Frontier, 1720–1750." MA thesis, Queen's University, 1990.
Baudrit, André. "Charles de Courbon, Comte de Blénac, 1622–1696." *Mémoires de la Société d'histoire de la Martinique* 2 (1967): 127–58.
Baugh, Daniel A. *British Naval Administration in the Age of Walpole.* Princeton: Princeton University Press, 1965.
– *Naval Administration, 1715–1750.* London: Naval Records Society, 1977.
Bédard, M-A. "La présence protestante en Nouvelle-France." *Revue d'histoire de l'Amérique française* 31 (1977): 325–49.
Bégon, Élisabeth. "Lettres de Madame Bégon." In *RAPQ pour 1934–35*, 187–278.
Beik, William. *Absolutism and Society in Seventeenth-Century France: State Power and Provincial Aristocracy in Languedoc.* Cambridge: Cambridge University Press, 1985.
– *Urban Protest in Seventeenth-Century France: The Culture of Retribution.* Cambridge: Cambridge University Press, 1997.
Bellin, Nicolas. *Le petit atlas maritime: Receuil de cartes et plans des quatres parties du monde.* 5 vols. Paris: Imprimerie Royale, 1764.
Benedict, Philip. "More than Market and Manufactory: The Cities of Early Modern France." *French Historical Studies* 20 (1987): 511–38.
Bently, Jerry H. "Sea and Ocean Basins as Frameworks of Historical Analysis." *Geographical Review* 89 (1999): 215–24.
Berbain, Simone. *Le comptoir français de Juda (Ouidah) au XVIIIe siècle.* Paris : Librarie Larose, 1942.
Bercé, Yves-Marie. *The Birth of Absolutism: A History of France, 1598–1661.* London: MacMillan Press, 1996.
– *Fête et révolte: Des mentalités populaires du XVIe au XVIIIe siècle.* Paris: Hachette, 1976.
Bézard, Yvonne. *Fonctionnaires maritimes et coloniaux sous Louis XIV: Les Bégon.* Paris: Albin Michel, 1932.

Black, Jeremy. *The English Press in the Eighteenth Century*. London: Croom-Helm, 1987.

Blackburn, Robin. *The Making of New World Slavery: From the Baroque to the Modern, 1492–1800*. London: Verso: 1997.

Bluche, François. *Louis XIV*. Paris: Fayard, 1986.

Bodin, Jean. *Six Books of the Commonwealth*. Abridged and translated by M.J. Tooley. Oxford: Basil Blackwell, 1956.

Boisnard, Luc. *Les Phélypeaux: Une famille de ministres sous l'ancien régime*. Paris: SEDOPOLS, 1986.

Bolster, W. Jeffrey. *Black Jacks: African-American Seamen in the Age of Sail*. Cambridge: Harvard University Press, 1998.

Bonnassieux, Pierre. *Les grandes compagnies de commerce*. Paris: Plon and Nourrit, 1892; reprint, New York: Burt Franklin, 1969.

Bonney, Richard. *Political Change in France under Richelieu and Mazarin, 1624–1661*. Oxford: Oxford University Press, 1978.

Bosher, J.F. *The Canada Merchants, 1713–1763*. Oxford: Clarendon Press, 1987.

– "Une famille de fleurance dans le commerce du Canada à Bordeaux (1683–1753): les Jung." *Annales du Midi* 95 (1983): 159–84.

– "French Colonial Society in Canada." *Transactions of the Royal Society of Canada*, series 4, 19 (1981): 147–64.

– *French Finances, 1770–1795: From Business to Bureaucracy*. Cambridge: Cambridge University Press, 1970.

– "French Protestant Families in Canadian Trade, 1740–1760." *Histoire sociale/Social History* 14 (1974): 179–201.

– "Government and Private Interest in New France." *Canadian Public Administration* 10 (1967): 244–57.

– "Huguenot Merchants and the Protestant International in the Seventeenth Century." *William and Mary Quarterly*, 3rd series, 52 (1995): 77–102.

– *Men and Ships in the Canada Trade, 1660–1760: A Biographical Dictionary*. Ottawa: National Historic Sites, 1992.

– "A Quebec Merchant's Trading Circles in France and Canada: Jean-André Lamaletie before 1763." In *Business and Religion in the Age of New France, 1600–1760: Twenty-Two Studies*, 372–98. Toronto: Canadian Scholar's Press, 1994.

– "Le ravitaillement de Québec en 1758." *Histoire sociale/Social History* 12 (1972): 79–85.

– "Sept grands marchands Catholiques français participant au commerce avec la Nouvelle-France (1660–1715)." *Revue d'histoire de l'Amérique française* 48 (1994): 3–27.

– "Shipping to Canada in Wartime, 1743–1760." In *Business and Religion in the Age of New France, 1600–1760: Twenty-Two Studies*, 464–86. Toronto: Canadian Scholar's Press, 1994.

– "The Treasurers of the Navy and Colonies under Louis x: Rochefort and La Rochelle." In *Business and Religion in the Age of New France, 1600–1760: Twenty-Two Studies*, 327–48. Toronto: Canadian Scholar's Press, 1994.

Bossu, M. *Nouveau voyages aux Indes occidentales; contenant une relation des différens peuples qui habitent les environs du grand fleuve Saint-Louis, appellé vulgairement le Mississippi*. Paris: Librarie Jay, 1768.

Bossuet, Jacques-Bénigne. *Politics Drawn from the Very Words of Holy Scripture*. Edited and translated by Patrick Riley. Cambridge: Cambridge University Press, 1990.

Boucault, Nicholas-Gaspard. "État présent du Canada, dressé sur nombre de mémoires et connaissances acquises sur les lieux, par le sieur Boucault, 1754." In *RAPQ pour 1920–21*, 11–50.

Boucher, Philip P. *Cannibal Encounters: Europeans and Island Caribs, 1492–1763*. Baltimore: Johns Hopkins University Press, 1992.

– *Les Nouvelles Frances: France in America, 1500–1815, an Imperial Perspective*. Providence: John Carter Brown Library, 1989.

– "Shadows in the Past: France and Guiana, 1655–57." In *Proceedings of the Sixth and Seventh Annual Meetings of the French Colonial Historical Society for 1980–1981*, edited by James Cooke, 13–26.

Bougainville, Louis-Antoine de. *Écrits sur le Canada: mémoires – journal – lettres*. Edited by Roland Lamontagne. Sillery, Qué.: Éditions du Pélican, 1993.

– "Mémoire sur l'état de la Nouvelle-France, 1757." In *RAPQ pour 1923–24*, 42–70.

Boulaye, Louis-Hyacynthe Polmier, sieur de la. "Mémoire du sieur de la Boulaye sur les colonies françaises d'Amérique." In *RAPQ pour 1965*, 73–86.

Boulle, Pierre. "The French Colonies and the Reform of their Administration During and following the Seven Years' War." PhD diss., University of California at Berkeley, 1968.

– "Some Eighteenth-Century French Views of Louisiana." In *Frenchmen and French Ways in the Mississippi Valley*, edited by John McDermott, 15–27. Urbana: University of Illinois Press, 1969.

Boutruche, Robert. "Bordeaux et le commerce des antilles françaises au XVIIIe siècle." In *Nos Antilles*, edited by Serge Denis, 83–124. Paris: Maison du Livre français, 1935.

Boxer, C.R. *The Dutch Seaborne Empire, 1600–1800*. London: Hutchinson, 1965; reprint, London: Pelican Books, 1988.

Braddick, Michael. *State Formation in Early Modern England, c. 1550–1700*. Cambridge: Cambridge University Press, 2000.

Brasseaux, Carl. "The Administration of Slave Regulations in French Louisiana, 1724–1766." *Louisiana History* 21 (1980): 139–58.

– *France's Forgotten Legion: Service Records of French and Adminsitrative Personnel Stationed in the Mississippi Valley and Gulf Coast Region, 1699–1769*. Baton Rouge: Louisiana State University Press, 2000. On CD-ROM).

– "The Moral Climate of French Colonial Louisiana." In *The French Experience in Louisiana*, edited by Glenn R. Conrad, 525–37. Lafayette: Center for Louisiana Studies, 1995.

Braudel, Fernand. *Civilization and Capitalism*. Vol. 1, *The Structures of Everyday Life: The Limits of the Possible*. Translated and revised by Sîan Reynolds. New York: Harper and Row, 1981.

– *The Identity of France*. Vol. 1, *History and Environment*. Translated by Sîan Reynolds. London: Collins, 1988.

– *The Mediterranean and the Mediterranean World in the Age of Philip II*. 3 vols. Translated by Sîan Reynolds. Rev. ed. New York: Harper and Row, 1972.

– *On History*. Translated by Sarah Matthews. Chicago: University of Chicago Press, 1980.

Brewer, John. *The Sinews of Power: War, Money, and the English State, 1688–1783*. Cambridge: Harvard University Press, 1990.

Bridenbaugh, Carl. *Cities in the Wilderness: The First Century of Urban Life in America, 1625–1742*. London: Oxford University Press, 1971.

Brière, Jean-François. "Pêche et politique à Terre-Neuve au XVIIIe siècle: La France, veritable gagnante au traité d'Utrecht?" *Canadian Historical Review* 64 (1983): 168–87.

– *La pêche française en Amérique du Nord au XVIIIe siècle*. Montréal: Fides, 1990.

Brisson, Réal. *La charpenterie navale à Québec sous le régime français*. Québec: Institut québécois de recherche sur la culture, 1983.

Brown, Richard D. *Knowledge Is Power: The Diffusion of Information in Early America, 1700–1865*. New York: Oxford University Press, 1989.

Brutalis, Jean-Auguste. *Inventaire du fonds de la chambre du commerce de Guienne*. Bordeaux: G. Gounouilhou, 1893; reprint, Bordeaux, 1989.

Buchet, Christian. *La lutte pour l'espace caraïbe et la façade atlantique de l'Amérique Centrale et du Sud (1672–1763)*. 2 vols. Paris: Publisud, 1991.

Burke, Peter. *The Fabrication of Louis XIV*. New Haven: Yale University Press, 1992.

Butel, Paul. *The Atlantic*. Translated by Iain Hamilton Grant. London: Routledge, 1999.

– *Les Caraïbes au temps des flibustiers: XVIe–XVIIe siècles*. Paris: Aubier Montaigne, 1982.

– *Les négociants bordelais: L'Europe et les îles au XVIIIe siècle*. Paris: Aubier, 1974.

Butel-Dumont, Georges M. *Histoire et commerce des Antilles anglaises.* Paris: 1758.

Cabantous, Alain. *Dix mille marins face a l'océan: Les populations maritimes de Dunkerque au Havre aux XVIIe et XVIIIe siècle (vers 1660–1794): Étude sociale.* Paris: Publisud, 1991.

Cahall, Raymond du Bois. *The Sovereign Council of New France.* New York: Columbia University Press, 1915.

Caldwell, Norman Ward. *The French in the Mississippi Valley, 1740–1750.* Urbana: University of Illinois Press, 1941.

Camus, Michel Christian. "Le general de Poincy, premier capitaliste sucrier des Antilles." *Revue française d'histoire d'outre-mer* 84 (1997): 119–25.

Canada. *Censuses of Canada, 1665 to 1871.* 5 vols. Ottawa: Printed by I.B. Taylor and Maclean, Roger, 1873–78.

Cantarra, François. "Les routes à Sillery sous le régime français." *Revue d'histoire de l'Amérique française* 49 (1996): 551–65.

Carey, James. *Communication as Culture: Essays on Media and Society.* Boston: Unwin Hyman, 1988.

Caron, Ivanhoë. "Historique de la voirie dans la province de Québec." *Bulletin des recherches historiques* 39 (1933): 198–215.

Carrière, Charles. *Négociants marseillais au XVIIIe siècle: Contribution à l'étude des économies maritimes.* Marseille: Institut Historique de Provence, 1973.

Cassel, Jay. "The *Troupes de la Marine* in Canada, 1683–1760: Men and Material." PhD diss., University of Toronto, 1987.

Castel de St-Pierre, Charles Iréné. *Abrégé de mémoire sur la réparation des chemins.* 1708; reprint [n.d., but c. 1716] (copy in Bibliothèque Nationale, Paris).

Cavignac, Jean. *Jean Pellet: commerçant de gros, 1694–1772: contribution à l'étude du négoce bordelais au XVIIIe siècle.* Paris: SEVPEN, 1967.

Censer, Jack R. *The French Press in the Age of the Enlightenment.* London: Routledge, 1994.

Champigny, Chevalier Jean de. *État présent de la Louisiane avec toutes les particularités de cette province d'Amérique, pour servir de suite à l'histoire des établissements des européans dans les deux indes.* La Haye: Frédéric Staatman, 1776.

Charbonneau, André, Yvon Desloges, and Marc Lafrance. *Québec: ville fortifiée du XVIIe au XIXe siècle.* Québec: Éditions du Pélican and Parks Canada, 1982.

– with the collaboration of Marc Lafrance. "Gaspard-Joseph Chaussegros de Léry (1682–1756)." In *Les villes françaises du Nouveau-Monde: Des premiers fonadateurs aux ingénieurs du roi (XVIe–XVIIIe siècles)*, edited by Laurent Vidal and Émilie d'Orgeix, 142–6. Paris: Somogy éditions d'art, 1999.

Charbonneau, Hubert, et al. *The First French Canadians: Pioneers in the St. Lawrence Valley*. Newark: University of Delaware Press, 1993.

Chard, Donald F. "The Price and Profits of Accomodation: Massachusetts-Louisbourg Trade, 1713–1744." In *Aspects of Louisbourg*, edited by Eric Krause, Carol Corbin, and William O'Shea, 209–27. Sydney, NS: University College of Cape Breton Press, 1995.

Charlevoix, Pierre-François-Xavier de. *Histoire et description générale de la Nouvelle France*. 3 vols. Paris: Giffart, 1744.

Chartier, Roger. *Cultural History: Between Practices and Representations*. Translated by Lydia G. Cochrane. Cambridge: Polity Press, 1988.

– "Introduction." In *The Culture of Print: Power and the Uses of Print in Early Modern Europe*, translated by Lydia G. Cochrane. Cambridge: Polity Press, 1989.

– "Texts, Printing, Readings." In *The New Cultural History*, edited by Lynn Hunt, 154–75. Berkeley: University of California Press, 1989.

– and Henri-Jean Martin, eds. *Histoire de l'édition française*. Vol. 2, *1660–1830: Le livre triomphant*. Paris: Promodis, 1988.

– and Hugues Neveux. "La ville dominante et soumise." In *Histoire de la France urbaine*, edited by Georges Duby, vol. 3, *La ville classique, de la Renaissance aux révolutions*, edited by Roger Chartier, 1–168. Paris: Éditions du Seuil, 1981.

Chartrand, René. *The French Soldier in Colonial America*. Ottawa: Museum Restoration Service, 1984.

Chaudhuri, K.N. *Trade and Civilisation in the Indian Ocean: An Economic History from the Rise of Islam to 1750*. Cambridge: Cambridge University Press, 1985.

Chauleau, Liliane. *Dans les Îles du Vent: la Martinique (XVIIe–XIXe siècle*. Paris : L'Harmattan, 1994.

– *La société à la Martinique au XVIIe siècle (1635–1713)*. Caen: n.p., 1966.

Chaussinand-Nogaret, Guy. *The French Nobility in the Eighteenth Century: From Feudalism to Enlightenment*. Translated by William Doyle. Cambridge: Cambridge University Press, 1989.

Chinard, Gilbert. *L'Amérique et le rêve exotique dans la littérature française au XVIIe et au XVIIIe siècles*. Paris: Société d'éditions "Les Belles Lettres," 1913.

Choquette, Leslie. "Corporatism or Physiocracy? The Trades of French Canada in the Seventeenth and Eighteenth Centuries." Paper presented at the Atlantic World Seminar, Harvard University, 1997 (Working Paper no. 97005).

– *Frenchmen into Peasants : Modernity and Tradition in the Peopling of French Canada*. Cambridge: Harvard University Press, 1997.

Clark, Charles E. *The Public Prints: The Newspaper in Anglo-American Culture, 1665–1740*. New York: Oxford University Press, 1994.

Clark, John G. *New Orleans, 1718–1812: An Economic History*. Baton Rouge: Louisiana State University Press, 1970.

– *La Rochelle and the Atlantic Economy during the Eighteenth Century*. Baltimore: Johns Hopkins University Press, 1981.

Clark, Stuart. "French Historians and Early Modern Popular Culture." *Past and Present* 100 (1983): 62–99.

Coates, Colin M. "Authority and Illegitimacy in New France: The Burial of Bishop Saint-Vallier and Madeleine de Verchères vs. the Priest of Batiscan." *Histoire sociale/Social History* 22 (1989): 65–90.

– "Representations of Authority in Louis XIV's New France." Paper presented to the Omohundro Institute of Early American History and Culture, Glasgow, July 2001.

Coclanis, Peter A. "'Drang Nach Osten': Bernard Bailyn, the World-Island, and the Idea of Atlantic History." *Journal of World History* 13 (2002): 169–82.

Le Code noir; ou Receuil des règlemens rendus jusqu'à présent. Paris: Chez Prault, 1767; reprint, Basseterre et Fort-de-France: Société d'histoire de la Guadeloupe et Société d'histoire de la Martinique, 1980.

Cohen, William. *The French Encounter with Africans: White Response to Blacks, 1530–1880*. Bloomington: Indiana University Press, 1980.

Cole, Charles Woolsey. *Colbert and a Century of French Mercantilism*. 2 vols. Morningside Heights, NY: Columbia University Press, 1939.

Collins, James B. *Classes, Estates, and Order in Early Modern Brittany*. Cambridge, UK: Cambridge University Press, 1994.

– *The State in Early Modern France*. Cambridge: Cambridge University Press, 1995.

Conrad, Glenn R. "Administration of the Illinois Country: The French Debate." In *The French Experience in Louisiana*, edited by Glenn R. Conrad, 442–59. Lafayette: Center for Louisiana Studies, 1995.

– "Alsatian Emigration to Louisiana, 1753–59." In *The French Experience in Louisiana*, edited by Glenn R. Conrad, 163–73. Lafayette: Center for Louisiana Studies, 1995.

– "Emigration forcée : A French Attempt to Populate Louisiana, 1716–1720." In *Proceedings of the Fourth Meeting of the French Colonial Historical Society*, edited by Alf Heggoy and James Cooke, 57–66.

Constant, Fred. *La retraite aux flambeaux: Société et politique en Martinique*. Paris : Éditions Caribéennes, 1988.

Corvington, Georges. *Port-au-Prince au cours des Ans*. Vol. 1, *La ville coloniale, 1743–1789*. Port-au-Prince, Haiti: Imprimerie Henri Deschamps, 1970.

Courville, Serge. "Espace, territoire et culture en Nouvelle-France." *Revue d'histoire de l'Amérique française* 37 (1983): 416–29.

Crane, Verner W. *The Southern Frontier, 1670–1732*. Philadelphia: Duke University Press, 1929.

Craton, Michael. *Testing the Chains: Resistance to Slavery in the British West Indies*. Ithaca: Cornell University Press, 1982.

Creole, Coeur. *Saint-Pierre, Martinique, 1635–1902*. Paris: Berger-Levrault, 1905.

Crespel, Emmanuel. *Voiages du révérend père Emmanuel Crespel dans le Canada et son naufrage*. n.p., 1742. (Copy in National Archives of Canada)

Crété, Liliane. *La traite des Nègres sous l'Ancien Régime*. Paris: Perrin, 1998.

Crouse, Nellis Maynard. *The French Struggle for the West Indies, 1665–1713*. New York: Columbia University Press, 1943.

Crouzet, François. *A History of the European Economy, 1000–2000*. Charlottesville: University Press of Virginia, 2001.

Crowley, Terence. "Government and Interests: French Colonial Administration at Louisbourg, 1713–1758." PhD diss., Duke University, 1975.

– "'Thunder Gusts': Popular Disturbances in Early French Canada, 1704–1797." *Canadian Historical Association. Historical Papers*, 1979, 11–32.

Curtin, Philip. *The Rise and Fall of the Plantation Complex* . 2nd ed. Cambridge: Cambridge University Press, 1998.

Dagnaud, G. *L'administration centrale de la Marine sous l'Ancien Régime* Paris: Librairie Chapelot, 1912.

Daney, Sidney. *Histoire de la Martinique depuis la colonisation jusqu'en 1815*. 3 vols. Facsimile of 1846 printing. Fort de France: Société d'histoire de la Martinique, 1963.

Dardel, Pierre. *Navires et marchandises dans les ports de Rouen et du Havre au XVIIIe siecle*. Paris: SEVPEN, 1963.

Dargent, Joseph. "Relation d'un voyage de Paris à Montréal en Canada en 1737." In *RAPQ pour 1947–48*, 9–17.

Darnton, Robert. *The Great Cat Massacre and Other Episodes in French Cultural History*. New York: Random House, 1985.

– *The Literary Underground of the Old Regime*. Cambridge: Harvard University Press, 1982.

Dart, Henry Plauché. "Cabarets of New Orleans in the French Colonial Period." *Louisiana Historical Quarterly* 19 (1936): 578–83.

– "A Criminal Trial before the Superior Council of Louisiana, May, 1747." *Louisiana Historical Quarterly* 13 (1930): 367–90.

– "The Legal System of Louisiana." *Louisiana Historical Quarterly* 2 (1919): 72–103.

Davies, K.G. *The North Atlantic World in the Seventeenth Century*. Minneapolis: University of Minnesota Press, 1974.

Davis, David Brion. *The Problem of Slavery in the Western Culture*. Ithaca: Cornell University Press, 1966.

– *Slavery and Human Progress*. Oxford: Oxford University Press, 1984.

Davis, Natalie Z. *Society and Culture in Early Modern France*. Stanford: Stanford University Press, 1975.

Davis, Ralph. *The Rise of the Atlantic Economies*. London: Weidenfeld and Nicolson, 1973.

Debbasch, Yvan. "Au coeur du 'Gouvernement des esclaves': La souveraineté domestique aux Antilles françaises (XVIIe–XVIIIe siècles)." *Revue française d'histoire d'outre-mer* 72 (1985): 31–53.

– "Le crime d'empoisonnement aux îles pendant la période esclavagiste." *Revue française d'histoire d'outre-mer* 50 (1963): 137–88.

Debien, Gabriel. "La Christianisation des esclaves des Antilles françaises aux XVIIe et XVIIIe siècle." *Revue d'histoire de l'Amérique française* 20 (1967): 525–55.

– "Les engagés pour les Antilles (1634–1715)." *Revue d'histoire des colonies* 38 (1951): 7–279.

– *Les esclaves aux Antilles françaises (XVIIe–XVIIIe siècles)*. Basse-Terre et Fort-de-France: Société d'histoire de la Guadeloupe et Société d'histoire de la Martinique, 1974.

Dechêne, Louise. "La croissance de Montréal au XVIIIe siècle." *Revue d'histoire de l'Amérique française* 27 (1973): 163–79.

– "L'évolution du régime seigneurial au Canada: Le cas de Montréal aux XVIIe et XVIIIe siècles." *Recherches sociographiques* 12 (1971): 143–83.

– *Habitants et marchands de Montréal au XVIIe siècle: Essai*. Paris: Plon, 1974; Montréal: Boréal, 1988.

– "Quelques aspects de la ville de Québec au XVIIIe siècle d'après les dénombrements paroissiaux." *Cahiers de géographie du Québec* 28 (1984): 485–505.

Delafosse, Marcel. "La Rochelle et le Canada au XVIIe siècle." *Revue d'histoire de l'Amérique française* 4 (1951): 469–511.

Delanglez, Jean. *French Jesuits in Colonial Louisiana (1700–1763)*. Washington: Catholic University of America Press, 1935.

– "Louisiana in 1717." In *Revue d'histoire de l'Amérique française* 3 (1949): 94–110, 256–69, 423–46.

Desbarats, Catherine. "Les deniers du roi dans l'économie canadienne du XVIIIe siècle." In *Vingt ans après* Habitants et marchands*: Lectures de l'histoire des XVIIe et XVIIIe siècles canadiens*, edited by Sylvie Dépatie, Catherine Desbarats, et al.,, 189–207. Montreal and Kingston: McGill-Queen's University Press, 1998.

Deschamps, Hubert. *Les méthodes et les doctrines coloniales de la France (du XVIe siècle à nos jours)*. Paris: Armand Colin, 1953.

Deslandes, André François Boureau. *Essay sur la marine et sur le commerce*. [Paris ?], 1743.

Desloges, Yvon. *A Tenant's Town: Quebec in the Eighteenth Century*. Ottawa: National Historic Sites, 1991.

– and Marc Lafrance. “Dynamique de croissance et société urbaine: Québec au XVIIIe siècle, 1690–1759.” *Histoire sociale/Social History* 21 (1988): 251–67.

Dessalles, Adrien. *Histoire générale des Antilles.* 5 vols. Paris: Librarie-Éditeur, 1847.

Dessalles, Pierre-Régis. *Les annales du Conseil souverain de la Martinique, ou tableau historique du gouvernement de cette colonie, depuis son premier établissement jusqu'à nos jours.* 2 vols. Bergerac: J.B. Puynesge, 1786; reprint, 4 vols., with introduction, sources, bibliography, and notes, by Bernard Vonglis, Paris: Éditions L'Harmattan, 1996.

Dessert, Daniel. *La royale: Vaisseaux et marins du Roi-Soleil.* Paris: Fayard, 1996.

Dickinson, John A. *Justice et justiciables: La procédure civile à la prévôté de Québec, 1667–1759* Québec: Presses de l'Université Laval, 1982.

Dictionary of Canadian Biography. Vols. 1–4. Toronto: University of Toronto Press, 1969–84

Dider-Neuville. *État sommaire des archives de la Marine antérieur à la Révolution.* Paris: L. Baudoin, 1898; reprint, Liechtenstein: Kraus, 1977.

Diderot, Denis, and Jean Le Rond d'Alembert, eds. *Encyclopédie, ou dictionnaire raisonné des sciences, des arts et des métiers.* 17 vols. Paris and Geneva: various publishers, 1755–1774.

Diefendorf, Barbara B. *Beneath the Cross: Catholics and Huguenots in Sixteenth Century Paris.* Oxford: Oxford University Press, 1991.

Documents Relative to the Colonial History of the State of New York. Edited by Edmund Baily O'Callaghan. Vols. 3–10. Albany: Weed Parsons, 1855–1858.

Domínguez, Virginia R. *White by Definition: Social Classification in Creole Louisiana.* New Brunswick: Rutgers University Press, 1986.

Donovan, Kenneth. “A Nominal List of Slaves and Their Owners in Île Royale, 1713–1760.” *Nova Scotia Historical Review* 16 (1996): 151–62.

– “Slaves and Their Owners in Île Royale, 1713–1760.” *Acadiensis* 35 (1995): 3–32.

Donzelot, Jacques. *The Policing of Families.* Translated by Robert Hurley. New York: Pantheon Books, 1979.

d'Orgeix, Émilie. “De l'éducation des ingénieurs militaires (1650–1750).” In *Les villes françaises du Nouveau-Monde: Des premiers fonadateurs aux ingénieurs du roi (XVIe–XVIIIe siècles)*, edited by Laurent Vidal and Émilie d'Orgeix, 49–54. Paris: Somogy éditions d'art, 1999.

– “L'architecture religieuse.” In *Les villes françaises du Nouveau-Monde: Des premiers fonadateurs aux ingénieurs du roi (XVIe–XVIIIe siècles)*, edited by Laurent Vidal and Émilie d'Orgeix, 63–7. Paris: Somogy éditions d'art, 1999.

Dorsey, Peter A. "Going to School with Savages: Authorship and Authority among the Jesuits of New France." *William and Mary Quarterly*, 3rd series, 55 (1998): 399–420.

Doyle, William. *The Oxford History of the French Revolution*. Oxford: Oxford University Press, 1989.

Drolet, Antonio. "La bibliothèque du College des Jésuites." *Revue d'histoire de l'Amérique française* 14 (1961): 487–544.

Droulers, Martine. "Saint-Loius-du-Maragnan et la France équinoxiale (1612–1615)." In *Les villes françaises du Nouveau-Monde: Des premiers fonadateurs aux ingénieurs du roi (XVIe–XVIIIe siècles)*, edited by Laurent Vidal and Émilie d'Orgeix, 88–90. Paris: Somogy éditions d'art, 1999.

Druke, Mary A. "Iroquois Treaties: Common Forms, Varying Interpretations." In *The History and Culture of Iroquois Diplomacy: An Interdisciplinary Guide to the Treaties of the Six Nations and Their League*, edited by Francis Jennings, William N. Fenton, Mary A. Druke, and David Miller, 85–98. Syracuse: Syracuse University Press, 1985.

– "Linking Arms: The Structure of Iroquois Intertribal Diplomacy." In *Beyond the Covenant Chain: The Iroquois and Their Neighbours in Indian North America, 1600–1800*, edited by Daniel K. Richter and James H. Merrell, 29–39. Syracuse: Syracuse University Press, 1986.

Dubé, Jean-Claude. *Claude-Thomas Dupuy, intendant de la Nouvelle-France, 1678–1738*. Montréal: Fides, 1969.

– *Les intendants de la Nouvelle-France*. Montréal: Fides, 1984.

Duchêne, Albert. *La politique coloniale de la France: Le ministère des colonies depuis Richelieu*. Paris: Payot, 1928.

Dufour, Pierre. *Esquisse de l'évolution physique du port de Québec dès origines à 1900*. Microfiche Report no. 23. Ottawa: Environment Canada, 1981.

Dumont de Montigny. *Mémoires historiques sur la Louisiane, contenant ce qui y est arrivé de plus mémorable depuis l'année 1687, jusqu'à présent*. 2 vols. Paris: J.B. Bauche, 1753.

Dunn, Richard. *Sugar and Slaves: The Rise of the Planter Class in the English West Indies, 1624–1713*. Chapel Hill: University of North Carolina Press, 1972.

Duplessis, Robert S. *Transitions to Capitalism in Early Modern Europe*. Cambridge: Cambridge University Press, 1997.

Durand, Georges. "What Is Absolutism?" In *Louis XIV and Absolutism*, edited by Ragnhild Hatton, 18–36. Columbus: Ohio State University Press, 1976.

Duviols, Jean-Paul. "Les cotes du Venezuela au XVIIIe siècle: Témoignage d'un contrebandier." *Caravelle* 32 (1979): 5–17.

Eccles, William J. "A Belated Review of Harold Adams Innis's 'The Fur Trade in Canada.'" In *Essays on New France*, 61–78. Toronto: Oxford University Press, 1987.

– *Canada under Louis XIV, 1663–1701*. Toronto; McClelland and Stewart, 1964.
– *The Canadian Frontier, 1534–1760*. Rev. ed. Albuquerque: University of New Mexico Press, 1983.
– *France in America*. Rev. ed. Markham, Ont.: Fitzhenry and Whiteside, 1990.
– "The Fur Trade and Eighteenth-Century Imperialism." In *Essays on New France*, 79–95. Toronto: Oxford University Press, 1987.
Édits and ordonnances Vol. 1, *Édits, ordonnances royaux, déclarations et arrêts du Conseil d'État du roi concernant le Canada*; vol. 2, *Arrêts et règlements du Conseil supérieur de Québec, et ordonnances et jugements des intendants du Canada*; vol. 3, *Complément des ordonnances et jugements des gouverneurs et intendants du Canada précédé des commissions des dits gouverneurs et intendants et des différents officiers civil et de justice*. Québec: Fréchette, 1854–56.
Eisenstein, Elizabeth L. *Grub Street Abroad: Aspects of the French Cosmopolitan Press from the Age of Louis XIV to the French Revolution*. Oxford: Clarendon Press, 1992.
– *Print Culture and Enlightenment Thought*. Chapel Hill: Hanes Foundation, 1986.
– *The Printing Press as an Agent of Change: Communications and Cultural Transformations in Early-Modern Europe*. Cambridge: Cambridge University Press, 1979.
Elliott, J.H. *Imperial Spain, 1469–1716*. New York: Mentor Books, 1966.
– *The Old World and the New, 1492–1650*. Cambridge: Cambridge University Press, 1970; Canto, 1991.
– *Spain and Its World, 1500–1700*. New Haven: Yale University Press, 1989.
Eltis, David. *The Rise of African Slavery in the Americas*. Cambridge: Cambridge University Press, 2000.
– Stephen D. Behrendt, David Richardson, Herbert S. Klein, eds. *The Trans-Atlantic Slave Trade: A Database on CD-ROM*. Cambridge: Cambridge University Press, 1999.
Engerman, Stanley L. "Europe, the Lesser Antilles, and Economic Expansion, 1600–1800." In *The Lesser Antilles in the Age of European Expansion*, edited by Robert L. Paquette and Stanley Engerman, 147–64. Gainesville: University Press of Florida, 1996.
Equiano, Olaudah. *The Interesting Narrative and Other Writings*. Edited, with introduction and notes, by Vincent Carretta. 1789; reprint, New York: Penguin Books, 1995.
Escarpit, Robert. *L'écrit et la communication*. Series "Que Sais-Je." Paris: Presses universitaires de France, 1973.
Esquemeling, John. *The Buccaneers of America*. 1687; reprint, New York: Dover, 1967.

Farge, Arlette. *Dire et mal-dire: L'opinion publique au XVIII siècle*. Paris: Seuil, 1992.

– *Fragile Lives: Violence, Power and Solidarity in Eighteenth-Century Paris*. Cambridge: Harvard University Press, 1993.

Fauteux, Aegidus. *Les Chevaliers de St. Louis en Canada*. Montréal: Éditions des Dix, 1940.

Fenton, William N. "Structure, Continuity, and Change in the Process of Iroquois Treaty Making." In *The History and Culture of Iroquois Diplomacy: An Interdisciplinary Guide to the Treaties of the Six Nations and Their League*, edited by Francis Jennings, William N. Fenton, Mary A. Druke, and David Miller, 3–26. Syracuse: Syracuse University Press, 1985.

Fernandez-Armesto, Felipe. "Origins of the European Atlantic." *Itinerario* 24: 111–28.

Fick, Carolyn. *The Making of Haiti: The Saint-Domingue Revolution from Below*. Knoxville: University of Tennessee Press, 1990.

Filion, Maurice. *La pensée et l'action coloniales de Maurepas vis-à-vis du Canada, 1723–1749: L'âge d'or de la colonie*. Ottawa: Leméac, 1972.

Flandrin, Jean-Louis. *Familles: Parenté, maison, sexualité dans l'ancienne société*. Paris: Hachette, 1976.

Fogel, Michèle. *Les cérémonies de l'information dans la France du XVIe au XVIIIe siècle*. Paris: Fayard, 1989.

Foster, Michael K. "On Who Spoke First at Iroquois-White Councils: An Exercise in the Method of Upstreaming." In *Extending the Rafters: Interdisciplinary Approaches to Iroquoian Studies*, edited by Michael K. Foster, Jack Campisi, and Marianne Mithun, 183–208. Syracuse: Syracuse University Press, 1985.

Fournier, Marcel. *Les Européans au Canada: Dès origines à 1765*. Montréal: Éditions du Fleuve, 1989.

Franquet, Louis, *Voyages et mémoires sur le Canada*. Québec: A. Coté, 1889.

Frégault, Guy. *La civilisation de la Nouvelle-France, 1713–1744*. Montréal: Fides, 1969.

– *Le XVIIIe siècle canadien: Études*. Montréal: HMH, 1970.

– *François Bigot, administrateur français*. 2 vols. Montr–al: Institut d'histoire de l'Amérique française, 1948.

– *Le grand marquis: Pierre de Rigaud de Vaudreuil et la Louisiane*. Montreal: Fides, 1952; reprinted 1962.

– *La guerre de la Conquête, 1754–1760*. Montréal: Fides, 1955; reprint, 1966.

– *Iberville le conquerant*. Montréal: Société des éditions Pascal, 1944.

Frostin, Charles. *Les révoltes blanches à Saint-Domingue aux XVIIe et XVIIIe siècles*. Paris: L'École, 1975.

Gadoury, Lorraine. "Démographie differentielle en Nouvelle-France: Villes et campagnes." *Revue d'histoire de l'Amérique française* 38 (1985): 357–78.

– *La noblesse de Nouvelle-France: Familles et alliances*. La Salle, Qué.: Éditions Hurtubise, 1992.
Galloway, Patricia K. "Louisiana Post Letters: The Missing Evidence for Indian Diplomacy." *Louisiana History* 22 (1981): 31–44.
Gareau, Jean Baptiste. "La prévôté de Québec: ses officiers – ses registres." In *RAPQ pour 1943–44*, 51–125.
Gauvreau, Danielle. *Québec: une ville et sa population au temps de la Nouvelle-France*. Sillery: Presses de l'Université du Québec, 1991.
Geggus, David. "The Causation of Slave Rebellions: An Overview." *Indian Historical Review* 14 (1987–88): 1–24.
– "The French and Haitian Revolutions, and Resistance to Slavery: An Overview." *Revue française d'histoire d'outre-mer* 76 (1989): 107–24.
– "The French Slave Trade: An Overview." *William and Mary Quarterly*, 3rd series, 58 (2001): 119–38.
– "The Major Port Towns of Saint Domingue in the Later Eighteenth Century." In *Atlantic Port Cities: Economy, Culture and Society in the Atlantic World, 1650–1850*, edited by Franklin W. Knight and Peggy K. Liss, 87–116. Knoxville: University of Tennessee Press, 1991.
Géraud-Llorca, Edith. "La Coutume de Paris outre-mer: L'habitation antillaise sous l'Ancien Régime." *Revue historique de droit français et étranger* 60 (1982): 207–59.
Gerzina, Gretchen Holbrook. *Black London: Life before Emancipation*. New Brunswick: Rutgers University Press, 1995.
Giddens, Anthony. "The Orthodox Consensus and the Emerging Synthesis." In *Rethinking Communication*, edited by Brenda Cervin, 53–65. Newbury Park, Ca: SAGE, 1989.
Gilroy, Paul. *The Black Atlantic: Modernity and Double Consciousness*. Cambridge: Harvard University Press, 1993.
Giraud, Marcel. "France and Louisiana in the Early Eighteenth Century." *Journal of American History* 36 (1949–50): 657–74.
– *Histoire de la Louisiane française*. Vol. 3, *L'époque de John Law (1717–20)*; vol. 4, *La Louisiane après le système de Law (1721–1723)*. Paris: Presses universitaires de France, 1966–74.
– *A History of French Louisiana*. Vol. 1, *The Reign of Louis XIV, 1698–1715*, translated by Joseph C. Lambert; vol. 5, *The Company of the Indies, 1723–1731*, translated by Brian Pearce. Baton Rouge: Louisiana State University Press, 1974–91.
– "Tendances humanitaires à la fin du règne de Louis XIV." *Revue historique* 209 (1953): 217–37.
Girod, François. *La vie quotidienne de la société créole: Saint-Domingue au XVIIIe siècle*. Paris: Hachette, 1972.

Gisler, Antoine. *L'esclavage aux Antilles françaises (XVIIe–XIXe siècles: contribution au problème de l'esclavage.* Fribourg: 1965; rev., Paris: Karthala, 1981.

Glazebrook, George Parkin deT. *A History of Transportation in Canada.* 2 vols. Toronto: McClelland and Stewart, 1938; reprint, 1964.

Glissant, Édouard. *The Fourth Century.* Translated by Betsy Wing. Lincoln: University of Nebraska Press, 2001.

Godechot, Jacques L. *Histoire de l'Atlantique.* Paris: Bordas, 1947.

Gosselin, Amédée. *L'instruction au Canada sous le régime français (1635–1760).* Québec: Laflamme & Proulx, 1911.

Gosselin, Auguste. *L'église du Canada depuis Monseigneur de Laval jusqu'à la Conquète.* 3 vols. Québec: Laflamme & Proulx, 1912.

Goubert, Pierre. *Louis XIV and Twenty Million Frenchmen.* Translated by Anne Carter. New York: Vintage, 1970.

– "Le tragique dix-septième siècle." In *Histoire économique et sociale de la France*, vol. 2, *Dès derniers temps de l'âge seigneurial aux préludes de l'âge industriel (1660–1789)*, edited by Fernand Braudel and Ernest Labrousse, 325–68. Paris: Presses universitaires de France, 1970.

Gould, Clarence. "Trade between the Windward Islands and the Continental Colonies of the French Empire." *Mississippi Valley Historical Review* 25 (1939): 473–90.

Gould, Eliga H. *The Persistence of Empire: British Political Culture in the Age of the American Revolution.* Chapel Hill: University of North Carolina Press, 2000.

– "A Virtual Nation: Greater Britain and the Imperial Legacy of the American Revolution." *American Historical Review* 104 (1999): 476–89.

Grahn, Lance R. "Cartagena and Its Hinterland in the Eighteenth Century." In *Atlantic Port Cities: Economy, Culture and Society in the Atlantic World, 1650–1850*, edited by Franklin W. Knight and Peggy K. Liss, 168–95. Knoxville: University of Tennessee Press, 1991.

Green, F.C. *The Ancien Regime: A Manual of French Institutions and Social Classes.* Edinburgh: Edinburgh University Press, 1958.

Greer, Allan. "Mutiny at Louisbourg, December 1744." In *Aspects of Louisbourg*, edited by Eric Krause, Carol Corbin, and William O'Shea, 70–110. Sydney, NS: University College of Cape Breton Press, 1995.

– *Peasant, Lord and Merchant: Rural Society in Three Quebec Parishes, 1740–1840.* Toronto: University of Toronto Press, 1985.

– *The People of New France.* Toronto: University of Toronto Press, 1997.

Griffiths, Naomi E.S. *The Contexts of Acadian History, 1686–1784.* Montreal and Kingston: McGill-Queen's University Press, 1992.

– "1600–1650: Fish, Fur and Folk." In *The Atlantic Region to Confederation: A History*, edited by Phillip Buckner and John G. Reid, 40–60. Toronto: University of Toronto Press, 1994.

Gruder, Vivian R. *The Royal Provincial Intendants: A Governing Elite in Eighteenth-Century France*. Ithaca: Cornell University Press, 1968.

Guet, I. *Origines de la Martinique: Le colonel François de Collart et la Martinique de son temps*. Vannes: Lafolye, 1893.

Haan, Richard L. "The Covenant Chain: Iroquois Diplomacy on the Niagara Frontier, 1697–1730." PhD diss., University of California at Santa Barbara, 1976.

Habermas, J. *The Structural Transformation of the Public Sphere: An Inquiry into a Category of Bourgeois Society*. Translated by Thomas Berger and Frederick Lawrence. Cambridge: Massachusetts Institute of Technology Press, 1989.

Hachard, Marie-Madeleine. *Relation du voyage des dames religieuses ursulines de Rouen à la Nouvelle-Orléans*. Edited and introduced by Gabriel Gravier. Rouen: Le Prévost, 1872.

Hale, John Rigby. *War and Society in Renaissance Europe, 1450–1620*. Baltimore: Johns Hopkins University Press, 1998.

Hall, David D. "The Ues of Literacy in New England, 1600–1850." In *Printing and Society in Early America*, edited by William L. Joyce, 1–26. Worcester: American Antiquarian Society, 1983.

Hall, Gwendolyn Midlo. *Africans in Colonial Louisiana: The Development of Afro-Creole Culture in the Eighteenth Century*. Baton Rouge: Louisiana State University Press, 1992.

Hall, N.A.T. "Maritime Maroons: Grand Marronage from the Danish West Indies." *William and Mary Quarterly*, 3rd series, 42 (1985): 476–98.

Hall, Stuart. "Cultural Studies: Two Paradigms." In *Media, Culture, and Society: A Critical Reader*, edited by Richard Collins. London: SAGE, 1986, 33–48.

– "Ideology and Communications Theory." *Rethinking Communication*, edited by Brenda Cervin, 40–52. Newbury Park, Ca: SAGE, 1989.

Hamelin, Jean. *Économie et société en Nouvelle-France*. Québec: Presses de l'Université Laval, 1960.

Hancock, David. *Citizens of the World: London Merchants and the Integration of the British Atlantic Community, 1735–1785*. Cambridge: Cambridge University Press, 1995.

Hanley, Sarah. "Engendering the State: Family Formation and State Building in Early Modern France." *French Historical Studies* 16 (1989): 4–27.

– *The "Lit de Justice" of the Kings of France: Constitutional Ideology in Legend, Ritual and Discourse*. Princeton: Princeton University Press, 1983.

Hardcastle, David. "The Military Organization of French Colonial Louisiana." In *The French Experience in Louisiana*, edited by Glenn R. Conrad, 345–59. Lafayette: Center for Louisiana Studies, 1995.

– "Swiss Mercenary Soldiers in the Service of France in Louisiana." In *The French Experience in Louisiana*, edited by Glenn R. Conrad, 368–77. Lafayette: Center for Louisiana Studies, 1995.

Hardt, Hanno. *Communication, History and Theory in America*. London: Routledge, 1992.

Hardy, James D., Jr. "The Superior Council in Colonial Louisiana." In *Frenchmen and French Ways in the Mississippi Valley*, edited by John Francis McDermott, 87–101. Urbana: University of Illinois Press, 1969.

– "The Transportation of Convicts to Colonial Louisiana." In *The French Experience in Louisiana*, edited by Glenn R. Conrad, 115–24. Lafayette: Center for Louisiana Studies, 1995.

Haring, C.H. *The Spanish Empire in America*. New York: Harcourt Brace, 1947; reprint, 1975.

Harris, Richard Colebrook. *The Seigneurial System in Early Canada: A Geographical Study*. 2nd ed. Madison: University of Wisconsin Press, 1968.

– ed. *Historical Atlas of Canada: From the Beginning to 1800*. Toronto: University of Toronto Press, 1987.

Harrison, Jane E. "'Adieu pour cette année': Seasonality and Time in New France." In *Proceedings of the Twenty-First Meeting of the French Colonial Historical Society* (1997), 93–110.

Haudrère, Philippe. "Quelques espaces du grand commerce maritime à la fin du XVIIe siècle (1690–1720)." In *La percée de l'Europe sur les océans vers 1690 – vers 1790*, edited by Étienne Taillemite and Denis Lieppe, 139–47. Paris: Presses de l'Université de Paris-Sorbonne, 1997. (*Revue d'histoire maritime*, no. 1, special ed., October 1997).

Hauser, Henri. *La pensée et l'action économique du Cardinal de Richelieu*. Paris : Presses universitaires de France, 1944.

Hayot, Émile. "Les gens de couleur libres du Ft-Royal, 1679–1823." *Revue française d'histoire d'outre-mer* 56 (1969): 145–63.

– "Les officiers du Conseil souverain de la Martinique et leurs successeurs les conseillers de la Cour d'appel, 1675–1830." Fort-de-France : Mémoires de la Société de la Martinique, 1964. (*Annales des Antilles*, special ed., 1964).

Headrick, Daniel R. *Tools of Empire: Technology and European Imperialism in the Nineteenth Century*. Oxford: Oxford University Press, 1981.

– *When Information Came of Age: Technologies of Knowledge in the Age of Reason and Revolution, 1700–1850*. Oxford: Oxford University Press, 2000.

Heinrich, Pierre. *La Louisiane sous la Compagnie des Indes, 1717–1731*. 1908; reprint, New York: Burt Franklin, 1970.

Herman, Edward S., and Noam Chomsky. *Manufacturing Consent: The Political Economy of the Mass Media*. New York: Pantheon Books, 1988.

Hintjens, Helen M. "What Is Freedom? Competing Notions of Rights and Responsibilities in the French Caribbean." *Itinerario* 25 (2001): 23–41.

Horton, Donald. "Gilles Hocquart, Intendant of New France: 1729–1748." PhD diss., McGill University, 1974.

Hrodej, Philippe. "L'Amiral Du Casse: De la stratégie de force au protectorat des colonies espagnoles d'Amérique (1690–1715)." In *La percée de l'Europe sur les océans vers 1690 – vers 1790*, edited by Étienne Taillemite and Denis Lieppe, 27–51. Paris: Presses de l'Université de Paris-Sorbonne, 1997. (*Revue d'histoire maritime*, no. 1, special ed., October 1997).

– "Saint-Domingue en 1690: Les observations du père Plumier, botaniste provençal." *Revue française d'histoire d'outre-mers* 84 (1997): 93–117.

Huber, Leonard M. *New Orleans: A Pictorial History*. New York: Crown, 1971.

Huetz de Lemps, Christian. *Géographie du commerce de Bordeaux à la fin de règne de Louis XIV*. Paris, Mouton, 1975.

Ingersoll, Thomas N. "Free Blacks in New Orleans." *William and Mary Quarterly*, 3rd series, 48 (1991): 173–200.

– *Mammon and Manon in Early New Orleans: The First Slave Society in the Deep South, 1718–1819*. Knoxville: University of Tennessee Press, 1999.

Innis, Harold A. *The Bias of Communications*. Toronto: University of Toronto Press, 1951; reprint, 1977.

– *Empire and Communications*. Revised by Mary Q. Innis. Toronto: University of Toronto Press, 1972.

– *The Fur Trade in Canada*. Toronto: University of Toronto Press, 1930; rev. ed., 1970.

Isambert, F.A., A.J.L. Jourdan, et al., eds. *Recueil général des anciennes lois françaises, depuis l'an 420 jusquà la révolution de 1789; contenant la notice des principaux monuments des Mérovingiens, des Carlovingiens et des Capétians, et le texte des ordonnances, édits, déclarations, lettres-patentes, réglemens arrêts du Conseil, etc ...* 29 vols. Paris: Belin-Le-Prieur, Verdiere, [1822–33]; reprint, Farborough, Eng.: Gregg, 1964.

Isherwood, Robert M. *Music in the Service of the King: France in the Seventeenth Century*. Ithaca: Cornell University Press, 1973.

J-C.B. [attributed to Bonnefons]. *Voyage au Canada fait depuis l'an 1751 et 1761* Paris: Aubier Montainge, 1978.

Jaenen, Cornelius. *Friend and Foe: Aspects of Franco-Amerindian Contact in the Sixteenth and Seventeenth Centuries*. Toronto: McClelland and Stewart, 1976.

– *The Role of the Church in New France*. Toronto: McGraw-Hill Ryerson, 1976.

– "Some Unresolved Issues: Lorette Hurons in the Colonial Context." In *Proceedings of the Twenty-First Meeting of the French Colonial Historical Society* (1997), 111–26.

Jennings, Francis. *The Ambiguous Iroquois Empire*. New York: W.W. Norton, 1984.

– *Empire of Fortune: Crowns, Colonies, and Tribes in the Seven Years War in America*. New York: W.W. Norton, 1988.

The Jesuit Relations and Allied Documents. Edited by Reuben Gold Thwaites. Vols. 67–9. Cleveland: Burrows Bros., 1900.

Johnson, Jerah. "New Orleans's Congo Square: An Urban Setting for Early Afro-American Culture Formation." *Louisiana History* 10 (1969): 117–37.

Johnston, A.J.B. *Control and Order in French Colonial Louisbourg, 1713–1758*. East Lansing: Michigan State University Press, 2001.

– "From 'port de pêche' to 'ville fortifiée': The Evolution of Urban Louisbourg, 1713–1758." In *Proceedings of the Seventeenth Annual Meeting of the French Colonial Historical Society, 1991*, edited by Patricia Galloway (1992), 24–43.

– *Religion in Life at Louisbourg, 1713–1758*. Kingston and Montreal: McGill-Queen's University Press, 1984.

Juchereau, Mère A.M.J. Saint-Ignace de. *Histoire de l'Hôtel-Dieu de Québec*. Montauban: Jérosme Legier, 1751.

Julien, Charles-André. *Les Français en Amérique de 1713 à 1784*. Paris : Centre de documentation et Société d'édition d'enseignement supérieur reunis, 1977.

Jumonville, Florence M. "Frenchmen at Heart: New Orleans Printers and Their Imprints, 1764–1803." *Louisiana History* 32 (1991): 279–310.

Kalm, Peter. *Peter Kalm's Travels in North America: The English Version of 1770*. Edited by by Adolph B. Benson. 2 vols. New York: Dover Publications, 1964.

Keene, David. "Fort de Chartres: Archaeology in the Illinois Country." In *French Colonial Archaeology: The Illinois Country and the Western Great Lakes*, edited by John A. Walthall, 29–41. Urbana: University of Illinois Press, 1991.

Keohane, Nannerl O. *Philosophy and the State in France: The Renaissance to the Enlightenment*. Princeton: Princeton University Press, 1980.

Kertzer, David I. *Ritual, Politics, and Power*. New Haven: Yale University Press, 1988.

Kesterton, W.H. *A History of Journalism in Canada*. Toronto: McClelland and Stewart, 1967.

Kettering, Sharon. "Patronage in Early Modern France." *French Historical Studies* 17 (1992): 839–62.

– *Patrons, Brokers and Clients in Seventeenth-Century France*. New York: Oxford University Press, 1986.

Keyes, John. "Un commis des trésoriers généraux de la marine à Québec: Lanoullier de Boisclerc." *Revue d'histoire de l'Amérique française* 32 (1978): 181–202.

Kim, Young Yum. "On Theorizing Intercultural Communications." In *Theories in Intercultural Communication*, edited by Young Yum Kim and William B. Gudykinst, 11–21. Newbury Park, Ca: SAGE Publications, 1988.

Klein, Herbert S. *African Slavery in Latin America and the Caribbean*. New York: Oxford University Press, 1986.

Klooster, Wim. *Illicit Riches: Dutch Trade in the Caribbean, 1648–1795*. Leiden: KITLV Press, 1998.

Knight, Franklin W., and Peggy K. Liss. "Introduction." In *Atlantic Port Cities: Economy, Culture and Society in the Atlantic World, 1650–1850*, edited by Franklin W. Knight and Peggy K. Liss, 1–22. Knoxville: University of Tennessee Press, 1991.

Konvitz, Josef W. *Cities and the Sea: Port City Planning in Early Modern Europe*. Baltimore and London: Johns Hopkins University Press, 1978.

Korn, Bertram Wallace. *Early Jews of New Orleans*. Waltham, Mass.: American Jewish Historical Society, 1969.

Krippendorf, K. "Power of Communication and Communication of Power." *Communication* 12 (1991): 175–96.

Labat, Jean-Baptiste. *Nouveau voyage aux isles de l'Amérique; contenant l'histoire naturelle de ces pays, l'origine, les moeurs, la religion, & le gouvernement des habitans anciens & modernes*. 6 vols. La Haye: P. Husson et al., 1724.

Lachance, André. "Les criminels, 1712–1759." In *Les marginaux, les exclus, et l'autre au Canada*, edited by André Lachance, 151–65. Montréal: Éditions Fides, 1996.

– "La désertion et les soldats déserteurs au Canada dans la première moitié du XVIIIe siècle." *Revue de l'Université d'Ottawa* 47 (1977): 151–61.

– "Les esclaves au 17e et 18e siècles." In *Les marginaux, les exclus, et l'autre au Canada*, edited by André Lachance, 201–8. Montréal: Éditions Fides, 1996.

– "Une étude de mentalité: Les injures verbales au Canada au XVIIIe siècle, 1712–1748." *Revue d'histoire de l'Amérique française* 31 (1977): 229–38.

– *La justice criminelle du roi au Canada au XVIIIe siecle: Tribunaux et officiers*. Québec: Presses de l'Université Laval, 1978.

– *La vie urbaine en Nouvelle France*. Montréal: Boréal, 1987.

Lafleur, Gérard. "Les Juifs aux Îles françaises du Vent XVIIe–XVIIIe siècles)." *Bulletin de la Société d'histoire de la Guadeloupe* 72 (1987): 77–131.

Lafrance, Jean. *Les épaves du Saint-Laurent (1650–1760)*. Montréal: Les Éditions de l'Homme, 1972.

Lahontan, Louis Armand de Lom d'Arce, Baron de. *Nouveaux voyages de M. le Baron de Lahontan, dans l'Amérique septentrionale* [1703]. In *Oeu-*

vres complètes, edited by Réal Ouellet, with Alain Beaulieu, vol. 2. Montréal: Presses de l'Université de Montréal, 1990.

Lamontagne, Roland. *La Galissonière et le Canada*. Montréal: Presses de l'Université de Montréal, 1962.

La Morandière, Charles de. *Histoire de la pêche française de la marine dans l'Amérique septentrionale*. 2 vols. Paris: Maissoneuve & La Rose, 1962.

Lanctot, Gustave. *L'administration de la Nouvelle-France*. Paris: Honoré Champion, 1929; reprint, Montreal: Éditions du Jour, 1971.

– "Le régime municipal en Nouvelle-France." *Culture* 9 (1948): 255–83.

Landsman, Ned C. "Nation, Migration, and the Province in the First British Empire: Scotland and the Americas, 1600–1800." *American Historical Review* 104 (1999): 463–75.

Langlois, Gilles-Antoine. "L'aventure urbaine de la Louisiane." In *Les villes françaises du Nouveau-Monde: Des premiers fonadateurs aux ingénieurs du roi (XVIe–XVIIIe siècles)*, edited by Laurent Vidal and Émilie d'Orgeix, 120–9. Paris: Somogy éditions d'art, 1999.

Laurent, Jeannine, and Jacques St. Pierre. *Les forts et chateaux Saint-Louis, 1620–1760*. Microfiche Report no. 40. Ottawa: Environment Canada, 1982.

La Vere, David. "Between Kinship and Capitalism: French and Spanish Rivalry in the Colonial Louisiana-Texas Indian Trade." *Journal of Southern History* 64 (1998): 197–218.

Le Blanc, François-Yves. "François Blondel et les îles d'Amérique (1666–1668)." In *Les villes françaises du Nouveau-Monde: Des premiers fonadateurs aux ingénieurs du roi (XVIe–XVIIIe siècles)* edited by Laurent Vidal and Emilie d'Orgeix, 156–61. Paris: Somogy éditions d'art, 1999.

– "Rochefort, arsenal modèle?" *Les villes françaises du Nouveau-Monde: Des premiers fonadateurs aux ingénieurs du roi (XVIe–XVIIIe siècles)*, edited by Laurent Vidal and Emilie d'Orgeix, 42–8. Paris: Somogy éditions d'art, 1999.

Lebrun, François. "Le calendrier agro-liturgique." In *Sociétés villageoises et rapports villes-campagnes au Québec et dans la France de l'ouest, XVIIe–XXe siècles: Actes du colloque Franco-Québecois de Québec*, edited by François Lebrun and Normand Seguin, 347–51. Trois Rivières: Centre de recherche en études québecoises, Université du Québec à Trois Rivières, en collaboration des Presses universitaires de Rennes II, 1987.

– *La Vie conjugale sous l'Ancien Régime*. Paris: Armand Colin, 1975.

Lemieux, Donald Jile. "The Office of 'Commissaire Ordonnateur' in French Louisiana, 1731–1763: A Study in French Colonial Administration." PhD diss., Louisiana State University, Baton Rouge, 1972.

Lemisch, Jesse. "Jack Tar in the Streets: Merchant Seamen in the Politics of Revolutionary America." *William and Mary Quarterly*, 3rd series, 25 (1968): 371–407.

Léon, Pierre. "La conquête de l'espace national." In *Histoire économique et sociale de la France*, vol. 3, pt. 1, *L'avènement de l'ère industrielle (1789–années 1880)*, edited by Fernand Braudel and Ernest Labrousse, 241–57. Paris: Presses universitaires de France, 1977.

– "La réponse de l'industrie." In *Histoire économique et sociale de la France*, vol. 2, *Dès derniers temps de l'âge seigneurial aux préludes de l'âge industriel (1660–1789)*, edited by Fernand Braudel and Ernest Labrousse, 217–66. Paris: Presses universitaires de France, 1970.

– and Charles Carrière. "L'appel des marchés." In *Histoire économique et sociale de la France*, vol. 2, *Dès derniers temps de l'âge seigneurial aux préludes de l'âge industriel (1660–1789)*, edited by Fernand Braudel and Ernest Labrousse, 161–215. Paris: Presses universitaires de France, 1970.

Le Page du Pratz, Antoine. *Histoire de la Louisiane, contenant la découverte de ce vaste pays; sa description géographique; un voyage dans les terres; l'histoire naturelle; les moeurs, coutumes et religion des naturels, avec leurs origines; deux voyages dans le nord du nouveau Mexique, dont un jusqu'à la mer du sud.* 3 vols. Paris: Chez de Buré, la Veuve Delaguette, et Lambert, 1758.

Lepetit, Bernard. *Chemins de terre et voies d'eau: Réseaux de transports et organisation de l'espace en France 1740–1840*. Paris: Éditions de l'École des hautes études en Sciences Sociales, 1984.

Le Roy Ladurie, Emmanuel. *Carnival in Romans*. Translated by Mary Feeney. New York: George Braziller, 1979.

Lewis, Gordon K. *Main Currents in Caribbean Thought: The Historical Evolution of Caribbean Society in Its Ideological Aspects, 1492–1900*. Baltimore: Johns Hopkins University, 1983.

Lézy, Emmanuel. "L'implantation française en Guyane, XVII–XVIIIe siècles." In *Les villes françaises du Nouveau-Monde: Des premiers fonadateurs aux ingénieurs du roi (XVIe–XVIIIe siècles)*, edited by Laurent Vidal and Émilie d'Orgeix, 90–5. Paris: Somogy éditions d'art, 1999.

Linebaugh, Peter, and Marcus Rediker. "The Many-Headed Hydra: Sailors, Slaves and the Atlantic Working Class in the Eighteenth Century." In *Jack Tar in History: Essays in the History of Maritime Life and Labour*, edited by Colin Howell and Richard Twomey, 11–36. Fredericton: Acadiensis Press, 1991.

Liss, Peggy K. *Atlantic Empires: The Network of Trade and Revolution, 1713–1826*. Baltimore: Johns Hopkins University Press, 1983.

Livet, Georges. "La route royale et la civilisation française de la fin du XVe au milieu du XVIIIe siècle." In *Les routes de France: depuis les origines jusqu'à nos jours*, edited by Guy Michaud, 57–100. Paris: L'Association pour la diffusion de la pensée française, 1959.

Lockridge, Kenneth. *Literacy in Colonial New England: An Enquiry into the Social Context of Literacy in the Early Modern West*. New York: Norton, 1974.

– *A New England Town: The First Hundred Years.* Enlarged ed. New York: Norton, 1985.

Lokke, Karl. *France and the Colonial Question: A Study of Contemporary French Opinion, 1763–1801.* New York: Columbia University Press, 1932.

Loncol, Jean Marie. "La Louisiane et les colonies espagnoles d'Amérique, 1731–1748." *Revue d'histoire de l'Amérique française* 18 (1964): 196–201.

Loque, Cal. "Transcending Coercion: The Communicative Strategies of Black Slaves on Antebellum Plantations." *Quarterly Journal of Speech* 67 (1981): 31–46.

Louis XIV, King of France. *Mémoires for the Instruction of the Dauphin.* Translated and introduced by Paul Sonnino. New York: Free Press, 1970.

Lunn, Alice Jean Elizabeth. "Economic Development in New France, 1713–1760." PhD diss., McGill University, 1942.

– "The Illegal Fur Trade Out of New France, 1713–60." *Canadian Historical Association Report*, 1939, 61–76.

Ly, Abdoulaye. *La Compagnie du Sénégal.* Paris: Éditions Présence africaine, 1958.

McAlister, Lyle N. *Spain and Portugal in the New World, 1492–1700.* Minneapolis: University of Minnesota Press, 1984.

McKay, Derek, and H.M. Scott. *The Rise of the Great Powers, 1648–1815.* London: Longman, 1983.

McKusker, John. *Essays in the Economic History of the Atlantic World.* London: Routledge, 1997.

McLennan, J.S. *Louisbourg from Its Foundation to Its Fall, 1713–1758.* London: MacMillan, 1916; reprint, Sydney, NS: Fortress Press, 1969.

McNeill, John. *Atlantic Empires of France and Spain: Louisbourg and Havana, 1700–1763.* Chapel Hill: University of North Carolina Press, 1985.

McQuail, Dennis. *Communication.* 2nd ed. London: Longman, 1984.

– *Mass Communication Theory: An Introduction.* 2nd ed. London: SAGE Publications, 1987.

Major, J. Russell. *From Renaissance Monarchy to Absolute Monarchy: French Kings, Nobles, and Estates.* Baltimore: Johns Hopkins University Press, 1994.

Malartic, Anne-Joseph-Hyppolyte de Maurés, Comte de. *Journal des campagnes au Canada de 1755–1760.* Paris: Plon, 1890.

Mancke, Elizabeth. "Another British America: A Canadian Model for the Early Modern British Empire." *Journal of Imperial and Commonwealth History* 25 (1997): 1–36.

Mandements, lettres pastorales et circulaires des évêques de Québec. Edited by Henri Têtu and C.O. Gagnon. 6 vols. Québec: A. Côté, 1887–90.

Margry, Pierre, ed. *Découvertes et établissements des Français dans l'ouest et dans le sud de l'Amérique septentrionale (1614–1754)*. 6 vols. Paris: Maisonneuve, 1879.

– *Relations et mémoires inédits pour servir à l'histoire de la France dans les pays d'outre-mer*. Paris: Challamel, 1867.

Marion, Marcel. *Dictionnaire des institutions de la France aux XVIIe et XVIIIe siècles*. New York: Ben Franklin, 1968.

Martin, Gaston. *Histoire de l'esclavage dans les colonies françaises*. Paris: Presses universitaires de France, 1948.

– "Nantes et la Compagnie des Indes (1664–1769)." *Revue d'histoire économique et sociale* 15 (1927): 231–53.

Marzagalli, Silvia. "The French Atlantic." *Itinerario* 23 (1999): 70–83.

Mathieu, Jacques. *Le commerce entre la Nouvelle-France et les Antilles au XVIIIe siècle*. Montréal: Fides, 1981.

– "Les relations ville-campagne: Québec et sa région au XVIIIe siècle." In *Société rurale dans la France de l'ouest et au Québec (XVIIe–XVIIIe siècles*, edited by Jacques Mathieu, 190–206. Montréal: Presses de l'Université de Montréal. 1981.

– and Serge Courville. *Peuplement colonisateur aux XVIIe et XVIIIe siècles*. Québec: CELAT, 1987.

Mattelart, Armand, and Michèle Mattelart. *Rethinking Media Theory*. Translated by James A. Cohen and Marina Urquidi. Minneapolis: University of Minnesota Press, 1992.

Maupassant, Jean de. "Les armateurs bordelais au XVIIIe siècle: l'Expédition de François Lavaud à la Louisiane (1761–1763)." *Revue philomathique de Bordeaux et du Sud-Ouest*, 1909, 159–78.

– *Un grand armateur de Bordeaux, Abraham Gradis (1699?–1780)*. Bordeaux: Feret & Fils, 1917.

May, Louis-Philippe. *Histoire économique de la Martinique (1635–1763)*. Paris: Librarie Rivière, 1930; reprint, Fort-de-France: Société de Distribution et de Culture, 1972.

Mémain, Réné. *La Marine de guerre sous Louis XIV: Le matériel: Rochefort, arsenal modèle de Colbert*. Paris: Hachette, 1937.

Ménétra, Jacques-Louis. *Journal of My Life*. With Introduction and commentary by Daniel Roche; translated by Arthur Goldhammer. New York: Columbia University Press, 1986.

Menkis, Richard. "The Gradis Family of 18th-century Bordeaux." PhD diss., Brandeis University, 1989.

Merrick, Jeffrey W. *The Desacralization of the French Monarchy in the Eighteenth Century*. Baton Rouge: Louisiana State University Press, 1990.

– "Patriarchalism and Constitutionalism in Eighteenth-Century Parelementary Discourse." *Studies in Eighteenth-Century Culture* 20 (1990): 317–30.

– "Politics on Pedestals: Royal Monuments in Eighteenth-Century France." *French History* 5 (1991): 234–64.
Mettam, Roger. *Power and Faction in Louis XIV's France*. Oxford: Basil Blackwell, 1988.
Mettas, Jean. "Pour une histoire de la traité des Noirs français: Sources et problèmes." *Revue française d'histoire d'outre-mer* 62 (1975): 19–46.
Meyer, Jean. *L'armement nantais dans la deuxième moitié du* XVIIIe *siècle*. Paris: SEVPEN, 1969.
– *Colbert*. Paris: Hachette, 1981.
– "Les décideurs: Comment fonctionne l'Ancien Régime." *Proceedings of the Annual Meeting of the Western Society for French History* 14 (1987): 81–97.
– "Des origines à 1763." In *Histoire de la France coloniale des origines à 1914*, edited by Jean Meyer, Jean Tarrade, Annie Rey-Goldzeigur, and Jacques Thobie, 12–196. Paris: Armand Colin, 1991.
– *La vie quotidienne au temps de la Régence*. Paris: Hachette, 1979.
Micelle, Jerry A. "From Law Court to Local Government: Metamorphosis of the Superior Council of French Louisiana." In *The French Experience in Louisiana*, edited by Glenn R. Conrad, 408–23. Lafayette: Center for Louisiana Studies, 1995.
Mims, Stewart L. *Colbert's West India Policy*. New Haven: Yale University Press, 1912.
Miquelon, Dale. "Canada's Place in the French Imperial Economy." *French Historical Studies* 15 (1988): 432–43.
– *Dugard of Rouen: French Trade to Canada and the West Indies, 1729–1770*. Montreal: McGill-Queen's University Press, 1978.
– "Envisioning the French Empire: Utrecht, 1711–13." *French Historical Studies* 24 (2001): 653–77.
– *The First Canada: to 1791*. Toronto: McGraw-Hill Ryerson, 1994.
– "Havy and Lefebvre of Quebec: A Case Study of Metropolitan Participation in Canadian Trade, 1730–60." *Canadian Historical Review* 56 (1975): 1–24.
– *New France, 1701–1744: "A Supplement to Europe."* Toronto: McClelland and Stewart, 1987.
Mississippi Provincial Archives: French Dominion. Vol. 3, collected, edited, and translated by Dunbar Rowland and A.G. Sanders. Jackson: Press of the Mississippi Department of Archives, 1932. Vols. 4–5, collected, edited, and translated by Dunbar Rowland and A.G. Sanders; revised and edited by Patricia K. Galloway. Baton Rouge: Louisiana State University Press, 1984.
Montesquieu, Charles de Secondat, Baron de. *The Spirit of the Laws*. Translated by Thomas Nugent. New York: Hafner, 1949; reprint, 1962.
Moogk, Peter. *La Nouvelle France: The Making of French Canada – A Cultural History*. East Lansing: Michigan State University Press, 2000.

– "Rank in New France: Reconstructing a Society from Notarial Documents." *Histoire sociale/Social History* 8 (1975): 34–53.

– "Reluctant Exiles: Emigrants from France in Canada before 1760." *William and Mary Quarterly*, 3rd series, 46 (1989): 463–505.

– "'Thieving Buggers and Stupid Sluts': Popular Culture in New France." *William and Mary Quarterly*, 3rd series, 36 (1979): 524–47.

Moore, Christopher. *Louisbourg Portraits: Life in an Eighteenth-Century Garrison Town*. Toronto: MacMillan, 1982.

– "The Other Louisbourg: Trade and Merchant Enterprise in Île Royale, 1713–58." *Histoire sociale/Social History* 12 (1979): 79–96.

Moore, John Hebron. "The Cypress Lumber Industry of the Lower Mississippi Valley during the Colonial Period." *Louisiana History* 24 (1983): 25–47.

Moreau de Saint-Méry, Médéric Louis Elie. *Description topographique, physique, civile, politique, et historique de la partie française de l'isle Saint-Domingue*, edited by Blanche Maurel and Etienne Taillemite. 3 vols. 1797; reprint, Paris: Société de l'histoire des colonies françaises et Librarie Larose, 1958).

Morgan, Edmund. "Slavery and Freedom: the American Paradox." *Journal of American History* 59 (1973): 5–29.

Morineau, Michel. "La vraie nature des choses et leur enchaînement entre la France, les Antilles et l'Europe (XVIIe-XIXe siècle)." *Revue française d'histoire d'outre-mer* 84 (1997): 3–24.

Morison, Samuel Eliot. *The European Discovery of America: The Northern Voyages, A.D. 500–1600*. New York: Oxford University Press, 1971.

– *The European Discovery of America: The Southern Voyages, A.D. 1492–1616*. New York: Oxford University Press, 1974.

Morrison, Kenneth M. *The Embattled Northeast: The Elusive Ideal of Alliance in Abenaki Euramerican Relations*. Berkeley: University of California Press, 1984.

Moureau, François. "La littérature des voyages maritimes: Du classicisme aux Lumières." In *La percée de l'Europe sur les océans vers 1690 – vers 1790*, edited by Étienne Taillemite and Denis Lieppe, 243–64. Paris: Presses de l'Université de Paris-Sorbonne, 1997. (*Revue d'histoire maritime*, no. 1, special ed., October 1997).

Mousnier, Roland. *The Institutions of France under the Absolute Monarchy, 1598–1789*. 2 vols. Translated by Brian Pearce. Chicago: University of Chicago Press, 1979.

Mukerji, Chandra. *Territorial Ambitions and the Gardens of Versailles*. Cambridge: Cambridge University Press, 1997.

Munford, Clarence. *Black Ordeal of Slavery and Slave Trading in the French West Indies, 1625–1715*. 3 vols. Lewiston, NY: E. Mellen Press, 1991.

– "Slavery in the French Caribbean, 1625–1715." *Journal of Black Studies* 17 (1986): 49–69.

Nasatir, Abraham P., and James R. Mills. *Commerce and Contraband in New Orleans during the French and Indian War: A Documentary Study of the Texel and Three Brothers Affairs.* Cincinnati: American Jewish Archives, 1968.

Nash, Gary B. *The Urban Crucible: The Northern Seaports and the Origins of the American Revolution.* Abridged ed. Cambridge: Harvard University Press, 1986.

Nash, R.C. "Irish Atlantic Trade in the Seventeenth and Eighteenth Centuries." *William and Mary Quarterly*, 3rd series, 42 (1985): 329–56.

Neatby, Hilda. *Quebec: The Revolutionary Age, 1760–1791.* Toronto: McClelland and Stewart, 1966.

Nicolai, Martin L. "A Different Kind of Courage: The French Military and the Canadian Irregular Soldier during the Seven Years' War." *Canadian Historical Review* 70 (1989): 53–75.

Nish, Cameron. *Les bourgeois-gentilshommes de la Nouvelle-France, 1729–1748.* Montréal: Fides, 1968.

Nordman, Daniel, and Jacques Revel. "La formation de l'espace français." In *L'espace français*, edited by Louis Bergeron, Patrice Bourdelais, Dominique Julia, et al., 53–173. Paris: Éditions du Seuil, 1989.

Olivier-Lacamp, Gael, and Jacques Legaré. "Quelques caracteristiques des ménages de la ville de Québec entre 1666 et 1716." *Histoire sociale/Social History* 12 (1979): 66–78.

O'Neill, Charles E. *Church and State in French Colonial Louisiana: Policy and Politics to 1732.* New Haven: Yale University Press, 1966.

Pagden, Anthony. *Lords of All the World: Ideologies of Empire in Spain, Britain, and France, c. 1500–1800.* New Haven: Yale University Press, 1995.

Pagés, Clément. "Relation d'un voyage de Paris en Canada [1741]." In *RAPQ pour 1947–48*, 21–8.

Palmer, R.R. *Catholics and Unbelievers in Eighteenth-Century France.* Princeton: Princeton University Press, 1939.

Parent, Jean-Claude. *L'histoire et le développement des chemins sous l'Ancien Régime au Canada, 1650–1760.* Research Microfiche no. 259. Ottawa: Environment Canada, n.d.

Pares, Richard. *War and Trade in the West Indies, 1739–1763.* Oxford: Oxford University Press, 1936.

– *Yankees and Creoles.* Cambridge: Harvard University Press, 1956.

Parker, David. *The Making of French Absolutism.* London: Edward Arnold, 1983.

Parkman, Francis. *France and England in North America.* Vol. 2, *A Half-Century of Conflict.* 1892; reprint, New York: Library of the United States, 1983.

Parry, J.H. *The Establishment of the European Hegemony: 1415–1715*. 3rd ed. New York: Harper & Row, 1966.

Patterson, Graeme. *History and Communications: Harold Innis, Marshall McLuhan, and the Interpretation of History*. Toronto: University of Toronto Press, 1990.

Peabody, Sue. "'A Dangerous Zeal': Catholic Missions to Slaves in the French Antilles, 1635–1800." *French Historical Studies* 25 (2002): 53–90.

– *'There Are No Slaves in France': The Political Culture of Race and Slavery in the Ancien Régime*. New York: Oxford University Press, 1996.

Pellegrin, Gabriel. "Mémoire sur la navigation du Canada [1757]." In *Public Archives of Canada Report, 1905*, vol. 1, pt. 5, 1–6. Ottawa, 1906.

Pelletier, Monique. "Sciences et cartographie marine." In *La percée de l'Europe sur les océans vers 1690 – vers 1790*, edited by Étienne Taillemite and Denis Lieppe, 265–91. Paris: Presses de l'Université de Paris-Sorbonne, 1997. (*Revue d'histoire maritime*, no. 1, special ed., October 1997)

Pérotin-Dumon, Anne. "Cabotage, Contraband, and Corsairs: The Port Cities of Guadeloupe and Their Inhabitants, 1650–1800." In *Atlantic Port Cities: Economy, Culture and Society in the Atlantic World, 1650–1850*, edited by Franklin W. Knight and Peggy K. Liss, 58–86. Knoxville: University of Tennessee Press, 1991.

– "Commerce et travail dans les villes coloniales des Lumières: Basse-Terre et Pointe-à-Pitre, Guadeloupe." *Revue française d'histoire d'outre-mer* 75 (1988): 31–78.

– *Être patriote sous les tropiques: La Guadeloupe, la colonisation et la révolution, 1789–1794*. Basse-Terre: Société d'histoire de la Guadeloupe, 1985.

– "French America." *International History Review* 6 (1984): 550–69.

Peters, John Durham. *Speaking into the Air: A History of the Idea of Communication*. Chicago: University of Chicago Press, 1999.

Petitjean-Roget, Jacques. "Les femmes des colons à la Martinique, XVII–XVIIIe siècles." *Revue d'histoire de l'Amérique française* 9 (1955): 176–235.

– *Le Gaoulé: La révolte de la Martinique, 1717*. Fort-de-France: Société de l'histoire de la Martinique, 1966.

– "Les Juifs à la Martinique sous l'Ancien Régime." *Revue de l'histoire des colonies* 43 (1956): 138–58.

– "Les protestants à la Martinique sous l'Ancien Régime." *Revue de l'histoire des colonies* 42 (1955): 220–65.

– *La Société d'habitation à la Martinique: Un demi-siècle de formation, 1635–1685*. 2 vols. Paris: Honoré Champion, 1980.

Petitot, A., and Monmerqué. *Collection des mémoires relatif à l'histoire de France depuis l'avènement de Henri IV jusqu'à la paix de Paris conclue en 1763*. 2nd series, vol. 68. Paris: Foucault, 1828.

Phillips, Roderick. "Family and Political Ideology in Eighteenth-Century France." *Proceedings of the Annual Meeting of the Western Society for French History* 16 (1989): 361–67.

Picard, Bernard. *Cérémonies et coutumes religieuses de tous les peuples du monde*. New ed. 3 vols. Amsterdam: 1783.

Pinon, Pierre. "Saint-Domingue: l'île à villes." *Les villes françaises du Nouveau-Monde: Des premiers fonadateurs aux ingénieurs du roi (XVIe–XVIIIe siècles)*, edited by Laurent Vidal and Émilie d'Orgeix, 108–19. Paris: Somogy éditions d'art, 1999.

– and Laurent Vidal. "L'urbanisme français au Nouveau Monde." In *Les villes françaises du Nouveau-Monde: Des premiers fonadateurs aux ingénieurs du roi (XVIe–XVIIIe siècles)*, edited by Laurent Vidal and Émilie d'Orgeix, 57–9. Paris: Somogy éditions d'art, 1999.

Pluchon, Pierre. "L'économie d''Habitation' à Saint-Domingue." In *La percée de l'Europe sur les océans vers 1690 – vers 1790*, edited by Étienne Taillemite and Denis Lieppe, 197–241. Paris: Presses de l'Université de Paris-Sorbonne, 1997. (*Revue d'histoire maritime*, no. 1, special ed., October 1997).

– *Nègres et juifs au XVIIIe siècle: Le racisme au siècle des Lumières*. Paris: Tallandier, 1984.

– ed. *Histoire de la colonisation française*. Paris: Fayard, 1991.

– *Histoire des Antilles et de la Guyane*. Toulouse: Édouard Privat, 1982.

Pocock, J.G.A. "The New British History in Atlantic Perspective: An Antipodean Commentary." *American Historical Review* 104 (1999): 490–500.

Poliquin, Daniel. *In the Name of the Father: An Essay on Quebec Nationalism*. Vancouver: Douglas and McIntyre, 2001.

Postlethwayt, Malachy [James MacPherson]. *A Short State of the Progress of the French Trade and Navigation*. London: Knapton, 1756.

Poussou, Jean-Pierre. *Bordeaux et le sud-ouest au XVIIIe siècle: Croissance économique et attraction urbaine*. Paris: Éditions de l'École des hautes études en sciences sociales, 1982.

Pratt, Mary Louise. *Imperial Eyes: Travel Writing and Transculturation*. London and New York: Routledge, 1992.

Pred, Alan. *Urban Growth and the Circulation of Information, 1790–1840*. Cambridge: Harvard University Press, 1973.

– "Urban Systems Development and the Long-Distance Flow of Information." *Economic Geography* 47 (1971): 498–524.

Price, Jacob M. "Economic Function and the Growth of American Port Towns in the Eighteenth Century." *Perspectives in American History* 8 (1974): 123–86.

– *France and the Chesapeake; A History of the French Tobacco Monopoly, 1674–1791, and of Its Relationship to the British and American Tobacco Trades*. Ann Arbor: University of Michigan Press, 1973.

Pritchard, James S. *Anatomy of a Naval Disaster: The 1746 French Naval Expedition to North America.* Montreal: McGill-Queen's University Press, 1995.

– "French Charting of the East Coast of Canada." In *Five Hundred Years of Nautical Science, 1400–1900,* edited by Derek Howse, 119–29. London: National Maritime Museum, 1981.

– *Louis xv's Navy, 1748–1762: A Study of Organization and Administration.* Montreal: McGill-Queen's University Press, 1987.

– "The Naval Career of a Colonial Governor: Charles de Thubières, Marquis de Caylus, 1698–1750." *Proceedings of the Sixteenth Meeting of the French Colonial Historical Society* (1990), 12–23.

– "The Pattern of French Colonial Shipping to Canada before 1760." *Revue française d'histoire d'outre-mer.* 63 (1976): 189–210.

– "Ships, Men, and Commerce: A Study of Maritime Activity in New France." PhD diss., University of Toronto, 1971.

– "The Voyage of the *Fier*: An Analysis of a Shipping and Trading Venture to New France, 1724–1728." *Histoire sociale/Social History* 6 (1973): 75–97.

Proulx, Gilles. *Between France and New France: Life Aboard the Tall Sailing Ships.* Toronto: Dundurn Press, 1984.

– "Soldat à Québec, 1748–1759." *Revue d'histoire de l'Amérique française* 32 (1979): 535–63.

Quéniart, Jean. *Culture et société urbaines dans la France de l'ouest au XVIIIe siècle.* Paris: Klincksieck, 1978.

– *Les hommes, l'église, et Dieu dans la France du XVIIIe siècle.* Paris: Hachette, 1978.

Quinn, David Beers. *North America from the Earliest Discovery to First Settlements: The Norse Voyages to 1612.* New York: Harper and Row, 1977.

Quinn, Frederick. *The French Overseas Empire.* Westport, Conn.: Praeger, 2000.

Ranum, Orest. *Paris in the Age of Absolutism: An Essay.* New York: Wiley, 1968.

Rapport de l'archiviste de la province du Québec. Edited by Pierre-Georges Roy. Quebec: Imprimerie du roi, Imprimerie du Québec, 1920–61.

Rawlyk, George A. *Nova Scotia's Massachusetts: A Study of Massachusetts–Nova Scotia Relations, 1630 to 1784.* Montreal: McGill-Queen's University Press, 1973.

Raynal, Abbé Guillaume-Thomas-François. *Histoire philosophique et politique des établissemens and du commerce des Européens dans les deux Indes.* 7 vols. Amsterdam, 1773–74.

"Records of the Superior Council [of Louisiana]." Various editors. Published in *Louisiana Historical Quarterly*, vols. 1–26.

Rediker, Marcus. *Between the Devil and the Deep Blue Sea: Merchant Seamen, Pirates, and the Anglo-American Maritime World, 1700–1750*. Cambridge: Cambridge University Press, 1987.
Reid, Allana Gertrude. "The Development and Importance of the Town of Quebec, 1608–1760." PhD diss., McGill University, 1950.
– "Intercolonial Trade during the French Regime." *Canadian Historical Review* 32 (1951): 236–51.
– "The Nature of Quebec Society during the French Regime." *Canadian Historical Association Annual Report*, 1951, 26–36.
– "Representative Assemblies in New France." *Canadian Historical Review* 27 (1946): 19–26.
Rennard, Jean. *Histoire religieuse des Antilles françaises des origines à 1914*. Paris: Société de l'histoire des colonies français et Librarie Larose, 1954.
– "Organisation des paroisses." In *Nos Antilles*, edited by Serge Denis, 131–59. Paris: Maison du Livre français, 1935.
Réno, Fred. "Re-sourcing Dependency: Decolonisation and Post-colonialism in French Overseas Departments." *Itinerario* 25 (2001): 9–22.
Reps, John W. *The Making of Urban America: A History of City Planning in the United States*. Princeton: Princeton University Press, 1965.
– *Town Planning in Frontier America*. Princeton: Princeton University Press, 1985.
Resbecq, H. Fontaine de. "L'administration centrale de la Marine." *Revue maritime and coloniale*, 1886, 412–61.
Rice, Anne. *Interview with the Vampire*. New York: Alfred A. Knopf, 1976.
Robinson, Willard B. "Maritime Frontier Engineering: The Defense of New Orleans." *Louisiana History* 18 (1977), 5–62.
Roche, Daniel. *France in the Enlightenment*. Translated by Arthur Goldhammer. Cambridge: Harvard University Press, 1998.
– *Les républicains des lettres: Gens de culture et Lumières au* XVIIIe *siècle*. Paris: Fayard, 1988.
Rochemonteix, Camille de. *La Père Antoine Lavalette à la Martinique*. Paris: Alphonse Picard & Fils, 1907.
Rocquebrune, R. La Roque. "La direction de la Nouvelle-France par le ministère de la Marine." *Revue d'histoire de l'Amérique française* 6 (1953): 470–88.
Rombouts, Stephen. "The Celebration of Public Events in Eighteenth-Century France." PhD diss., Vanderbilt University, 1986.
Roncière, Charles de la. *Histoire de la Marine Française*. Vol. 4, *En quète d'un empire colonial*; vol. 5, *La Guerre de trente ans–Colbert*. Paris : Plon, 1910–34.
Roussier, Paul. "Fêtes d'autrefois à la Martinique." In *Nos Antilles*, edited by Serge Denis, 217–40. Paris: Maison du livres français, 1935.

– "Instructions données à l'intendant des Îles françaises du Vent le 25 août 1716." *Revue de l'Histoire des colonies* 17 (1924): 67–106.

Roux, Antoine de. "La création urbaine en Martinique et en Guadeloupe aux xviie et xviiie siècles." *Les villes françaises du Nouveau-Monde: Des premiers fonadateurs aux ingénieurs du roi (xvie–xviiie siècles)*, edited by Laurent Vidal and Émilie d'Orgeix, 99–107. Paris: Somogy éditions d'art, 1999.

Roy, Pierre-Georges. *Les lettres, les sciences et les arts au Canada sous le régime français*. Paris: Jouve, 1930.

– "Les secrétaires des gouverneurs et intendants de la Nouvelle-France." *Bulletin des recherches historiques* 61 (1935): 74–107.

– *La ville de Québec sous le régime français*. 2 vols. Québec: Redempti Paradis, 1930.

Rule, J.C. "The Administrative History of the Reign." In *The Reign of Louis xiv: Essays in Celebration of Andrew Lossky*, edited by Paul Sonnino, 95–109. Atlantic Highlands, nj: Humanities Press International, 1990.

– "Colbert de Torcy, an Emergent Bureaucracy, and the Formulation of French Foreign Policy, 1698–1715." In *Louis xiv and Europe*, edited by Ragnhild Hatton, 261–88. Columbus: Ohio State University Press, 1976.

– "Jérôme Phélypeaux, Comte de Pontchartrain, and the Establishment of Louisiana, 1696–1715." *Frenchmen and French Ways in the Mississippi Valley*, edited by John McDermott, 179–97. Urbana: University of Illinois Press, 1969.

Saintard. *Lettres d'un citoyen sur la permission de commercer dans les colonies, annoncé pour les puissances neutres*. [Paris?], 1756. (Copy in Bibliothèque Nationale, Paris).

Saintoyant, J. *La colonisation française sous l'Ancien Régime*. Paris: La Renaissance du livre, 1929.

Saint-Simon, Duc de. *Mémoires*. Edited by Yves Cloirault. Vol. 4. Paris: Éditions Gallimard, 1985.

Salone, Émile. *La colonisation de la Nouvelle-France: Étude sur les origines de la nation canadienne française*. Paris: Guilmoto, 1905.

Sanger, Victoria. "La ville *ex nihilo*: un modèle Vauban?" In *Les villes françaises du Nouveau-Monde: Des premiers fonadateurs aux ingénieurs du roi (xvie-xviiie siècles)*, edited by Laurent Vidal and Emilie d'Orgeix, 37–41. Paris : Somogy éditions d'art, 1999.

Satineau, Maurice. *Histoire de la Guadeloupe sous l'Ancien Régime, 1635–1789*. Paris: Payot, 1928.

Savary des Bruslons, Jacques. *Le parfait négociant ou instruction générale pour ce que regarde le commerce des marchandises de France, et des pays étrangers*. Paris: Éstiene et Fils, 1673; reprint, 1749.

Savelle, Max. *The Origins of American Diplomacy: The International History of Angloamerica, 1492–1763*. New York: MacMillan, 1967.

Scammell, Geoffrey V. *The First Imperial Age: European Overseas Expansion, 1400–1715*. London: Unwin Hyman, 1989.

Schaeper, Thomas. "Colonial trade Policies Late in the Reign of Louis XIV." *Revue française d'histoire d'outre-mer* 67 (1980): 203–15.

– *The French Council of Commerce, 1700–1715: A Study of Mercantilism after Colbert*. Columbus: Ohio State University Press, 1983.

Schnakenbourg, Christian. "Statistiques pour l'histoire de l'économie de plantation en Guadeloupe et Martinique (1635–1835)." *Bulletin de la Société d'histoire de la Guadeloupe* 31 (1977): 3–121.

Scott, Julius S. "Afro-American Sailors and the International Communication Network: The Case of Newport Bowers." In *Jack Tar in History: Essays in the History of Maritime Life and Labour*, edited by Colin Howell and Richard Twomey, 37–51. Fredericton: Acadiensis Press, 1991.

Seguin, Robert-Lionel. *La Civilisation traditionnelle de l'habitant aux XVIIe et XVIIIe siècles*. Montréal: Fides, 1967.

– *La vie libertine en Nouvelle-France au XVIIe siècle*. 2 vols. Ottawa: Leméac, 1967.

Severin, Werner J., and James W. Tankard Jr. *Communication Theories: Origins, Methods, and Uses in the Mass Media*. 3rd ed. White Plains, NY: Longman, 1972.

Singer, Marshall. *Intercultural Communication: A Perceptual Approach*. Englewood Cliffs, NJ: Prentice-Hall, 1987.

Smelser, Marshall. *The Campaign for the Sugar Islands, 1759: A Study of Amphibious Warfare*. Chapel Hill, NC: University of North Carolina Press, for the Institute of Early American History and Culture, 1955.

Socolow, Susan Migden. "Introduction." In *Cities and Society in Colonial Latin America*, edited by Louisa Schell Hoberman and Susan Migden Socolow, 3–18. Albuquerque: University of New Mexico Press, 1986.

Solow, Barbara L. "Introduction." In *Slavery and the Rise of the Atlantic System*, edited by Barbara L. Solow, 1–20. Cambridge: Cambridge University Press, 1991.

Stallybrass, Peter, and Allon White. *The Politics and Poetics of Transgression*. London: Methuen, 1986.

Standen, S. Dale. "Charles, Marquis de Beauharnais de la Boische, Governor of New France, 1726–1747." PhD diss., University of Toronto, 1975.

– "Politics, Patronage, and the Imperial Interest: Charles de Beauharnais's Disputes with Gilles Hocquart." *Canadian Historical Review* 60 (1979): 19–40.

Stanley, George F.G. *New France: The Last Phase, 1744–1760*. Toronto: McClelland and Stewart, 1968.

Steele, Ian K. *The English Atlantic, 1675–1740: An Exploration of Communication and Community*. New York: Oxford University Press, 1986.

– *Guerillas and Grenadiers: The Struggle for Canada, 1689–1760*. Toronto: Ryerson Press, 1969.

– "Moat Theories and the English Atlantic, 1675–1740." *Canadian Historical Association. Historical Papers*, 1978, 18–33.

– *The Politics of Colonial Policy: The Board of Trade in Colonial Administration, 1696–1720*. Oxford: Clarendon Press, 1968.

Stein, Robert. *The French Slave Trade in the Eighteenth Century*. Madison: University of Wisconsin Press, 1979.

– *The French Sugar Business in the Eighteenth Century*. Baton Rouge: Louisiana State University Press, 1988.

Stelter, Gilbert A. "Military Considerations and Colonial Town Planning: France and New France in the Seventeenth Century." In *Settlements in the Americas: Cross-cultural Perspectives*, edited by Ralph Bennett, 210–37. Newark: University of Delaware Press, 1993.

Stevens, John D., and Hazel Dicken Garcia. *Communications History*. Beverly Hills, Ca: SAGE Publications, 1980.

Strayer, Brian E. *Lettres de Cachet and Social Control in the Ancien Régime, 1659–1789*. New York: Peter Lang, 1992.

Surrey, Nancy Maria Miller. *The Commerce of Louisiana during the French Regime, 1699–1763*. New York: Columbia University Press, 1916; reprint, New York: AMS, 1968.

Symcox, Geoffrey W. "The Navy of Louis XIV." In *The Reign of Louis XIV: Essays in Celebration of Andrew Lossky*, edited by Paul Sonnino, 127–42. Atlantic Highlands, NJ: Humanities Press International, 1990.

Taillemite, Étienne. "Introduction." In *Inventaire analytique de la correspondence générale avec les colonies: Départ (Série B)*, edited by E. Taillemite. Paris : Ministère de la France d'outre-mer, 1959.

Tannenbaum, Frank. *Slave and Citizen*. New York: Vintage Books, 1946.

Tarrade, Jean. *Le commerce colonial de la France à la fin de l'Ancien Régime: L'évolution du régime de l'exclusif de 1763 à 1790*. 2 vols. Paris: Presses universitaires de France, 1972.

Tessier, Georges. *Diplomatie royale française*. Paris: Picard, 1962.

Thibault de Chanvalon, Jean-Baptiste. *Voyage à la Martinique, contenant diverses observations sur la physique, l'histoire naturelle, l'agriculture, les moeurs, & les usages de cette isle, faites en 1751, & dans les années suivantes*. Paris: J.B. Bauche, 1763.

Thornton, John. *Africa and Africans in the Making of the Atlantic World, 1400–1800*. 2nd ed. Cambridge: Cambridge University Press, 1998.

Thorpe, Fred. *Remparts lointoin: La politique française des travaux publics à Terre-Neuve et à l'Île Royale, 1695–1758*. Ottawa: Éditions de l'Université d'Ottawa, 1980.

Tranchepain, Révérend Mère St Augustin de. *Relation du voyage des premières Ursulines à la Nouvelle Orléans et de leur établissement en cette ville*. New York: J. M. Shea, 1859.

Trénard, Louis. "De la route royale à l'âge d'or des diligences." In *Les routes de France: depuis les origines jusqu'à nos jours*, edited by Guy Michaud, 101–32. Paris: L'Association pour la diffusion de la pensée française, 1959.

Trigger, Bruce G. *The Children of Aataentsic: A History of the Huron People to 1660*. Montreal and Kingston: McGill-Queen's University Press, 1987.

– "The Historians' Indian: Native Americans in Canadian Historical Writing from Charlevoix to the Present." *Canadian Historical Review* 68 (1986): 313–42.

Trudel, Marcel. *Beginnings of New France, 1524–1663*. Toronto: McClelland and Stewart, 1973.

– *Dictionnaire des esclaves et de leurs propriétaires au Canada français*. Montreal: Hurtibise-HMH, 1990.

– *L'esclavage au Canada français: Histoire et condition de l'esclavage*. Québec: Presses de l'Université Laval, 1960.

United States Navy. *Distance between Ports, 1965*. H.O. Publication no. 151. Washington: U.S. Naval Oceanographic Office, 1965.

Usner, Daniel H., Jr. *Indians, Settlers, and Slaves in a Frontier Exchange Economy: The Lower Mississippi Valley before 1783*. Chapel Hill: University of North Carolina Press, 1992.

Vachon, André. *L'administration de la Nouvelle-France, 1627–1760*. Québec: Presses de l'Université Laval, 1970.

Vaillé, Eugène. *Histoire générale des postes françaises*. Vol. 5, *La Ferme générale et le groupe Pajot-Rouillé (1691–1738)*; vol. 6, *La Ferme générale et le groupe Grimod-Thiroux (1738–1789)*. Paris: Presses universitaires de France, 1951–53.

Van Ruymbeke, Bertrand. "Charlesfort, Fort-Caroline et la Floride huguenote (1562–1565)." In *Les villes françaises du Nouveau-Monde: Des premiers fonadateurs aux ingénieurs du roi (XVIe–XVIIIe siècles)*, edited by Laurent Vidal and Émilie d'Orgeix, 74–7. Paris: Somogy éditions d'art, 1999.

– "Un refuge avant le Refuge? La 'Floride huguenote' et les origines de la Caroline du Sud." In *Coligny, les protestants, et la mer*, edited by Martine Acerra and Guy Martinière, 235–45. Paris : Presses de l'Université de Paris-Sorbonne, 1997, 235–45.

Vassières, Pierre de. *Saint-Domingue: La société et la vie créole sous l'Ancien Régime (1629–1789)*. Paris: Perrin, 1909.

Vergé-Franceschi, Michel. "L'amirauté de France dans la deuxième moitié du XVIe siècle: Un enjeu entre catholique et protestants." In *Coligny, les protestants, et la mer*, edited by Martine Acerra and Guy Martinière, 35–43. Paris : Presses de l'Université de Paris-Sorbonne, 1997.

– *Marine et éducation sous l'Ancien Régime*. Paris: Éditions du Centre national de la recherche scientifique, 1991.
– *La marine française au XVIIIe siècle*. Paris: SEDES, 1996.
Véron de Forbonnais, François. *Essai sur l'admission des navires neutres dans nos colonies*. [Paris?], 1759. (Copy in Bibliothèque Nationale, Paris).
Verrette, Michel. "L'alphabétisation de la population de la ville de Québec, 1750–1849." *Revue d'histoire de l'Amérique française* 39 (1985): 51–76.
Villiers du Terrage, Marc de. *Histoire de la fondation de la Nouvelle-Orléans (1717–1722)*. Paris: Imprimerie Royale, 1917.
– *The Last Years of French Louisiana*. 1913; reprint, Lafayette: Center for Louisiana Studies, 1982.
Voltaire. *Candide*. Translated by Lowell Blair. New York: Bantam Books, 1981.
Vovelle, Michel. *Les métamorphoses de la fête en Provence de 1750 à 1820*. Paris: Aubier/Flammarion, 1976.
Vries, Jan de. *The Economy of Europe in an Age of Crisis, 1600–1750*, Cambridge: Cambridge University Press, 1976.
Wade, I.O. *The Clandestine Organization and Diffusion of Philosophic Ideas in France from 1700 to 1750*. Princeton: Princeton University Press, 1938.
Wallerstein, Immanuel. *The Modern World System: Capitalist Agriculture and the Origins of the European World Economy in the Sixteenth Century*. Vol. 1. New York: Academic Press, 1974.
Walsh, H.H. *The Church in the French Era: From Colonization to the British Conquest*. Toronto: Ryerson Press, 1966.
Walthall, John A., and Thomas E. Emerson. "French Colonial Archaeology." In *French Colonial Archaeology: The Illinois Country and the Western Great Lakes*, edited by John A. Walthall, 1–13. Urbana: University of Illinois Press, 1991.
Watts, David. *The West Indies: Patterns of Development, Culture and Environmental Change since 1492*. Cambridge: Cambridge University Press, 1987.
Webster, Jonathan. "Merchants of Bordeaux in Trade to the French West Indies, 1664–1717." PhD diss., University of Minnesota, 1973.
Wesseling, H.L. "Gabriel Hanotaux: A Historian in Politics." *Itinerario* 25 (2001): 65–84.
Westfall, William. "The Ambivalent Verdict: Harold Innis and Canadian History." In *Culture, Communication, and Dependency: The Tradition of H.A. Innis*, edited by William H. Melody, Liora Salter, and Paul Heyer, 37–51. Norwood: Ablex Publishing, 1981, 37–51.
White, Richard. *The Middle Ground: Indians, Empires, and Republics in the Great Lakes Region, 1650–1815*. Cambridge: Cambridge University Press, 1991.

Williams, Raymond. *Communication*. Rev. Ed. London: Chatto & Windus, 1966.
Wilson, Samuel. *Bienville's New Orleans: A French Colonial Capital, 1718–1768*. New Orleans: n.p., 1968.
– "Ignace François Broutin." In *Frenchmen and French Ways in the Mississippi Valley*, edited by John McDermott, 231–94. Urbana: University of Illinois Press, 1969.
Woods, Patricia Dillon. *French-Indian Relations on the Southern Frontier, 1699–1762*. Ann Arbor: UMI Press, 1980.
Wraxall, Peter. *An Abridgment of the Indian Affairs*. Edited and introduced by Charles McIlwain. Cambridge: Harvard University Press, 1915; reprint, New York: Benjamin Blom, 1968.
Young, Kathryn A. "Crown Agent-Canadian Correspondent: Michel Sarazin and the Académie Royale des Sciences, 1697–1734." *French Historical Studies* 18 (1993): 416–34.
– *Kin, Commerce, Community: Merchants in the Port of Québec, 1717–1745*. New York: Peter Lang, 1995.
Zitomersky, Joseph. "Ville, État, implantation et société en Louisiane française." In *Colonies, Territoires, Sociétés : L'enjeu français*, edited by Alain Saussol and Joseph Zitomersky, 23–48. Paris: L'Harmattan, 1996.
Zoltvany, Yves F. "Esquisse de la coutume de Paris." *Revue d'histoire de l'Amérique française* 25 (1971): 365–84.
– "The Frontier Policy of Philippe de Rigaud de Vaudreuil, 1713–1725." *Canadian Historical Review* 48 (1967): 227–50.
– *Philippe de Rigaud de Vaudreuil, Governor of New France, 1703–1725*. Toronto: McClelland and Stewart, 1974.

Index